CANADIAN INDUSTRIAL RELATIONS:

S.M.A. Hameed

Butterworth and Co. (Canada) Ltd.
Toronto, Canada

Syed M.A. Hameed
Professor of Industrial Relations
Faculty of Business Administration and Commerce
University of Alberta

Canada:
Butterworth & Co. (Canada) Ltd.
2265 Midland Avenue
Scarborough, Ontario, M1P 4S1

England:
Butterworth & Co. (Publishers) Ltd.
88 Kingsway
London, WC 2B 6AB

Australia:
Butterworths Pty. Ltd.
586 Pacific Highway
Chatswood, N.S.W. 2067
Australia

New Zealand:
Butterworths of New Zealand Ltd.
Law Society Building
26-28 Waring Taylor Street
Wellington 1, New Zealand

South Africa:
Butterworth & Co. (S.A.) (Pty.) Ltd.
152-154 Gale Street
Durban, Natal
South Africa

ISBN 0-409-83500-5

1   2   3   4   5   79   78   77   76   75

Printed and bound in Canada
by Alger Press Limited.

TO

MORAD

YAVAR

AYESHA

Preface

In December 1966, the late Prime Minister Lester B. Pearson established a Task Force on Labour Relations, which commissioned a large number of research projects. Since the completion of these reports, industrial relations -- both as a discipline and as a field of research -- has acquired a valuable Canadian content. Unfortunately, the findings of many of the studies have not reached the students, particularly those in undergraduate courses.

Many task force researchers have contributed to this volume. I am indebted to them for preparing updated summaries of their task force reports. Others, not associated with the task force but representative of the large volume of research developed in more recent years, have prepared articles specifically for this text. The selected articles from these two sources fit neatly within a systems framework. Also included here is a case for simulated contract negotiations, which makes this reader comprehensive for instructional purposes.

I wish to acknowledge Mr. David Godden of Butterworth & Company (Canada) Ltd. for the confidence and support given to the preparing of this volume. I also wish to mention Mrs. Audrey Milligan and Mrs. Sharon Gibney, for their valuable assistance in the preparation of the manuscript.

S.M.A. Hameed
University of Alberta
February 1975

Introduction

In contemporary Canadian society, more and more individuals are becoming aware of the complexity of the power relationship between labour and management. They are also recognizing that rapid technological changes and current inflationary trends are adding a new wage-employment dimension to union demands. Other elements, too, are complicating the industrial relations scene, such as the restructuring of social values, public policy experimentation with the right of strike in the public sector, and the role of government agencies in the resolution of collective bargaining disputes.

The Canadian public in general, and the students of industrial relations in particular, are unable to understand the pressures on the process of collective bargaining. Many people are disturbed by the strikes in schools, hospitals and postal services. They question the role of unions in the society and feel that the public policy is ineffective in protecting the public interest.

Systems Approach

The complexity of those issues mentioned above can be analyzed and understood only if we place the industrial relations problems in the context of the total Canadian society. Piecemeal and fragmented explanations create confusion. For instance, some experts emphasize the need for changing goals and values; others would like to see modifications in the laws governing the process of collective bargaining. Still others advocate the construction of a "humanistic democracy" in which the rights and opportunities of individuals would expand. However, these approaches are partial, unidimensional and nonoperational. We first need to develop a total approach and clearly define what we want to change, that is, our dependent variables. Then we must determine the factors that may bring about these changes, that is, the independent or causal variables.

By adopting a systems approach we can visualize the Canadian society as a composite of five interdependent systems: economic, social, political, legal and IR. Our enquiries and concerns can then be placed within the framework of a relevant system to examine the influence of its components and the components of other systems, which consist of inputs, a conversion mechanism and outputs.

Let us take the complexity of issues described earlier and

observe how the systems approach can help in better understanding them. The following factors were mentioned in the opening paragraph: (1) power relationship between labour and management; (2) technological changes; (3) inflationary trends; (4) social values; (5) public policy; (6) collective bargaining; and (7) strikes. The relationship among these factors is not defined in the way they appear before us, and therefore a search for a viable solution for any of them is greatly impaired. However, in a systems framework, each of them can be assigned to one of the five Canadian systems mentioned above. For example, power relationships between labour and management are an element of the conversion mechanism in the IR system. Effects of technological changes and inflationary trends are an output of the economic system. Social values and public policy are outputs of the social and political systems, respectively. Collective bargaining is a conversion mechanism of the IR system and strikes are an output of that same system. How does this identification and assigning of issues to appropriate Canadian systems aid our understanding of them? Because the output of one system becomes an input in other systems, and because there is a causal relationship among the components of each system, these issues acquire a defined relationship and each becomes explainable.

Let us take strikes as an example and observe what causal factors affect their behaviour and incidence. By now, we know that strikes are an output of the IR system. Placed in a systems framework, they are determined by the following factors: (1) inputs (i.e., participation of labour, management and government; inputs from other systems, such as technological change, inflation, social values, public policy; and inputs from outside the society, such as the policies of the multinational corporations, and wage settlements in the U.S.); (2) internal environment (i.e., goals and ideology of the participants); and (3) a conversion mechanism (i.e., collective bargaining and the power relationship).

Many more examples can be given to demonstrate the usefulness of the systems approach. Basically, it can systematize our knowledge and define the interrelationship among issues. It can help us find solutions because we know the causal variables and their influence on the dependent variables.

Organization of this Book

As a logical follow-up to the systems approach, the selected articles are distributed in five parts. Part I contains an analysis of industrial relations, both as a discipline and as a field of research. The scope and the multidisciplinary character of IR are discussed in chapter 1. An integrated theory, defining the systems, their components and the interrelationship

among the components, is developed in chapter 2. Essentially,
this chapter becomes the basis for the organization of the
remainder of the book.

Inputs in the IR System from Other Systems

The five systems outlined in the theory have been identified in
the Canadian society. Part II contains six articles, discussing
the output from each of the systems as it becomes an input in
the IR system. Arthur Kruger, in chapter 3, discusses the
effects of technological change (an output of the economic system) on the participants of the IR system. By analyzing a large
number of case studies, he observes that advance notice, company-
paid retraining, internal transfer based on seniority, attrition,
and joint committees are among the most widely used arrangements
for coping with worker displacement. Bernard Solasse and Jean
Sexton, in chapter 4, are concerned with a specific phenomenon,
namely, the implications of economic affluence for the members
of the Confederation of National Trade Unions in Quebec. They
suggest that in order to meet the consumption needs of its
members, CNTU advocates the formation of a vast cooperative sector. R. R. March, in chapter 5, presents a survey of public
opinion (output of the social system) toward unions, strikes,
and other related topics. He concludes that regionalism and
union membership are strong determinants of public attitude.
Richard U. Miller, in chapter 6, studies the political affiliation of the trade unions, particularly the role of the NDP in
the political system. In chapter 7, Innis Christie analyzes
unfair labour practices, such as employer participation in the
formation of a trade union, use of the "yellow dog" contracts,
failure to bargain in good faith, and others. He concludes,
on the basis of his interviews, that there is moderate satisfaction with the existing law of unfair labour practices. In
chapter 8, M.A. Zaida, drawing from survey and research data,
discusses the influence of the Canadian minimum wage on employment and wage differentials. His conclusions are that implementation of the minimum wage has affected employment in low-
wage industries and areas and has tended to narrow wage
structures. In chapter 9, J. Douglas Muir provides an historical development of labour-management relations. He discusses
such important issues as the legal status of the trade unions,
union security, bargaining rights and obligations, and picketing.

Inputs in the IR System from the Participants

Inputs in the IR system from the participants, that is, labour,
management, and government, constitute the subject matter of
part III. In chapter 10, Francis J. McKendy studies the history
and structure of the labour movement. He speculates that in
years to come, unions will become larger through mergers. International unions, if they continue to serve the interest of the

workers, will remain viable. In chapter 11, C. P. Thakur has
captured the salient structural features of the contemporary
labour movement. Through a set of interesting charts, he explains the membership growth historically and the current union
affiliation.

The second participant in the IR system is management.
Laurent Belanger, in chapter 12, provides the results of his
interviews with top managers of twenty-five of the largest
corporations and an equal number of medium and small businesses.
The purpose of his interviews was to survey management attitudes
toward their associations, unions and strikes. Managerial need
for job satisfaction among Francophone-Anglophone and male-female
managers is measured by Rabindra N. Kanungo, in chapter 13, by
using Maslow-type need categories. He concludes that Francophone
and female managers derive greater satisfaction on the job than
Anglophone and male managers.

The third participant in the IR system is government. We all
know that one of the fundamental measures of governmental intervention in the IR system is the determination of appropriate
bargaining units. In chapter 14, E. E. Herman evaluates the
effect of public policy and the board certification practices to
arrive at a conclusion that flexibility, innovation, creativity
and experimentation are needed for ensuring an appropriate
bargaining unit. In chapter 15, W. B. Cunningham looks at
another significant measure of governmental intervention, namely,
the role of compulsory conciliation boards. He concludes that
the provinces that abolished or reduced the use of compulsory
boards in recent years have not shown an increased strike
incidence. On the contrary, this measure has spelled some benefits for the process of collective bargaining.

Inputs in the IR System from Outside the Society

John Crispo, in chapter 16, demonstrates great insight into the
controversy of American-dominated corporations and trade unions
in Canada. In his opinion, multinational corporations and international unions need to reconcile their dual loyalties if the
concept of internationalism in industrial relations is to become
more acceptable.

Mechanisms for Converting Inputs into Outputs

In the IR system, there are three possible mechanisms for converting inputs to outputs: (1) collective bargaining; (2) continuing formal or informal labour-management interaction; and
(3) compulsory arbitration. Collective bargaining is the most
widely used conversion mechanism in Canada. Accordingly, part
V of this book contains five articles on this topic. There is
also one article each on joint labour-management councils and

compulsory arbitration in Australia.

Robert J. Christy, in chapter 17, explains the influence of
the size and scope of bargaining units on the process and outcome of collective bargaining. The analysis of his data indicates that British Columbia and the Atlantic Provinces have a
higher centralized bargaining structure (i.e., multi-establish-
ment or multicorporate) than other regions. Robert Rogow, in
chapter 18, examines the changing employment status of the
foreman and suggests that public policy is not generally
sympathetic to supervisory unionism and collective bargaining.
Managerial opposition is also stronger in this case than it is
in the case of rank-and-file bargaining. Shirley B. Goldenberg,
in chapter 19, looks at a higher level of managerial employees,
namely, professional workers. According to her, Alberta,
British Columbia, Newfoundland, Nova Scotia and Prince Edward
Island do not give professionals the legal right to bargain
collectively in the private sector. However, the number of
those who have this right is greater now than it was a decade
ago. Stephen G. Peitchinis, in chapter 20, examines a special
case of collective bargaining: the railway industry. He points
out that, due to the refusal of management, "there has been no
real collective bargaining on the railways". In such circumstances, it seems advisable that an impartial tribunal be
established to rule if one of the parties refuses to bargain on
an issue. Problems in the chemical industry are of a different
nature. In chapter 21, G. E. Eaton suggests that this is a
high growth and high wage industry. Although it is not extensively organized, experimentation with coordinated bargaining and
joint bargaining is occurring.

No studies on plant-level, informal interaction between
labour and management are included in this book. However, a
study by Aranka E. Kovacs, chapter 22, describes the formation,
objectives and scope of joint labour-management councils. Her
research indicates that these bodies perform a useful function.
Accordingly, she has recommended that a Canadian Industrial
Relations Council be established.

Compulsory arbitration is an accepted conversion mechanism
in the Australian industrial relations system. In chapter 23,
J. E. Isaac suggests that if the large-scale work stoppages of
the 1890s had not occurred, Australia might have adopted "free"
collective bargaining. However, compulsory arbitration has
been flexible and beneficial in establishing a national wage
policy.

Included in part V is a set of rules (chapter 24), by J.
Lewiski and G. Swimmer, for simulated contract negotiations.
This simulation provides an opportunity for the students to

develop a "feel" for the collective bargaining process, by applying their textbook knowledge to an experimental situation. The game has been developed over a period of two years and has evoked an extremely favourable response from the students.

Outputs of the IR System

The most important outputs of an IR system are wages, hours of work, fringe benefits, a web of rules and even strikes and lock-outs. Part VI contains six articles dealing with most of these topics.

Gerald E. Starr, in chapter 25, examines the role of unions and collective bargaining in the determination of wages. The union-nonunion wage differentials for the male and female basic labour rate, and wage levels for skilled and white-collar workers are studied by separating control variables from union-impact variables. In chapter 26, G. L. Reuben narrows the discussion of wage determination down, focussing on the manu-facturing industry. His study examines wage determinants within major industries, and then broadens its scope to show how these major industries affect wage determination in the country as a whole. In chapter 27, Morley Gunderson focusses entirely on male-female wage differentials, concluding that "sex discrimina-tion in employment is clearly a prevailing phenomenon". S.M.A. Hameed (chapter 28) suggests that labour movement and long-term productivity trends have been responsible for the reduction of working hours. He argues that the same factors will lead to a four-day, thirty-two-hour work week by the late 1980s.

By analyzing and testing relevant strike statistics since 1900, Stuart M. Jamieson (chapter 29) arrives at a series of original and unexpected results. For example, he finds no correlation between business cycles and cycles of industrial conflict. Similarly, he finds no correlation in the behaviour of strike activity between Canada and the United States. The incidence of work stoppages is analyzed from a different angle by F. R. Anton (chapter 30). He has analyzed the rationale and the implications of a government-supervised strike vote and con-cludes that there is no evidence to indicate that strikes can be avoided because of a vote requirement.

A collective agreement is an output of the IR system. What it contains must be enforced and honoured by both labour and management for its entire duration. J. Douglas Muir, in chapter 31, argues that "conflict may arise out of honest differences in interpreting the agreement". Therefore, all agreements must, by law, contain a grievance procedure that allows the settlement of a dispute, in the last stage, through a binding arbitration.

Conclusion

Rapid technological changes, increasing union drive to organize white-collar and professional workers, continuing rivalry between the CLC and the CNTU, and the union effort to negotiate on several nonwage items are some of the inputs in the Canadian IR system. The ability of an IR student to understand and analyze the implications of these inputs depends largely on his or her grasp of the conceptual framework presented in this book. The selection of articles and the organization of the book provide workable guidelines for the understanding of public and private decision making, enabling the reader to effectively handle the growing complexity of the IR system.

Note that part IV of the book, dealing with the inputs from outside the society, contains only one article, thus indicating the need for further research in this area. Another area that needs attention is the analysis of fringe benefits; no suitable articles on collectively bargained and legally required fringe benefits appear to exist. Except in these two areas, the book is quite comprehensive and complete. Students taking an introductory course in industrial relations will find it useful; executive and industrial relations practitioners will also find it both interesting and informative.

CONTRIBUTORS AND THEIR AFFILIATIONS

Frank R. Anton — Department of Economics
University of Calgary

L. Belanger — Department of Industrial Relations
Laval University

I. Christie — Faculty of Law
Dalhousie University

R.J. Christy — Unemployment Insurance Canada
Ottawa

Dr. J. Crispo — Faculty of Administrative Studies
University of Toronto

W.B. Cunningham — Department of Economics and Political Science
Mount Allison University

G.E. Eaton — Department of Economics and Political Science
York University

Shirley B. Goldenberg — Department of Industrial Relations
McGill University

Morley Gunderson — Centre for Industrial Relations
University of Toronto

Dr. S.M.A. Hameed — Faculty of Business Administration and Commerce
University of Alberta

E. Edward Herman — Department of Economics
University of Cincinnati

J.E. Isaacs — Faculty of Economics and Politics
Monash University, Australia

Stuart Jamieson — Department of Economics
University of British Columbia

R.N. Kanungo — Faculty of Management
McGill University

A.E. Kovacs — Department of Economics
University of Windsor

Arthur M. Kruger — Department of Political Economy
University of Toronto

J. Lewiski — Government of Saskatchewan
Regina

R.R. March   Department of Political Economy
                      McMaster University

F.J. McKendy   Economics and Research Branch
                      Canada Department of Labour
                      Ottawa

R.U. Miller   Industrial Relations Research Institute
                      University of Wisconsin

Dr. J.D. Muir   Faculty of Business Administration and Commerce
                      University of Alberta

Stephen G. Peitchinis Faculty of Business Administration
                      University of Calgary

G.L. Reuber   Vice-President, (Academic) and Provost
                      University of Western Ontario

Robert Rogow   Department of Economics and Commerce
                      Simon Fraser University

Jean Sexton   Department of Industrial Relations
                      Laval University

B. Solasse   Department of Industrial Relations
                      Laval University

G. F. Starr   Ontario Department of Labour
                      Toronto

Gene Swimmer   School of Public Administration
                      Carleton University

Dr. C.P. Thakur Faculty of Business Administration and Commerce
                      University of Alberta

M.A. Zaidi   Faculty of Law
                      Dalhousie University

TABLE OF CONTENTS

Management

Government

PART IV: INPUTS IN THE IR SYSTEM FROM OUTSIDE THE SOCIETY... 177

PART V: MECHANISMS FOR CONVERTING INPUTS TO OUTPUTS........ 187

PART VI: OUTPUTS OF THE IR SYSTEM.......................... 283

PART I: A THEORETICAL FRAMEWORK

1. Perspectives of Industrial Relations

by S. M. A. Hameed

The student taking an industrial relations course for the first
time has generally had one or more introductory courses in
economics, sociology or other social sciences. On first exposure to IR, he or she is mystified by the comparative lack of
clarity on some of the basic questions. For example, is IR an
autonomous discipline, comparable to other social sciences?
What is the scope of its study? What is its origin? How do we
define its subject matter? Does it have an integrated theory?

Attempts have been made to answer most of these questions in
this chapter. Since developing an integrated theory is of utmost
importance, chapter 2 has been exclusively devoted to the last
question. The remainder of the book presents a comprehensive
survey of the industrial relations discipline as it has evolved
in Canada.

Is IR an Autonomous Discipline?

Any branch of knowledge can acquire the status of an autonomous
discipline if it satisfies three basic criteria. First, there
must be a unity of focus in the enquiries of that branch of
knowledge. Even the most complex phenomena under study must
emanate from or be traceable to a predefined nucleus of objectives. An economist, for instance, may be engaged in such
disparate activities as examining the fiscal policies of the
Canadian government or analyzing the population trends in India.
Nevertheless, his enquiries converge on one basic economic
concern, this being to observe "human behaviour as a relationship
between ends and scarce means which have alternate uses".

Similarly, the focus of IR is on human behaviour as a relationship among individuals, formal, informal, public and
private groups in a work-related environment. This makes IR
noticeably different from other social sciences, as it studies
work-oriented human behaviour *in its totality*. IR studies the
entire work pattern of an individual as he enters the labour
market, earns monetary and nonmonetary rewards, develops a work
perception and motivation, communicates and participates in the
structure and process of the formal and informal groups at work,

1

abides by the work regulations imposed both by management and by government, and receives various work-related benefits, such as unemployment and worker compensation, retraining allowances, and finally, as he leaves the labour market, retirement benefits. Thus, the phenomena under study are varied and complex, but unified in their focus on human hehaviour, interaction and attitudes in the work-related environment.

Second, there must be continuity in the relationship of phenomena under study. Ultimately, all human knowledge is interrelated. But because of gaps in human knowledge and the limited comprehension of the human mind, discontinuity or a weakening of relationships between phenomena becomes discernible. These discontinuities form the boundaries of a discipline. Some phenomena tend to spill over these boundaries to become the subject matter of another discipline if the first criterion, that is, unity of focus, applies. With the widening of human awareness, new concerns and new areas of investigation are identified, and consequently, new disciplines emerge, such as biochemistry, social psychology, or industrial relations.

A periodic restructuring of knowledge is therefore imperative because of the discoveries of new frontiers, emergence of new problems, and need for changed policies. A comprehensive study of human behaviour in a work-related environment is not possible in the absence of an autonomous discipline of IR because its related phenomena spill over the boundaries of existing social sciences. The continuity in the relationship of phenomena is thus weakened vertically, as seen in table 1.1, and strengthened horizontally.[1] In other words, labour economics, industrial psychology, industrial sociology, labour law and personnel management have a stronger and common link in the analysis of work-related behaviour than they have with their parent disciplines.

Third, a theoretical framework identifying dependent and independent variables and establishing lines of causality is essential for explaining and possibly predicting various phenomena. It is not sufficient to have partial theories that are not linked together. In essence, a discipline needs a unified theory to integrate different components of the subject matter and establish a centrality of theme.

The horizontal slicing of knowledge, constituting a separate and autonomous IR discipline, is now complete with an integrated theory that conceptually connects these segments of knowledge. More about the integrated theory of IR will be explained in the next chapter.

IR meets all three criteria and therefore, is an autonomous discipline. According to Irving Sabghin: "... second only to politics and public administration, Industrial Relations represents the most complete symbiosis of the behavioural sciences into one field." It is heartening to note that graduate programs in IR have survived over a decade in some of the leading universities in Canada and the United States. Its future existence and growth are no longer threatened.

The Scope of Industrial Relations

Many allied social sciences, at one time or another, are faced with the problem of determining the scope of their study. Should they remain secluded in the pursuit of truth for its own sake or should they also make policy recommendations? If the intent is to achieve scientific rigour the scope of the subject may be restricted. Thus, it is often argued that a social science should remain neutral between different ends and study "what is" rather than "what ought to be". Such positive and normative bias has led to unnecessary controversy. IR is relatively free from this polemic. It was formalized as a practical subject, concerned with the accommodation of conflicting interests within the work-related environment. In this pragmatic sense it is not an idle pursuit of truth for its own sake. An IR researcher may not "furnish a body of settled conclusions, immediately applicable to policy",[2] but even when he is conducting a purely scientific study his ultimate purpose is to state the implications that can be readily utilized in

---

TABLE 1.1 Traditional Social Science Disciplines

Content Segments	Economics	Psychology	Sociology	Law	Commerce
Typical	Public Finance	Clinical Abnormal Child Psy.	Family Criminology Organization	Torts Criminal	Accounting Marketing
	International				
Majors	Agricultural	etc.	etc.	Wills Estates etc.	Business Finance etc.
Industrial Relations	Labour Economics	Ind.Psy.	Ind.Soc.	Labour Law	Personnel Management

Source: L. Reed Tripp, "The Industrial Relations Discipline in American Universities", *ILRR* (July 1964).

understanding a conflict situation (i.e., strikes and lockouts), and making value judgements.[3]   Therefore, the IR knowledge is "for the healing" rather than a "purely formal technique of reasoning, an algebra of choice".[4]

A number of examples can be furnished to indicate that scientific studies conducted in IR have often been in the nature of making policy recommendations. To cite a few: the Kerr and Seigal study of the longshoremen and textile workers indicated the limitations in the Human Relations School;[5]   Reynolds's study of the labour market behaviour rejected the classical theory of the labour market;[6]   and Smith's Work Theory suggested that the personality and behavioural factors are defined in the work situation. These are examples of IR studies which, though emphasizing formal methods of scientific investigation, do not refrain from making value judgements. This establishes a healthy tradition of utilizing IR knowledge both for purely academic theorizing and for policy purposes, thus defining the scope of IR in a broader context. In other words, IR is capable of yielding *a priori* results, containing scientific truth, and is also suitable for making policy recommendations. The student of physics or chemistry might study his subject with a view to arriving at the truth, but leaving the question of practical application of results to others. But varying degrees of labour-management cooperation, strikes, and dispute settlements demand value judgements, in some form or another, from IR researchers, teachers and practitioners. They cannot help responding to this demand, as industrial relations, in a broader sense, is a concern of every citizen in an industrialized society. The scope of industrial relations, thus defined, includes both academic theorizing and operational policy making.

The Origin and Growth of IR

The origin and growth of IR is difficult to trace historically because the body of knowledge developed separately in two areas. Labour economics dealt with the history and development of the trade union movement, and management science concentrated on the managerial and organizational functions. A third area also existed, relating to the role of the practitioner distinct from the role of the academic social scientist. For example, conciliation briefs and arbitration awards provide a basic understanding of the conflict-resolution process. Following the strikes and labour unrest in the years immediately after World War II, formal efforts were made to establish a new discipline of Industrial Relations. Subsequently a cross-communication developed among those areas represented by the economist, social psychologist and lawyer-practitioner, as they used the same thought process.

In terms of individual contributions to IR, one may safely

go as far back as Adam Smith.[7] He started the first formal investigation of the problems of men at work. *Wealth of Nations,*
Book I, is entitled, "Of the causes of improvement in the
productive power of labour, and of the order according to which
its produce is naturally distributed among the different ranks
of the people".[8] Like all pioneering studies, Adam Smith's
writing also dealt with selected problems of work place.
Totality of work-place behaviour, which has, in recent years,
become the focus of IR study, was obviously not the concern of
Wealth of Nations. It only dealt with topics like division of
labour, productivity and market characteristics.

A full-fledged contribution to IR had to wait a long time.
At the turn of this century, a number of notable writers focussed
their attention on different facets of labour-management
relations. Commons at Wisconsin and Barnett at Johns Hopkins did
the pioneering work in the U.S., parallel to the Webbs' contribution to British industrial relations. Studying the changing
nature of property rights in the Anglo-American experience,
Commons noted how the form or structure of an economy changes as
a society moves from feudalism to a modern, market-oriented
economy.[9] In so observing, he provided a rich historical and
institutional background for the study of IR. One of his
greatest contributions to the growth of IR study is his treatment of work behaviour in its totality. He went beyond the
intellectual tradition of the German historical school[10] and
combined not only economics and jurisprudence but many other
branches of human knowledge. His interpretation of union and
management interaction has the "psychological dimensions of
thinking, feeling, willing, persuading, coercing, commanding,
obeying and expectation; its ethical and legal dimensions of
rights, duties, liberties and exposure and its political or
governmental dimensions of authority and authorization in the
use of physical power, economic or moral power, according to
common rules that set the limit and direction of conduct".[11]

Another valuable aspect of Commons's writings, which helped
in the development of IR study, was his recognition of the
element of conflict. His approach to the resolution of conflict
was neither Marxian nor similar to that taken by the Human
Relations School. In both, IR loses much of its efficacy and
justification as a separate and viable branch of human knowledge.
To Commons, society appeared as a metaphysical entity that
breeds conflict. No one can ever eliminate conflict forever.
*All that is possible is to establish a foundation for a legal
determination of reasonableness by securing an advance accommodation of conflicting interests through voluntary agreement.*[12]
Thus he emphasized a pragmatic approach for the IR researcher,
to provide society with the largest possible number of alternatives of conduct or possibilities of action. Herein lies the
utility of IR study and the ever-widening scope for research.

George Barnett, in his early study of printers, noted the impact of technology on the development of unions.[13]   His interests in the unions lay essentially in the statistical aspects of the movement. He emphasized empiricism as a method of studying union growth. This could be considered a departure from Commons's historical-institutional method of study, but in fact Commons also used empiricism to a great extent. There were other points of similarity between these two founding fathers of IR. For example, Commons and Barnett were both impressed by the United States Industrial Commission and were also interested in the working of the Whittley Committees in England.

Ely, Blum, Seager and Millis are among those notable writers who enriched IR and marked the end of an earlier phase characterized by a virtual monopoly of economists, lawyers and political scientists. Psychologists and sociologists stepped into this field in a formally recognizable fashion with the beginning of the Hawthorne experiments at Western Electric. Taylor, Gantt, Emerson and Gilbreth, who started the pioneering phase of scientific management, are often treated with indifference by the economists. But for a balanced treatment of this subject it is essential that their contributions, representing the management philosophy of the pre-World War I period, be duly acknowledged.

However, there are reasons for the cold treatment given the scientific management group. First, they regarded labour as a commodity or a machine. Secondly, in their scheme of things there was no place for unions as an important part of the IR system.

The succeeding phase of Administrative Organization and its exponents, namely Gullick and Urwick, Mooney and Reily, Mary Parker Follet, and R. C. Davis, are also noteworthy. The field of personnel management had emerged prior to the 1920s and the human element in business was being recognized, but it was only in the thirties that the Human Relations School marked the beginning of an impressive phase in IR development history. Greater attention was now being paid to the modern industrial worker. His problems were interpreted in terms of breaking systems of values and his sense of losing social relatedness. Mayo, Roethlisberger and Dickson[14] provide the main interpretations of the results of the Hawthorne studies. According to Mayo, "the group factors operating to determine individual motivation are spontaneous social influences defined generally by the specific group structure".[15]   This assumption provided the basis not only for Human Relations but also for Group Dynamics. Kert Lewin popularized the term *group dynamics* and pioneered a new technique of research. Following these research studies, numerous other behavioural research studies at Michigan, Harvard and Yale were conducted, signifying the growing influence of hehavioural research in IR.

With the increased participation of psychologists and sociologists, it now became possible to understand the dynamic group interaction at the work place and its importance in achieving higher levels of output. While this new phase brought psychologists and economists closer, their points of view were still divided on the issue of conflict resolution within the work situation. William F. Whyte, one of the chief exponents of the Human Relations School, realized that Mayo had indeed underplayed the element of conflict and that the existence of unions within the plant community makes the IR system more realistic and operational.[16]   He tended to agree with some of the union advocates that informal group behaviour is not the only clue to the problem of industrial peace;[17] one must also study the formal union structure and its functioning within the plant. These signs of mutual acceptance and agreement among the labour economists and social psychologists ushered in a third phase in IR growth, shifting the multidisciplinary approach to a new plane. In this phase behavioural scientists have shown a deeper insight into personality factors and in-plant behaviour. Chris Argyris and Bakke, the notable Yale researchers, are active participants in the Industrial Relations Research Association (IRRA), and seem willing to carry the IR program into the future along with the labour economists. Notable in this group are Clark Kerr, John Dunlop, Arthur Ross, Lloyd Reynolds, Sumner Slichter, Richard Lester, and Neil Chamberlain.

Industrial Relations Defined

John T. Dunlop stated that "the field of IR purports to concern itself with a totality of behaviour. It cannot be content with a single aspect, the economic or the psychological."[18]   Similarly, L. Reed Tripp, in a foregoing table, illustrated that IR utilizes only those parts of traditional disciplines that structure and determine its multidisciplinary character. An understanding of the totality of work-related behaviour requires a study of the complex relationship among individuals, formal, informal, public and private groups. The purpose of the study is to determine the nature of interaction, degree of cooperation or conflict, and the process of decision making, as it concerns allocation of rewards to participating individuals and groups.[19]   The rewards could be negative or positive, monetary or psychological, social or political in nature. The process of decision making is unilateral, bilateral or trilateral, as is explained in the following diagram.

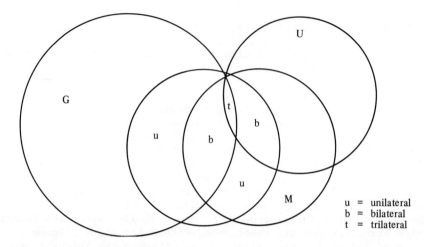

The decisions in the work-related environment are sometimes
made unilaterally by the management or the government (areas
marked *u* in the diagram). At other times, union and management
or management and government make joint decisions in a unilateral
fashion (areas marked *b*). There are also occasions when all
three participants make decisions, trilaterally (areas marked *t*).

The participating individuals and groups include various
categories of workers, hierarchies of management and their
associations, unions, government agencies, and even the public, in
an indirect sense. However, the interaction is primarily between
labour and management to seek accommodation over the profit-
oriented goals of management and the reward-oriented goals of
employees. Certain components of these goals are in harmony but
others are in conflict, making the process of accommodation
continuous and ongoing. The spectrum of employee rewards is wide
and varied, extending from various forms of wage payment to
fringe benefits and the purely psychological feeling of job
security. The profit-oriented goals of management, on the other
hand, are also complex, ranging from subcontracting, technological change to hiring, layoff, discharge, demotion and transfer of employees. Because of this wide range of issues and
multiplicity of possibilities that exist for their resolution,
IR becomes an interesting study of the uniformities underlying
human interactions. To deal with a situation when a conflict of
goals is recognized, formal, informal, public or private methods
of accommodation are invoked.

The above discussion suggests that in the definition of IR
the following five elements must be present. First, labour and
management have to interact in the work-related environment in
order to produce goods and services. Second, there is an
inherent conflict between certain goals of the interacting
groups. Third, the process of accommodation is continuous and
ongoing because of the nature and frequency of conflicts.

Fourth, the methods of accommodation include formal, informal, public and private actions. Fifth, the accommodation or compromise is necessary to determine the allocation of rewards to interacting groups, primarily the workers. Given these elements, we may say that IR is a discipline that studies human behaviour as a relationship among individuals, formal, informal, public and private groups who interact in a work-related environment to reach a compromise over the allocation of rewards.

Notes

1. Professor Tripp indicated slicing of knowledge in table 1.1. The concept of continuity in the relationship of phenomena and the strengthening effect horizontally is my interpretation of the existing IR status. See L. Reed Tripp, "The Industrial Relations Discipline in American Universities", *LRR*, July 1964.

2. J. M. Keynes, *The General Theory of Employment, Interest and Money* (New York: Harcourt Brace & Co., 1951).

3. See P. Streeten, "Economics and Value Judgement", *Quarterly Journal of Economics*, November 1950, p. 95.

4. Ibid.

5. Kerr and Seigal, "The Inter Industry Property to Strike -- An International Comparison", in A. Kornhauser, *The Industrial Conflict* (New York: McGraw-Hill Inc., 1956), p. 189.

6. L. G. Reynolds, *The Structure of Labor Markets: Wages and Labor Mobility in Theory and Practice* (New York: Harper, 1961).

7. For a detailed discussion on the subject, see J. Douglas Brown, "University Research in IR", *IRRA Annual Proceedings* (28-29 December 1952).

8. Adam Smith, *An Enquiry Into the Nature and Causes of Wealth of Nations* (Edinburgh: A. and C. Black, 1850).

9. K. Parsons, "The Basis of Commons' Progressive Approach to Public Policy", in *Labor, Management and Social Policy,* ed. G. G. Somers (Madison: University of Wisconsin Press, 1963).

10. See Mark Perman, *Labor Union Theories in America* (Illinois: Row, Peterson and Co., 1958).

11. John R. Commons, *Legal Foundations of Capitalism* (Madison: University of Wisconsin Press, 1959).

12. N. Feinsinger, "Law and the Public Interest in Labor-Management Relations", in *Labor, Management and Social Policy,* ed. G.G. Somers.

13. George E. Barnett, *Chapters on Machinery and Labor* (Cambridge: Harvard University Press, 1943).

14. Roethlisberger and Dickson, *Management and the Worker* (Cambridge: Harvard University Press, 1943).

15. K. U. Smith, *Behaviour, Organization and Work: A New Approach to Industrial Behavioural Science* (Madison: College Printing and Typing Co. Inc., 1962).

16. See W. F. Whyte, "Human Relations -- A Progress Report", in *Complex Organizations,* ed. Amitai Etzioni (New York: Holt, Rinehart and Winston, 1961).

17. Kerr and Seigal, "The Inter Industry Property to Strike".

18. John T. Dunlop, "Research in IR: Past and Present", *IRRA Proceedings*, 1954.

19. Alton Craig suggested that IR is concerned with "the allocation of rewards to employees for their services". See Alton W. J. Craig, "A Model for the Analysis of Industrial Relations Systems" (mimeographed), 1967.

2. An Integrated Theory of Industrial Relations

by S. M. A. Hameed

The status of IR as an autonomous discipline was discussed in chapter 1 in relation to three criteria, namely, unity of focus, continuity in the interrelationship of phenomena, and the development of an integrated theory. The purpose of this chapter is to demonstrate that a large number of theories in IR are conceptually linked together.

There are three levels of theories that deal with unionism, collective bargaining, and industrial relations. At the most fundamental level, John R. Commons,[1] Selig Perlman,[2] and Frank Tannenbaum[3] are the major theorists who explain the phenomenon of worker participation in unions in terms of economic, psychological and social factors, respectively. At the intermediate level are theories of collective bargaining by Neil Chamberlain,[4] Joseph Shister,[5] Reed Tripp[6] and others[7] who explain the process of wage determination and decisions on matters of industrial jurisprudence, through a matrix of economic and institutional factors. At the highest level of conceptualization, there are theories of industrial relations by John T. Dunlop,[8] Gerald G. Somers,[9] Jack Barbash,[10] Kerr, et al[11] and others[12] who have analyzed labour, management and government interaction within an environmental context.

A unifying theme integrates the existing theories of unionism, collective bargaining and industrial relations. This theme, implicit in the definition of IR, is to observe human behaviour as a relationship among individuals, formal and informal, public and private groups who interact in a work-related environment to reach a compromise on the allocation of rewards. To be more specific, it is the compromise over the allocation of rewards which is basic to the formation of unions, collective bargaining processes and governmental decisions.

For some of the concepts in this chapter, I am indebted to Alton W. Craig, "A Model for the Analysis of Industrial Relations Systems" (mimeographed), 1967. Excerpts from my paper "A Theory of Responsive Bargaining", *Labour Law Journal*, August 1973, also appear in this chapter.

A Generalized Framework

In a democratic society, decisions pertaining to the allocation
of rewards are largely made on the basis of compromise rather
than compulsion. They are made in private and public sectors,
among groups and individuals, and are not confined to the IR
system. For instance, wages are determined in the unionized
sector of the economy through the process of collective
bargaining. They are left to the market forces and individual
or informal bargaining in the economic system. A variety of
employee benefits, such as governmental pension schemes,
unemployment insurance compensation, and workmen's compensation are determined in the political system. Other fringe
benefits, such as paid vacations, holidays and sick leave, may
be determined through collective bargaining in the IR system or
unilaterally decided by the employers in the economic system.
Thus, the IR system is one of five systems where wages,
employee benefits and other nonmonetary rewards are determined.
A generalized framework is therefore necessary to encompass
other existing systems.

Any society, developing or industrialized, may be regarded as
a composite of five systems: (1) economic; (2) social; (3)
political; (4) legal; and (5) industrial relations. These
systems are interdependent and have conceptual similarities in
their structures and processes.

Components

Each system, whether it is economic or social, legal or political,
has the same components as the IR system. These are: (1) internal environment; (2) inputs; (3) a conversion mechanism; and
(4) outputs. Figure 2.1 will be helpful in understanding the
character and function of these components.

FIGURE 2.1

Components of the Five Societal Systems

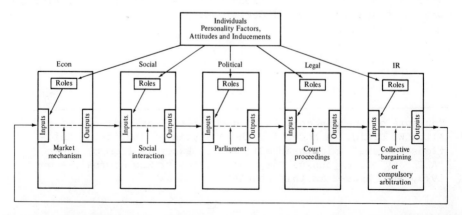

Internal Environment

The character, potential, and function of each system is basically dependent upon its internal environment. It has nonphysical attributes like goals and ideology and/or physical properties such as natural resources and ecology. Both these categories can and do change as a result of various inputs (individual participation, inputs from other systems, and inputs from outside the society). In the determination of the output of a system internal environment plays a significant role.

To illustrate, let us examine the internal environment of the five systems in Canada. The economic system has a high level of technology and abundant mineral, forest, and agricultural resources. For the most part, a cold climate makes agriculture, construction, and shipping seasonal in nature. The product and labour markets, due to long distances, are generally decentralized. The goals of the economic system are to maintain full employment, stable prices, balance of payments, and equitable income distribution. Its ideology is primarily free enterprise.

The ideology of the Canadian social system is, broadly speaking, egalitarianism. This is an understanding which is shared generally by individuals, formal and informal groups in their interaction pattern. The social goals are diverse and complex but in a generic sense they include welfare and rehabilitation of the aged, the poor and the delinquent, stability in the family structure, and social tolerance of racial, ethnic, and minority groups.

The Canadian political system ideologically rests on a popular concensus in making democratic decisions. Formation of governments and parliamentary procedures recognize the principle of majority rule. The goals of the system include defence, maintenance of law and order, and protection of public interest.

The ideology of the legal system is "equality before law". The goals of the system are to establish reasonable standards of justice through a web of rules and regulations.

Inputs

Each system receives three kinds of inputs: (1) individual participation; (2) inputs from other systems; and (3) physical or nonphysical inputs from outside the society.

Individual Participation

Individuals participate in formal and informal, public and private groups and in larger systems because of certain inducements offered by these groups that tally with the individuals' attitudes, educational or cultural background. Figure 2.1 illustrates that an individual's participation in each of the five systems depends upon the urgency and hierarchy of his or her needs. Thus, need satisfaction is the stimulus for participation in any system. For instance, given Maslow's need hierarchy, one would assume that an individual will participate in the economic system for food and shelter; in the social system for status, prestige and affiliation; in the political system for power and dependence; in the legal system for protection and security. It appears that the IR system satisfies the residual needs not satisfied in other systems. Consequently, participation in this system is a function of unsatisfied needs in other systems.

When an individual participates in a system for the satisfaction of some of his needs, he plays one or more roles available in that system. For instance, the economic system contains the roles of consumers and producers, buyers and sellers. Similarly, the social system offers a variety of roles in the family, the church, and voluntary organizations; while the political system has participative roles at different levels of governments, political parties, and civil service. The legal system has judges, lawyers, and clients, and the IR system has labour, management, and government functionaries. The aggregate level of participation in any system is variable, as individuals may drop in and out of that system or qualitatively reduce or increase their degree of participation. Thus the development of a system depends partly on the level and degree of individual participation.

Inputs from Other Systems

There is an interdependence among the systems, as output from one system becomes input in another system. As an example, we can examine the inputs from economic, social, political and legal systems as they affect the IR system.

The Economic System. Of great significance for the IR system is the output of the economic system. In a generalized sense, one could say that the output of an economic system is the state of the economy, that is, recession, boom, stagflation or depression. Different levels of prices, profits and unemployment, indicative of the state of the economy, have an impact on the IR system. For example, during a recession, when the profits are low and unemployment is high, unions will have a low bar-

gaining power. In a more specific context, given the internal
environment of the Canadian economic system, employees in the
seasonal industries, like construction or shipping, many exhibit
a high degree of militancy during the active season, to obtain
higher wages and other benefits.

The Social System. The output of the social system, relevant
for the IR system, may be described as social values and public
opinion. If the ideology of the Canadian social system is a mix
between egalitarianism and social Darwinism, unions as a collectivity can find little acceptance or sympathy. Unions appear as
a minority group, defying the norms of a nation of property
holders. At times, a prolonged labour dispute or an inflationary wage settlement could intensify the social disapproval
of union activities and the output of the system may be a
negative public opinion, forcing political and legal systems to
take action.

The Political System. Being receptive to the outputs from
other systems, the political system continuously produces
suitable legislation and executive orders. This output is
extremely pertinent to the functioning of the IR system. The
basic ideology of the Canadian political system's being democratic freedom has helped in the passage of legislation and
Orders-in-Council (P.C. 1003 and Industrial Relations and
Dispute Investigation Act), which have recognized the workers'
right to organize, bargain collectively and even strike in
nonessential industries. In the case of emergency disputes or
prolonged strikes, the Canadian government intervenes in order
to protect the public interest.

The Legal System. The output of the legal system that has
an impact on the IR system is couched in judicial decisions.
In the early history of the Canadian and American trade union
movement, courts played an important role in handling conspiracy charges. Justice Shaw of Massachusetts ruled in the case
of Commonwealth vs. Hunt (1842) that unions were no longer
conspiracies. In instances of picketing, illegal strikes,
and the interpretation of existing labour relations and labour
standards acts, courts still play a significant role. It may
be remembered that statutory law is an input and common law
is an output of the legal system.

Inputs from Outside the Society

The industrial relations system is heavily affected by inputs
from outside the society. Countries are no longer closed
because of national boundaries; there are inflows and outflows
of raw materials, finished goods, short-term and long-term
capital, technical assistance, and scientific, legal and
social innovations (see figure 2.2).

FIGURE 2.2   Input - Output Flow between IR System and
              Systems of Other Societies

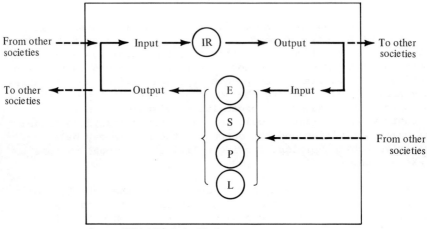

Source: IRRA 1973 Spring Meeting

    In the Canadian society the economic system continues to
receive capital inflows from the U.S. and immigration from a
large number of countries around the world. The political
system has borrowed legislative ideas from Great Britain and
the U.S. which affect the IR system. For instance, the
Conciliation Act of 1900 was based on similar legislation in
the U.K. The IRDI Act of 1948 has many provisions that were
originally passed in the American Wagner Act of 1935. The IR
system has received financial and organizational help from the
U.S. in the formation and development of its international
unions. Many Canadian social values and attitudes are a
reflection of those in the U.S.

Conversion Mechanisms

Each system has one or more mechanisms for converting inputs
to outputs. These mechanisms could be technical, market, or
institutional processes or simply formal or informal group or
individual interaction patterns. Only those mechanisms relevant to the IR system will be discussed. We would do no more
than simply identify the mechanisms in different systems,
reserving a somewhat longer discussion to mechanisms in the IR
system.

    In Canada, wages and working conditions for a large section
of the work force are determined by the market mechanism.
Generally, it is the employer who, in keeping with the market
forces, determines the level of wages, nature of fringe bene-

fits, and working conditions. In the social system, it is the
concensus and public opinion that acts as a conversion mechanism
and determines the social desirability and prestige associated
with various occupations. Thus, mobility between occupations
may not be determined entirely by the wage differential but by
the varying degrees of social acceptance and prestige attached
to a wide range of occupations.

The conversion mechanism in the political system is the parliament that produces legislation governing minimum wage, maximum
hours, statutory holidays, pensions, workmen's compensation,
unemployment insurance compensation and social assistance. There
is a separate body of legislation that provides a framework for
conducting labour-management negotiations. The conversion
mechanism in the legal system consists of court proceedings at
different levels.

Of the conversion mechanisms in the IR system, collective
bargaining and compulsory arbitration must be recognized as two
possible alternatives. Collective bargaining is by far the most
prevalent mechanism throughout Europe and North America. Compulsory arbitration is used in Australia, New Zealand and a
number of developing countries. Collective bargaining is essentially a voluntary, bilateral process that converts inputs to
outputs. If settlement is not obtained through a bilateral
negotiation, third parties such as government conciliators or
private mediators assist the parties. A breakdown in collective
bargaining may result in a possibility of a strike or lockout.
That possibility does not exist under compulsory arbitration,
as the dispute is decided through an award that becomes binding
on both labour and management parties.

Output

The output of the IR system may be defined as a web of rules
(Dunlop), conflict resolution (Somers), or productivity, efficiency or allocation of monetary or nonmonetary rewards (Craig).
In addition to these positive outputs, the IR system at times
produces negative outputs such as strikes or lockouts. They
become an input in all the systems and are recycled. In normal
circumstances they are resolved in the IR system with the help
of conciliatory or mediatory services. But, if the strikes
become prolonged or threaten public interest, other systems
react. Social systems may produce a strong public opinion,
political systems may legislate a back-to-work order and the
legal system may invoke emergency dispute settlement clauses.
In short, the IR system, or any system for that matter, does
not function in isolation.

We have indicated earlier that the focus of the IR system is

on rewards, including wages, hours of work, paid vacations,
holidays, sick leave, pensions, unemployment insurance compensation, worker's compensations, medical insurance, occupational
recognition, and other nonmonetary rewards. Many but not all of
these are an output of the IR system. Economic, social and
political systems produce some of these rewards. Therefore it
is important that the IR system is conceptualized in the
totality of all other systems.

Integration of the IR Theory

We have argued so far that systems are interdependent. We go a
step farthur and suggest that the components in each system are
also *integrated* and *causal*. These two characteristics are significant in conceptualizing a unified and integrated theory of IR.

The components described throughout this chapter may now be
presented in the form of the following equations:

$$I_1 = f\ (P) \qquad\qquad\qquad (1)$$

$$C = f\ (I_1,\ I_2,\ I_3,\ E) \qquad\qquad (2)$$

$$E = f\ (I_1,\ I_2,\ I_3) \qquad\qquad (3)$$

$$O = f\ (I_1,\ I_2,\ I_3,\ E,\ C) \qquad\qquad (4)$$

where P = personality factors, including knowledge, education
and past experience helping in the establishment of an induce-
ment-response equilibrium; I_1 = input (participation of
individuals); I_2 = inputs from other systems in the same
society; I_3 = inputs from outside the society; C = conversion
mechanisms; E = internal environment; and O = output.

The four interdependent equations outlined above constitute
a conceptual framework, applicable to all the five systems in
any society. This has two primary advantages: (1) it places
the IR system at a conceptual parity with the other systems,
making it possible to analyze economic, social, political and
legal developments within the same conceptual framework; and
(2) it broadens the scope of analysis, that is, in case a
researcher wishes to understand the origin and nature of outputs from other systems being fed into the IR system, he can
do so without altering his tools of analysis.

The equations can be developed into theories of unionism,
collective bargaining and industrial relations. For instance,
equation 1 is a theory of unionism, equation 2 is a theory of
collective bargaining, and equation 4 constitutes a theory of
industrial relations.

Theory of Unionism. According to equation 1, an individual
will participate in a system if his attitudes, education and past
experience are in harmony with the inducements offered by that
system. We also indicated earlier that the IR system satisfies
the residual needs not satisfied in other systems. Applying
these broad elements of a participation theory to the phenomenon
of union membership, we find that workers will join a union only
when there is harmony between the nature of inducement (job
security, higher wages, etc.) offered by the union and their
level of education, attitudes and past experience. Further, if
participation in other groups, organizations or systems satisfies
the socio-economic and psychological needs of a worker, he will
not join the union. The phenomenon of white-collar and profes-
sional-worker unionism can be explained with the help of this theory.

Theory of Collective Bargaining. Equation 2 explains that the
bargaining mechanism (C) is affected by the following factors:
(1) the nature of participation or interaction (I_1) between
labour, management and government; (2) the inputs from economic,
social, political and legal systems (I_2);   (3) the inputs from
outside the society (I_3), such as volume of trade or inflow of
capital; and (4) the internal environment (E), which includes
the goals and ideology of labour and management. It also suggests
that the mechanism itself may change, say, from collective
bargaining to compulsory arbitration to binding voluntary arbitration or anything else, if the above causal variables changed.

Theory of Industrial Relations. Equation 4 explains that
the output of the IR system is affected by all those factors
described in the theory of collective bargaining, plus the
nature of the conversion mechanism itself.

Conclusion

This chapter has attempted to provide a conceptual framework for
integrating all three levels of IR theory. By placing the IR
system at par with other systems, it has broadened the scope of
analysis, as a researcher may undertake a second level of
investigation into the nature and causes of inputs coming from
other systems. Thus the same tools of analysis are helpful in
the understanding of other systems.

The conceptual framework has included the inputs from outside the society, meaning that societies need not be treated
as closed entities but as integrated and dynamic ones. This
will be particularly useful for the IR system where the
analysis of the operation of the multinational corporations
demands a broader framework.

The variables used in our equations are broad and unspecified, but depending on what is to be explained, appropriate equations may be defined in operational terms.

An interdependence exists among the variables included in our four equations. The lines of causality are defined in each equation, implying a potential for making predictions for the future.

Notes

1. John R. Commons, *A Documentary History of American Industrial Society,* 11 vols. (Glendale, California: Arthur H. Clark Company, 1910-1911).

2. Selig Perlman, *The Theory of the Labour Movement* (New York: Macmillan, 1928).

3. Frank Tannenbaum, *A Philosophy of Labour* (New York: Alfred A. Knopf, 1951).

4. Neil W. Chamberlain, *Collective Bargaining* (New York: McGraw-Hill, 1951).

5. Joseph Shister, "Collective Bargaining", in *A Decade of Industrial Relations Research, 1946-1956* (New York: Harper and Brothers, 1958).

6. L. Reed Tripp, "Collective Bargaining Theory", in *Labor Management and Social Policy*, ed. G. G. Somers (Madison: University of Wisconsin Press, 1963).

7. S. M. A. Hameed, "A Theory of Collective Bargaining", *Industrial Relations*, vol. 25, no. 3 (August 1970).

8. John T. Dunlop, *Industrial Relations Systems* (New York: Holt, Rinehart and Winston, 1958).

9. G. G. Somers, "Bargaining Power and Industrial Relations Theory", in *Essays in Industrial Relations Theory*, ed. G. G. Somers (Ames, Iowa: Iowa State University Press, 1969).

10.Jack Barbash, "The Elements of Industrial Relations", *British Journal of Industrial Relations* 4 (October 1964).

11.Kerr, et al., *Industrialism and Industrial Man* (Cambridge, Mass.: Harvard University Press, 1960).

12.Alton W. Craig, "A Model for the Analysis of Industrial

Relations Systems" (mimeographed); also S. M. A. Hameed, "Theory and Research in the Field of Industrial Relations", *British Journal of Industrial Relations,* vol. V, no. 2 (July 1967).

13. See Herbert G. Henerman, Jr., "Toward a General Conceptual System of Industrial Relations: How Do We Get There?", in *Essays,* ed. G.G. Somers.

PART II: INPUTS IN THE IR SYSTEM FROM OTHER SYSTEMS

3. Human Adjustment to Technological Change:
    An Economist's View
    by Arthur A. Kruger

Introduction

Over the past decade,[1] there has been considerable discussion of
the problems of adapting workers to change. The debate was
sparked by the rise in unemployment levels in Canada and the
United States in the period 1957-1961, and the accompanying
spread of new technology symbolized by the computer. Economists began to discuss the issue of structural unemployment -- a
special type of unemployment resulting from rapid shifts in
technology and consumer demand.[2] The proponents of the struc-
turalist position pressed for the development of manpower
programmes to speed the adjustment of labour supply to these
demand changes. Others urged a more radical rethinking of the
relative roles of work and leisure. They wanted programmes
designed to prepare men not for new jobs but for a future in
which work would be insignificant and output would be procured
largely by machines.[3]

    Much of this debate centred on the question of whether or
not technological change was proceeding at a rate so different
from the past that it posed entirely new adjustment problems
requiring vastly different institutions and attitudes from
those developed previously.

    This debate, as well as the experience of change and worker
displacement in many industries, influenced the thinking of
corporate and union officials as well as governments. In collective bargaining the emphasis shifted somewhat to matters such
as work rules, seniority rules, the age of retirement, the level
of pension benefits, severance pay, and supplementary unemployment benefits. All of these mechanisms were commonly found in
existing collective agreements. Unions sought to use these
readily available devices to facilitate the adaptation of
workers to displacement. Managements were reluctant to give
way because they feared that such programmes committed companies

---

to unpredictable costs, and also because they often inhibited
the firms in applying new technology.

In some cases, union leaders and management worked out bold
new programmes designed to facilitate worker adjustment to
technological change without unduly inhibiting the corporation's
ability to implement change.   The most interesting and important
cases on this continent are described in appendices II, III, and
IV of my report to the Task Force on Labour Relations.[4]

Governments also responded by rethinking the role of voca-
tional training in education, and by expanding programmes for
adult retraining.   Research was undertaken on forecasting manpower requirements.   Other new areas of state activity opened
up, including manpower mobility assistance and subsidies to
encourage industrial expansion in depressed areas.

Technological Change -- Costs and Benefits

Each party, confronted with the prospect of change, will attempt
to assess the likely costs and benefits of the innovation.   On
the basis of this appraisal, the parties will determine the
attitudes toward the change and toward the pace of adoption of
change.   This section will examine the costs and benefits of
technological change as viewed by each of the parties.   With
this we can see the limits of management's willingness to make
concessions in order to receive worker and union approval for
change, as well as the factors influencing worker and union
attitude to change.   The factors determining the economic
costs and benefits for society will also be examined.

Technological Change and Labour Displacement

Popular discussion of the subject often assumes that technological change is inherently labour displacing.   This is not
necessarily true either at the macro- or microlevel.   At the
macrolevel the degree of unemployment created by such changes
is a function of the level and composition of aggregate demand,
the degree of competition and mobility in markets, as well as
the pace of discovery and implementation of new methods.   It
is not possible to untangle the portion of unemployment
attributable to technological change and that owing to other
sources.

There is some evidence that on balance, technological change
in Canadian manufacturing has tended to be labour displacing
in the sense that the required labour input per unit of output
has fallen.   However, total employment has held up because of
buoyant aggregate demand from a variety of sources, including

expanded sales as a result of lower costs and lower prices for the products.

There is no inherent reason to expect technological change either to create or to destroy jobs in the aggregate. The impact of such change at the aggregate level depends on a variety of other factors, primarily the government's monetary and fiscal policies. What is certain is that technological change will create adjustment problems, both for labour and for management. Such changes will require workers to change their occupations, plants, firms, industries or geographic locations. However, technological change is not the only source of dislocation. Such forces as the discovery of new sources of raw materials or changes in the level of aggregate demand or the composition of aggregate demand will have similar displacement effects. It is worker displacement, rather than technological change per se, that generates problems for workers, management, governments and collective bargaining. We should bear in mind that much of the debate about automation and many of the collective bargaining experiments designed to cope with technological change reflect the concern over the broader problem of adjusting displaced workers, whatever the source of displacement.

Management and Technological Change

Most economists assume that the prime motive influencing the behaviour of corporate management in the marketplace is the desire to increase profits. The decision on whether or not to make changes in the firm and the timing of change will reflect this desire. Obviously no innovation will be adopted unless it is expected to raise profits, either through lowering production costs or improving product quality so as to permit the firm to increase sales or raise the product price.

Popular discussion of the problem of technological change focusses on the discovery of new types of capital equipment that usually are assumed to be rapidly adopted and labour displacing. But the problems of technological change do not always emerge so suddenly and so dramatically. Usually there is a long time lag between the discovery of a new process and the application of that process.

Technological change in a given industry is not the sole nor even necessarily the most important source of worker displacement in that industry. Workers may also be displaced because of: (1) shifts in product demand resulting from changes in income, tastes, relative product prices or scope of markets; (2) shifts in the level of product output resulting from changes in costs of production which may occur as a result of technological change, but which also take place as a result of changes in factor markets; and (3) shifts in relative factor prices resulting in changes in factor proportions.

In these cases, technological change in other sectors (rival or complementary products or in factor markets) may be responsible for the worker displacement in a given industry. Other forces, such as the pace of economic growth, tariffs and trade agreements, changes in the nature of competitive conditions in various markets (including the labour market), and a variety of government activities may also initiate the pressure that ultimately generates worker displacement in a given sector. Here the firm or industry may be faced with unexpected pressures for rapid change.

The Worker and Technological Change

Normally, workers have little incentive or opportunity for initiating technological change. (There are exceptions to this, notably the Scanlon Plan or other similar plans.) Rather, they are confronted with the prospect of change and react to management's decision in this area.

For workers, technological change is usually viewed with fear and suspicion. They see few benefits arising from it. Even where they are persuaded that change is the source of economic growth and benefits everyone in the long run, they feel -- often with justification -- that changes in their own particular firm or industry bring nothing but dislocation and problems for them. If this view appears to be shortsighted, it is nonetheless understandable. Long-run general benefits are not as tangible and important as immediate losses, both monetary and psychic. (Lord Keynes once noted that in the long run we are all dead.)

There are cases, of course, where technological change results in upgrading of workers in pay and in the nature of the work, but workers seldom anticipate such favourable impact from change.

Workers focus on the costs rather than the benefits of change. The costs include not only such monetary ones as loss of income resulting from unemployment or a downgrading in occupation, but also the psychic discomforts incurred in adjusting to a new occupation, new coworkers, a new employer, a different community, and so on.

In summary, workers seldom see benefits arising from change; rather, they focus on costs (both monetary and psychic) associated with adjustment to change. Given this perspective, it is understandable that the normal worker response to the prospect of change is fear and hostility.

Union policies reflect worker concern over displacement. In
part, this demonstrates the democratic structure of many unions
and also the desire of union leaders to ensure union survival
and power. Where technological or other changes appear to
threaten the employment of union members or to enhance
management's power to resist union bargaining pressures,
unions will oppose change. Where no such threat is in prospect
but workers must adjust to change, unions will accept change but
attempt to influence its pace or to secure arrangements that
facilitate worker adaptation.[5]

The objectives of union members and their leaders normally
are in harmony, permitting agreement on strategy toward change.
However, in some cases, the institutional objectives of union
leaders and the goals of some or all of the membership may conflict. Union leaders may sacrifice potential benefits for displaced workers (who will leave the union) in the interest either
of greater benefits for those who remain employed or of enhanced
bargaining power for the union. (John L. Lewis's policy in the
coal industry provides an example of this.) Union leaders may
be prepared to see their members hurt in cases where union
power or survival is threatened. In such situations, they may
risk the prospect of loss of employment for many members for
the prospect, however slight, of holding power. Through their
ability to present selectively the issues to the rank and file,
they often get membership support for such risky ventures.
(The ITU strike at the Toronto newspapers provides a vivid
example of this.)

In some cases, union leaders are compelled to choose between
the interests of conflicting groups within the union. Should
older workers' jobs be protected by seniority at the expense of
younger workers? Should older workers be compelled to retire
to permit the younger workers to hold their jobs? Should a
curb be placed on overtime work (or other work-sharing arrangements be imposed) to spread work over a larger group of members,
or should a smaller group get the opportunity to enjoy larger
incomes?

The Government Interest in Change

Certain areas of government concern with change are well
known.[6] Modern governments are committed to policies promoting
economic growth. Technological change is a crucial variable
determining the growth rate. Unemployment is also a matter of
public concern. Governments have accepted the objective of
reducing unemployment to an "acceptable level" and of assisting

those temporarily unemployed. The state, therefore, is concerned lest change result in an undue amount of unemployment.
As part of the growth and stabilization goals, the governments
seek to check inflationary pressures and preserve the exchange
value of our dollar. Cost cutting, technological and other
changes contribute to these goals. Keynesian policies designed
to raise aggregate demand are the primary device for checking
unemployment or inflation.

It is relatively easy to measure the cost of public information, training, mobility, and local incentive programmes that
form the core of public policy in this area. It is more difficult to measure the social benefits of these policies. This
involves such matters as value judgements on the weight to be
placed on the suffering of the unemployed, the benefits of
maintaining community ties, and so on. There are also serious
measurement problems (even after these value judgements are
made) in determining the impact of these policies in such
areas as relative and absolute prices, including factor prices
such as wage rates and salaries.

Case Studies

The results of the case studies are summarized in tables 3.1,
3.2 and 3.3. Table 3.1 (in the appendix) cross-classifies
the firms (or industries) and the contractual clauses. Table
3.2 (in the appendix) indicates the nature of the environment
applicable in each case. (I have used judgement in many of
these designations. Anyone who wishes to disagree can readily
adjust this table and the following one.) The results of these
two tables are then combined in table 3.3 (in the appendix),
where the frequency of various contract provisions is plotted
against the environmental characteristics.

We will turn first to an examination of table 3.1. It is
obvious that the most widely used arrangements for coping
with worker displacement in the companies studied are advance
notice, company-paid retraining, internal transfer based on
seniority, attrition, and joint committees. Somewhat less
common but fairly popular are induced attrition, relocation at
company expense, and severance pay. Still less common are
displacement funds, short-week benefits, rate retention, S.U.B.,
and work spreading. Rare are the instances of shared-cost
retraining, relocation without allowance, preferential hiring,
and productivity sharing.

The Plautz (Ontario) industry data disclose similar results.
Advance notice is by far the most common device. It is found
in all industry groups except one, and most companies that
have any provisions at all provide for advance notice.

Seniority and severance pay are also important. Rate retention
and preferential hiring get heavier emphasis than in the other
cases, largely because of their inclusion in many paper and metal
fabricating contracts, respectively. If these cases were not
included, these provisions would not be significant. Somewhat
surprising is the small number of attrition cases in the sample.
One suspects that attrition must be the practice in many of
these cases although it does not appear in the collective
agreements, or is not explicitly tied to technological change.

These findings are not surprising. Seniority is a long-
established device for rationing employment opportunities and has
become an accepted practice even in many nonunion establishments.
Employers have always engaged in on-the-job training, both for
new workers and for employees transferring among jobs within the
firm. The use of seniority in job transfer almost invariably
assumes some retraining obligation for the company. Similarly,
attrition is a long-standing device for coping with displacement,
although contractual arrangements to provide for this are of
more recent vintage. Advance notice is a prerequisite for the
effectiveness of many other arrangements (e.g., retraining,
relocation, joint committees, etc.) and is used in most cases
where any kind of displacement machinery appears. Joint
committees almost invariably are established once the principle
of advance notice is accepted. Notice per se is of little use
unless it is followed by discussion of ways of using the time
available before the change to good advantage. If anything, a
more careful analysis of practice in these cases would almost
certainly show that these procedures are even more widely
followed than our data indicate.

The other kinds of arrangements are somewhat newer and have
not been as widely accepted. Severance pay and preferential
hiring have a somewhat longer history than most of these other
arrangements. One suspects that they are often used even where
no mention is made of them in the collective agreement. Benefits such as relocation grants, work spreading, S.U.B., rate
retention, productivity sharing, and displacement funds are
newer to collective bargainings. Some (such as S.U.B., or
rate retention) are resisted by management. Productivity
sharing has been viewed with suspicion by many unions.

Little will be said about table 3.2. Readers should note
that not only is our total sample small but that certain
environmental characteristics are hardly represented at all.
For example, most of our cases involve firms in oligopolistic
product markets, with only four competitive and two monopolistic cases. Only two of our cases involved instances of
multiemployer bargaining units. Only four firms had a labour
force of under five hundred. When these weaknesses are combined with the rather off-handed way in which some of the
classification was done, it should be obvious that the data in

table 3.3 must be interpreted with caution.

Other Proposals -- An Evaluation

The extensive discussion of technological change in recent years
has generated a number of proposals for handling the problem.
The Freedman Report (report of the Industrial Enquiry Commission
on Canadian Railways "Run Through") and the statements by the
Economic Council of Canada provide two widely publicized
examples of such proposals. It is impossible to treat all of
the plans here but I feel that some consideration should be
given to these two widely discussed Canadian schemes. Some
reference will be made to other plans as well.

The Freedman Report

Although Freedman addressed himself to a particular displacement
problem in a single industry, there has been considerable discussion of his proposals and their possible extension beyond the
railway case. Freedman deals with several contentious issues,
including: (1) the residual right versus common-law approach to
collective agreements; (2) the rights of unions and workers
threatened by displacement; (3) the rights of a community
threatened by displacement; (4) the responsibilities of companies, unions, and the state in assisting worker adjustment to
displacement. We will deal with each of these in turn.

(1) Freedman concedes that under existing law, the residual
rights doctrine prevails and supports management's contention
that it can make any changes unilaterally unless specifically
restricted by the terms of contract. He sees the necessity of
preserving management's residual rights, yet also accepts the
merit in the union's contention that workers have property
rights in their jobs which must be respected. The conflict is
particularly sharp in the event of technological change.
Freedman proposed that management give thirty days' advance
notice of such change and discuss with the union methods of
facilitating adjustment. He proposes further that if an
arbitrator finds that the proposed change will result in substantial displacement, and if the parties cannot agree on
arrangements for implementing the change, the company be compelled to delay the introduction of new processes until after
the agreement expires and the union can bargain over the issue
with the support of a strike threat.

    Both proposals are radical. While many companies might
accept advance notice, few would like to be compelled to do
so by law. More significant is the second proposal, which
would result in delaying any major changes until the expira-

tion of agreements. This in effect destroys management's residual rights where major technological change is the issue. It
may also result in sizeable economic losses to the company as a
result of the imposed delay. To overcome this objection, Mr.
Marchand has proposed that in the event management asks to
implement a major change, the contract expires immediately and
the parties open negotiations on this and related issues, with
a view to concluding a new agreement.

These proposals deserve consideration. As stated earlier,
companies usually know of impending changes long before they are
prepared to implement them. A legal requirement of thirty days'
advance notice should not prove to be unduly onerous. As for
making such change negotiable, the "Marchand amendment" is
preferable to the original Freedman plan. Marchand's proposal
makes major change negotiable without necessarily imposing
undue delays.

There are several problems raised by these proposals. First,
there is the difficulty of distinguishing between a major change
(where residual rights govern) and a "material" change. Then
there is the danger that management may implement change in
stages, with each step involving a minor alteration but with
"material" change occurring over time. Arbitrators may have
problems deciding these questions. Any adequate decision will
involve lengthy hearings which themselves impose delays.

(2) The report says that unions and workers have the right to
advance notice (as discussed above) in the event of technological
change. Displaced workers should be assisted in geographic
mobility by the company. Specifically, moving costs -- including
loss of capital value of housing or expenses in breaking leases
--should be covered. Freedman contends that these workers should
not bear the full cost of change and that management must be
prepared to spend some of its economic benefits resulting from
the change on these workers. He *implies* that if the cost of
assisting displaced workers in this way exceeds the benefits to
the company of making the change, then the change should not be
made. He limits himself to the railways and does not face up to
the problems of industries where import competition or entry are
more likely to create pressures for technological change. He
neglects the evidence on the unwillingness of workers to move
even if incentives are provided. The report devotes little
attention to other adjustment programmes.

(3) In cases where a single firm is a major employer in a
community, company decisions may adversely affect the community,
destroying considerable investment in social overhead capital
(schools, roads, etc.). Freedman recognizes the community
interest in these cases and recommends advance notice to the
community. In the railway case, he suggests a device for

delaying change in such cases, but his proposal is not immediately applicable to other industries. He does not resolve the
problem of ensuring the protection of community interests. Nor
does he really treat systematically the question of forcing
companies to consider these social costs in their decisions.
The subject of "externalities" is of great importance in
assessing many private decisions (pollution, safety, etc., as
well as worker displacement) and one that economists recognize
as extremely difficult to treat analytically. If all social
costs had to be considered before any change could be made, few
innovations would ever be adopted. On the other hand, if external effects are completely ignored, many socially undesirable
changes will occur.

(4) Companies, unions and governments are urged to accept some
responsibility for promoting change and facilitating worker adaptation to change. Management's responsibilities as seen by the
report have been indicated above. Unions are encouraged to
cooperate with management and to accept necessary changes in
their philosophy and structure. Freedman was particularly concerned about union insistence on narrow seniority units on the
railways, which frustrated attempts to cope with displacements.

   The state was to assist in manpower adjustment and was to
reimburse companies for any economic losses resulting from imposed delays in implementing change. This would induce companies
to accept delay and to work out arrangements with communities and
unions to minimize their hardships. One wonders how one could
establish the size of this subsidy and prevent serious abuses
by companies. There is enough time, in most situations, to permit adequate advance notice without any loss by the company or
any necessity for compensation. If compensation is to be paid,
the onus should be on the companies concerned to demonstrate
losses attributable to imposed delays that would not otherwise
have occurred.

   In summary, the Freedman Report is thoughtful and thought
provoking. It combines a diagnosis of the problems of the
parties immediately involved with consideration of social costs
and social concerns. The analysis is neither explicit nor precise on this matter, but Freedman does demonstrate an awareness
of the complex problem. Although his principal concern is the
railways, much of the discussion has broader significance. I
would be prepared to accept compulsory advance notice. There
is merit in the suggestions that material change should be
subject to the bargaining process (including the threat of
stoppage) and that it is unreasonable to permit unilateral
management action on major changes during the term of contract.
Unless something is done here, we may anticipate bitter strikes
over the principle of residual rights. Although I am critical
of the report's failure to cope adequately with the problem of

introducing social costs into management's decisions, I concede
that this is a problem where our analytical tools remain under-
developed.

The Economic Council

The Economic Council of Canada has issued three publications relevant to this topic. The first and most significant was *A Declaration on Manpower Adjustments to Technological and Other Change,*
issued in November 1966. The Council discusses the various
provisions that have been used in collective bargaining and urges
wider adoption of these adjustment provisions. The declaration
adds to our earlier list of contractual arrangements the use of
portable pensions to facilitate labour mobility. Great stress
is placed on the need for advance notice and joint consultation.
The declaration states that normally management knows of impending change well in advance of implementation, so that advance
notice is not unduly burdensome. The fact that representatives
of management joined union officials in signing the declaration
lends support to our earlier argument that economic theory
suggests the existence of a substantial time lag in most cases.
The Council statement notes that public policies designed to
promote full employment are *the* key to the success of *any* programmes designed to facilitate the adjustment of displaced
workers.

The basic role of Keynesian policies in this matter is something that almost all economists can agree on. Other programmes
are designed to shift displaced workers to vacant positions.
No such shift is possible unless the vacancies exist or are
created. The spread of portable (vested) pensions would be
useful. However, it would tend to raise the cost of pension
plans and perhaps limit the ability to resort to induced attrition. There is little to quarrel with in this declaration but
there is little that is new, revolutionary or thought provoking.

The Council issued another statement in February 1967. This
document, entitled *Toward Better Communications Between Labour
and Management*, asserts repeatedly that better communication
provides good results for all concerned and contributes to a
long list of goals, including adjustment to displacement.
Little proof is offered in support of these statements. In my
opinion, much that is said shows either naivete on the part of
those formulating the document, or a preference for concensus
on general, rather harmless assertions rather than careful
examination of the problems. Improved communications can make
a material difference only where the parties have shared
objectives unknown to themselves which can be discovered by
discussion. Where there is genuine disagreement, communications
per se are unlikely to help much and indeed can be harmful by

pointing out areas of disagreement that were not apparent.

In March 1967, the Council published Jean-Real Cardin's study *Canadian Labour Relations in an Era of Technological Change*. Cardin argues that the failure of collective bargaining in this area is largely the result of the interaction of outmoded union and management philosophy and archaic institutional structures. Bargaining units are relatively small and the focus in bargaining is on the goals of "actors" at the microlevel (firm, craft, etc.). Adversary roles are emphasized, with discussion confined to the infrequent periods when contracts must be redrawn.

His solution lies in broadening both the bargaining units and the perspective of the parties. The Swedish system appears to be his model of the ideal, although he does not explicitly state this.

Although much can be gained by expanding bargaining units so that mobility is facilitated, there is little in Cardin's proposals likely to improve the situation. Our unions and companies are unlikely to accept national bargaining on the Swedish pattern. Here the presence of international corporations and international unions does make a difference, although other factors also operate to inhibit centralization. Cardin puts great stress on the desirability of communication per se, something I have already questioned. Finally, we should not confuse the functions of the state (with or without the participation of interest groups) in setting macropolicies and the function of unions and collective bargaining in seeking to assist workers in coping with what is unique to their own situation. In the drive for centralization, we may lose much that is healthy and useful in our currently decentralized arrangements. In our attempt to remake collective bargaining so that it can cope with displacement, we may destroy its ability to perform what it has done so well in the past.

Cardin's basic proposals are unlikely to be followed. It is doubtful that they would be effective.

Summary

The following appear to be the major findings of this study.

(1) Measuring the rate of technological change at the macro- or microlevel is difficult.

(2) The employment impact of technological change is almost impossible to separate from other factors causing displacement.

(3) Technological change is *not* inherently labour displacing.

(4) Normally, in cases of major change, there is a considerable period between the decision to alter technology and the actual implementation of this decision.

(5) Dislocation can arise from a variety of sources in addition to technological change. The problem we face is dislocation regardless of its source, and not technological change per se.

(6) Firms making the change may not always be highly profitable. Often they act under the stimulus of losses.

(7) Where entry into an industry is possible (or import competition exists), new entrants (or foreign competitors) use the latest techniques with no demand on them to compensate displaced workers. Older firms shifting to new techniques are asked to implement costly assistance programmes. Often these firms are simultaneously burdened by the competitive disadvantage of heavy fixed charges associated with the pruchase and use of older techniques. This twofold pressure to overcome the burden of fixed costs and to assist displaced workers, when competitors face neither pressure, can create serious hardships for these firms.

(8) Worker costs and benefits associated with change depend on worker values, prior training and experience, and conditions in the relevant labour markets. Hardest hit are the lowest skilled and the least willing to move. Management's decisions are motivated primarily by profit maximization. The government's approach is contingent on the relative importance attached to a variety of social and economic goals, as well as on the political pressures of the moment.

(9) Most of the studies of collective bargaining and displacement are of two kinds. Some are limited to case descriptions. Others proclaim general principles or panaceas on the strength of hunches rather than tested hypotheses. Definition, methods of classification and methods of analysis are not comparable. No theoretical structure guides the studies. Thus little can be done to integrate them or to employ their findings in testing hypotheses. This report contains a deficient but nonetheless valuable beginning to a more systematic attack. There is some evidence that certain of the environmental variables are significant in predicting the likelihood of particular kinds of contractual provisions.

(10) Our cases also produced other findings.

(i) Displacement that does not involve moving out of one's community or shifting to another employer (or union) is easiest to cope with through collective bargaining.

(ii) Workers do not take advantage of mobility grants. This means that when displacement occurs in an area with few alternative employment opportunities, collective bargaining is virtually impotent in assisting workers.

(iii) Workers are not likely to accept retraining unless they are certain that training is tied to a specific job vacancy, preferably at a firm that employs them and provides the retraining.

(iv) Limited seniority units, particularly in multiunion situations, inhibit adjustment arrangements. Although there have been some notable instances of success in altering union policies, these are few in number and more than matched by the cases of failure to adjust even in the face of severe displacement problems.

(v) More use should be made of the facilities of the Manpower Centres and of company and union contacts in the labour market to facilitate worker adjustment. The Ontario Hydro and General Steelwares cases might be emulated by others.

(vi) Displacement funds have not accomplished much of significance thus far.

(vii) Attrition is a mechanism for allocating the burden of displacement and not a remedy.

(11) The Freedman Report touches on a number of important issues and makes some interesting proposals. It urges compulsory advance notice arrangements and rejects management's residual rights in cases where a change will result in material displacement. These are radical suggestions. The report touches on the question of community costs associated with such change and the need to bring consideration of these to bear on management's decisions. This issue is not resolved in the report.

The work of the Economic Council of Canada thus far is disappointing. The Council has pressed for wider use of some of the procedures followed in the cases we have examined. It has pushed some questionable panaceas that have little basis in careful analysis and little likelihood of ever being implemented. The most valuable contribution it has made is in pointing out the crucial role of government aggregate-demand policies in determining the degree of possible success of collective bargaining in this area.

TABLE 3.1

Contractual Provisions for Worker Displacement, by Industry

Company or Industry	A. Advance Notice	B. Avoding Layoff	Natural Attrition	Induced Attrition	Retraining	−Co. Paid	−Shared Cost	Relocation	−With Allowance	−Without Allowance	Transfer (Seniority)	Work Spreading	C. Income Maintenance	Severance Pay	S.U.B.	Preferential Hiring	Rate Retention	−Permanent	−Temporary	Short-week Benefits	D. Productivity Sharing	E. Joint Committees	−Creative	−Administrative	F. Estab. of Fund	No. of Plants Studied
Alberta Telephone	X		X	X		X			X														X			
Bowater	X					X					X						X						X			
Can. Johns-Mansville	X	X				X					X						X						X			
CNR − London, Ont.	X		X	X		X			X		X			X									X			
Casavant Freres	X					X					X												X			
Cleyn & Tinker	X	X				X					X						X						X			
General Steelwares	X	X	X			X			X		X			X									X			
Hydro − Ont.	X	X				X					X					X							X			
Imperial Oil	X	X	X					X	X		X			X											X	
Moirs Ltd.	X	X									X															
Pacific Press	X	X				X					X			X									X			
American Motors									X			X									X		X			
Armour	X		X			X			X		X			X	X								X	X		
Basic Steel											X												X			
Domtar	X	X	X			X			X		X												X	X		
Imperial Oil − loco	X	X	X			X					X			X					X				X	X		
Kaiser Steel		X				X									X				X	X	X		X	X		
Pacific Maritime		X	X							X									X					X	X	
Quebec Iron																							X			
Railways-Kellock		X				X					X					X		X	X							
PLAUTZ (a)																										
Chemical industry	3			−		1					5	−		3		2	3				1					94
Machinery industry	3			2		1					4	−		−		5	−				−					106
Meat products industry	6			−		−					−	−		6		−	2				−					33
Metal fab. industry	13			8		5					18	−		2		12	2				−					252
Paper & allied industry	55	1		2		−					2	−		21		−	25				−					99
Petrol. & coal industry	2			1		−					1	−		−		−	1				−					11
Primary metals industry	7			4		−					8	−		2		2	5				−					92
Printing, etc. industry	33	6		6		−					−	4		19		−	1				−					231
Rubber industry	3			−		−					7	−		−		2	−				2					29
Trans. equip. industry	−			2		9					7	−		−		8	−									76

a. For the Plautz cases, I have indicated the number of establishments studied in each industry and the number with each kind of provision in each industry.

TABLE 3.2

Environmental Characteristics of
Unionized Companies
and Industries

Company or Industry	Competitive	Oligopoly	Monopoly	Co. Dominated	Many Employers	Expanding	Contracting	One Plant	More than One	One Company	More than One	One Union	More than One	Craft Union(s)	Industrial Union(s)	Small (under 500)	Large (over 500)	Old
	Product Market			Labour Market		Employment Opportunities		Scope of Collective Bargaining — Employer				Union				Labour Force		
Alberta Telephone			X		X	X				X	X		X		X		X	
Bowater		X		X			X	X		X			X	X	X		X	
Can. Johns-Mansville		X		X			X	X		X		X			X		X	
CNR — London, Ont.		X			X					X	X		X	X	X	X		
Casavant Freres								X		X		X			X	X		
Cleyn & Tinker	X			X			X		X	X		X			X			
General Steelwares		X			X	X			X	X		X			X	X		X
Hydro — Ont.			X	X					X	X			X	X			X	
Imperial Oil		X			X		X		X	X		X		X			X	
Moirs Ltd.				X			X	X		X		X	X				X	
Pacific Press		X		X				X		X			X	X	X		X	
American Motors		X			X		X		X	X		X			X		X	
Armour	X				X		X		X	X			X		X		X	
Basic Steel		X		X			X	X		X		X			X		X	
Domtar		X		X	X		X		X	X			X	X	X		X	
Imperial Oil — loco		X				X				X		X			X	X		
Kaiser Steel		X			X	X		X		X		X			X		X	
Pacific Maritime					X	X					X	X			X		X	
Quebec Iron		X			X	X		X	X			X			X		X	
Railways-Kellock		X			X					X			X	X	X		X	
Chemcial industry		X																
Machinery industry		X																
Meat products industry	X																	
Metal fab. industry		X																
Paper & alliod industry		X																
Petrol. & coal industry		X																
Primary metals industry		X																
Printing, etc. industry	X																	
Rubber industry		X																
Trans. equip. industry		X																

TABLE 3.3

Frequency of Contractual Provisions for Worker Displacement, Related to Company or Industry Environment

Company or Industry Environment	Product Market			Labour Market		Employment Opportunities		Scope of Collective Bargaining — Employer / Union								Labour Force			Total No. of Cases
	Competitive	Oligopoly	Monopoly	Co. Dominated	Many Employers	Expanding	Contracting	One Plant	More than One	One Company	More than One	One Union	More than One	Craft Union	Industrial Union	Small	Large	Old	
A. Advance notice	2	8	2	6	7	2	7	6	8	14	0	5	9	6	11	4	9	1	14
B. Avoiding layoff																			
Natural attrition	1	9	2	5	7	4	5	5	0	13	1	6	8	6	12	4	10	1	14
Induced attrition	0	5	1	1	7	3	3	1	0	7	1	3	5	2	8	3	5	1	8
Retraining																			
– Co. paid	2	10	2	6	9	4	5	6	1	15	0	6	9	6	14	4	11	1	15
– Shared cost	0	1	0	0	1	0	1			1	0	0	1	0	1		1		1
Relocation																			
– with allowance	1	5	1	1	6	2	4	0	6	7	0	2	5	2	7	2	5	1	7
– without allowance		0	1	1	0	0	1	0	1	0	1	1	0	0	1		1		1
Transfer (seniority)	2	11	1	7	9	2	8	6	9	15	1	6	10	7	14	4	12	1	16
Work spreading	0	3	0	0	3	1	2	0	3	2	1	2	1	0	3	0	3		3
C. Income maintenance																			
Severance pay	1	6	0	1	6	1	3	2	5	6	1	3	4	2	7	3	4	1	7
S.U.B.	1	3	0	1	4	2	3	1	3	3	2	4	1	0	5	0	5		5
Preferential hiring	0	1	1	1	1	–	–	0	1	2	0	0	2	2	0	0	2		2
Rate retention b	1	2	0	3	0	0	3	2	1	3	0	2	1	1	2	1	2		3
– permanent		1	0	0	1			0	0	1	0	0	1	1	0		1		1
– temporary		3	0	0	3	1		2	0	3	0	2	1	1	2		2		3
Short-week benefits	0	2	0	1	2	1	1	1	1	1	2	3	0	0	3	0	3		3
D. Productivity sharing	0	2		0	2	1	1	1	1	2	0	2	0	0	2	0	2		2
E. Joint committees																			
– creative	2	11	2	7	9	4	7	6	10	15	1	8	8	5	15	4	12	1	16
– administrative		2	0	0	3	1		1	1	2	1	2	1	0	3	1	2		3
F. Establishment of fund	1	3	0	1	3	2	2	1	2	3	1	2	2	1	4	0	4		4
Total no. of cases	2	13	2	7	12	5	9	7	11	18	2	9	11	7	18	4	15	1	20

a. NOTE: Some companies have both craft and industrial unions.

b. Rate retention covers cases where it is unclear whether it is permanent or temporary. Where this is clear it is so listed. Thus total cases of rate retention of any kind is 7.

Notes

1. This study was financed by a grant from the Task Force on
Labour Relations. A somewhat more comprehensive version of
this paper was submitted to the task force as Project no. 45.

   The author is indebted to Mr. E. Lightman, a graduate student
at the University of California (Berkeley, California), who
provided invaluable assistance in this study. Mr. Lightman did
most of the work in assembling the materials for the case
studies on which some of the findings of this study are based.

2. For an excellent discussion of this subject see J. W. L.
Winder, "Structural Unemployment", in *The Canadian Labour Market:
Readings in Manpower Economics*, ed. A. Kruger and N. M. Meltz
(Toronto: University of Toronto, Centre for Industrial Relations,
1968).

3. See "The Triple Revolution", *Advertising Age* (6 April 1964);
or G. Piel, *Consumers of Abundance* (Centre for the Study of
Democratic Institutions, 1961).

4. Arthur Kruger, *Human Adjustment to Industrial Conversion*,
Project no. 45, Task Force on Labour Relations (Ottawa, 1968).

5. An example of this difference in union attitude is the
difference in the reaction of the railway firemen and the boilermakers to the introduction of the diesel engine. For the
firemen, the change meant the destruction of their skill and
union, whereas the boilermakers had alternative jobs to go to
where their skill was utilized and where they often remained
within their union. The firemen fought the innovation longer
and harder than did the boilermakers. (I am indebted to
Professor John Dunlop of Harvard University for this example.)

6. For further discussion of the basis for government concern
and for an evaluation of public policy in this area, see Kruger
and Meltz, *The Canadian Labour Market*, particularly the articles
by Kruger, Winder and Drummond. For further discussions of
public policy goals, see Economic Council of Canada, *Fourth
Annual Review* (Ottawa: Queen's Printer, 1967), p. 2.

4. The Confederation of National Trade Unions (CNTU) and the Affluent Society*

by Bernard Solasse and Jean Sexton

This research[1] is intended to describe the problem of unionism and consumption at the CNTU, its background, the general shape of the question, and the stages of its progress. We tried to go beyond the daily activities and official positions of the CNTU to the broader but less immediately obvious concerns, which were significant in restating the CNTU's position and ideology as a trade union confederation. The primary motive of this study was also to study the behaviour of the union member as a consumer.

A review of the research objectives led us to view the question from a broader base, to take into account the fact that the Confederation of National Trade Unions was only one of many organizations interested in this type of problem. Some of the groups, independent of the union movement per se include the *Fédération des caisses d'économie du Québec*, the *Fédération des magasins CO-OP du Québec*, and the *Fédération des associations coopératives d'économie familiale*.

The first part of the study is a general introduction to the objectives and actions of the CNTU, and its relations with the other cooperative groups in the field of consumption.

The second part is devoted to a study of the scope of the CNTU initial experience as such, that is, the activity of its Family Finance Service (*Service du Budget Familial*), which provides assistance to members in debt, directs the education of the union member as a consumer, and provides the training of CNTU officials.

The third part discusses the relations, objectives, attitudes, and activities of the CNTU and its adjunct cooperative organizations.

The behaviour of union members as consumers has not been studied per se. Initial hope to obtain a large amount of precise information for this study was only partially satisfied. The sole scientific, and very interesting, work available on this topic was M. A. Tremblay and G. Fortin's *Les comportements économiques de la famille salariée du Québec*[2]. There was, at the time of our research, no comprehensive study by a union on this subject, in spite of the extensive work done by the CNTU in this general area.

---

* Reproduced by permission of Information Canada.

The method was simple, descriptive, empirical, and based on the available material, complemented by a series of interviews.

The Results of the Research

Instead of a formal conclusion, research results were grouped around three main themes: (1) the emergence of an awareness by wage earners as consumers; (2) the extension of the field of union interest and activity; and (3) the necessity of expanding the field of research in industrial relations.

(1) The Emergence of an Awareness by Wage Earners as Consumers

(i) The actions taken by the CNTU in the field of consumption were not a planned part of union policy, but a specific response to the needs of union members as consumers. In other words, this experience is not the result of an initiative taken by the CNTU, but the consequence of an awareness by the union members.

Their awareness was tied to actual situations and distress: indebtedness and its consequences to daily family life, the threat of seizure of their possessions, and the fear of judicial procedures.

(ii) This awareness is not the expression of an intellectual or ideological development. It does not lead spontaneously to the revaluation of this affluent society, into which every wage earner, unionized or not, seems to be integrated by sharing its value system, which influences that wage earner's needs as a consumer.

However, there seems to be a certain continuity between the improvement of the wage level and working conditions asked for at the bargaining table, on the one hand, and rising expectations to consume more and more in accordance with economic growth and development, on the other. The motives for union demand and personal indebtedness are often identical: a certain number of goods not necessarily useful per se but important to possess in this "keep up with the Joneses" society.

The CNTU and the ACEF's efforts to educate their members do not contest this continuity. They do not ask their students to give up their hopes in the field of consumption, but instead propose means of reaching these goals at the lowest cost possible for each and every individual involved in the experience, by balancing the family budget, using credit unions, and purchasing goods at cooperative stores. In addition to this, both organizations invite their members to distinguish between two levels of consumption, individual and collective, and propose to extend the field of preoccupation regarding the latter to social security, health insurance, and cooperative housing. Their basic ideal is for an affluent society, free of speculation and usury, and where profit is not a synonym for exploitation.

(iii) This awareness has led the union member to turn spontaneously to the union organization for help in resolving his problems, even if they are personal. The union becomes the organization one can "count on" and "have confidence in". This marked interest in the union for such purposes is a spontaneous reaction, and not the result of any serious thought's bringing forward a precise definition of the union organization, its role and its functions.

(2) The Extension of the Field of Union Interest and Activity

Undoubtedly, the experience undertaken by the CNTU in the field of consumption is a sign of increased interest within the union organization.

(i) In other respects, the action of the CNTU seems related to a certain type of leadership and illustrates, in a more general way, the evolution of the notion of union democracy.

In order to respond to the expectations and needs of the union members in the field of consumption, in the absence of clearly defined "policy and orientation", the executive of the CNTU has hired a director for its Family Finance Service. He will enjoy a great deal of freedom of action within the organization, reporting to the executive board, if not to the president alone.

These decisions and practices illustrate both the evolution of the role of the union agents in labour organizations and their real influence and power, and the evolution of union democracy. The CNTU is not unique in this area; this exists in various degrees in other union organizations in North America, as well as in Europe.

The power and influence of these agents seems considerable, as their work touches a new field in which the elected union leaders coming from the rank and file are not particularly competent.

This is only one aspect of a general trend to concentrate the position and power within the union organization in the hands of the administrative machinery. This movement cannot be explained only in terms of efficiency. To a certain extent, it is a reaction to the emergence of new problems arising at a higher level. Necessary solutions to these problems require a more global action by the labour movement at the political level and also the setting of agreement with other organizations.

Union democracy, under these conditions, is less and less a

democracy of direct participation, where the union members themselves state the policies and orientations of their organizations. Rather, it is more and more an indirect democracy, where the members are called on by their elected representatives to approve or disapprove the policies and orientations decided by the executive and the technical advisors.

This type of democracy is not without its influence on the behaviour of the union agents. They must administer and pay great attention to the desires and wishes expressed by the union members. For certain permanent employees, paid by the union and aware of the influence they exercise on the definition of policies of the movement, the temptation is strong to solicit an electoral mandate. But in doing so they risk a confrontation with the leaders coming from the rank and file, whose past experience is prestigious in the eyes of the union members.

(ii) The impact of the information and education acquired by the Family Finance Service of the CNTU on the orientations of this central union is another important topic for comment.

Information and education tend toward the realization of practical objectives. Immediate usefulness is one of the major preoccupations of the CNTU. But this leads to a certain number of fundamental investigations on the affluent society and the correctives this organization can offer it. The evolution of themes and content of the information and education effort have been underlined. From an initial moralizing approach, the CNTU progressively gets to a more economic and political stage. Exploitation of the consumer becomes the correlation of exploitation of the producer. To put an end to the exploitation, the CNTU advocates a growing intervention of the legislature and the formation of a vast cooperative sector where the decision-making power will be exercised by the workers themselves.

It would be convenient to distinguish various levels of analysis: the important role of the director of the Family Finance Service of the CNTU has been stressed. Its ideas have been accepted by the executive congress, but in a less radical form. This denotes the existence of a certain gap between the preoccupations of the one responsible for the Family Finance Service and those of the directors of the CNTU.

At the level of the rank and file, it is hard to gauge the interest aroused by these positions. A choice exists between two hypotheses: in the first case, the rank and file would be interested in the practical aspects of experience and their own immediate benefits; in the second case, they add, to those practical propositions, a real desire to work for the realization of more profound social reforms. It is still too soon to contrast profitably these hypotheses.

(iii) Beyond the specific experience undertaken by the CNTU

in the field of consumption, it seems that this organization has changed its orientation to advance toward a new multifunctional and renewed conception of union action.

Strictly economic and professional union activities at the firm level would not be out of date but would be complemented by other actions, undertaken this time on the political level, in response to more general objectives: the upholding of purchasing power, development and economic growth, the reduction of unemployment, etc.

This revaluation of unionism is less the consequence of a voluntary and fundamental ideological reorientation than the consequence of the necessary adaptation of a society on the road to rapid socialization. Here the centres of decision making have shifted and the working of the system requires greater cooperation on all levels.

(3) The Necessity of Expanding the Field of Research in Industrial Relations

The institutionalization of labour-management relations and the relative stability engendered may lead one to consider industrial relations as a closed system. This, however, is an underestimation of a society undergoing rapid evolution with dynamic consequences.

This study lacks in not being able to express clearly the behaviour, aspirations, and hopes of unionists. The unionist is simultaneously producer, consumer, and citizen, and it is here that one must seek the explanation of the CNTU policy in the field of consumption.

Notes

1. Bernard Solasse, *Syndicalisme, consommation et société de consommation,* Study no. 3, Task Force on Labour Relations (Ottawa: Privy Council, 1968), p. 47.

2. M.A. Tremblay and G. Fortin, *Les Comportements économiques de la famille salariée du Québec* (Quebec: Laval University Press, 1964), p. 405.

5. Public Opinion and Industrial Relations*

by R. R. March

What is the attitude toward labour unions in general? It appears
that the Canadian public has a vague feeling that unions are, in
principle, a "good thing", (although when specific union
activities are discussed, a discrepancy appears). In October
1956, 70 per cent of those sampled thought that labour unions
had been beneficial for Canada, while only 12 per cent
thought they had been detrimental. The same level of support
for labour unions was indicated again in September 1961, when
66 per cent approved of them and only 23 per cent disapproved.
As is to be expected, union members indicated substantially more
support for unions than did nonunion members (85 per cent to 70
per cent). But the 15 per cent difference is not as large as
one might expect, nor is there a substantial difference among
various socio-economic groups.[1]

The regional variations for approval of unions are fascinating. Support for unions was lowest in Alberta (49 per
cent), rather low in Ontario (67 per cent), and exceptionally
high in Quebec (83 per cent), Saskatchewan (89 per cent) and
New Brunswick (100 per cent -- but with a sample of only ten).
These strong variations in support for the principle of unions
underscore the significance of regional variations in Canada,
and the relative weakness of social class as a determinant of
public opinion.[2]

Although the right of unions to exist is not seriously
questioned in Canada, the right to organize in unions is another
matter. It appears that there is even greater support for the
abstract principle of the "right" to organize in unions, as
opposed to the vague acceptance of the right for unions to
exist. The translation of the vague principles of union
existence and the right to organize in a union, into the
coercion or workers to unionize is another matter, as we shall
see later.

But let us return to our examination of the principle of
organizing a union. The right to organize a union is not
seriously questioned in principle, for in September 1959, 82
per cent of those sampled supported the right of workers to
organize into unions, only 8 per cent opposed this right, while
11 per cent were undecided.

There are no significant differences between union and nonunion members concerning the right to organize in unions.
Union members replying affirmatively totalled 95 per cent,

---

* Reproduced by permission of Information Canada.

while nonunion members supported the principle by 90 per cent.[3]

Given such levels of support, it appears that the right to organize in unions is open to question in Canada about as much as Motherhood. In March 1973, the Galleys Poll asked an unusual question, partly in response to the drive taking place to organize white-collar workers. The question was: "Labour unions, so far, have mainly organized what are called 'blue-collar workers' -- those who are paid by hourly rates, that is, labour. A movement now is to organize into unions 'white-collar workers', that is, workers in offices who are paid a salary. Do you think that this would be a good idea or not?"

A bare majority of Canadians (51 per cent) endorsed the idea of white-collar workers organizing into unions. For every five adults who thought it was a good idea, about three opposed it.[4]

Sales and clerical workers, most involved in the new union program, revealed no more enthusiasm for such unionization than did executive or professional people. In each segment 51 per cent were agreeable to the plan but over 30 per cent objected to it. Farmers and others divided equally on the question, with 37 per cent on either side of the argument.

On the average, about one in five Canadians cannot as yet decide what they think about the unionization of salaried workers. However, certain activities of unions are regarded as divisive. This is especially true when the element of coercion is examined. That is, the public, while generally well disposed toward unionism, does not support *compulsory* features of union tactics. For example, a sample of Canadians was asked, on 28 July 1954, whether an employer should be able to hire anyone, whether or not the worker belonged to any union. Only 16 per cent supported the statement that the worker must belong to a union, whereas 73 per cent said that employers should have the right to hire anyone. The Canadian public in 1954 certainly opposed the idea of a "closed shop".[5]

Union and nonunion members are sharply divided on this issue of coercion, with 63 per cent of union members, compared to 90 per cent of nonunion respondents, opposed to the requirement that an individual must belong to a union. The differences are even sharper among those in favour of a closed shop. Only 37 per cent of nonunion members were opposed. If we control for size, the ratio of support for a closed shop between union and nonunion members is of the order of nine to one.

Finally, on this question of a closed shop, there are no very large regional differences, or differences among social classes. It would appear, then, that the support for a closed shop is a union artifact, or a part of union psychology. Still, the fact that only 37 per cent of union members support the concept indicates that the unions have not sold their members on this idea.

Another facet of the structure of public opinion on unions is
the rather strong shift since 1954 toward increasing criticism
of labour leaders. In 1954, more of those sampled thought that
organized labour was wisely led (38 per cent) than that it was
unwisely led (34 per cent). Some 28 per cent were undecided.
In 1957, the opinions were similar, with slightly more opting
for "wisely led" than "unwisely led", but the undecided
element increased sharply from 28 per cent to 38 per cent. By
February 1964, the proportion of critical respondents had
increased sharply, and in June 1966, and August 1966, had increased sharply again, to 44 per cent. The undecided element
dropped, but still remained significantly large.

As would be expected, union members were much less likely to
criticize union leadership. In 1957, for example, 71 per cent
of union members thought that unions were wisely led. However,
by 1964, only 25 per cent of union members approved of union
leaders, while 75 per cent disapproved! In fact, nonunion
members were more favourably disposed to union leaders than
were union members themselves. Two years later, in 1966, there
was a shift back to the more normal pattern of support for
union leaders, but even so, a slight majority of union members
still disapproved of union leadership (52 per cent opposed, 48
per cent in favour). Nonunion members continued to disapprove
of union leaders (a ratio of two to one).

It is apparent, then, that although the general public
approves of unions, approval does not extend to union leaders.
Moreover, union members themselves have become very critical
of their own leaders. Much industrial unrest is likely the
result of poor leadership by union officers.

Usually the respondents questioned concerning the degree
of wisdom of union leaders were requested to provide specific
criticism of unions, if they had any. In 1957, some two-thirds
of union members would offer no criticism, while only one-third
of nonunion members refused critical comment.

There were few very specific criticisms of unions; and there
were no special differences between union and nonunion members.
They both tended to rank their criticisms in the same order.
For example, both groups ranked as first the criticism that
unions demand "too much"; secondly, that unions are "too
prone to strike"; and thirdly, that unions are "too strong".[6]

The regional variations in the total of critical remarks are
more interesting. The three Prairie Provinces are by far the
most critical of unions, with only 13 per cent of Manitoba, 22
per cent of Saskatchewan, and 22 per cent of Alberta respondents offering no comment. Tolerence of unions was strongest
in Quebec (78 per cent), while British Columbians were the next

most tolerant (55 per cent). The Quebec results are most surprising, given the purported antiunion bias of that province.
Finally, the ranking of criticism is not significantly different
among the provinces, with union "demands", "strength" and
"proneness to strike" again singled out as the most serious
flaws.

In 1973, opinion had shifted somewhat. Criticism now
focussed on union power rather than demands. Some felt that
unions had "become too powerful, abuse their power, have too
much control, and are too political" (25 per cent), 11 per cent
said they "cause too many strikes, won't work unless they get
what they want", while 10 per cent argued that unions "raise
cost of living by higher wages, help to cause inflation, demand
too much, and are greedy, against common good".[7]

The public in general also appears to think that there are
"too many troublemakers and agitators among union leaders". In
March 1954, 40.8 per cent of those sampled agreed that there
are "too many agitators", and in November 1964, this proportion
increased to 47 per cent. In August 1966, the proportion remained approximately the same, at 42 per cent.

These facts indicate that public opinion, as determined by
the CIPO, has hardened against union leaders, although the
general climate of opinion favours unions themselves. Much of
the criticism is directly related to a few unions whose leaders
dominated the news in those years. Respondents who were
critical of unions were asked to name the unions they "had in
mind" when they criticized the unions. Of those replying, 23
per cent named the Teamsters and/or Jimmy Hoffa; 15 per cent
singled out the Steelworkers. Railway unions were mentioned
by 6 per cent, miners by 3 per cent, and auto workers by 3 per
cent. Another 8 per cent condemned the C I O and C L C (2
per cent rather than a specific union, while 8 per cent named
the I W A . Another group (16 per cent) damned "all of them".
Some 20 per cent could name no unions. It is the large
industrial and service unions that are most criticized. This
is not unexpected, because these unions are also the most
visible ones; that is, when they go on strike they disrupt
the lives of many citizens.

This is not to imply that the public has any coherent or systematic critical philosophy of unions. In the few instances
when the CIPO attempted to probe for specific criticisms of
labour unions, the following concepts were proferred by the
public to explain their criticism: calling of strikes,
dictatorial leadership, excessive power, excessive agitation
and demands, and rackets. Even so, none of these criticisms
is held by a significant proportion of the public; they remain
vague predispositions.[8]

Because of these criticisms, a significant portion of the

public (38 per cent) in 1961 felt that "laws regulating labour unions are not strict enough". Only 11 per cent thought the laws were too strict.[9]

There appears to be no significant variation among regions, union-nonunion respondents, or socio-economic classes with respect to the degree of strictness of laws regulating labour unions. The only interesting regional difference is among those who felt that the laws were "about right". Here, once again, Quebec respondents were the most satisfied with present laws (52 per cent), with Nova Scotia (40 per cent, N of 5) and British Columbia respondents (35 per cent) next in order of satisfaction.

In 1966, the majority of the public sampled felt that laws regulating labour unions were not strict enough (33 per cent), while 16 per cent thought they were too strict; 22 per cent regarded them as just right, while 30 per cent were undecided.[10]

The same people in the 1966 sample were also asked to assess the strictness of laws for business activity. Their replies indicate that they were just as unhappy with the weakness of the laws regulating business as they were with laws regulating labour unions.[11] Incredibly, there was absolutely no difference in the attitude of union and nonunion respondents with respect to the strictness of laws regulating business![12]

When we investigate in more detail this public distrust of union activity, it is important to know what objects of union-labour activity the public accepts as legitimate. It will be seen that it is the style of labour-management negotiations that upsets the public and not the objects of labour activity. For example, the public is very well disposed toward higher wages for labour in general. Most of those sampled in August 1963, June 1966, and August 1966 favoured increased wages. In 1963, the margin was almost two to one in favour of higher wages, but in 1966, the margin in favour had increased to three to one![13]

Once again, union and nonunion members do not differ greatly in the degree of their approval for high wage demands. Union members support these demands by a clear majority of 57 per cent, with nonunion respondents slightly less approving at 42 per cent. These two groups differ most strongly at the No end of the scale in preference, with only 6 per cent of union members opposed to high wage demands, compared with 20 per cent of nonunion respondents opposed.

When the replies are analyzed by socio-economic class, a strong correlation results. That is, the higher the status of the group, the less likely it is to support high wage demands.[14]

This is not to say that the public regards higher wages as

the most important object of labour activity. In a series of
questions begun in 1949, the CIPO asked samples of the Canadian
public to state, first, what labour should *not* press for from
employers. Higher wages (35 per cent) and shorter working hours
(35 per cent) were most often cited as undesirable objectives.
However, when asked to state what was the most important object,
security of employment was always cited as the most important
(85 per cent in 1949, 39 per cent in 1956, 56 per cent in
1961,[15] and 82 per cent in 1967).[16]

When asked to provide positive statements in favour of labour
unions, only 9 per cent claimed that unions could "ensure job
security; help employment". The greatest boon of unions was
seen to be their ability to "protect the workers from exploitation; preserve the right of workers; help the little man" (19
per cent), while 12 per cent cited "keep wages up; provide fair
wages; fringe benefits".[17] It is the psychological support of
unions, rather than their ability to deliver the goods, that
seems to be most important in the minds of the public. A very
confusing point is that 48 per cent could not offer a single
argument in favour of unions.

Unemployment

It is axiomatic that Canadian social scientists, journalists,
and practicing politicians acknowledge regional differences in
public opinion. They are also in agreement that provincial
governments, because of their size and history, are almost
equal in public consciousness to the federal government. If
this argument holds true, then we would expect to see these
differences reflected in the replies to questions concerning
the relative roles of various levels of government in Canada.

However, with the exception of Quebec, the data do not fulfill expectation. Regardless of how the data is controlled,
whether by province, socio-economic status, or membership in a
union, the Canadian public is remarkably alike in its views on
the role of two of the three main levels of government in
Canada. Moreover, the public -- despite the theories of
Maritime and Western Canada separatism promoted by soothsayers
-- looks to the federal government to provide leadership in
the area of unemployment. For example, in December 1963, a
sample was asked: "As you perhaps know, there is quite a bit
of unemployment just now. Which level of government do you
feel should take the main responsibility for tackling this
problem - municipal, provincial, or federal?" The replies
were: municipal, 6 per cent; provincial, 15 per cent; federal,
39 per cent; all three levels equally, 33 per cent; none,
0.6 per cent; and can't say, 12 per cent.[18]

The only significant deviation from the tendency to look to
the federal government for responsibility in the area of

unemployment is in Quebec. But the low support in Quebec for federal activity was masked by the large proportion of the sample (55 per cent) who opted for the ambiguous reply, "all" levels of government are responsible for ending unemployment.

This general agreement on the level of government responsible for solving unemployment breaks down, however, when the adequacy of measures being taken are questioned. Here social class and regionalism lead to differences of opinion. For example, when asked whether they felt that the "steps being taken by our various governments to tackle this problem are adequate or inadequate", the same sample split thusly: adequate, 23 per cent; inadequate, 55 per cent; no opinion, 21 per cent.[19]

The same level of dissatisfaction with the federal government concerning unemployment endeavours was indicated by another sample in May 1961, where 30 per cent felt it was adequate; 54 per cent, inadequate; and 12 per cent, no opinion. Much the same socio-economic and regional differences were evidenced as in the previous sample.

Those who felt the federal government was not doing enough "to help solve the unemployment situation" were asked to state, "What more do you think they should be doing?" The largest proportion (21 per cent) suggested the old panacea of more public works; another 15 per cent wanted protection of jobs by: (1) keeping out foreign goods (7 per cent); and (2) restricting immigration (8 per cent). Ten per cent suggested the creation of new industries, while 8 per cent advocated opening up the north. Five per cent attacked automation, and only 4 per cent supported more sophisticated economic-social measures, such as increasing education and training, and reorganizing finances in order to enable the government to spend more money (10 per cent). Fifteen per cent made no suggestion.

It would appear, then, that the public looks to the federal government, especially, for solutions to unemployment; is critical of the government's efforts; but can only suggest stop-gap measures. (See CIPO, July 1960 for similar stop-gap suggestions.) This dependence on government initiative is a long-standing one in Canada. For example, in July 1954, when people were asked, "Do you think business firms in this country will be able to provide enough jobs for everyone during the next five years, or will the government have to step in and provide work?", only 21 per cent thought business firms could provide enough jobs, whereas 65 per cent looked to the government to step in (14 per cent were undecided).[20]

For some inexplicable reason there was no sharp division of opinion between union members and nonunion citizens about the necessity of government action to provide jobs. However, there was a sharp difference among citizens when social class is considered. Here, those at the lowest end of the scale were quite persuaded (84 per cent) that the government would have to provide employment, while those at the other end of the scale gave only 66 per cent support for the idea.

There is additional evidence that the public tends to look toward government leadership in the area of economic development. For example, when asked to evaluate the relative success of various leaders in improving living standards, more (31 per cent) named government leaders than any other group. Opinion was evenly divided on the role of labour leaders (25 per cent) and businessmen (25 per cent).

Union members cited labour leaders (45 per cent) as having done the most, then government (30 per cent) and finally businessmen (22 per cent), while nonunion members cited government first (40 per cent), businessmen second (32 per cent), and finally union leaders (25 per cent). Obviously, there is a sharp difference of opinion here between union and nonunion respondents, and this difference on the relative roles of labour, business and government perhaps underlies the ambivalence of the public with respect to responsibility for the improvement of living standards in Canada.

Again, in May 1956, 31 per cent of a sample thought that leaders in government "had done the most to improve the living standards of the people in (Canada)", whereas 25 per cent credited this to leaders in labour unions, and only 25 per cent to business. Sixteen per cent had no opinion.[21]

The public is also divided in its opinion about the relative weight of influence of various segments of the social system. For example, the respondents of a survey conducted in May 1960 stated that capitalists, industrialists, and big business (23 per cent), and the rich upper class (19 per cent) were the groups in the population getting the most out of the current prosperity, whereas only 9 per cent thought labour was benefiting most. Farmers were mentioned by 0.8 per cent; the middle class, by 9 per cent; professional groups, by 7 per cent; businessmen, by 5 per cent; government and politicians, by 5 per cent; and others, by 6 per cent. Some 4 per cent thought all groups were doing well; only 11 per cent had no opinion.[22]

A question asked in 1955 indicates what groups the public thinks *have* the most influence on the federal government, and also what groups the public thinks *should* have the most influence.

In other polls, only labour and big business were compared as to which "has the most influence on the laws passed in this country". In these polls, big business does not fare well and appears to be more criticized than unions. However, the choice of wording is unfortunate. Would the results have been different had the question been, "big business" and "big labour unions", and "big government"?

In 1972, the Gallup Poll finally made these finer distinctions. When the three most visible social-governmental groups were compared simultaneously, big labour received heavy disapproval as being the "... biggest threat to Canada in years to come...."[23] The replies were: big government, 22 per cent; big business, 27 per cent; and big labour, 36 per cent. But opinion is very changeable. In the context of the inflationary crisis of 1973-1974, public opinion would probably be less critical of unions, with big business becoming the great scapegoat.

Strikes

The issue that most bedevils public opinion about labour-union activity is probably the strike. The CIPO has asked many questions of the public about strikes, and the tactical use of pickets, injunctions, etc. To begin with, the "right to strike" has strong support, in general. In November 1963 (CIPO 299, question 13(a) 63.7 per cent of those sampled supported the right to strike; 28.5 per cent opposed; and 7.8 per cent had no opinion.

Further analysis indicates that the right to strike is strongly supported by union members (82 per cent), while there is lesser support (65 per cent) among nonunion people. However, it is surprising to discover that the lower the social class, the lower the support for the right to strike! It may be that the abstract concept of the "right to strike" is regarded as fundamental to democratic society, and so those who are most educated are also the most articulate about "rights". No doubt the upper socio-economic groups would argue the proposition in these terms.

However, only 45 per cent of the same sample thought that the strike "has not outlived its usefulness as a means by which workers can press for their demands", whereas 38 per cent of the same sample thought that the strike weapon had "outlived its usefulness"; 8 per cent gave ambiguous answers; and 9 per cent had no opinion.

The public, in 1966, did not support the principle of sympathy support by other unions in the picket line. Some 59 per cent wanted the right of other unions to join picket lines restricted, only 24 per cent supported sympathy picketing, 2 per cent gave qualified answers, and 15 per cent were undecided. However, strong support was given to the principle of court injunctions to restrict the numbers in a picket line. Some 54 per cent approved of such court injunctions; only 25 per cent disapproved; 3 per cent gave qualified answers; and 18 per cent had no opinion.

The public has even indicated a willingness to support such drastic action as limiting the duration of a strike to seven days! In January 1966, 73 per cent favoured such a proposal. The question was: "It has been suggested that no strike be permitted to go on for more than seven days. If after seven days the union and the employer cannot reach an agreement, a government-appointed committee would decide the issue and both be compelled to accept the terms." Only 19 per cent opposed such compulsory arbitration, while 7.8 per cent had no opinion. There was surprisingly strong support for this proposition even among union members (65 per cent). It is obvious that few people like lengthy strikes. One should have the right to strike, but not for long periods.

The public appears, also, to believe in restricting the right to strike in certain categories of employment. For example, when asked in January 1966 whether "workers in public utilities such as transportation, gas, hydro, and so on, should be allowed to strike or not", only 29 per cent agreed to allow them to strike; 60 per cent wished to prevent strikes in these cate-gories; 2 per cent gave qualified answers; and 9 per cent had no opinion.

Those who supported the right to strike gave as their reasons that: "everyone has the right to strike" (50 per cent); "a strike is all right, is justified -- with proper bargaining" (20 per cent); "a strike is their only weapon" (11 percent); "they have to uphold the union" (5 per cent); "no particular reason" (2 percent); other reasons (1 per cent). Those who opposed the right to strike cited these reasons: "the public suffers" (54 per cent); "disrupts the country -- raises the cost of living" (16 per cent); "can settle it peacefully" (7 per cent); "they are well paid -- the more they get the more they want" (12 per cent); "don't believe in strikes or unions" (14 per cent).

The public, in April 1963, appeared to be less concerned by strikes in such communications industries as newspapers, tele-phone, radio, and TV. But again, there is sharp disagreement on this issue between union and nonunion members.

We can summarize our findings on the issue of strikes in the following way. In general, there is not very strong support for the right to strike (64 per cent in favour). This right is supported more strongly by union than nonunion members, but even the union members' level of support is only 82 per cent. There are strong regional variations in opinion on this issue, with lowest support in the Province of Quebec, and highest in the Maritimes (with the exception of Prince Edward Island). The public would like to see some alternative to the strike weapon, or at least a drastic curtailment of the length of a strike. This proposition receives support even among a majority of union members.

Conclusion

A survey of Canadian public opinion on industrial relations over the last two decades indicates that regionalism and whether an individual is or is not a member of a union are crucial determinants of public attitudes toward industrial relations. If this is so, and certainly the evidence presented in the previous pages supports this contention, then the task of government is made very difficult if it hopes to provide some uniformity in the handling of disputes.

There is one irreducible element in the picture. While the principle of labour unions is not questioned seriously, there is very strong dissatisfaction with the traditional methods, such as strikes, used to settle disputes. There is strong approval of government intervention in strikes, particularly *federal* government intervention. It would also appear that key communications media such as railroads and seaways would like to see some alternative to the strike.

Notes

1. See table 1a, in R. R. March, *Public Opinion and Industrial Relations,* Task Force on Industrial Relations (Ottawa: Privy Council Office, July 1968).

2. R. Alford, *Party and Society* (Chicago: Rand McNally & Co., 1963), pp. 250-284.

3. R. R. March, *Public Opinion,* table 2, p. 4.

4. *Toronto Star,* 5 May 1973.

5. R. R. March, *Public Opinion,* table 3, p. 5.

6. Ibid., table 5, p. 9.

7. *Toronto Star,* 24 January 1973.

8. R. R. March, *Public Opinion*, table 6, p. 12.

9. Ibid., table 7, p. 13.

10. Ibid., table 8, pp. 14-15.

11. Ibid., table 9, p. 15.

12. Ibid., table 10, p. 16.

13. Ibid., table 11, p. 17.

14. Ibid., table 12, p. 17.

15. Ibid., table 13, p. 19.

16. *Ottawa Citizen*, 13 May 1967.

17. *Toronto Star*, 20 January 1973.

18. R. R. March, *Public Opinion*, table 19, p. 27.

19. Ibid., table 20, pp. 28-29.

20. Ibid., table 21, pp. 30-31.

21. Ibid., table 22, p. 33.

22. Ibid., table 23, pp. 34-35.

23. *Toronto Star*, 22 July 1972.

6. Political Affiliation of the Trade Unions

by Richard U. Miller

Introduction

Labour organizations on the North American continent, almost from their beginning, have sought their objectives through economic means. Negotiations with employers, reinforced by such weapons of economic power as strikes, boycotts, picketing, and union security arrangements, have long been the norm. Thus, marked by its narrow focus, North American unionism has been characterized, sometimes derisively by its European counterparts, as business or "bread and butter" unionism. One consequence of this is the tendency for observers of the trade union scene to fail to discern broader social goals, beyond limited economic self-interest, and the frequent resort to political mechanisms to attain both economic and social objectives. In this chapter, a brief review will first be undertaken of trade union mechanisms for political intervention; secondly, the results of such intervention will be evaluated; and finally, an attempt will be made to ascertain whether in the future, the balance will shift away from economic action toward greater political intervention.

Historical Evolution of Political Intervention

In the early years of Canadian labour history, trade unions often found themselves confronted by resistant employers and hostile governments. Under these circumstances fledgling unions were not able, at times, to muster sufficient economic power to achieve their demands. As a consequence, limited political intervention was acceptable within the framework of the Gomperistic philosophies of the American parent internationals to which the Canadian workers belonged.[1] Among the political practices employed to supplement collective bargaining were legislative lobbying, submissions of proposals, and endorsation of candidates. These, of course, were the tools of a nonpartisan political action made famous by the admonition of Samuel Gompers, long-time president of the American Federation of Labour, to limit political action to a policy of rewarding friends and punishing enemies, without regard for party membership. This outlook effectively excluded trade unions from becoming associated with particular parties for joint action, and also frowned upon labour leaders' offering themselves as candidates for public office.

Dissent from the official policies of limited political action emerged, however, at nearly every convention of the old Trades and Labour Congress, and within the Canadian branches of the American international unions which formed the bulk of the TLC's constituent organizations. In 1906, for example,

59

encouragement was given by the TLC to the formation of provincial labour parties. And again in 1917 the policy was relaxed even further to permit the creation of a federal Canadian Labour Party.[2]

In 1923, however, the electoral failures of the CLP strengthened the hand of the pro-Gompers factions within the TLC, who forced a reestablishment of the policies governing the Congress up to 1906. As far as politics were concerned the TLC was to leave "the labour political autonomy in the hands of the established labour political parties" and to "continue to act as the legislative mouthpiece for organized labour ... independent of any political organization...."[3] The Congress was to be rigidly nonpartisan until the late 1930s, when the organization of industrial workers rent the fabric of organized labour, producing a schism within the TLC and ultimately a rival labour centre, the Canadian Congress of Labour.

Turn Toward Direct Political Action

Economic catastrophe, the inefficacy of nonpartisan political action, the limited economic power of the newly organized unskilled and semiskilled factory workers, and more radical labour leadership created the conditions under which a sizeable segment of labour was to shift its political stance from the 1930s onward. The only element lacking was a viable political option and this was soon supplied by the Cooperative Commonwealth Federation.

The CCF had been organized in 1933 with a very limited participation from the trade unions.[4] A major obstacle to participation was the association with the CCF of the All Canadian Congress of Labour, which was viewed by the TLC and its internationals as a rival, radical and illegitimate labour organization. As well, the dominance by middle-class, highly educated United Churchmen served as an additional impediment to union support of the CCF.

It was in the midst of this scene that the organization of the mass-production factory workers was begun after 1935, resulting in the creation of such industrial unions as the United Autoworkers, United Steelworkers, and Meatpackers unions. Although these labour organizations too were branches of American internationals, their leaders were much more politically oriented, often holding socialist or communist beliefs. In 1940, these unions affiliated within a new labour centre, the Canadian Congress of Labour, to challenge the supremacy of the TLC.

Early in the decade of the 1940s with the merger of ACCL and the CCL, federal and especially provincial CCF political success, along with growing defections of TLC affiliates from the centre's

political policy, brought the issue of elective political action
back to the forefront. The CCL gave the CCF its endorsement and
an estimated 100 local unions affiliated. Moreover, the main
source of income for the party became the labour movement.[5] The
hallowed traditions of Gompers were being laid aside apparently,
and a new philosophy of labour action forged.

It perhaps should come as no surprise that in the end the movement toward direct political action was to be weak and diffuse,
with the issue still in doubt more than thirty years later.
Despite a parliamentary political system and the attractive
model of the British Labour Party, the weight of Gompersian
tradition and international unionism soon diffused the move
toward trade union support for the CCF. A hard core of labour
participation remained until the CCF's demise in 1958, but the
bulk of organized labour drew back as early CCF electoral
successes became an endless cycle of defeats. Only in Saskatchewan was the party's promise fulfilled.

The New Democratic Party and Labour

It is an historical irony that even as direct political action
seemed to be waning, events were conspiring to bring it renewed
emphasis. Among these events, greatest significance should be
attached to the 1956 merger of the TLC and CCL, creating the
Canadian Labour Congress. The leadership of the combined
centres almost immediately endorsed political action, authorizing the nascent Congress' Political Education Committee to
seek the creation of a "new party".[6] The CCF's electoral
disaster in 1958, in which it lost seventeen of its twenty-five
federal seats, prompted a series of joint discussions with the
CLC, which terminated with the official dissolution of the
CCF and the subsequent creation of the New Democratic Party in
July 1961.

The new party was conceived to be "a broadly based people's
political movement, which embraces the CCF, the labour movement,
farm organizations, professional people and other liberally
minded persons interested in basic social reform...."[7]

In this respect the NDP was cast in much the same mold as the
CCF had been at its birth. The CCF throughout its life had
never managed to mold these diverse units into a cohesive whole.
The farmers thought the CCF clubs too radical, the CCF clubs
viewed the labour leaders as "power-hungry right wingers",
labour leaders conversely accused CCF'ers of middle-class, ivory
tower, utopian dreaming, and the rank-and-file union members
expressed a clean-cut refusal to support any segment of the
party.[8]

No mass union support of the CCF materialized, and instead,
whatever labour participation was involved became a continuing

source of suspicion, tension and resentment. In a reaffirmation of the old axiom that those who do not learn from history are forced to repeat it, the NDP from its inception set a parallel course to that of the CCF. It was to be a "new" party unable to escape its past, and therefore, with almost the identical internal tensions that had beset its progenitor. As we shall see below in an examination of union affiliation, finances, and party relations, labour participation in the NDP is not without its problems.

Union Affiliation

The number of union members continues to grow in Canada year by year, reaching over 2.5 million in 1973.[9]   It is of some interest to note, therefore, that the proportion of union members affiliated with the NDP through their organizations has continued to decline from a high of 14.6 per cent in 1964 to 11.0 per cent in 1973. Moreover, the geographic and organizational concentration of union affiliations that typified NDP at its beginning continues in much the same form. For example, in 1968 Ontario accounted for over 80 per cent of union affiliation. In 1974 that was still true. Three unions, the Steelworkers, Autoworkers, and Food and Allied Workers, accounted in 1968 for 68 per cent of union membership. If any change had occurred by 1974 concentration within the three was a percentage point or two higher.[10]

These statistics indicate that however much the leadership of the CLC and the larger national or international unions may support affiliation with the NDP, these feelings are shared for the most part neither by the local union leadership nor by rank-and-file members. Illustrative of the sentiments of individual members are the results of a survey carried out among its affiliates by the International Association of Machinists in 1971, which disclosed that while 70 per cent of the respondents considered themselves "working class", only 40 per cent normally thought of themselves as NDP. Even more striking was the fact that only 38 per cent felt unions should support a political party.[11]   Analysis of the voting records of union members seems to indicate that even a smaller percentage actually vote NDP.[12]

NDP - Trade Union Tensions

As pointed out above, the relationships between NDP and organized labour have not run smoothly, either since the party's founding in 1961 or during the lifetime of its sire, the CCF. In this respect, points at issue seem to have been basically of three types: (1) structural; (2) philosophical; and (3) those stemming from the accession of the NDP to power, most notably in British Columbia.

First of all it is important to note that unlike the other parties on the Canadian political scene, the NDP and its predecessor have sought to erect a political organization capable of housing both individuals and groups. In this respect the British Labour Party constituted a model both to emulate and avoid. The financial and voting support of the trade unions was desired without simultaneously giving up administrative control. Thus bloc voting at NDP conventions was not to be allowed, the CLC itself was not to affiliate, and local unions were to be given much smaller proportional representation at party meetings and conventions. At the federal level, for example, while the constituency associations were to be permitted one delegate per fifty individual members, the affiliated union organizations were allotted only one delegate per one thousand members.

Given approximately 275,000 affiliated union members in 1973 as against 73,000 individual members, it would seem that the riding associations would be entitled to more than five times as many federal delegates, leaving the party machinery firmly in control of the latter segment of the NDP.[13]   Attendance at federal conventions, when taken together with the fact that a large proportion of the party's income is drawn from union sources, places the intraparty roles of the unions in a far different light. Thus, in reality, the ridings and the organized labour affiliates are much more evenly balanced, with the likelihood of passage of an issue opposed by labour at a party meeting or caucus quite low.

Union influence within the party becomes particularly clear as one examines the NDP's financial structure. The $90,000 contributed by union affiliates in 1972, for example, constituted 44 per cent of the party's federal general revenue and fell short of that contributed by individual members by only $12,000.[14]
In fact, of the more than $365,000 spent by the NDP in the 1972 federal election over $200,000 was collected from union sources.[15]   Moreover, if one were to place a value on the unpaid manpower and other resources supplied by trade unions during the course of the election, the total dollar contributions of organized labour would greatly exceed the figure reported above. Finally, at its July 1973 federal convention the affiliation dues were raised from five cents to ten cents per capita, which while increasing the party's revenues, would also raise the unions' influence.

The massive extent of "real" trade union participation in the party has left the constituency groups with the dilemma of creating a formula by which trade union electoral support can be maintained and even increased, while perhaps at the same time containing or diluting union power within the party. The efforts have been for the most part unsuccessful, leading to charges of "taxation without representation" as well as dysfunctional power struggles. Moreover, if anything, trade union influence has continued to grow, not diminish, despite these efforts.

These structural tensions have also been exacerbated by the fact that the bulk of the affiliated trade union party membership is in turn structurally connected to U.S.-based international unions. The federal Department of Labour estimated recently, for example, that in 1973 slightly over 56 per cent of the 2.5 million organized workers in Canada belonged to the internationals and that eight of the twelve largest unions in Canada were U.S. headquartered.[16]   Given that it is precisely these same internationals holding affiliation with the NDP, the party has been subjected to much criticism for being union-dominated by U.S. labour "bosses". In an era of growing Canadian nationalism, this image likely has a serious negative electoral impact.

A second major source of intraparty tension is a long-standing philosophical debate over party ends and means: the union sectors have been a force holding first CCF and then NDP to the political centre for nearly forty years in the face of both "old" left and "new" left efforts to move toward a pronounced socialist position. The most recent emergence of this was the struggle that began in the late 1960s, particularly within the Ontario provincial party. General disillusionment with accepted North American institutions, a crisis within the federal party leadership, and a desire from various segments of the party's intellectual base to present a more articulated alternative to the other parties led to a spate of position papers -- most notably the "Manifesto for an Independent Socialist Canada". The manifesto argued:

On the road to socialism, aspiration for independence or feelings of nationalism and particularly anti-imperialism, should be taken into account in their own right. For to pursue independence in a serious way in Canada is to make visible the necessity and desirability of socialism.[17]

Centred in a group self-proclaimed as the Waffle supporters of the attempt to "radicalize", the NDP succeeded in gaining positions on the federal executive and concessions from the party leadership. By 1972, the growth of the Waffle to constitute almost a party within a party and its strident voice provoked the affiliated unions to counterattack. Condemned as displaying a "sneering, contemptuous attitude toward official trade unionism and the labour leadership", the Waffle was effectively given the choice of disbanding or being purged. In August 1972, a majority of the Waffle quit the NDP to create a new organization, the Movement For An Independent Socialist Canada.[18]

In retrospect, the Waffle clearly elicited a sympathetic philosophical response from many individual constituency members as well as a sprinkling of trade unionists. Yet the bulk of organized labour and, most importantly, the leadership of the Canadian sections of the Steelworkers, Autoworkers, and Food and

Allied Workers did not share this view. When the latter group,
uneasy from the beginning, finally perceived the Waffle as a
threat, ideologically and structurally, the intraparty power of
trade unions was made manifest.

The third dimension of trade union-party tensions are those
ensuing from the issues which the election of NDP governments
would pose for trade union affiliates. Upon assumption of
power, the necessities of representing all constituencies may
bring the party into conflict with special interest groups such
as unions. The arguments over incomes policies and labour
legislation which have characterized recent British Labour
Party governments provide salient examples of the potential
sources of disagreement between NDP governments and unions in
Canada. At the federal level, NDP governments are still a
"dream of power". The party has been denied even the luxury
of constituting the opposition. The possibilities for conflict
of this kind, however, were indicated at the 1972 CLC convention,
where the former federal leader of the NDP, David Lewis, condemned "extravagant" bargaining demands as tending only to raise
false hopes in workers, and called for restraint on the part of
labour leaders.[19] Lewis argued that these false hopes led to
frustration and strikes when employers were unable to fulfill
the demands. Also urged by Lewis was increased autonomy for
Canadian affiliates from their international parents: "Full
self-reliance of Canadian labour is one of the potent weapons
in the struggle for Canadian self-reliance".[20] Had NDP come
to power in 1974, continued articulation of these views would
have led organized labour and the party into their first serious
confrontation. Even short of achieving power the relations
between labour and the NDP leadership were reported as not
entirely satisfactory from labour's side. Whether the 1974
change in both NDP and CLC leadership will provide a more
harmonious basis for the relationship still remains to be tested.

Thus if party-labour relations under NDP governments are to be
evaluated, it must be at the provincial level. Here the electoral successes have been much more pronounced, with governments
now (1974) under NDP control in British Columbia, Manitoba, and
Saskatchewan. However, in both the latter two provinces
organized labour has not been a key factor in the party's political achievements. For example, in the spring of 1974,
affiliated union membership in Saskatchewan was only 5,326 and
in Manitoba, 11,546.[21] This constituted about 10 per cent and
12 per cent respectively of the organized workers of the two
provinces. In both cases also, the total number of organized
workers is relatively small.

For British Columbia, on the other hand, the unionized work
force is quite large, nearly 300,000 members, with a correspondingly important segment of these workers affiliated with
the NDP. It is significant, therefore, that in this particular
province the party-trade union relationship apparently began to

founder within a few short months after the NDP took power in
August of 1972. In addition to a series of strikes against
provincially owned or controlled companies, arguments also
arose over Premier Barrett's choice for labour minister, the
creation of a commission of enquiry to examine the province's
labour laws, and the proposed appointment of a chairman
identified with the Conservatives.[22] Although the tensions, at
least superficially, diminished after that, the results of the
1974 federal election from the standpoint of British Columbia
raise some doubts about labour satisfaction and solidarity
with the party. Not only did the NDP's popular vote fall
proportionately (12 per cent) but also, nine of the eleven
federal seats held after the 1972 election were lost.[23] While
other factors may have contributed to the NDP losses, disharmony
between the party and the trade unions undoubtedly played its
part.

Québécois Trade Unions and Québécois Politics

With over 900,000 trade union members, Quebec labour is clearly
a force with great potential political power. This potential
has yet to be realized, however, and thus the actual magnitude
of the power remains an enigma. The two major labour centres,
the Quebec Federation of Labour and the Confederation of
National Trade Unions, have swung back and forth between no
political action, nonpartisan activity, party-connected political action, and finally, direct mass action epitomized by the
so-called common front. Until 1946, for example, the CNTU was
apolitical officially but supportive of the Union National
generally. From 1946 onward, however, the confederation became
increasingly interventionist in provincial politics such that
by 1961, as the NDP was being created, the appearance was given
of an impending affiliation. A delegation from the CNTU
attended the founding convention of the NDP and the confederation's president, Gerard Picard, became associate president of
the NDP.[24]

The marriage of the CNTU and NDP was not to be, however, as
the successor to Picard, Jean Marchand, moved the CNTU away
from the NDP toward the liberals. Marchand himself became an
important figure within the National Liberal Party, although
the confederation itself stopped short of a formal linkage.

The QFL for its part has endorsed the NDP from the latter's
beginning to the present time. It has not supported the party,
however, in any effective manner. In 1974, for example, union
affiliations amounted to only 5,800 members, almost half what
it had been ten years earlier.[25] The leadership has chosen
instead to unofficially support the Parti Québécois and to
direct its efforts at the provincial level to legislative submissions and "lobbying", and at the Montreal municipal level to
direct action. The 1972 common front of the CNTU, QFL and

Teachers Union (CEQ) set in motion the use of the general strike
as a political weapon amidst the student rhetoric of Marxist
economics. Whether this reflects a widespread desire to discard
the former moderate, reformist union goals in Quebec for revolutionary, socialist strategies is unclear. What is clear is
that the NDP is not a viable political entity in the province
and that the conservative, Gomperistic political orientation
marking most Anglo-Canadian unions has been rejected by their
French Canadian counterparts.

Conclusion

It is evident from the above that apart from the Province of
Quebec, neither the centrality of economic objectives attained
by economic means nor the belief that political action is best
undertaken independently and directly through legislative or
parliamentary representations is under challenge. If anything,
both sets of norms have been strengthened by the most recent
electoral failure of the NDP (1974) and the repression of the
common front in Quebec in 1972. To paraphrase a "counterculture"
proverb, "Samuel Gompers is not dead, he is merely living in
Ottawa under an assumed name."

    In view of this it is interesting to note that the hard-core
NDP nevertheless continues undaunted by the lack of federal
success. In November of 1974, it was reported that the CLC had
held a working conference on political action in Ottawa which
resolved that "labour must become fully involved in the life of
the New Democratic Party instead of merely playing a supporting
role".[26] It is thus equally clear, whatever the outcome, that
those CLC leaders emotionally attached to the British Labour
Party model will continue to support the NDP, whether local
officers and rank-and-file members share the commitment or not.

Notes

1. For a more detailed historical review of union political
action, see: Gad Horowitz, *Canadian Labour in Politics*
(Toronto: University of Toronto Press, 1968); H. A. Logan,
Trade Unions in Canada (Toronto: Macmillan, 1948); Clifford
A. Scotton, *Canadian Labour and Politics* (Canadian Labour Con-
gress,   ); Richard U. Miller, "Organized Labour and
Politics in Canada", in R.U. Miller and A.F. Isbester,
Canadian Labour in Transition (Toronto: Prentice-Hall, 1971).

2. H. A. Logan, *Trade Unions,* p. 430.

3. Ibid., p. 431.

4. The two standard sources on the early days of the CCF are:
S.M. Lipset, *Agrarian Socialism* (Berkeley: University of

California Press, 1950); and Dean McHenry, *The Third Force in Canada* (Berkeley: University of California Press, 1950). See also Gerald L. Caplan, "Insight: Perspective on Party Conflict", *New Democrat,* May-June 1973, pp. 8-11.

5. Leo Zakuta, "Membership in a Becalmed Protest Movement", *Canadian Journal of Economics and Political Science* 24 (May 1958), p. 198. But see also G.L. Caplan, "Insight", who disputes this.

6. CLC, *Report of Proceedings,* First Convention(23-27 April, 1956), p. 49. Cf. also Stanley Knowles, *The New Party* (Toronto: McClelland and Stewart, 1961).

7. S. Knowles, *The New Party*, p. 127.

8. G.L. Caplan, "Insight", p. 10.

9. Canada Department of Labour, *News,* 7 August 1974.

10. CLC, Department of Political Education.

11. As reported in *Labour Gazette*, April 1972, pp. 200-201.

12. *The New Democrat,* July-August 1968, p. 3.

13. Desmond Morton, *NDP: The Dream of Power* (Toronto: Hakkert, 1974), p. 155.

14. Khayyam Z. Paltiel, "Party and Candidate Expenditures in the Canadian General Election of 1972", *Canadian Journal of Political Science,* June 1974, p. 347.

15. Ibid.

16. Canada Department of Labour, *Labour Gazette,* October 1974.

17. As quoted in D. Morton, *The Dream of Power*, pp. 92-93.

18. D. Morton, *The Dream of Power*, pp. 134-135.

19. "Labour Facing Greatest Challenge", *Labour Gazette*, August 1972.

20. Ibid.

21. CLC, Department of Political Education.

22. *Toronto Star*, 26 February 1973.

23. *Vancouver Sun*, 10 July 1974, p. 37.

24. Guy Lortie, "Evolution de l'action politique de la CSN", *Relations Industrielles*, vol. 22, no. 4, pp. 535-538.

25. CLC, Department of Political Education.

26. CLC, *Canadian Labour Comment*, 1 November 1974, p. 4.

7. The Law of Unfair Labour Practices*

by Innis Christie

Introduction

The term *unfair labour practice* is generally used to denote an antiunion practice prohibited by labour relations legislation. While there are provincial variations that may be important in particular cases, broadly similar prohibitions, intended to protect the rights of employees to organize and bargain collectively, are found in the Canada Labour Code and the statutes of all the provinces. What are these prohibitions? What sanctions are imposed for their breach? By what institutions of government are they administered? Finally, how effective are they? To the first three of these questions a labour lawyer can give answers which are both complex and precise, and closely tied to the labour statute of the province in which he is practicing. A less technical response is also possible, and is offered here.

Blatant antiunion intimidation occurs most frequently on the fringes of industrial society, in the areas of the country or sectors of the economy where unionism is not accepted in principle, and among employers who are barely surviving financially. However, employers who accept the basic tenets of free collective bargaining may fear that out of simple ignorance, or because they have been misled by the union, their employees will not act wisely in choosing a bargaining agent. They may feel that the "true" facts must be put before the employees; that union propaganda must be counteracted. An employer with these concerns may have no wish to exceed the limits of the law but there is, nevertheless, a danger that his antiunion influence will be considerable because of the pervasive feeling among employees that they are vitally dependent for their jobs on employer good will. Unfair labour practice sections have been included in all Canadian labour relations statutes to limit this influence and generally to prevent interference with the right of employees to choose their union. These provisions have proven difficult to apply, but they are crucial to the effective operation of Canadian labour legislation.

The question of the effectiveness of unfair labour practice laws cannot be answered with any pretence of precision, but some insight is afforded by a study entitled "Unfair Labour Practices: An Exploratory Study of the Efficacy of the Law of Unfair Labour Practices in Canada", by I. Christie and M.R. Gorsky, published by the Queen's Printer in 1970. The study was commissioned by the Privy Council Task Force on Labour

---

* Reproduced by permission of Information Canada.

Relations, commonly known as the Woods Task Force, which reported in 1968. The study took the form of a survey of informed opinion, for the most part of lawyers active in labour relations, but it also surveyed the opinions of the chairmen and senior officials of the boards that administer labour relations laws across Canada, of academic labour lawyers, and of some union representatives who frequently appear as counsel before labour relations boards.

Eight Unfair Practices: The Specifics

(1) Employer Interference in the Formation of a Trade Union

The legislation of all Canadian jurisdictions prohibits an employer from interfering in the formation of a trade union. Normally, "interference in formation" would consist of the employer's paying or otherwise encouraging "loyal" employees to establish an organization that would be responsive to the employer's wishes rather than truly representative of the interests of the employees. The labour relations statute in every jurisdiction in Canada provides for prosecution for such activities. In most provinces prosecution requires the consent of the Minister of Labour and in some -- Ontario and New Brunswick, for example -- the consent of the Labour Relations Board. Consent is normally given upon showing that there has been, prima facie, a breach which is continuing.

Prosecution, however, is not an effective remedy for employer interference in the formation of a trade union. The main reason for formation of an employer-dominated union is to forestall the certification of a legitimate union, and to do this the competing organization must itself gain certification or sign a binding collective agreement with the employer. The real and effective protection, therefore, against such activities on the part of the employer is the section of the labour statute that directs the labour relations board to refuse to certify such a dominated trade union and provides that an agreement signed by such an organization does not constitute a collective agreement. In other words, when a union is held to be employer dominated, its presence does not constitute a bar to the certification of another trade union.

There was a strong consensus among those interviewed in the Unfair Labour Practices Study that dominated unions are no longer a significant problem in Canada. Denial of certification to such a union and the refusal to give binding effect to its collective agreements were considered to be effective deterrents.

(2) Employer Interference in the Selection of Bargaining Agent

Intimidation or firing for union membership may be thought of as

a severe form of interference with the "selection" by employees
of their bargaining agent, but the concern for the moment is
with interference stopping short of that.   Not every province
has legislation expressly prohibiting mere "interference" by an
employer "in the selection of a trade union" by his employees,
but the Labour Relations Act of Ontario does, in just those
terms.   On the other hand, the Ontario Labour Relations Act, like
most others, provides that nothing in the act is to affect an
employer's freedom of expression.   In the absence of any obvious
attempt at intimidation it may require a judgement of extreme
delicacy to determine whether an employer has illegally inter-
fered with the "selection" of a bargaining agent by his employees
or has, in fact, simply exercised his right to freedom of expression.   Depending on the circumstances, interference with
selection may take the form of a notice, posted by the employer,
which goes beyond simply stating the facts and exhorts the
employees to reject the union, the sending of letters to individual employees, or assembling them for a speech.   Individuals
are sometimes summoned for interviews, or simply interrogated
on the shop floor as to union membership or their sympathies in
the matter.   In each case the words used, any natural implications, the overall context, and even such things as the union's
opportunity to speak in reply must be considered in determining
whether the employer has used his influence to interfere with
selection.   The Unfair Labour Practices Study showed that
neutrals and lawyers who act principally on behalf of the unions
in Ontario felt that there was a considerable amount of interference by employers in the selection of bargaining agents.
Their opinion must, however, be taken in context.   It appeared
from the interviews that the Ontario Labour Relations Board has
taken a much stricter view of permissible interference than
that taken in Quebec, the west or the Maritimes.   Those interviewed in Quebec and the Maritimes did not feel there was a
great deal of illegal interference, but this was probably because their understanding was that an employer could counter
the union's organizing campaign with anything short of intimidation.   In fact, of course, in small industries where there is
a high level of paternalism, as there continues to be in the
Atlantic Provinces, an employer's expression of his wishes need
not be backed by any patent threat to be effective.

It was suggested, however, by those interviewed in the Unfair
Labour Practices Study that the fear of certification without a
vote is only an effective deterrent against interference by the
employer where, in his own estimation, any such interference
would be no more than marginally effective.   In other words,
if the employer thinks that by interfering he can prevent the
union from gaining the support of even 50 per cent of the work
force he may decide that on balance it is in his interest to do
so.   The solution may lie in the provision of the new British
Columbia Labour Code, under which the board of that province
has the power to certify where there has been improper interference, even though there is no evidence that the union has

or ever had even a bare majority of the employees as members.

Labour and management partisans and neutrals interviewed in the course of the Unfair Labour Practices Study shared the opinion that although employer interference in selection is almost never prosecuted as such, it should be continued to be specified as an unfair labour practice subject to prosecution to ensure that the policy of the law is made clear.

Difficulties in the application of the law against interference in the selection of a bargaining agent may arise in connection with limitations that the employer puts on the union's freedom to carry on organizing activities on his premises. Broadly speaking, an employer has the right to prohibit such activities during working hours and is not required to permit full-time union organizers on his premises. The general understanding, however, is that labour statutes in Canada do not permit an employer to discipline employees who "talk union" on his premises unless they are in breach of a reasonable prohibition of all nonwork communication. There is, moreover, a requirement in the law of some provinces -- Ontario and British Columbia, for example -- that where employees not only work but live on the employer's property he must, upon direction from the Labour Relations Board, permit access to them by a labour union representative. Bush workers are those most obviously affected.

The Unfair Labour Practices Study disclosed a general consensus in favour of the operation of the laws relating to the employer's right to control access to his premises, as it affects union organization.

(3) Intimidation: Threats to Compel Employees to Refrain from Becoming or Cease to be Members, Officers or Representatives of Trade Unions

Employer pressure in many of its forms may, of course, go beyond mere "interference with selection" and constitute intimidation. Particularly where employees have been interviewed or interrogated individually about their union affiliations, boards have been ready to find that there has been intimidation.

Under the Canada Labour Code and the labour statutes of all Canadian provinces employers are prohibited from using threats or intimidation to persuade their employees not to support a union. Prosecution is provided for, but even where an employer's activity is sufficiently serious to constitute "intimidation", prosecution is almost never resorted to. Occasionally, a union will seek and obtain consent to prosecute from the Minister of Labour or the provincial labour relations board, depending on which is required under the specific law of the particular jurisdiction, but the general view is that little is to be gained from prosecution. What the union wants in such situations

is to be certified. As in the case of lesser forms of interference with the selection of a bargaining agent, the real
sanction lies with the labour relations board and the exercise
of its power to certify with a vote.

(4) Yellow Dog Contract

Canadian labour relations legislation commonly provides that no
employer shall seek to impose in any contract of employment a
condition that restrains an employee from being a member of a
trade union. The sanction against such activity is prosecution,
following consent by the Minister of Labour or the provincial
labour relations board, as the case may be. Those interviewed
in the Unfair Labour Practices Study stated, almost unanimously,
that such contracts are no longer a problem. There were a few
who said they had seen such conditions in writing and some who
alleged that oral promises to the prohibited effect are sometimes
extracted from employees. It was generally felt that the legislative prohibition helped to explain the absence of the practice
and should be retained.

(5) Refusal to Hire, Discrimination in Employment, and Firing
   for Union Activities

Firing a union activist removes a union supporter who might tip
the balance in favour of the union in a vote, it rids the
employer of an employee who may be winning others over to the
union, and it operates as a powerful threat against other
employees to prevent them from continuing as or becoming union
members. The prohibition against firing for union activities
is, therefore, the most important of the unfair labour practices.

An employer is prohibited from dismissing an employee *because*
he is a union supporter. Thus the unfair labour practice is
necessarily framed in terms of motive, because it is generally
agreed that an employer has to have the right to discipline or
discharge members of his work force for proper cause, in
accordance with the normal standards prevalent in industrial
society.

"*Because* he is a union supporter" is the phrase used in most
of the statutes, and motive is the key element in the offence.
Since motive is what goes on in the employer's mind, a serious
problem of proof emerges. Normally the law deals with the
problem of proof of motive by providing that the presence of
the required motive may be presumed where specified external
circumstances exist. Canadian unfair labour practices legislation has done this in a variety of ways. The Canada Labour
Code provides that a written complaint alleging discriminatory
firing is in itself evidence of the offence. This would appear
to cast on the employer the burden of introducing at least some
evidence to show that there was no discriminatory firing. The
Ontario Labour Relations Act is silent on the matter of onus,

but the Ontario board has held, in many cases, that where there is a union-organizing campaign and it is proved that the employer knew of it at the time he dismissed an employee, the onus is on the employer to establish that he did not dismiss that employee for union activities. In other words, the Ontario board has reversed the onus of proof on the issue of motive. In several other jurisdictions, including Quebec, this reversal of onus has been specifically enacted in the labour relations legislation. The net result is that the employer must prove some plausible grounds other than union activities for the dismissal. Of course, if he expressly based dismissal on grounds of union activities it will not avail him to prove that there were other grounds upon which he could have fired the employee.

The same problems of motive arise in connection with refusal to hire and discrimination on the job, and the same procedural solutions have been provided by legislatures and labour relations boards. Because there is less at stake, such cases do not come to the fore nearly as frequently as discriminatory firing, but the reasons for the probibition of such activities, the sanctions, the methods of enforcement, and the problems of proof are, in broad terms, the same. In fact, there is no unfair labour practice harder to detect and prove than discrimination in hiring by an employer. Here, more than in the case of any other unfair labour practice, it was the opinion of those interviewed in the Unfair Labour Practices Study that no law can be effective against a subtle and well-advised employer.

Discrimination against employees for union membership is not only an unfair labour practice, and therefore an offence against the labour relations legislation subject to prosecution, but also an offence under the Criminal Code. However, the obstacle of meeting the criminal onus, of proving beyond a reasonable doubt that an employer fired or otherwise discriminated against an employee *because* of union membership or activities, is virtually insuperable. There have been very few prosecutions under the Criminal Code and most of those interviewed in the Unfair Labour Practices Study did not even know that the code provision existed. Nevertheless, there was a variety of opinion to the effect that prohibition by the Criminal Code constitutes a useful statement of an important nation-wide principle.

Where a discriminatory firing occurs during the fourth stage of the collective bargaining relationship, that is, where there is a collective agreement between the parties, the normal procedure is for the matter to go to arbitration. Virtually all collective agreements provide for arbitration in any situation where it is alleged that an employee was dismissed without just cause. In order to prove just cause an employer must go beyond proving that he acted without antiunion motive, which is theoretically all he need do in an unfair labour practice case. On the other hand, if the grievor -- the dis-

missed employee -- can prove the antiunion motive the dismissal
could not be held by an arbitrator to have been for just cause.

The labour legislation in every Canadian jurisdiction, on its
face, permits a complaint of unfair labour practice to be made
to the labour relations board even though a collective agreement is in force. In most provinces, however, the board would
rule that the matter should be decided by an arbitrator.
Special circumstances may give rise to an exception. The
Ontario board has held that where an employee has been dismissed
for activities against the interests of the union which is party
to the collective agreement and which would have to support him
in an arbitration proceeding, he may take his complaint straight
to the Labour Relations Board.

Both labour and management people interviewed in the Unfair
Labour Practices Study almost unanimously favoured the conciliatory approach to resolving unfair labour practices cases.
Procedures like that under section 79 of the Ontario Labour
Relations Act, under which a field officer attempts to bring
the parties into agreement, and only where he fails does the
matter go to the Labour Relations Board, met with general
approval.

The majority of the persons interviewed in the Unfair Labour
Practices Study felt that the powers exercised by the Ontario
board under section 79 and equivalents in other jurisdictions
were not excessive. Neutrals and labour people generally
thought that the board should be given even greater discretion
and flexibility of operation. There were a very significant
number of dissents from management people, including some of
the most competent lawyers in the field, who felt that the
board had so much discretion that the law was rendered uncertain
and subject to the vagaries of internal accommodation on the
Labour Relations Board.

(6) Changing Wages and Working Conditions to Undercut the Union

The labour relations laws of several jurisdictions prohibit any
change in wages and working conditions by the employer, without
the consent of the Labour Relations Board, from the time an
application for certification is made. In other jurisdictions
such changes are prohibited only from the time notice to bargain
has been given. This "freeze" continues in effect until the
conciliation procedure has been completed and the waiting period
until the union may legally strike has elapsed.

The major sanction for breach of the prohibition against any
change in wages or working conditions is prosecution for breach
of the labour statute, which requires consent of the Minister
of Labour in some jurisdictions and of the Labour Relations
Board in others. In addition, in some jurisdictions -- Nova
Scotia, for example -- the Labour Relations Board has power to

award compensation to any employee who has lost money as a
result of such a change in wages or conditions. Normally,
however, a prohibited change would be one that would put more
money in the pockets of individual employees, rather than
causing them loss. The change is prohibited, after all, because
it can be used to persuade employees that they do not need the
assistance of a union.

It was the unanimous opinion of Labour people interviewed in
the Unfair Labour Practices Study that the freeze on wages and
working conditions, commencing at the date of an application
for certification, is desirable. The protection was regarded
as important and labour was strongly of the opinion that to
delay its effect until notice to bargain had been given is to
allow the union to be undercut at the time when it is most
vulnerable. In general, this position was supported by the
neutrals interviewed.

The general management view was that the protection against
change in wages and working conditions should apply only from
the date of notice to bargain and not from the date of application for certification. In general, it was claimed that management does not really think it can "buy" employees by improving
conditions and that the prohibition is therefore unnecessary.
The feeling was that such a provision is subject to abuse by
unions. Certification applications may be rather drawn-out
proceedings, so a freeze from the time of application may have
a severe effect, such as making a company uncompetitive in the
wage market. The employees can suffer if the company is
prevented from making changes that are obviously due. While it
was recognized that any such change could be effected by gaining
the union's consent, it was felt that the seeking of consent
would involve a *de facto* recognition of the union and that the
union would inevitably bargain over the giving of consent. This,
it was said, would be contrary to the general intention of the
labour relations legislation, in that it would, in effect, force
an employer to bargain with the union while the union's application for certification was still pending.

(7) Failure to Bargain in Good Faith

The labour relations statute of every Canadian jurisdiction requires that once there is a certified bargaining agent, either
side may give the other notice to bargain, after which the
parties must meet and bargain in good faith or, as several
provincial statutes express it, "make every reasonable effort
to conclude a collective agreement". Failure to bargain in
good faith is not usually included under the heading "Unfair
Labour Practices" in Canadian Labour legislation and in most
acts no specific penalty is provided. Failure to bargain
simply constitutes a breach of the statute, which, in theory,
subjects the breaching party to prosecution and a fine, provided
the consent of the Minister of Labour or the Labour Relations

Board, as the case may be, has been obtained. In some jurisdictions -- Nova Scotia, for example -- a complaint of failure
to bargain in good faith may be made to the Minister of Labour
or to the Labour Relations Board. On the face of the statute
this adds little, because all the minister or the Labour
Relations Board can do in such circumstances is direct the
recalcitrant party to do what he is obliged to do under the
statute in any case. However, the reality may well be that such
intervention is effective to get negotiations started or renewed.

Prosecution for failing to bargain in good faith is virtually
unknown in Canadian labour relations, although there have been
a few cases where refusal to bargain was particularly blatant
and therefore provable in court. Partly, this may be due to the
fact that the legislation in every Canadian jurisdiction imposes
compulsory conciliation upon the parties. Where management and
union have met with a conciliation officer, however fruitlessly,
it may be difficult to prove a failure to bargain in good faith
because the requirement of good faith does not require either
party to make any concessions.

The general opinion expressed by those interviewed in the
Unfair Labour Practices Study was that there was little that the
law could or, in the opinion of the management people interviewed, should do to ensure good-faith bargaining. Labour
opinion placed more value on legal intervention in the bargaining
process, but the prevailing attitude was one of cynicism,
particularly among the labour lawyers interviewed. Union representatives felt that the legislation might be effectively
strengthened in some way. Management people interviewed generally
held that at the negotiation stage the collective bargaining relationship is, and should be, one of power. They felt that
compulsory conciliation under Canadian legislation is more
desirable than the relatively highly structured and legalistic
approach to "bargaining in good faith" taken in the United
States. Compulsory conciliation was seen by labour people and
neutrals, on the other hand, as an adjunct, rather than an
alternative, to the legal requirements of good-faith bargaining,
but almost no one was in favour of introducing sophisticated
sets of legal standards to be applied by a court or a labour
relations board in determining whether or not the good faith
obligation had been breached.

There was a suggestion that conciliation officers should be
alert to evidence of bad faith and should withdraw immediately
from negotiations upon the faith's evidencing itself, thus permitting strikes and picketing at an earlier time than is generally now the case. (The right to strike is delayed a set number of
days after the conclusion of conciliation efforts.) The general
opinion was that conciliation officers should not be given power
to penalize a party not bargaining in good faith, because the
exercise of such a power would destroy an officer's usefulness
as a conciliator.

(8) Employer Interference in the Administration of Trade Unions

As was pointed out at the beginning of this discussion of specific unfair labour practices, under Canadian labour laws employers are prohibited from participating in the formation of a trade union. In the Canada Labour Code and under the legislation of most provinces, the same section of the statute prohibits employers from participating in or interfering with the administration of a trade union or the representation of employees by the trade union. Participation in the formation of a trade union is an unfair labour practice which occurs at the organization stage, when an employer may attempt to forestall certification of a legitimate union by establishing a "house" union. Interference in the administration and functioning of the union may occur later, as when a trade union that was legitimate when it established its bargaining rights becomes dominated by the employer.

Conclusion

In the past several years, a new Canada Labour Code has been enacted and there have been major new labour relations statutes passed in Alberta, British Columbia, Manitoba, New Brunswick, Nova Scotia, Newfoundland, and Prince Edward Island. In spite of these opportunities, the law relating to unfair labour practices has not changed significantly since 1968, when the Unfair Labour Practices Study was done for the Privy Council Task Force on Labour Relations, although the accommodative or conciliatory approach to unfair labour practices has been adopted in those provinces that did not have an equivalent of section 79 of the Ontario Labour Relations Act. Labour relations boards across the country have been given primary jurisdiction over unfair labour practices, with provision for an attempt by a board officer to settle any complaint before it comes before the board for adjudication. The new British Columbia Labour Code has gone farthest in eliminating prosecution as a sanction for unfair labour practices, putting the administration of the law relating to unfair labour practices almost entirely in the of the provincial Labour Relations Board.

The Unfair Labour Practices Study indicates that the lack of any radical changes in the law of unfair labour practices reflects moderate satisfaction with the way the law works, and not any notion that it is unimportant.

In the case of labour people there was a large element of what can best be described as "resignation to the inevitable". Neutrals, particularly labour board chairmen and vice-chairmen, were not greatly concerned with any lack of efficacy in the unfair labour practice provisions and, except in the area of individual rights, management's view was that everything was working well. These broad generalizations are subject to the

caveat that the "satisfaction" tended to disappear when the
questioning became more specific and satisfaction was most
markedly lacking among those who had given the matter the
greatest consideration. There were, in fact, disturbingly few,
even in the select group interviewed, who indicated through
constructive suggestions or knowledge of alternatives that they
had ever considered the law of unfair labour practices from a
critical point of view. There were a number of exceptions, of
course, principally labour relations board people, highly
specialized lawyers (mainly in Toronto) and academics.

It has been widely accepted that unfair Labour practices may
be subtle and difficult to prove and that merely penalizing the
employer who commits an unfair labour practice does little for
an employee who has lost his job, or for the future continuing
relationship between the union and the employer. Accommodation
between the parties, therefore, has been accepted as the primary
goal, and compensation -- effected through a broad range of
remedial powers vested in Labour Relations Boards -- as the
secondary goal. The fact remains, unfortunately, that some
employers apparently continue to calculate that the gains from
defeating unions through unfair labour practices far outweigh
the likely costs.

8. Impact of the Federal Minimum Wage Law*

by M.A. Zaida

Introduction

Controversy has surrounded the subject of minimum wage legislation
from the Factory Acts of nineteenth-century Great Britain through
its early twentieth-century North American beginnings in the states
and provinces and the eventual passage of federal minima: the Fair
Labor Standards Act of 1938 in the United States and the Canada
Labour (Standards) Code in 1965. Such legislation represents an
attempt by society to maintain certain values and standards not
being achieved within the existing institutional framework. In
most western societies it is believed that those supplying labour
services are entitled to at least a subsistence wage (somehow defined) in order that workers and their dependents may avoid abject
poverty; those able to work should not, it is felt, need to burden
the rest of society with costs of their care. Substandard wages
may occur because employers exploit the unequal bargaining power
of workers, failing to pay them their "true worth"; or, alternatively, low wages may subsidize inefficient management practices.
In either case, government intervention to raise wages would increase total social welfare.

However, despite the seeming desirability of the social objectives of minimum wage laws, they have provoked more controversy
than any other area of labour legislation. Wage setting has an
easily recognizable money dimension, with important implications
for employment, wage structures, costs, productivity, and prices;
yet there is much disagreement among economists as to the nature
and magnitude of these effects. Economic analysis provides no
definite predictions concerning the effects of a minimum wage. To
date, empirical studies on the impact of minimum wages have yielded

This paper is based on a study prepared in 1968 and published in
1970 under the title, *A Study of the Effects of the $1.25 Minimum
Wage under the Canada Labour (Standards) Code,* Task Force on Labour
Relations, Study no. 16, March 1970. The reader is referred to the
original study for a theoretical analysis of minimum wages, as well
as a review of theoretical and empirical literature regarding the
minimum wage. For a recent study of minimum wage setting in a
Canadian province, where jurisdiction over most Canadian industry
lies, see: Frank Whittingham, *Minimum Wages in Ontario: Analysis
and Measurement Problems,* Industrial Relations Centre, Queen's
University, Research Series, no. 11, 1970. Research assistance
provided by Ms. Elizabeth Bryant is gratefully acknowledged.
*Reproduced by permission of Information Canada.

diverse results as well. The effects of increased wages on costs, output, prices, employment, and the wage structure are dependent upon, among other things, the type of firm or industry studied, the geographical location, and the general level and trend of economic activity. Thus, we must appeal to the facts in order to determine the impact of a minimum wage in a particular instance. Accordingly, in the remainder of this paper we will attempt to analyze the available Canadian data in order to draw some inferences about the impact of the Canadian federal minimum wage on employment and on wage differentials.

The Canadian Federal Minimum Wage

The Canada Labour (Standards) Code was enacted in 1965 and took effect on July 1 of that year. In 1970 it was incorporated into the Canada Labour Code, which consolidated federal labour legislation regarding industrial relations, fair employment practices, industrial safety, and labour standards. The code, which is enforced by the Minister of Labour, is unique among wage laws in that it incorporates minimum standards for vacations and holidays as well as for wages and hours. It provided initially for a minimum wage of $1.25 per hour ($1.00 for youths under seventeen); a standard eight-hour day and forty-hour week, with time-and-a-half for overtime; a maximum forty-eight-hour week; eight holidays with pay; and two weeks' paid vacation after every completed year of employment. The level of the minimum wage has increased several times, as it may be raised by order of the Governor in Council. As of December 1972, it stood at $1.90 per hour, with a $1.65 minimum for those under seventeen.

Coverage under the code is limited to those industries and undertakings over which parliament has exclusive legislative authority as specified in the British North America Act; these are activities deemed to be of a national, interprovincial or international nature. Specifically, the federal jurisdiction industries (FJI) are: rail, air, road, and water transportation; services incidental to water transportation; pipeline operations; telephone and cable communications; radio and television; grain elevators and grain milling; banking; hotels; uranium mining; the federal Crown corporations (e.g., the CBC, Air Canada, the Canadian National Railway); and defined operations that have been declared to be to the "general advantage" of Canada or of two or more provinces. On the average, these industries tend to be characterized by relatively high wages and by a large service sector component; the degree of unionization varies markedly. Employment in FJI in mid-1965 amounted to about 382,000, or approximately 5 per cent of nonagricultural employment in Canada.

Survey

The data used to analyze the impact of the Canadian federal minimum wage were collected by the Canada Department of Labour from questionnaires sent to all firms under federal jurisdiction. In May 1965, two months before the minimum wage was to take effect on July 1, and again in May 1966, ten months after the effective date, the department carried out two surveys.

First, the Working Conditions Survey determined the *total* number of workers in FJI. The number was found to be 381,668 in 1965 and 391,313 in 1966.

Secondly, the Wage Survey was designed to determine the distribution of earnings of those workers in FJI whose wages per hour (or hour-equivalent, in the case of salaried employees) were $2.50 or less. Included in the wage rate were additional earnings such as cost of living allowances, shift premiums, bonuses, etc. This survey involved two major limitations. On the one hand, response was voluntary. Consequently, out of 4,573 questionnaires sent out in 1965, only 2,455, or 54 per cent were returned. A similar response pattern evolved in 1966. Since we wanted to determine the response of firms to the implementation of the minimum wage law, we decided to study only firms who had returned the questionnaires in both 1965 and 1966. Only 1,511 firms satisfied this requirement; these constituted our matched sample. It will be apparent that the large number of rejections of questionnaires and the sizeable nonresponse introduced features that may well distort some of the findings. However, it should be noted that in 1965 these 1,511 firms represented 78 per cent of the total FJI employment.

Also, since the sample was restricted to individuals earning up to $2.50 per hour, the upper portion of the frequency distribution of earnings was missing. Hence, a number of constraints were imposed on the analysis, since some of the more powerful tools of statistical inference could not be used.

It should also be noted that a large portion of our sample consisted of relatively high-wage and unionized industries, whereas previous studies on the minimum wage have generally dealt with low-wage and nonunionized industries. Furthermore, no special surveys were made of uncovered firms.

The main difficulty with most minimum wage studies, including this one, is the problem of segregating the effects of minimum wages from other influences on economic institutions. Changes in prices, wages, employment, and output are the result not only of changes in wage laws, but also of the interaction of shifting consumer tastes, management investment decisions, the pattern of government taxation, spending, and countless other influences. None of these forces comes to a halt when a minimum wage law is enacted. Unfortunately, in this study as in others, we were not able to hold other things constant while analyzing the impact of minimum wages, and therefore the results presented here should be interpreted with great care.

In particular, it is important to note the state of the Canadian economy during the period in question. As the Economic Council of Canada pointed out in its 1967 report:

As of June 1967, the Canadian economy had been expanding without a significant reversal since the business cycle trough in March 1961. The expansion had thus lasted 75 months. This represents probably the longest uninterrupted expansion in Canadian business cycle history. It also constitutes the largest expansion in terms of the absolute rise in the volume of total output and total employment. Since 1961, Canada has in fact experienced what could appropriately be described as a Great Expansion.[1]

From 1961 to 1966, real Gross National Product increased by 35 per cent and employment by 18 per cent, while unemployment dropped from 7.1 per cent to 3.6 per cent;[2] this represented the lowest unemployment rate since the mid-1950s. In 1967, unemployment again began to rise. Thus, from the standpoint of employment the federal minimum wage of 1965 was enacted at a propitious time, indeed.

It is important to note the variation in the price level, since if prices are stable the effect of a minimum wage can be analyzed with more confidence. While the early 1960s showed only small year-to-year changes in prices, the situation changed markedly starting about 1965, when the Consumer Price Index rose 2.5 per cent over 1964. After 1965, the rate of change of the price level continued to rise, reaching the annual rate of 4.1 per cent in 1968.

It is clear that under conditions of such large year-to-year price changes the impact of a minimum wage is considerably softened, the more so the longer the time period in question. This circumstance, like the low level of unemployment at the time of enactment, will limit the generality of our conclusions in this study.

Findings

As noted above, total employment in FJI rose from about 382,000 in 1965 to about 391,000 in 1966, a rise of 2.5 per cent. This suggests that at first sight the federal minimum wage had no noticeable impact on employment. However, it is difficult to establish this with certainty, since available techniques do not allow us to distinguish effects of the minimum wage from long-term trends in employment levels.

Employment changes in major labour-force groups are shown in table 8.1.

In order to examine the impact of the minimum wage on various sectors of the economy, we will now proceed to analyze the data provided by the 1,511 firms constituting our matched sample. For industries, provinces, and areas, two hypotheses will be tested: (1) that the impact of the minimum wage on employment and wage structures should be felt most in low-wage industries and areas; and (2) that the narrowing of the wage distribution in an industry or area is highly correlated with the percentage of workers below the minimum wage. The final hypothesis to be tested is (3) that male-female and office-nonoffice wage differentials will narrow.

TABLE 8.1

Total FJI Employment in 1965 and 1966

	1965	1966	% Change
Total	381,668	391,313	2.5
Males	297,105	293,537	-1.2
Females	84,578	97,776	15.6
Nonoffice	222,450	214,007	-3.8
- Males	204,845	196,682	-4.0
- Females	17,605	17,395	-1.2
Office	159,218	177,236	11.3
- Males	92,241	96,855	5.0
- Females	67,226	80,381	19.6

By Industry

As shown in table 8.2, total employment by industry for the 1,511 firms in our sample rose in eleven of fifteen cases (the railroad industry could not be studied on account of deficiencies in the data available to us). It declined in only four cases: Services Incidental to Water Transportation, Hotels, Federal Crown Corporations (Other), and Miscellaneous Industries. In two of the four industries the percentage decline was large: Services Incidental to Water Transportation and Federal Crown Corporations (Other). In some industries there were sizeable increases, particularly in Air and Water Transportation, Telephone Communications, Grain Elevators and Grain Milling, and Pipeline Operations.

In order to determine whether the wage distribution for some industries had changed more than for others we adopted the following formula:

$$\left(\frac{50\%ile - 10\%ile \text{ in } 1966}{\text{median in } 1966}\right) - \left(\frac{50\%ile - 10\%ile \text{ in } 1965}{\text{median in } 1965}\right)$$

designated the "coefficient of relative narrowing". The nature of the formula is such as to show a negative coefficient if the wage distribution has narrowed and a positive coefficient if it has widened. This formula--which has been used in similar form in various minimum wage studies, such as that by Kaun[3]--requires that at least the lower half of the wage distribution be known in order to be usable. Since our data showed the wage distribution up to only $2.50 per hour, we had to reject nine industries characterized by high earnings, where over half of the industry's work force earned more than $2.50 per hour (see table 8.3, column 1).

TABLE 8.2

Total Employment in FJI, by Industry, May 1965 and May 1966, for the 1,511 Firms in the Matched Sample

Industry	Total Employment in May 1965 (1)	Total Employment in May 1966 (2)	Change in Employment between 1965 and 1966 (3)	Col. 3 as % of Col. 1 (4)
Rail transportation	n.a.[a]	n.a.[a]	n.a.[a]	n.a.[a]
Air "	14,782	17,552	2,770	18.74
Road "	17,605	17,872	267	1.52
Water "	8,816	9,746	930	10.55
Services incidental to water transport	11,497	9,010	-2,487	-21.63
Pipeline operations	722	986	264	36.57
Telephone communications	36,857	41,241	4,384	11.89
Cable communications	551	569	18	3.27
Radio and TV	13,096	13,968	872	6.66
Grain elevators and grain milling	15,872	17,162	1,290	8.13
Banking	77,088	78,772	1,685	2.18
Hotels	1,274	1,214	- 60	- 4.17
Uranium mining	1,364	1,469	105	7.70
Federal Crown corp.:				
Mfg.	3,932	4,049	117	2.98
Other	10,016	8,653	-1,363	-13.61
Miscellaneous	2,923	2,870	- 53	- 1.81

Note: The above employment data refer to total employment of the 1,511 firms constituting our matched sample.

a Railroads had to be omitted because of shortcomings in the data made available to us.

TABLE 8.3

Measures of Changes in the Wage Distribution by Industry,
between May 1965 and May 1966

Industry	Available Range in Percentiles[a]	Changes in Absolute Wage Distribution, in cents[b]	Coefficient of Relative Narrowing	% of Workers Below Minimum May 1965[c]
	(1)	(2)	(3)	(4)
Rail transportation	n.a.	n.a.	n.a.	n.a.
Air "	10 - 30	2	n.a.	n.a.
Road "	10 - 70	9	-.021	3.56
Water	10 - 70	-3	-.016	4.80
Services incidental to water transport	10 - 30	-10	n.a.	n.a.
Pipeline operations	10 - 20	-12	n.a.	n.a.
Telephone communications	10 - 60	-6	-.058	6.76
Cable communications	10 - 40	0	n.a.	n.a.
Radio and TV	10 - 40	-1	n.a.	n.a.
Grain elevators and grain milling	10 - 75	-4	-.019	9.45
Banking	10 - 80	3	-.031	18.70
Hotels	10 - 90	-27	-.140	56.44
Uranium mining	10	n.a.	n.a.	n.a.
Federal Crown corp.:				
Mfg.	10 - 30	-7	n.a.	n.a.
Other	10 - 40	-14	n.a.	n.a.
Miscellaneous	10 - 20	-5	n.a.	n.a.

Notes

a The upper limit of the "available range" is the highest possible decile for each industry for earnings of up to $2.50 per hour. That is, if the 4th decile earned, say, $2.28, the 5th decile, $2.47, and the 6th decile, $2.62, then this industry would have an available range of 0 to 50. Since we exclude the lowest 9% of the industry, it would have an available range of 10 to 50.

b The figures show whether the wage distribution over the available range, shown in column 1, has narrowed (-) or widened (no sign).

c This column shows the number of workers earning less than $1.25 per hour in May 1965 as a percentage of industry employment in the matched sample.

This left only the following six industries: Road and Water Transportation, Telephone Communications, Grain Elevators and Grain Milling, Banking, and Hotels.

It will be observed from table 8.3 that the coefficient of relative narrowing was negative in each of the six cases, thus supporting our expectation that the wage distribution had narrowed. The magnitude of the coefficient is much larger for hotels--an industry known to have relatively low earnings, as indicated by the fact that the available range included 90 per cent of the work force--than for the other five industries. This lends support to our first hypothesis. However, of the four industries experiencing employment declines, only hotels fall in the low-wage category as defined by the available range index. For the six industries, our second hypothesis is also supported, since in table 8.4 the relationship between column 3 (the coefficient of relative narrowing) and column 4 (the percentage of workers below the minimum in 1965) yields a correlation coefficient of -.92, or an r^2 of .85.

By Province

Table 8.4 illustrates that employment in the 1,511 firms constituting our matched sample rose in all provinces. However, the increase ranged from a low of .11 per cent in Manitoba to a high of 8.94 per cent in British Columbia. The pattern of employment increases in table 8.4 suggests that there tends to be a direct relationship between the general level of wages in a region and the increase in employment, which would support hypothesis (1). The growth rates for provinces generally believed to be low wage, such as Newfoundland, Prince Edward Island, Nova Scotia, New Brunswick, and Quebec are on the average substantially lower than for the remaining provinces, with the exception of Manitoba. This implies that employers in the low-wage provinces may be slower in hiring additional workers as a result of incremental wage costs, while employers in high-wage regions are hurt much less by minimum wage provisions. This may partly explain the observed growth differentials, though of course other variables, such as regional variations in economic activity, are important as well.

Table 8.5 presents the same information as table 8.3, for provincial rather than industrial data. The coefficient of relative narrowing is negative in all provinces, suggesting that the wage distribution has narrowed over the lower half of the wage distribution analyzed. The magnitude of the coefficient is larger for the low-wage Atlantic Provinces on the whole than for the remaining provinces. Newfoundland is an exception, possibly due to the fact that relatively few firms from that province were included among the 1,511 firms and those that did enter into the sample were from relatively high-wage industries. In general, however, these results would also tend to support hypothesis (1). Hypothesis (2), as well, is supported, since the correlation between columns 3 and 4 in table 8.5 is -.88, giving an r^2 of .77.

TABLE 8.4

Total Employment in FJI, by Province, May 1965 and May 1966, for the 1,511 Firms in the Matched Sample

Province	Total Employment in 1965	Total Employment in 1966	Change in Employment between 1965 and 1966	Col. 3 as % of Col. 1
	(1)	(2)	(3)	(4)
Canada	299,019	308,812	9,793	3.28
Newfoundland	6,700	6,724	24	.36
Prince Edward Island	850	869	19	2.24
Nova Scotia	8,502	8,724	222	2.61
New Brunswick	8,152	8,209	57	.70
Quebec	91,939	94,246	2,307	2.51
Ontario	116,968	121,133	4,165	3.56
Manitoba	21,583	21,606	23	.11
Saskatchewan	9,662	10,008	346	3.58
Alberta	14,836	15,293	457	5.78
British Columbia	19,827	21,600	1,773	8.94

Note: The above employment data refer to *total* employment of the 1,511 firms constituting our *matched sample*.

TABLE 8.5

Measures of Changes in the Wage Distribution, by Province, between May 1965 and May 1966

Province	Available Range in Percentiles	Changes in Absolute Wage Distribution in cents	Coefficient of Relative Narrowing	Number of Workers Earning up to $1.25/h. as % of Total FJI Employment in Province, in May 1965
	(1)	(2)	(3)	(4)
Canada			--	--
Newfoundland	10 - 70	- 6	-.032	9.22
Prince Edward Island	10 - 80	- 2	-.077	19.65
Nova Scotia	10 - 90	-20	-.068	17.14
New Brunswick	10 - 80	- 5	-.045	10.71
Quebec	10 - 90	- 7	-.030	6.57
Ontario	10 - 60	- 3	-.031	6.14
Manitoba	10 - 70	- 4	-.027	6.74
Saskatchewan	10 - 70	- 2	-.026	12.15
Alberta	10 - 80	2	-.041	12.42
British Columbia	10 - 70	-10	-.015	8.05
	10 - 60	5		

Note: For explanations of column headings, see notes for table 8.3.

High vs Low-Wage Areas

Since the Canada Department of Labour does not classify regions within provinces as high wage or low wage, it was necessary to establish a method for such a classification. We decided to select the fifty-eight cities listed in *Wage Rates, Salaries, and Hours of Labour,* published by the Canada Department of Labour, and chose nine occupations which we felt offered substantial employment opportunities within federal jurisdiction industries. Then we arranged the fifty-eight cities for each of the nine occupations in descending order of wages, and selected the highest thirteen cities for these nine occupations as representing our high-wage area. Similarly, the lowest thirteen constituted our low-wage sample. The thirty-two cities in the middle range were dropped in order to obtain a more clear-cut separation between high- and low-wage areas.

We then calculated total employment in our sample of FJI firms in the two groups of cities constituting the high-wage and low-wage areas, respectively, and obtained the following results:

TABLE 8.6

High- and Low-Wage Areas: Employment and Wage Distribution Changes

	Total Employment, May 1965	Total Employment, May 1966	Change between 1965 and 1966	Change Expressed as % of 1965 Empl.	Available Range in Deciles	Change in Absolute Distribution, in cents
	(1)	(2)	(3)	(4)	(5)	(6)
High-wage	21,700	21,934	234	1.07	10-50	2
Low-wage	4,064	3,657	-407	-10.02	10-80	-10

Note: The above data refer to total employment of firms from our matched sample which were located in the high-wage and low-wage cities selected.

The table clearly indicates major differences between the high-wage and low-wage labour markets. In the former, employment rose by about 1 per cent, while it declined in the latter by some 10 per cent. Furthermore, the absolute wage distribution (which, it will be remembered from table 8.3, refers to the available range, column 5 above) rose by $.02 over the 10-50 range for high-wage areas, and declined by $.10 for the low-wage areas. These results, then, lend further support to hypothesis (1), that minimum wage legislation tends to have a stronger impact on employment and wage structures in low-wage areas than in higher-wage areas.

Male-Female Differentials

To test hypothesis (3) regarding narrowing of male-female wage differentials, we compared earnings of women and men for various selected percentiles of the wage distribution for both 1965 and 1966. Since males are generally known to earn more on the average than females, the ratio ($\frac{\text{earnings of females}}{\text{earnings of males}}$) will be less than one for earnings of females of any percentile compared with earnings of males of any percentile no lower than the female percentile studied. In other words, if the 20th percentile of females is compared with, say, the 20th percentile of males, the ratio should be less than one. Similar ratios result if various other percentiles are used.

TABLE 8.7

Earnings Ratios for Males (M) and Females (F) for Various Percentiles, in 1965 and 1966.

		1965					1966		
	F 10	F 50	M 10	M 50		F 10	F 50	M 10	M 50
F : 10	1	.718	.713	.505	F : 10	1	.770	.765	.557
F : 50		1	.994	.703	F : 50		1	.994	.724
M : 10			1	.707	M : 10			1	.728
M : 50				1	M : 50				1

Note: F = Female; M = Male; F : 10 refers to the 10th %ile of females, etc.; the entry .718 in 1965, for example, states that earnings of the 10th %ile of females were 71.8% of the earnings of the 50th %ile of females.

The data in table 8.7 clearly show that, in general, women were able to improve their position compared to men. The magnitude of such improvements ranged from about 2 to more than 5 percentage points. For example, in 1965 the 10th percentile of females earned only .505 (or about half) as much as the 50th percentile of males. By 1966 the fraction had risen to .557, amounting to a gain of 5.2 percentage points. The above narrowing in favour of women is, of course, only relevant if it is the result of a genuine economic improvement, since the ratio can also rise as a result of decreased employment of the lowest-paid females. However, the fact that table 8.2 shows the total FJI employment of women increasing considerably from 1965 to 1966, while the employment of men declined, would suggest that this did not occur. Thus is appears that women were able to improve their earnings position *vis-a-vis* men; also, low-wage men (the 10th percentile) profited compared to the 50th percentile of men, since the earnings ratio rose from .707 in 1965 to .728 in 1966.

Office-Nonoffice Differentials

In essence this comparison, presented in table 8.8, is merely a variation of the above female-male earnings comparison. We have used the ratio of earnings in office employment to earnings in nonoffice employment to measure earnings differentials between these two groups.

TABLE 8.8

Earnings Ratios for Office (O) and Nonoffice (NO) Workers for Various Percentiles, in 1965 and 1966.

	1965					1966			
	O 10	O 50	NO 10	NO 50		O 10	O 50	NO 10	NO 50
0 : 10	1	.620	.838	.605	0 : 10	1	.672	.884	.646
0 : 50		1	1.351	.976	0 : 50		1	1.316	.962
NO: 10			1	.722	NO: 10			1	.731
NO: 50				1	NO: 50				1

Note: O = office; NO = Nonoffice workers; 0:10 refers to the 10th %ile of office workers, etc.; the entry .838 in 1965, for example, states that earnings of the 10th %ile of office workers were 83.8% of the earnings of the 10th %ile of nonoffice workers.

This table shows that the 10th percentile of office workers were able to improve their earnings position compared to nonoffice workers, and also relative to the 50th percentile of office workers; this lowest-paid group of office workers is generally known to be overwhelmingly female. However, the 50th percentile of office workers lost relative to nonoffice workers. Since from table 8.2 we observe that over half of office workers in total FJI employment are male, as well as the large majority of nonoffice workers, we can infer that the position of male office workers worsened relative to male nonoffice workers.

In conclusion, we observe that while the implementation of the federal minimum wage had no noticeable impact on the overall level of employment, it did seem to affect employment levels in low-wage industries, provinces, and cities, and in general to narrow wage structures. These results emphasize once again the necessity of analyzing the effects of minimum wages in particular situations.

Notes

1. Economic Council of Canada, *Fourth Annual Review* (1967), pp. 11-12.

2. *Ibid.*, p. 12.

3. David E. Kaun, "Economics of the Minimum Wage: The Effects of the Fair Labor Standards Acts, 1945-1969" (Ph.D. thesis, Stanford University, 1964).

9. Highlights in the Development of the Legal System*

by J. Douglas Muir

Public Policy Prior to 1900

The nineteenth century can be viewed as an era of laissez-faire. During this period, emphasis was primarily given to economic freedom and free competition in the marketplace. This general attitude, and the legislation that emerged from it, tended to restrict the development of the trade unions. It was considered that any combination of workers for the purpose of influencing wage levels would hamper free competition. The Combines Acts of 1799, 1800 and 1825 in Britain are prime examples of the legislative approach taken during this period. These statutes were designed to outlaw combinations of either employers or employees so as to protect free competition and allow wages and prices to be established by the natural laws of supply and demand. As such, trade unions, which were obviously conspiring to affect wages, were illegal. It was within such a restrictive framework that trade unions in both Britain and Canada had to organize workers and attempt to bargain with management. Thus, it is not surprising that trade union development during the nineteenth century was slow and primarily restricted to the specialized-craft trades.

A breakthrough in the prevailing antiunion attitude occurred in Britain in 1871, when parliament passed both a Criminal Law Amendment Act and a Trade Unions Act. The Canadian parliament followed the British pattern and in 1872 passed the Canadian Trade Unions Act and the Canadian Criminal Law Amendment Act. The introduction of these statutes was used to bring an end to the prosecution of printers who were striking in Toronto. These statutes also freed both the British and the Canadian trade unions from the existing restraint of trade criminal conspiracy restrictions. Members of trade unions were no longer liable to prosecution for criminal conspiracy merely because the purpose of the trade union resulted in a restraint of trade. Thus trade unions were effectively legalized in Canada in 1972. In addition, new statutes permitted peaceful picketing and established that labour-management agreements were no longer invalid due to restraint of trade restrictions. Further amendments in 1890 clarified that no one could be convicted of a conspiracy for refusing to work with a workman (nonunion, for example) or for an employer (who may be refusing to recognize the union, for example).

Without going into the details, it is important to note that the nineteenth century development of the Canadian attitude toward unions and collective bargaining was by no means smooth and

---

*Reproduced from *Labour Gazette*.

easy. There were a number of tests of the constitutionality of
the statutes and of the meaning and application of both restraint
of trade and civil conspiracy. In any event, by 1900 Canadian
law recognized the legality of combinations of workers and the
use of both the strike and peaceful picketing. In addition, it
exempted trade unions from the anticombines laws and protected
unions from liability for restraint of trade.

The Development of Provincial Responsibilities, 1900 to 1935

The legislation during the latter part of the nineteenth century
was designed primarily to free unions from restrictions placed
upon their organizating activities. Little had been done about
collective bargaining rights, responsibilities and procedures.
The first statute to attempt to deal with these areas was the
1900 Conciliation Act. This statute was almost identical to the
1896 British Conciliation Act and was, in Canada, quite ineffective. For while the British statute developed out of a voluntary
recognition and bargaining relationship that was the practice in
Britain, the Canadian statute was imposed upon Canadian employers
who were generally opposed to having any relations with unions.
The 1900 statute was designed to promote and encourage the settlement of labour-management disputes by voluntary conciliation,
and therefore did not require employers to recognize or bargain
with the union. The only sanction given to the conciliator was
his right to publish his recommendations in the hopes that public
pressure would influence the parties. Since there was no compulsory element in this statute, very little use was made of the
government's conciliation services. It should be noted that this
1900 statute also established the Federal Department of Labour
and marked the entry of the federal government into legislation
designed to control collective bargaining.
     During the early 1900s, two further steps were taken in the gov-
ernment's move to require labour and management to use the conciliation services. The first, in 1903, followed the 1901 strike by
trackmen and established compulsory conciliation for railways through
the Railway Labour Disputes Act. The second followed the serious
strike in the Lethbridge coal fields in 1906, which led to the enactment of the Industrial Disputes and Investigation Act in 1907.
The IDI Act required compulsory investigation by a conciliation
board and the postponement of the right to strike until after the
completion of the conciliation process. Again, the only sanction
available to the conciliation board was through publication of the
conciliation recommendations. As with the Conciliation Act, the
basic weakness of the IDI Act was its failure to require the employer to either recognize or bargain with the union. Thus labour-management relations were still based upon the voluntariness of the
parties. It should be noted that between the Conciliation Act and
the Industrial Disputes Investigation Act, the main characteristic
of Canadian public labour policy was established: namely, the postponement of the right to strike until after the parties have been
exposed to the process of conciliation. This is still an important
principle in the Canadian approach to dispute resolution, and is
one of the features that make our system uniquely "Canadian", dis-

tinguishing it from either the American or British approach to dispute resolution.

It was during this same period that the second unique feature
of the Canadian industrial relations system developed. This was
the removal of the major responsibility for labour-management
relations from the federal government and its allocation to the
provincial governments. Thus Canada has eleven sets of statutes
and regulatory bodies dealing with labour-management relations
(ten provincial and one federal). This decentralization of its
labour policy distinguishes Canada from both the United Kingdom
and the United States.

The problem of allocating responsibility for labour-management
relations stems from a question of interpretation of the British
North America Act. It was not surprising, given the state of
development of unionism in Canada in 1856, that the BNA Act did
not specifically assign responsibility for labour-management relations. Initially the Federal Department of Labour attempted to
avoid the constitutionality question by only applying the IDI Act
in provincial and municipal disputes with the consent of the parties. The constitutionality of the IDI Act was tested and upheld
in the Quebec courts in 1912, but in another case (Toronto Electric Commissioners vs Snider, 1925) the Privy Council ruled that
the IDI Act was unconstitutional. The council determined that
labour-management relations involved the civil rights of the employers and employees in a province and therefore was an area of
legislative jurisdiction expressly given to the provinces by section 92 of the BNA Act. As a result of this decision the federal
government's jurisdiction is now restricted to: (1) industries
such as interprovincial railways, telegraphs, shipping, and tele-
phones; (2) industries falling in the federal government's residual
power of section 91, BNA Act (*i.e.*, matters not within the legislative jurisdiction of any province); (3) undertakings connecting
provinces or extending beyond the limits of a province (for example, connecting Canada to another country); (4) work for the
general advantage of Canada (for example, Ontario's Chalk River
atomic energy plant); and (5) times when a state of emergency is
declared (as during World Wars I and II). Therefore, the federal
government's authority is now for the most part restricted to
industries that are national or interprovincial in scope, which
limits federal jurisdiction primarily to the service industries
in the transportation and public utility fields.

Following the Snider case, the IDI Act was amended to limit
its application to areas of federal jurisdiction. However, by
1932 all provinces, except Prince Edward Island, had passed enabling legislation so that the federal IDI Act could be applied
within the provinces.

The Depression and War Years: 1935-1945

The economic conditions of the 1930s placed governments under considerable pressure to find solutions to relieve the effects of the
depression. As a result of the "new deal" economic philosophy,

governments considered giving recognition and bargaining rights to the unions. In so doing, unions would force wages up and the resulting increase in purchasing power in the hands of the consumer would help counteract the depression. The major step in this direction was taken in the United States, when the Wagner Act was passed in 1935. This act, for the first time, gave the American unions the right to organize, to bargain and to strike, and protected the unions from various unfair labour practices of management.

In Canada, the pressures of the depression clearly showed the weakness of the IDI Act--the failure to provide both freedom and independence to the trade unions themselves and a management obligation to actually bargain with the unions. Without these essentials, collective bargaining was not working well. As a result of the economic pressures of the depression, many companies were simply refusing to bargain with the unions and therefore the conciliation and other provisions of the IDI Act were useless. At this time, pressure was developing from the unions to have these legislative deficiencies rectified. Since the Canadian labour movement was now heavily influenced by the U.S. international unions, it is not surprising that Canada turned to the American legislation to find a solution. In 1937, the Canadian Trades and Labour Congress presented a draft statute, based on the Wagner Act, which they proposed be adopted by the provincial legislatures. By 1939, six provinces (not including Ontario, Prince Edward Island and Quebec) had passed legislation incorporating Wagner-style union rights and protection in addition to the IDI Act form of conciliation requirements.

With the start of the war in 1939, the federal government's jurisdiction was extended to include the regulation of labour relations in all industries associated with the war effort; this included most of Canada's industrial and manufacturing sector. In 1940, the government issued a statement of principles, which were basically four in number: (1) the workers' rights to organize; (2) their freedom to negotiate; (3) the settlement of disputes without work stoppage through negotiations and conciliation; and (4) a procedure for resolving employee grievances. These principles were initially applied through separate Orders-in-Council but were subsequently incorporated in the 1944 Wartime Labour Relations Regulations (PC 1003). Without going into the details of these regulations, it is fair to conclude that they contained many of the features now incorporated in our provincial and federal labour statutes. After the passage of PC 1003 seven provinces (not including Saskatchewan and Quebec) passed legislation making the order applicable to those industries not connected with the war effort and still under provincial jurisdiction. Thus by 1944, there was again a high degree of uniformity of labour policy in Canada.

The Postwar Period: 1945-1974

Two developments during the war period assisted in ensuring the continuation of the wartime labour policies into the postwar period. The first was the almost doubling in size of the trade union movement and the second was the pattern of stable union-management relationships which had developed during the war. In 1946, the federal government convened a conference of labour ministers in an attempt to establish uniformity of legislative control over labour-management problems. At this conference the ministers agreed, with a few minor exceptions, that Canadian public labour policy should include the following principles: (1) employee freedom of association and union recognition; (2) compulsory bargaining rights for certified unions; (3) postponement of the right to strike until after government intervention through conciliation; (4) prohibition of unfair labour practices by both employers and unions to protect individual rights and the collective bargaining process; (5) establishment of legal status and enforceability to the collective agreement; (6) provision for resolving disputes arising out of the collective agreement without resorting to the strike; and (7) establishment of regulatory bodies with investigation and control powers in the form of boards of industrial relations.

At the federal level these principles were incorporated in the Industrial Relations and Disputes Investigations Act, in 1948. Although the war was over, the Wartime Labour Relations Regulations (PC 1003) remained in effect until repealed by this IRDI Act. Very shortly after this all provinces (except Prince Edward Island and Saskatchewan and, to a degree, Quebec) brought their labour legislation into line with the policy expressed in 1946 and contained in the IRDI Act. Although some of the provinces have pursued independent policies in certain areas, the basic principles forming public labour policy have remained the same from province to province throughout the 1950s and most of the 1960s.

By the middle of the 1960s pressure was again building within the Canadian industrial relations system. This time the pressure resulted primarily from the expansion of the bargaining units from local to industry-wide and national in scope, coupled with the growing interdependence of firms within the industrial sector. As a result of these two developments, the impact of the strike upon the public had been magnified. Another development that also placed pressure on the system was the expansion of unionism into the government and public services sectors and into white-collar and professional groups. All of these developments led to a demand from the public for greater protection and for the governments to adopt some system for speedily resolving emergency disputes.

The years 1965 and 1966 were very bad ones for our industrial relations system. During this time there were major strikes in virtually all sectors of the Canadian economy. In fact, there were over eleven hundred strikes and lockouts in all, and the resulting man-days lost almost equalled the total man-days lost due to strikes for the entire previous six-year period. These strikes caused much public hardship and the governments were under pressure to "do something". The federal government reacted by appointing a Task Force on Labour Relations. This task force conducted an intensive study of the Canadian industrial relations problems and presented recommendations to the government in December 1968. However, it took until July 1971 for the federal government to enact a new Canada Labour Code to replace the 1948 Industrial Relations and Disputes Investigation Act. Between 1971 and 1973, most of the provinces have also either enacted new labour statutes or revised their existing legislation.

Public Labour Relations Policy in Canada: 1974

As previously mentioned, considerable effort has been made since the 1925 Snider Case decision to standardize the labour relations policy in Canada. The remainder of this paper will determine the degree to which such standardization of labour policy still exists in Canada.[1] In so doing, attention will be focussed on the labour policy principles agreed upon among the ministers of labour in 1946, and those changes recommended by the task force in 1968.

Legal Status of Trade Unions

A number of provinces have definite statutory provisions giving trade unions legal status before the courts. Even without such provisions it has been held that unions were legal persons by virtue of recognition under the labour statutes. In Alberta, British Columbia, Manitoba, Prince Edward Island, and New Brunswick, unions are legal entities capable of suing and being sued for purposes specified in the act. Under the Canada, Nova Scotia and Ontario statutes both trade unions and employer organizations may be prosecuted for offences under the acts. Unions in Quebec are legal entities capable of suing and being sued if they are registered under the Professional Syndicates Act. As such, trade unions in Canada are legal entities and may be accountable for their illegal acts, such as illegal strikes and unfair labour practices.

Freedom of the Individual

It was not until the 1944 Wartime Labour Relations Regulations that Canada had an explicit policy designed to protect the worker from coercion and intimidation from either the union or from management. The 1944 policy, which is now contained in all jurisdictions, gives the worker the right to be a union member and to participate in its lawful activities. It also makes it an unfair labour policy for either the union or management to try to compel anyone to join or not join a union or to continue or discontinue his union membership.

The statutes in most provinces require that the unions make their annual financial statements available to their members. In addition, the Alberta and New Brunswick statutes ensure that no worker is disciplined or expelled from the union without a full and proper hearing (except for nonpayment of union dues). Thus, while all jurisdictions have some provisions designed to protect the individual workers' rights, there is room in this area for

further legislative developments. So far, very little of the 1959
Landrum Griffin Act protections in the United States have found
their way into our Canadian legislation.

Union Security

By the 1960s all jurisdictions had, either directly or indirectly,
authorized labour and management to negotiate a clause making
union membership a condition of employment. In addition, all
statutes also permitted labour and management to introduce closed
shop and/or voluntary revocable checkoff of dues provisions into
the collective agreements. Thus, the kind and degree of union
security has been totally dependent upon the bargaining power of
the union.

In 1968, the task force recommended that compulsory irrevocable
checkoff of union dues be given to the unions as a right. In 1971,
the federal government gave the unions the legislated right to
check off union dues provided it is revocable upon thirty days'
notice by the employee. New Brunswick is the only jurisdiction
to establish the checkoff as a union right.

Certification of the Union

Basic to the Canadian system is the certification of a trade union
as the bargaining agent for a group of employees, provided the
Board of Industrial Relations finds the union to be appropriate,
the unit of employees appropriate and that a majority of employees
in the unit are members in good standing of the union. Certification gives the union exclusive jurisdiction to bargain for those
in the unit, protects its jurisdiction from raiding by other unions,
compels management to recognize and bargain with the union, and
gives the union the right (provided all the conditions are fulfilled) to call a strike under the statute. A system for certi-
fying unions is contained in the statutes in all jurisdictions.
However, the procedures and requirements vary widely from jurisdiction to jurisdiction.

The task force recommended that exclusive bargaining rights
should also be available to unions through voluntary recognition
by the employer. So far, only the federal government, Ontario,
New Brunswick, and Alberta have followed this recommendation.

Extension of Bargaining Rights to New Groups

The task force recommended that bargaining rights be extended to
small groups of employees normally excluded from the provisions
of the labour acts. These groups include: (1) supervisory and
junior managerial employees; (2) those employed in a confidential
capacity in matters relating to labour relations; (3) security
employees and private police; (4) public law enforcement officers
and firefighters; and (5) members of licensed professions. Some
of the governments have followed the recommendation of the task
force and have given bargaining and other rights to these special
groups. For example, police and firemen have been given the right

to bargain in all jurisdictions but they only have the right to strike in British Columbia. Problems are resolved by arbitration in most other jurisdictions. Similarly, government employees have bargaining rights in all jurisdictions but may strike in British Columbia, Saskatchewan, Quebec, Nova Scotia, Newfoundland, and the federal jurisdiction. Government workers have access to arbitration in other jurisdictions except Alberta, New Brunswick and Ontario. Supervisory and managerial employees only have bargaining and strike rights in British Columbia and Manitoba. Professional employees (excluding teachers) have bargaining rights in British Columbia, Saskatchewan, Manitoba, Ontario (engineers only), Quebec, New Brunswick, and the federal jurisdictions. They may strike only in Saskatchewan, Manitoba, Quebec, New Brunswick, and the federal jurisdictions. Finally, hospital workers may bargain in all jurisdictions but are prevented from striking in Ontario and Prince Edward Island.

Bargaining Rights and Obligations

Once a trade union has been certified as the bargaining agent, it is obligated, in all jurisdictions, to meet with management and bargain collectively, with the intention of concluding a written agreement covering wages and working conditions. In all jurisdictions there are certain requirements affecting the bargaining process. They are as follows.

(1) *Notice of intention to bargain.* All jurisdictions provide that a notice of intention to renegotiate an existing agreement must be served between the parties from within two months prior to the expiry date of the agreement in Nova Scotia, Ontario, Prince Edward Island and Quebec to up to between two to four months prior to the expiry date in other provinces.

(2) *Time limit to commence negotiations.* Once the notice of intention to bargain has been served, negotiations must commence within eight days in Quebec, up to within a maximum of twenty days in New Brunswick, Newfoundland, Nova Scotia, Prince Edward Island, Alberta, and the federal jurisdictions.

(3) *Bargaining representative.* In British Columbia, Alberta, and Newfoundland, employers must appoint a person who is a resident of the province with authority to bargain, conclude and sign the collective agreement on behalf of the employer. This provision is designed particularly for extraprovincial companies.

(4) *Duration of an agreement:* All jurisdictions require that a collective agreement be for a duration of at least one year. However, there is nothing in any of the statutes to prevent the parties from negotiating agreements of a longer duration.

Government Intervention During Negotiations

In all jurisdictions it has been required that strike action be postponed until after there has been some form of government intervention in the form of conciliation. However, this requirement has now been removed in Manitoba. The predominant pattern has been a two-stage conciliation process, involving first a conciliation officer and then, if necessary, a conciliation board. Recently there has been a trend toward reducing the conciliation process to a single stage, except in emergency or highly public-sensitive disputes. The situation now is that a conciliation officer may be appointed if requested by one of the parties, or the Minister of Labour in all jurisdictions except Nova Scotia and Prince Edward Island may appoint a conciliation officer to a dispute, even if not requested to do so by one of the parties. Similarly, if the conciliation officer fails, the minister may appoint a conciliation board, although he is no longer required to do so except in Nova Scotia. The trend has been toward fewer and fewer conciliation boards.

The New Brunswick statute now allows for preventative mediation, which is the early introduction of a mediator or conciliator into the bargaining process. This is done where it is felt that he may be able to help prevent a dispute from developing.

Strikes

In order for a legal strike to take place in all jurisdictions, the following conditions must be met: (1) bargaining rights must have been acquired by the union, either by certification or voluntary recognition; (2) the conciliation procedure must have been completed and have failed (no longer required in Manitoba); (3) where a strike vote is required (as in Nova Scotia, New Brunswick, and Prince Edward Island), it must have been taken and approved by a majority voting in the unit; (4) the existing collective agreement must have expired; and, where necessary, (5) the required notice (such as the two-day advance notice in Alberta and Nova Scotia) must have been given to the employer, or the "cooling-off" period (such as the sixty days in Quebec or fourteen days in Nova Scotia and Alberta) expired. An interesting innovation has been introduced in Saskatchewan, where the government now has the right to conduct a second strike vote in any strike that lasts for thirty days or more. Except in the emergency dispute area, this is the only statute that provides for any specified action to be taken after a strike commences. The other statutes leave it to economic forces and informal mediation. Finally, the new federal statute allows the board to ban any strike during the seven days immediately preceding a federal election.

Picketing

The statutes tend to avoid involvement in the problems of picketing, except in British Columbia, Newfoundland, New Brunswick, and Alberta.

Usually this subject is dealt with by the courts. The most developed statute is in British Columbia, where picketing is allowed only in connection with legal strikes and may occur only at the employer's place of business by union members or persons authorized by the union. The intent of the picketing can only be to persuade persons not to enter the employer's place of business or to do business with the employer. In addition, the acts associated with picketing must be legal and not violate the criminal code.

The Labour Relations Board

As expressed by the ministers of labour in 1946, one of the basic principles for sound industrial relations rests in the functioning of a regulatory board with powers to investigate and control the application of the labour relations statutes. As such, each province has established a labour relations board with duties and powers as specified in the statute. In all cases, these boards have the power to determine: (1) whether a person is an employee for the purposes of the statute; (2) if a person is a member of a trade union; (3) if an organization is an appropriate trade union for bargaining purposes; and (4) if a collective agreement has been entered into or is in operation and whether or not a party is bound by it. In addition, the British Columbia, Alberta, New Brunswick, Nova Scotia, Saskatchewan, and Ontario boards have been given the power to handle unfair labour practices. The New Brunswick and Alberta boards may now hear jurisdictional dispute problems. In all jurisdictions the board's decisions are final and binding and are not subject to review by the courts, except on procedural matters. However, the boards themselves may review, rescind or amend any of their own orders or decisions.

Other Legislative Developments

There are three other major areas of legislative developments in Canada. First, there is the development of specific provisions in British Columbia, Alberta, Ontario, Quebec, Nova Scotia, New Brunswick, and Prince Edward Island to deal with labour relations problems unique to the construction industry. Most of these provisions are patterned after the Ontario statute and are designed to encourage and control multitrade and multiparty bargaining. The Ontario statute goes so far as to bring the construction industry within the emergency dispute provisions so that the board may issue injunctions against otherwise lawful strikes. Second, there are the provisions governing successor rights in the Ontario, New Brunswick, Alberta, Saskatchewan, and federal statutes to safeguard unions against mergers, takeovers, etc. Finally, a number of the statutes (such as Alberta, Ontario and Quebec) have emergency disputes provisions which enable the government to take action to outlaw a threatened or actual strike where it will seriously injure the health, safety or welfare of the public. Most of these provisions are directed to the utility and hospital sectors but their scope is widening to include other sectors (such as construction in Ontario).

Mention should also be made that strikes or lockouts are not permitted during the life of an agreement. Thus, all contracts must have a binding-arbitration grievance procedure in them. This restriction has been changed, in that the British Columbia, Saskatchewan, and federal statutes now provide for bargaining during the life of the contract when the employer introduces technological changes that substantially affect employment.

Summary

As indicated throughout the foregoing outline, there is still a considerable degree of consistency in the labour policy expressed by the legislation of the various provinces. Thus, in spite of the Snider Case decision and the breaking up of the Canadian industrial relations system into eleven jurisdictions, there remains a common base and standard of labour policy throughout Canada. It is recognized that there are many procedural differences and some policy differences among the provinces. However, there is not a great deal of conflict between the policies expressed by our eleven jurisdictions. Perhaps this has something to do with the nature of our labour relations problems and the level of cooperation that exists between the various ministers of labour.

Note

1. This analysis is based on the Canada Labour Code (1971), Labour Code of British Columbia (1973), Alberta Labour Act (1973), Saskatchewan Trade Union Act (1973), Labour Relations Act of Manitoba (1973), Ontario Labour Relations Act (1970), Quebec Labour Code (1969), Industrial Relations Act of New Brunswick (1972), Nova Scotia Trade Unions Act (1972), Prince Edward Island Labour Act (1971), and Newfoundland Trade Union Act (1968).

PART III: INPUTS IN THE IR SYSTEM FROM THE PARTICIPANTS

10. History and Structure of the Labour Movement in Canada

by Francis J. McKendy

A century or so ago, Canada's economy was largely agricultural, with a few large concentrations of population and industry. However, a few labour unions existed in the early 1800s. There are, for example, records of several craft unions in the Maritime Provinces that existed before the end of the War of 1812. There is evidence, too, of the existence of a printers' union in Quebec City as early as 1827, and a few shoemakers' unions in Montreal in the 1830s. Printers were organized in Toronto also at about this time, according to one labour historian, and in Hamilton in 1833. Little by way of broadening the base of organization among workers beyond individual local units was evident until the latter half of the last century, however.

According to Forsey, the first "outside" unions in Canada were of British origin. The Amalgamated Society of Engineers established its first local in Canada in 1851; and the Amalgamated Society of Carpenters and Joiners became, in 1860, the first permanent union in the building trades.

The development and growth of unions in Canada, however, have been most heavily influenced by events and developments in the United States, and in the decade preceding Confederation, unions that had been operating south of the border began to form locals in Upper Canada. This was the beginning of "international unionism" as we know it in Canada today.

There have been many attempts over the years to "nationalize" the labour movement in Canada, in spite of the fact that Canadian locals of international unions have, generally speaking, a large degree of autonomy. This inclination is still very much alive among some labour unionists, and there are pressures being exerted in some quarters to sever international connections and to work toward an all-Canadian union movement.

It is interesting to note that, in this connection, the Canadian Labour Congress, the larger of the two central labour bodies in Canada, adopted certain criteria at its 1970 convention calling for minimum standards of self-government by its international affiliates operating in Canada.

The question of international unionism--its advantages and disadvantages--is a timely topic; but it is only one of the many interesting tangents that would take this chapter beyond its scope. For those interested in greater detail, I would refer them to John Crispo's *International Unionism*, published by McGraw-Hill in 1967.

During the past ten to fifteen years, the proportion of union members in Canada belonging to international unions, although constituting a substantial majority, has shown a consistent downward trend: from 73 per cent of total union membership in 1958 to 71 per cent in 1963, 67 per cent in 1968, and 62 per cent in 1971. This downward shift in proportion is attributable not to a decline in the membership of international unions in Canada, but rather to the rapid growth in the membership of national unions; and this has been caused, in large measure, by the extension of collective bargaining into new sectors--particularly the Public Service at both provincial and federal levels.

Despite this trend, it must be recognized that, with certain notable exceptions--including that portion of the labour movement represented by the Confederation of National Trade Unions and a few large national unions affiliated with the CLC--the international character of the labour movement in Canada is its most unique feature.

As I indicated earlier, the beginning of the union movement began prior to Confederation with the formation of scattered Canadian locals of unions that were already active in the U.S. The first attempt after Confederation to form a national federation of unions was in 1873, when thirty locals in Ontario united to form the Canadian Labour Union. Conventions were held by this organization for several years, but it failed to prosper.

Meanwhile, the Knights of Labour, formed in the U.S. in 1869, organized a Canadian Assembly in 1881; the Knights attempted to organize workers regardless of skill or occupation, and by the end of the 1880s they claimed a membership of 16,000.

At the second convention of the Knights of Labour Assemblies in 1886, the Dominion Trades and Labour Congress was established, and in 1893 this became the Trades and Labour Congress of Canada, which retained its identity until 1956, when the Trades and Labour Congress of Canada and the Canadian Congress of Labour merged to become the Canadian Labour Congress.

Just after the turn of the century, the international unions in the Trades and Labour Congress that held affiliation with the American Federation of Labor in the U.S., gained control of the Congress, and measures were taken, by amending the constitution, to eliminate "dual unionism" (more than one union in a given trade or industry). Accordingly, the District Trade Assemblies of the Knights of Labour and a number of purely Canadian unions were expelled in 1902. These expelled unions, together with others, then formed a new federation--the National Trades and Labour Congress, which became, in 1908, the Canadian Federation of Labour.

Another schism in the Canadian labour movement, centred in the West, culminated in the formation in 1919, of an organization called the One Big Union. This union sought to organize workers by industry rather than by trade, and it gained prominence after the Winnipeg General Strike in 1919.

The One Big Union proclaimed a doctrine of revolutionary unionism similar in some respects to that of the Industrial

Workers of the World, one of several unions organized as left-wing revolutionary movements in the U.S. just after the turn of the century, in opposition to the conservative policies of the craft unions and the American Federation of Labor. The I.W.W. exerted an influence on the union movement in Western Canada in the early 1900s. The One Big Union claimed a membership of about 41,000 at the time of the Winnipeg General Strike, but owing to internal conflicts, and opposition from federal and provincial governments and the Trades and Labour Congress, it soon began to decline. More detailed information about the One Big Union is contained in the report of the Royal Commission to "Enquire into and Report upon the Causes and Effects of the Winnipeg General Strike", by H.A. Robson, Commissioner.

About the time these events were taking place, attempts were being made in the Province of Quebec to federate the unions that had, for a number of years, been organizing in accordance with the social philosophy of the Roman Catholic Church.

The origin of this development can be traced to a lockout in Quebec City in 1900 that involved a number of shoe manufacturers and three local unions. The then Archbishop of Quebec was appointed to arbitrate the dispute, and he recommended that the unions revise their constitutions in accordance with the social principles set forth in Leo XIII's Encyclical of 1891, *Rerum Novarum*. The suggestions of the Archbishop called for, among other things, the appointment of chaplains to guide the deliberations of unions.

The first such union was formed in 1912 among pulp and paper workers, and other units soon began ot form among various occupational and industrial groups. In 1918, in Quebec City, these unions--or *syndicats*, as they were called--united under the name National Central Trades Council. This event was followed in the same year by a conference for the entire province, and at a founding convention in Hull in 1921, a permanent organization, the Canadian and Catholic Confederation of Labour, was formed. We shall see later how this organization evolved into the Confederation of National Trade Unions.

Another attempt to Canadianize the labour movement took place in 1927, when dissident elements of the Canadian Federation of Labour, the Canadian Brotherhood of Railway Employees, and what remained of the One Big Union united to form the All-Canadian Congress of Labour.

The Great Depression of the 1930s brought its difficulties to the labour movement, however, and both the All-Canadian Congress and the Trades and Labour Congress experienced declining membership. At the same time, certain elements in both congresses were expressing dissatisfaction with their leadership.

The Communist Party in Canada formed a new revolutionary labour federation, the Workers' Unity League, during this period. It remained active for a few years during the early thirties and had some success in organizing various groups of longshoremen, loggers, fishermen, and hard-rock miners in British Columbia, and mining, smelting, automobile and textile workers, and Great Lakes seamen in Ontario and Quebec.

The league's success was short-lived, however, and the organization was disbanded in 1934. Some of its members and officials eventually became active in the Trades and Labour Congress and the All-Canadian Congress of Labour.

In 1935, the U.S. passed the Wagner Act, whereby labour was legally permitted to join unions and to bargain with employers. Soon afterward, agitation for similar legislation began to mount in Canada.

In the same year, a number of unions in the American Federation of Labor formed the Committee for Industrial Organization. These events sparked organizational activity in previously unorganized areas in Canada, and the newly formed Committee of the American Federation of Labor provided assistance. In 1936, however, certain unions belonging to the committee were suspended from the American Federation of Labor for "dual unionism", and their expulsion the following year gave rise to a new federation in the United States--the Congress of Industrial Organizations. In Canada, under pressure exerted by unions affiliated with the American Federation of Labor, the Trades and Labour Congress expelled the Canadian branches of CIO unions in 1939.

Although defections had weakened the All-Canadian Congress of Labour, in the 1930s the organization had begun to raise the hopes of labour for new policies for industrial unionism, political action, and government intervention in economic affairs. The Canadian branches of the CIO unions joined the ACCL at its 1940 convention, the constitution was changed, and a new body--the Canadian Congress of Labour--came into being.

During the late 1940s after World War II, the Trades and Labour Congress of Canada and the Canadian Congress of Labour became involved in controversy over the issue of communist influence among their affiliates. Both congresses had experienced rapid membership gains, and certain Communists had secured key positions in a number of affiliates.

In the Canadian Congress of Labour, there was conflict between its executive and the left-wing leaders of several of its large affiliated unions. Resolutions put forward by these leaders were usually defeated in convention, however.

In the Trades and Labour Congress, there was a more conciliatory policy toward the left-wing elements during and after the war, and Communists held key positions of leadership in some TLC affiliates and in the congress itself. The TLC, however, disagreed with the views of its U.S. counterpart, the American Federation of Labor, and regarded the issue as one of Canadian autonomy rather than ideology.

The first open break came in 1949, when the CCL took action to expel two major Canadian affiliates. These same unions in the U.S. were, along with some others, subsequently expelled from the CIO. Meanwhile the TLC, after a good deal of infighting in its own ranks and with its U.S. counterpart, the American Federation of Labor, took similar action and cooperated with the international executives of several unions in ridding the organization of left-wing leadership.

In 1955, the AFL and CIO merged to form one federation, and in April 1956, the Canadian counterparts, the Trades and Labour Congress of Canada and the Canadian Congress of Labour, at a joint convention in Toronto, merged under the name Canadian Labour Congress.

Meanwhile, in Quebec, the Canadian and Catholic Confederation of Labour was undergoing significant changes in policy and viewpoint, and in the late 1950s, it appeared that a merger with the Canadian Labour Congress might take place. This, however, did not materialize, mainly because of differences in opinion as to how the confederation would fit structurally and autonomously into the CLC, and how it would maintain its own internal structures within such a merger. Instead, at its 1960 convention, the Canadian and Catholic Confederation of Labour changed its name to the *Confédération des syndicats nationaux* (Confederation of National Trade Unions) and adopted a new statement of principles that, although affirming adherence to Christian principles, did not refer specifically to the social doctrines of the Roman Catholic Church.

Today, these two central labour bodies, the Canadian Labour Congress and the Confederation of National Trade Unions, are made up of unions that account for 85 per cent of the total membership in Canada, the remainder being composed of unaffiliated national and international unions and independent local organizations.

The schism that took place recently in the Confederation of National Trade Unions can be traced back to the mid-1960s, with the organization of white-collar workers in government and hospital services and the proposal by President Pepin to open a "second front" going beyond collective bargaining activities and becoming more oriented toward political action. The more traditional elements in the CNTU, representing workers in the industrial sectors, lost their majority in the governing bodies of the confederation, and they were not too pleased by the new orientation given the organizations by relative newcomers.

The orientation of the CNTU, expressed by the "moral reports" of the president at several conventions in the 1960s, indicates that the confederation was changing its philosophy from the American type of business unionism to one resembling of a European-style operation, with more input into political and social affairs. (The so-called moral report is the statement of policy of the organization contained in the addresses of the president to conventions.) Three of these reports, "A Society for Man", presented in 1966, "The Second Front", delivered in 1968, and "A Liberty Camp", put forward in 1970, all indicate the predominance of the thinking of the more politically minded professionals and white-collar workers within the confederation.

In the early 1960s, the CNTU was in general accord with the Quebec government of the time, approving and even participating in such decisions as the nationalization of hydro, the regionalization of school boards, and new labour legislation. When the so-called quiet revolution began to lose its momentum, the CNTU believed that the government was falling short of its expectations, and the confederation gradually moved toward a more independent attitude, opening what might be called a "second front" to seek implementation of the unsatisfied expectations of the "quiet revolution".

Among other reasons for conflict within the CNTU were: the large number of university-educated persons on the permanent staff; leaders who were not close enough to blue-collar members; the money spent on consumer education, political education, and the Lapalme affair; and, in general, the attitude toward matters judged outside the ambit of collective bargaining.

Before dealing with the structure of the Canadian labour movement, I would like to mention that the Canada Department of Labour has maintained an unbroken series of statistics on union membership since 1911. A few examples will illustrate how union membership has grown since that time, and indicate something of its composition.

There were 133,000 union members in Canada in 1911. By the end of World War I, this figure had more than doubled to 368,000. There was some falling off in the 1920s and during the depression years, however, and it was not until the first year of World War II that the 1919 level was again reached. Membership increased rapidly during the war years, and by 1946 the total was 832,000. At mid-century it went over the 1,000,000 mark, and then crept up during the 1950s and the first half of the 1960s to 1,500,000.

Since then it has continued to climb; by January 1968 it had exceeded 2,000,000, and at last count, January 1971, it was 2.2 million. These figures do not include certain groups which, although they may not all call themselves unions, are more and more carrying on union functions through some form of collective bargaining. I refer mainly to professional organizations such as teachers and nurses.

If these were added--and it is reasonable in view of their collective bargaining activities that they should be--the total membership in Canada of collective bargaining organizations, whether called "unions" or not, would be about 2,500,000. There are, of course, among nonagricultural paid workers, some untapped or relatively untapped sources of new union membership. It is significant to note that during the last convention of the Canadian Labour Congress, held in Ottawa in May 1972, the decision was taken to apply more resources and money toward organizing white-collar workers. The effectiveness of this effort may have a substantial effect on union membership over the next few years.

The first part of this article dealt with the historical development of the union movement in Canada, mainly in terms of the broadest form of labour organization: the central labour bodies such as the CLC, the CNTU, and similar union organizations that have played a part in the evolution of the movement.

These central labour bodies are really "organizations of unions" rather than unions, in the sense that they do not normally perform union functions, such as collective bargaining, per se. They are concerned with coordinating, at the national level, the activities of their affiliated unions, including the relations between the labour movement and government, and the establishment of relations with organized workers on an international (in this case meaning worldwide) scale. Their policies are developed in open conventions held every two years. Each year, they present briefs to the federal government in which they state their organizations' positions on a wide range of economic, social, and political issues as well as national and international affairs. They deal with such topics as labour legislation, human rights, housing, and trade policy.

Although the CLC is regarded as a counterpart of the AFL-CIO in the U.S., and although most international unions operating in Canada are affiliated with the centrals in both countries, the CLC is really an autonomous national labour centre; in fact, it frequently differs substantially from its U.S. counterpart on international and other issues. The CNTU, of course, by its very makeup as an indigenous movement, is also an autonomous centre, with its member organizations operating almost exclusively in Quebec.

The basic unit of labour organization in a particular locality is the "local"--sometimes called lodge, branch, or, in the case of CNTU affiliates, the *syndicat*. Locals, or their equivalents, have their own constitutions, and the members pay dues to and participate in the affairs of the local, including the election of officers, financial and business affairs, and the relations between local and employer.

Local unions normally have a good deal of autonomy, and, in the Canadian industrial relations system, most collective bargaining takes place between the local and the employer of its members. (There are certain exceptions to this practice in which bargaining is conducted on a national or regional scale, and in some cases by combinations of unions or locals and associations representing employers.)

Locals may vary in size, depending on the type of union to which they belong and the size of the establishments in which their members are employed. They may be of three types: (1) a local of a national or international union; (2) one chartered directly by a central labour body; or (3) an independent association not connected with any other labour organization. The equivalent of the local in the CNTU is the *syndicat*, normally identified by including in its name the industry and locality in which it operates. The locals of most national and international unions outside the CNTU are identified by the name of the union to which they belong and by a local number.

The union is the unit of a labour organization that organizes and charters locals in the industries and trades as defined in its constitution, sets general policies for its locals, assists them in the conduct of their affairs, and co-coordinates their activities. It is financed by locals through per capita dues and assessments. Unions hold regular conventions for delegates from their locals, at which general policies are set and officers elected.

The equivalent of a union in the CNTU organization is the *Fédération*. *Fédérations* are organized primarily along industry lines, and in 1971 there were twelve in number.

Among the substructures of union organization are district councils--organizations of locals of a union in a particular area, formed to coordinate the activities and administer to the needs of those locals. District councils may hold meetings of delegates from each member local to deal with matters of mutual interest and to elect district officers. They are also known as "joint boards" or "conference boards".

Another part of the substructure, most frequently found among unions organized along craft lines, is the Allied Trades Federation. It is an organization of unions or of locals in a particular area in the same industry, coordinating the activities of the members and dealing with jurisdictional questions. Policies are established and officers are elected at meetings attended by delegates from member organizations. Trades federations may also be known as union councils, union federations, or joint councils; as previously mentioned, they are most frequently found in industries organized along craft lines.

Another part of the substructure is the local labour council. This is an organization formed by a labour central at the city level and functioning in the same manner as a provincial federation, but within the scope of a city. The councils are financed through per capita taxes on affiliates.

This brings us to the level of the central labour bodies or congresses, which, as mentioned, are national coordinating bodies that speak for the labour movement as a whole.

The CLC, being a national organization, has a provincial federation in each province. Provincial federations are made up of member unions of the congress in each province. They act, in the provinces, similarly to the way the CLC acts on a national basis, presenting briefs to the provincial governments and coordinating the activities of member locals. Provincial federations do not, however, charter locals. All locals of CLC unions in the provinces are urged to affiliate with provincial federations, but it is not mandatory. Provincial federations of labour are financed by per capita fees from their member locals, and, as with other substructures, are entitled to send delegates to the congress's conventions.

In the Confederation of National Trade Unions, whose operation is almost entirely in Quebec, there are regional councils. These might be considered as equivalent, on a geographic basis, to the provincial federations of the CLC.

The supreme governing body of both congresses is the Convention, held at two-year intervals. In the CLC, the governing body between conventions is the Executive Council, comprising the president, secretary-treasurer, two executive vice-presidents, six general vice-presidents, and nine vice-presidents-at-large. The Executive Council meets at least four times a year. The Confederal Bureau of the CNTU has a function similar to that of the CLC's Executive Council.

In the Confederation of National Trade Unions, the governing body between confederations is the Confederal Council, comprising the general president, the general secretary, the general treasurer, the general vice-president, the general director of services, one representative of each federation, eight representatives of central councils, and one representative of staff members of the confederation. This body also meets at least four times a year.

In the CLC, the Executive Committee, comprising the president, the secretary-treasurer, two executive vice-presidents, and the general vice-president are responsible for the administration of the affairs and activities of the Congress, meeting at least six times a year for this purpose.

The CLC is affiliated with the International Confederation of Free Trade Unions, an international body composed of 121 affiliates in 94 countries in North, Central and South America, Europe, Asia, the Middle East, Africa and Australia. Canada has two members on the Executive Board, and the total membership of the ICFTU is 48,000,000.

The Confederation of National Trade Unions speaks internationally through affiliation with the World Confederation of Labour, which has 81 affiliates in 72 countries in the Americas, Europe and Africa. The total membership of the World Confederation of Labour is 15,000,000. The CNTU is usually represented on the executive of this organization by its president.

The structure of the Canadian labour movement as an operating concern is somewhat complex. Eighty five per cent of all Canadian union members are in organizations affiliated with either of the two principal labour congresses, the CLC or the CNTU. Between these two congresses there has been much rivalry, arising out of jurisdictional matters and general philosophy. The CNTU has always been opposed to international unionism as espoused by the CLC and its predecessors, although the reason for this opposition has undergone some change throughout the years of the CNTU's existence. The CNTU has been less concerned than the CLC about such matters as raiding, believing that interunion competition is a desirable thing because it gives dissatisfied workers a choice. The CNTU has also believed in a more tightly controlled type of confederation, in contrast to the more loosely knit character of the CLC.

Despite their differences, there have been occasions when the Quebec Federation of Labour, the Quebec wing of the CLC, and the CNTU have cooperated in pursuit of mutually desired government action. A recent example of this was the "common front", made up of CNTU and QFL affiliates and the Quebec Teachers' Corporation, together representing 210,000 government employees seeking better conditions for hospital workers, civil servants, teachers, and hydro and liquor board employees, and taking joint strike action in support of their demand.

Following this strike action in April and May 1972, a rift occurred in the CNTU over the issue of political action. A breakaway of the more conservative elements under the leadership of the so-called three D's (Dion, Dalpe and Daigle, all former officials in the CNTU) followed, and a new federation, the *Confédération des syndicats démocratiques* was formed on a platform of independence from party politics. This new organization has been recruiting membership from erstwhile affiliates of the CNTU and, as of October 1972, was reported in the press as having more than 30,000 members.

There are some who interpret the joint action by the Quebec Federation of Labour and the other two Quebec-based organizations as indicative of a possible restructuring of the Quebec labour movement, which might, it is suggested, be composed of like-thinking organizations and officials of the Quebec Federation of Labour and the more militant wing of the Confederation of National Trade Unions on the one hand, and the more conservative elements, including the CSD, on the other.

In any discussion of the structure of unions in Canada, the very size of that part of the labour movement that is international, and the diverse relationships that result from this fact, make the international aspect of union structure the most interesting and unique feature of our union movement.

There are 99 international unions in Canada, whose membership is deployed among 5,000 local unions; this is about half the total number of locals in the country. Many people are inclined to regard the Canadian labour movement as merely a part of the U.S. movement. In support of this thesis, they cite the fact that Canadian locals operate under the same union constitutions, are represented at international conventions on the same basis as American locals, pay the same per capita dues to international headquarters, and are entitled to the same strike pay and other benefits for their members.

There are, of course, differences among international unions in policies respecting such matters as strike and contract authorization. In collective bargaining matters, however, Canadian locals or sections of the internationals enjoy a large degree of autonomy, particularly in those unions formerly in the CIO before the 1955 merger, and in construction unions formerly affiliated with the American Federation of Labor. Most international unions with locals in Canada have Canadian representatives--either vice-presidents or board members--on their executives.

There are many differences in the de facto relationships between Canadian locals belonging to international and United States locals of the same union. Canada is a sovereign power, with a different form of government and different industrial relations legislation, but with largely similar economic problems. The Canadian Labour Congress, however, is a separate and autonomous Canadian central labour body.

Most executives of international unions recognize those political and legal differences and acknowledge that Canadian problems can best be handled by Canadian officers. This is reflected in the sometimes greater degree of autonomy and control enjoyed by the Canadian sections of internationals in Canada than is the case with their counterparts in the U.S. The Canadian sections of a good many internationals are organized as separate Canadian districts. This is especially true of the internationals with large Canadian memberships. (A good example is the Steelworkers; and, even in a declining union like the United Mine Workers, there have been for many years two separate districts in Canada, one in the east and one in the west.)

The trend toward separate Canadian districts is likely to continue as a result of the guidelines put forward by the Task Force on Labour Relations and subsequent declarations by the CLC.

The Eleventh Report of the Standing Committee on External Affairs and National Defence Respecting Canada-United States Relations noted, with pleasure, the resolution of the CLC, at its Edmonton convention in 1970, dealing with minimum standards of self-government for Canadian sections of international unions. The committee, recognizing the wide diversity in international union constitutions, outlined several objectives as desirable. They are as follows.

(1) Canadian members and locals of international unions should be recognized as the Canadian section of the international.
(2) The Canadian section of the international union should have the machinery and the authority to deal with all matters of concern to the Canadian members and locals. As a general principle, international headquarters should not put a Canadian local under trusteeship without the advice of the Canadian headquarters.
(3) In particular, Canadian members and locals of international unions should have complete authority with regard to their collective bargaining program, to the settlement of disputes, and to the conclusion of collective agreements, which should not require approval in the United States.
(4) Canadian officers of international unions should be elected by Canadians, either by delegates at conventions or by the Canadian membership.
(5) As far as is possible, machinery should be provided so that control over expenditures and staff in Canada rests with the Canadian section and its officers. Financial statements in reasonable detail, giving members a clear view of the financial operations of the union, should be made available to all members.
(6) Generally, all steps should be taken to give Canadian sections of international unions full authority to deal with all matters-- whether they are concerned with the internal administration of the Canadian locals, or with general social and economic policy, or with collective bargaining--without any control from the outside.

The indications are that unions in Canada are here to stay for a long while, and will continue to play a significant part in the economic affairs of our country. The structure of the union movement will depend to a large extent on the kind of political, economic and legislative environment in which it will have to operate. It is generally conceded that a free union movement is an essential part of a democratic society; and free collective bargaining is, on the whole, a sound system of allocating the output of our resources and efforts.

It is fair to speculate that unions will become larger; mergers are being encouraged within the movement so that unions will be in a better position to provide the kind of services demanded by their members in a modern industrial society. The problem of international unionism in Canada, if indeed it is a problem, is likely to be left to the unions themselves to solve. Workers are generally pragmatic and they will, given the choice, join the union that serves them best.

Pressure to make corporations more socially conscious--whether it be in terms of industrial relations policies, environmental control, or other fields--will have an effect on unions and their attitudes. And unions will, I believe, be responsive to initiatives--wherever they originate--to promote the common good of all Canadian citizens, as well as the citizens of other parts of the world that are less fortunate, economically, than we.

11. The Structure of the Labour Movement

by C.P. Thakur

Introduction

In this late twentieth century, the trade union is much too familiar an organization. However, the degree of popular esteem accorded it differs from situation to situation. In a liberal
democratic country like Canada, effective trade unionism is a
major symbol of a voluntary, decentralized and pluralistic society. The affluent Canadian free enterprise economy is prepared
for, and even receptive to, the pressures from organized labour.
Its structurally reformed (mixed) capitalist system, in itself
partly due to the contributions of organized labour as a counter-
vailing force to owner-employers/managers, has learned, howsoever
grudgingly, to live with this popular institution. This has no
doubt happened at considerable emotional, and even some economic,
cost to them. But it has brought substantial gains for them, as
well as for the system itself. Its continued smooth working and
its acceptability by the society could have been doubtful in the
absence of the reforms from time to time. More particularly, the
Canadian industrial relations system assigns a key actor-status
to trade unionism. Its state-guided, and industrial peace-ori-
ented, collective bargaining framework provides a crucial role
for trade unions in determining the rules of work. More than one
forum is open to them for interacting with other key actors in
the system, around issues ranging from policy making to the mun-
dane, job-related ones. The framework of political democracy
allows it a legitimate and significant role, even in the larger
macroquestion of power sharing among the major competing interests in the society. The competitive party system allows a
greater bargaining power to an articulate, strategically placed,
and organized working community.

From the preceding it would appear that the organized labour
is a force to reckon with in the Canadian society. This is true
both at the economic and political levels. It must, however, be
emphasized here that this is an index of both (1) its progress
and achievements, on the one hand; and (2) the challenge to its
potential to contribute in future, on the other.

But in both these areas there is a surprising mixture of facts
as well as fictions. Organized labour is known as "big labour"

The author wished to acknowledge the assistance of Mr. G. Muguran
in the preparation of charts and figures for this chapter, and
Professor Albert N.B. Nedd for his help in preparing the first
table.

121

in terms of popular thinking, at any rate. Its "bigness" is a
source of satisfaction for some, but is, at the same time, a basis
for awesome exasperation, depending upon one's interest and status as an observer of the politico-economic scene.

Objectives

The purpose of this chapter is to present facts, and dispute some
fictions relating to the current status of trade unionism in
Canada. Data will be presented with a view to moderating excessive popular concerns and skepticism as well as undue enthusiasm
where the trade union movement is concerned. We will first present the relevant data on its size, then analyze its structural
features, and finally comment on their implications in the context of industrial relations. Emphasis throughout will be more
on current and prospective aspects, but relevant references to
past perspective will also be made.

Growth of Trade Unionism

In the year 1972 over one in three (34.4 per cent) nonagricultural
workers, and over one in four (27.6 per cent) civilian labour-
force members belonged to the organized category of the industrial
community. A total of 437 unions, with 10,462 locals, and a membership of 2,370,641 constitute today a major power centre in the
Canadian society. Its significance must be understood in terms
of facts: (1) that they are largely located in the strategic sector of the economy; and (2) that they constitute the urban, relatively educated, and more articulate section of the society.
With their combined power they are in a position to help or even
hurt the process of economic and political management in the
country.

But this broad picture of a particular year conveys only a
part of the story. The fact that (1) the movement has not
achieved its present status overnight; (2) there have been ups
and downs in its career; and (3) it has not been characterized
by a uniform degree of organizational dynamism throughout its
history must be appreciated for its realistic assessment. Chart
11.1 illustrates the broad pattern of organizational growth.

Between isolated and local attempts by certain skill groups,
around 1816, and the emergence of the dominant national federating body, the Canadian Labour Congress, in 1956, the story of
the labour movement in Canada is rather complex.[1] Periods of
severe frustrations have alternated with those of satisfying
achievements. In this process of social evolution, various
forces have made their contribution; not all of them, however,
in the same direction.

The inherent pressure of industrial-urban transformation re-
leased forces of spontaneous institutional response from the
workers in the form of organized protection of their interests.

CHART 11.1

Growth of Trade Unionism in Canada

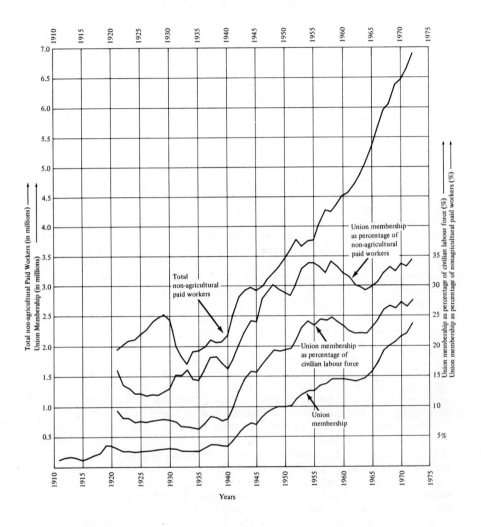

Years

Later, they received support from liberal and progressive sections of the society. External sources contributed largely to this response; indeed the Canadian labour movement has been international in character from a very early stage. The first external influence came from the United Kingdom. This was partly through: (1) the efforts of some British trade unions in starting their Canadian branches; (2) the inflow of propensity to unionize and related organizational know-how, through a large body of the immigrant work force from the United Kingdom; and (3) a receptive attitude of the colonial government in Canada to the emerging institution of the kind already familiar in the mother country.

Subsequently, the major source of influence was from the United States of America. Several factors substantially helped in the transmission of influence. First, the relatively established and growing trade union movement in the U.S.A. extended its operation into the Canadian labour market. This was with a view to strengthening its bargaining power in relation to the industrial corporations willing to take advantage of the less organized, and hence cheaper, labour across the border to the disadvantage of the U.S. labour. Secondly, the "demonstration effect" of the wage and benefit gains of organized activity to the American workers made the message of unionism appealing to Canadian workers, too. Thirdly, the extension of professionalized personnel practices through the Canadian branches of major U.S.-based corporations encouraged, at the same time, a degree of management tolerance toward union activity.

Another significant factor influencing the course of unionism in Canada has been the government labour policy. A gradual, delayed, but nevertheless protective and promotive policy of government[2] substantially helped the labour movement. In this area, too, the British, and later (to a greater extent) the U.S. government policies had their influence. It is important, however, to remember that the attitude of the Canadian government as well as employers toward trade unionism was primarily prompted by the economic needs of the situation from time to time. The significance of coal mining and railway transportation for the economy, and the risks of industrial unrest in these industries, are not unrelated to their less hostile attitude to trade unionism. The vulnerability of an export-oriented product market, and the industrialists' wish to take advantage of the prosperity resulting from the world wars further explain this tendency.

But this should not create the impression that the trade union movement did not have to pay a price in the course of its development. The bitterness of the struggle was acute enough, due to employer hostility and the partisan and indifferent attitude of the government, especially in early years.

During the twenties, the movement had a limited base. Its craft character was marked, and the hostilities from employers remained its principal handicap. Public policy had eliminated some of the major obstacles to its growth, but it was not marked by an appreciation of the need to consciously foster its development. Finally, the depression of 1929 brought the major economic blow. The labour market setting turned exceedingly adverse to union activity. The need for its protective role was no doubt paramount, but in a state of reducing job opportunities, few workers were left with a desire to join unions. Even the unions were hardly in a position to demonstrate their effectiveness in protecting jobs or earnings.

During the late thirties and early forties, however, the movement forged ahead. Four factors helped in this regard: (1) revival of economic activity in general and wartime prosperity in particular, encouraged industrialization in the country; (2) the size of the unionizable base expanded; (3) employers were willing to come to terms with the movement; and (4) the rival U.S. trade union federations were engaged in a competitive struggle in organizing the Canadian labour force. The emergence of the Congress of Industrial Organizations, with its concern for industrial rather than craft unionism, brought momentum to union growth. By 1953, the degree of unionism touched the 33 per cent mark; since then the movement has stayed around that level. We will refer to this stagnation of the last two decades later in the chapter.

Efforts of Unification

While the movement as a whole was growing, there were also distressing internal features. The divisive forces drew their support from a variety of sources.[3] First, the division within the U.S. movement extended itself to the Canadian scene. The movement echoed the struggles between both the Knights of Labour and AFL, and the AFL and the CIO. Attempts were made to retain a degree of neutrality, but unsuccessfully. Secondly, their struggles finally shaped around craft and industrial kinds of unionism promoted by the AFL and the CIO, respectively. Their corresponding affiliates in Canada, the TLC and CCL, faithfully carried the struggle on this side of the border. Thirdly, a major challenge to union unity came from the uniquely Canadian linguistic, religious, and regional problem through the Quebec-based union activity. The interest of the Catholic Church and the fears of a French-speaking minority provided the basis of a separatist labour movement. This was further fed by the wider regional undertones of the national policy. The last source of internal factionalism came from ideological sources. From time to time, thoughts of radical persuasion did influence the sections of the movement.

Nevertheless, positive forces within the movement, aided by the external developments like the merger of the AFL and the CIO, created a climate for the formation of the Canadian Labour Congress in 1956 after the merger of the two leading and rival Canadian federations, the TLC and the CCL. This marked a major achievement on the path to unification, but much remained to be done. There were the problems of (1) the intractable issue of merger of the CNTU, the Quebec-based federation; and (2) the existence of several independent unions, both small and large. Organized labour in Canada still does not have one common forum.

TABLE 11.1

Summary of Attempts to Bring Canadian Trade Unions Within One National Body

Year	Name of the Organization	Geographic Scope	Philosophy/Policy	Outcome
1873	Canadian Labour Union	Ontario	Unite all unions in Canada	Failed due to depression
1881	Knights of Labour	Canada	Organize workers into trades and district assemblies	
1883	Canadian Labour Congress	Canada	Unite independent union within K of L	Not successful
1887	Trades and Labour Congress (TLC) of Canada	Canada	Canadian wing to the American Federation of Labor--craft unionism	Continued until merger with CCL to form CLC in 1956
1908	Canadian Federation of Labour (CFL)	Canada	Nationalism and industrial unionism--opposed to TLC	Could not continue
1919	One Big Union (OBU)	Western Canada	Revolutionary industrial unionism--opposed to TLC-type craft unionism	Could not survive due to internal dissensions, opposition from government and TLC
1920	Canadian Federation of Labour (Revived again)	Canada	Opposed to craft as well as revolutionary radical unionism--against TLC and OBU	Suffered due to general decline of union movement

TABLE 11.1 (cont'd)

Year		Country		
1927	All Canadian Congress of Labour	Canada	Complete independence of Canadian labour movement	Could not succeed due to depression and inadequate nationalism
1930–1934	Workers' Unity League	Canada	Revolutionary ideology-Communist sponsored	Disbanded by the Communist party
1936	Canadian Federation of Labour (a new body)	Canada	Reaction to internal conflicts within the AIC, Canadian Congress of Labour	Lost workers' support
1940	Canadian Congress of Labour (CCL)	Canada	Industrial unionism--rival to TLC formed by CIO affiliates expelled by TLC and remaining units of ACCL	Merged with TLC to form CLC in 1956
1956	Canadian Labour Congress (CLC)	Canada	International business/economic unionism	Continuing

Table 11.1 tries to briefly summarize the course of unification efforts within the Canadian trade union movement until the creation of the CLC in 1956.

Regional Distribution of Unionism

The fact that 34.4 per cent of nonagricultural workers are being unionized does not mean that all regions of the country are characterized by a uniform degree of unionism. Unionism is an institutional response to industrialism and urbanism. Regions differ in terms of degree of industrialization and urbanization; therefore there has to be a corresponding difference in the degree of unionism. Such factors as: (1) the size of the unionizable work force; (2) its locational concentration or dispersal; (3) its propensity to respond to unionization; and (4) the magnitude of efforts put in by union organizers all contribute to the final regional picture. Table 11.2 gives a factual account of regional distributions of unionization in Canada.

TABLE 11.2

Interregional Distribution of Unionism

	1967		1971	
Region	No. of Union Members	% of Total Members	No. of Union Members	% of Total Members
Atlantic	120,707	6.28	155,084	6.95
Quebec	569,430	29.65	653,673	29.30
Ontario	721,581	37.57	878,938	39.39
Prairies	198,151	10.32	243,434	10.91
B.C.	240,228	12.51	280,114	12.55
Other[a]	70,550	3.67	20,000	0.90
Canada	1,920,647	100.00	2,231,243	100.00

Source: Figures for 1967 from *Canadian Industrial Relations*, Report of the Task Force on Labour Relations, 1968; for 1971, from Department of Labour, *Labour Gazette*.

a Figures for tables 11.2 and 11.3 are not from the same basic data.

Table 11.2 broadly conforms to the industrial and urban characteristics of the regions. The figures confirm the fact that unionization is the product of industrialism. With a better balance in the spread of industrialization as a result of current conscious attempts for regional development, we can reasonably expect a corresponding change in the regional structure of unionism in Canada. The other possibility could be a vigorous effort to organize the nonindustrial and rural work force too.

Success in this effort, although unlikely, would definitely influence the interregional picture of the union movement. This is partly evident, at any rate, in the white-collar and public-employee categories.

Industrial Distribution

The nonagricultural work force has been the traditional client of union movement. However, within this category too, there are differences. The manufacturing and transportation workers have responded more readily. Their clustering in larger sizes, in relatively more accessible and fewer locations, has aided this process. The early and prolonged efforts of various construction skill groups to protect the quality of craftsmanship, and control training and hiring significantly helped union development in this industry. A possible variation in the extent of protest among workmen in different industries can partly explain their responses to unionism.

TABLE 11.3

Interindustry Distribution of Trade Union Membership

Industry Group	1967		1971	
	No. of Union Members	% of Total Members	No. of Union Members	% of Total Members
Agriculture	865	0.05	344	0.02
Forestry	43,907	2.29	32,574	1.45
Fishing and trapping	3,285	0.17	2,304	0.10
Mines	57,929	3.02	73,582	3.30
Manufacturing	758,802	39.51	785,603	35.21
Construction	209,558	10.91	246,206	11.03
Transportation and utilities	361,605	18.83	377,145	16.90
Trade	78,416	4.08	86,970	3.90
Finance	890	0.05	2,615	0.12
Service industries	169,382	8.82	281,978	12.64
Public administration	206,788	10.77	339,216	15.20
Others	29,278	1.52	2,706	0.12
	1,920,647	100.00	2,231,243	100.00

Source: Department of Labour, *Labour Gazette,* February 1968 and July 1973.

Table 11.3 presents the interindustry structure of unionism in Canada. The picture conforms to the earlier discussion. However, a better showing by the service industry is the result of a new course this movement is currently taking. There has been a proportionately faster growth of the number of employees in the service and public employment sectors of the economy. These groups have naturally invited the attention of union organizers, with apparent growing success. The CUPE, with 157,919 members, and PSAC, with 129,652 members, are the second- and third-largest unions, respectively.

The Structure of Trade Unions by Affiliation

The Canadian trade union movement is not a unified one. Due to the competitive existence of more than one federating body the movement stands divided. The principal division is along national and international lines, but within the national sector of the movement there are further divisions. In addition, there are several independent unions. The three principal federating bodies are: (1) the AFL-CIO; (2) the CLC; and (3) the CNTU. Three points need to be emphasized here. First, the AFL-CIO and the CLC have some overlapping affiliating jurisdiction. A majority of the CLC affiliates are also the affiliates of the AFL-CIO; and these are some of the large unions in the manufacturing group, like the United Steelworkers Union, the United Automobile, Aerospace and Agricultural Implement Workers Union, etc. Second, there are some international as well as national unions with several locals, but without any affiliation to the three leading federations, like the International Brotherhood of Teamsters, Chauffeurs, Warehousemen and Helpers. Third, the CNTU affiliates are confined to the Province of Quebec only.

Figures 11.1 and 11.2 present the related pictures. As a result of this division within the movement, we have a large variation in the size category of unions. There are few very large unions, but many small ones. The small ones are able to survive only because they get support from their international affiliates. Chart 11.2 presents the facts relating to the size category of trade unions in Canada. It must be noted that only ten unions in Canada have a membership of over 50,000.

Nationalism and Internationalism

The issue of international unionism vis-à-vis autonomous national unionism has been a controversial one in Canada for a variety of reasons. Strong positions, backed by facts as well as emotion, have been taken in defence of both kinds of unionism. Historically, internationalism has been the dominant feature of unionism in Canada. This is mainly due to the contribution of the U.S. labour movement in organizing the Canadian workers, and the need to deal with multinational corporations with plants in both the countries. However, as in other walks of Canadian like, the tide of nationalism is growing higher in this field, too. The

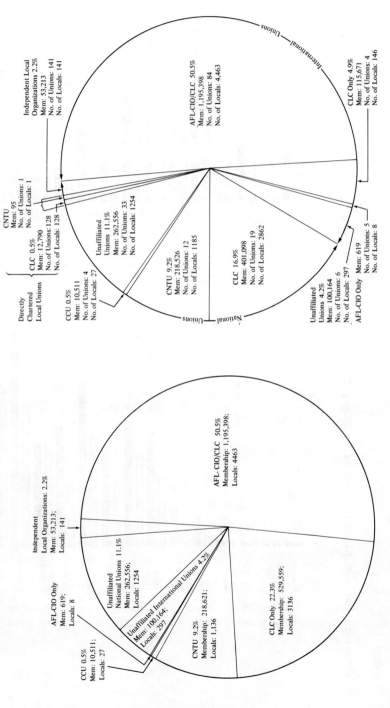

FIGURE 11.1

Union Membership by Congress Affiliations, 1972

FIGURE 11.2

Union Membership by Type of Union and Affiliation, 1972

CHART 11.2

International and National Unions by Size, 1972

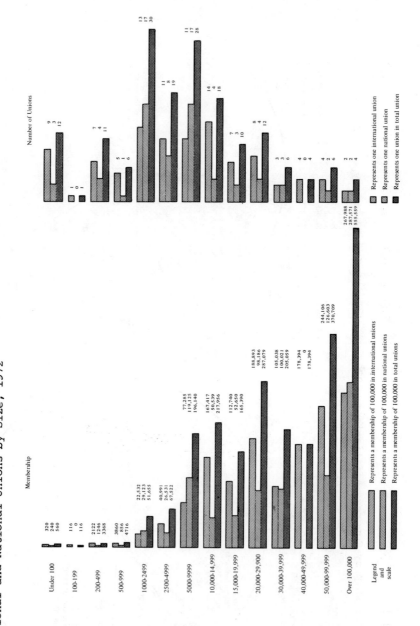

earlier figure 11.2 gives the current position, and table 11.4
indicates the direction of change.

TABLE 11.4

Union Situation by Affiliation

	1968			1972		
Type of Affiliation	No. of Unions	No. of Locals	% Total Members	No. of Unions	No. of Locals	% of Members
International	108	4,967	66.9	99	4,914	59.6
National	54	3,990	29.4	68	5,278	37.7
Directly chartered locals	193	193	1.2	129	129	.5
Independent locals	123	123	2.5	141	141	2.2
			100.0			100.0

Source: Labour Organizations in Canada, 1968 and 1972.

Note: This table shows that: (1) the percentage share of national unions out of total membership has increased from 29.4 to
37.7 between 1968 and 1972; (2) the international unions have
lost some membership, their percentage share falling from 66.9
to 59.6; and (3) the entire loss of about 10 per cent of the
membership of international unions is not necessarily the corresponding gain to the nationalist ones, but it does indicate
a weakening of internationalism.   This is due to: (1) a vigorous
struggle on behalf of purely nationalist unions to enroll new
members; (2) a disillusionment of some Canadian units of international associations, and a consequent breakaway tendency; and
(3) development of new national unions in the white-collar and
professional categories in recent years.   Nevertheless, nearly
60 per cent of the unionized work force remains committed to
internationalism.

The Structure of the CLC Group of Unions

The CLC group of unions constitutes the majority of organized
labour in Canada, representing over three-quarters of the union
members.   The majority of the CLC affiliates are affiliated with
the major international federation of the AFL-CIO.   Between the
three federal bodies and the local unions there are several
other intermediary bodies.   The interorganizational links are
rather complex, and they range from strong to nominal contact.
Chart 11.3 presents the structural details of the CLC group of
unions.

CHART 11.3

The Structure of the CLC Segment of the Canadian Labour Movement

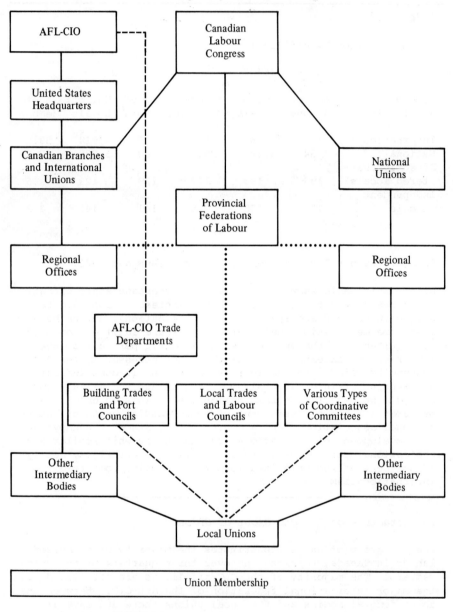

Source: Adapted from John H.G. Crispo, *International Unionism: A Study of Canadian-American Relations* (Toronto: McGraw-Hill, 1967), p. 167.

Division of Activities Among Different Levels of Union Bodies

Chart 11.3 indicates the complex relationships among a large number of union bodies. There is a functional division of activities
among them. The top bodies like the CLC or the AFL-CIO have essentially five functions: (1) lobbying at the government or other
levels; (2) international activities relating to the ILO, the
International Trade Secretariats, etc.; (3) fraternal or other
contacts with the world labour movement; (4) coordination among
the affiliates for organizational work; and (5) research, educational and other services to member organizations.

   The last two functions, in the case of many large national or
international unions, are performed by their national/Canadian or
international offices. Most of the Canadian unions are not in a
position to perform their bargaining and service functions without these services from the federal, national or international
offices.

   At the bottom of the structure, the locals constitute the base.
They are in direct touch with members. Their functions are mainly
three: (1) to bargain and enter into agreements; (2) to keep
watch on contract administration, and handle grievances; and (3)
to implement the organizational programs at the local level,
like enrolling new members or aiding in organizing nonunion
plants.

   At the middle level are the provincial federations and the
city and local councils which are the coordinating bodies. The
provincial federations get involved in the lobbying task at the
level of the provincial governments, too; and also devote some
time to organizational matters.

Concluding Implications

All the features of the trade union movement discussed in this
chapter have a bearing on the industrial relations scene in
Canada. After nearly a century and a half of unionism, several
main questions arise: (1) What are the strengths and weaknesses
of organized labour? (2) How do we characterize its current
status? (3) How far is it playing its desired role in the national industrial relations framework? (4) What challenges is the
movement likely to face? (5) What kinds of structural and organizational changes would equip it to perform its task better?

   It is worthwhile reiterating some of the features of the movement here, and commenting on their implications in the context
of these questions.

(1) The movement has made considerable progress, but in recent
years has apparently stagnated. In a dynamic economic setting,
the size of the work force changes, there are sectoral and structural changes within the working community, and the relative
power position of key actors is unlikely to remain in the previous state of balance. A movement like trade unionism must
find ways to continue to improve and consolidate its position

accordingly. It is not sufficient to say that organizable sections of the work force are reasonably well covered, and that the
remaining ones are difficult to reach. This amounts to a mere
rationalization of poor organizing performance. But there is
encouraging evidence of awareness of this problem within the movement.

(2) Some regions, and particularly some industries, are much better organized, and in many respects account for the large part
of the story of union movement. This also distracts attention
from the paramount need for organizational protection to workmen
in the poorly unionized regions and industries. In the absence
of a better-balanced spread of the movement, the labour market
will increasingly stand the risk of being characterized by separate high-wage vis-à-vis low-wage regions and industries. This
institutional imbalance in the market will handicap its functioning as a rational labour- and skill allocating mechanism across
regions and industries. A further possibility is that the better-
organized ones are able to look after their interests effectively,
while the poorly organized or unorganized ones remain vulnerable
to the risks of exploitation. This will have unintended effects
on other aspects of the economic and social scene as well.

(3) There are only a very few large unions in Canada; most of
them are small. The few larger ones make the headlines on a day
to day basis. This inadvertently again distorts the popular image
of unionism, and even misguides public opinion. Workers covered
by large unions are better protected, enjoy qualitatively much
better service from them, and invariably face even a less hostile
employer/manager. But this again encourages a degree of compla-
cency and indifference on the part of all concerned toward the
fate of those less protected.

    Small unions are poor in resources, cannot have the required
professional skills, and are no match for the employers in terms
of bargaining power. They therefore have their unwelcome consequences for the worker, the union organization, and also the
industrial relations system. Beyond doubt, there is a case for
a limited number of large and well-equipped unions. A planned
program of organizational mergers is long overdue.

(4) A similar case arises for an expeditious arrangement for a
common forum at the national level. The negotiations between the
CNTU and the CLC have been unduly procrastinated. With due regard to the mutual concerns, ways must be found to forge a common platform. The recent autonomy acquired by the Quebec Federation of Labour may contain the seeds of aggressive regionalism,
at the cost of the strength and effectiveness of the movement as
a whole. It must be remembered that one of the leading arguments
used by the Quebec Federation of Labour was the threat to its
activities from the CNTU.

(5) The Canadian Labour Congress is the creation of its affiliates.
It has certain definite functions to perform. Its real status as
the apex body is dependent on: (i) the effective execution of the
tasks assigned to it; and (ii) its success in projecting an image
of an increasingly useful body to its affiliates.

The task of political lobbying on behalf of organized labour is getting more difficult in an inflationary economy. Failure in this regard is hurting both the workers and the union movement. Antiunion lobbies are getting a more receptive ear from the government, the mass media, and the common citizen.

Similarly, the tasks of organizational coordination--like sorting out of jurisdictional disputes, promoting mergers, and encouraging coordination in bargaining problems--call for more urgent and vigorous improvement.

This is also true of the CLC's research and educational services. The extent and quality of these services do not compare with those in several other countries, and they are far too inadequate for the need. It is unlikely that the movement will retain its dynamism and vigour without adequate investment in skill generation.

(6) A continuing commitment to international unionism remains an area of concern. The present stress through which the CLC is passing, due to pressures from the two rival camps, is a challenge to its organizational ingenuity. The useful support from the powerful U.S. trade union movement is welcome, and has been of great advantage historically. But a reasonable degree of autonomy and functional effectiveness for the CLC and its national affiliates in relation to Canadian affairs is the minimum requirement to withstand the pressure. The last Vancouver convention brought urgency to the need for speedy progress in this regard. It may be mentioned in passing that growing economic problems are currently turning the U.S.A. to a protectionist policy. The U.S. unions are solidly behind this trend, which has already experienced adverse reactions from the Canadian unions. International unionism will require much goodwill from all concerned, and considerable internal skills. In the ultimate analysis the quarrel is on the relative share of new jobs, too.

(7) The strike as a weapon is facing severe attacks, unfettered collective bargaining is under a cloud, employers are getting better organized, and workers continue to need the protective umbrella of trade unions. Union leaders should keep asking the question, Is the movement being regeared on a sustained basis for the emerging challenges?

(8) At any rate, the macropicture of achievements indicates that much remains to be done. The trends in real wages, the ratios of real wages to productivity, and wages to profit, the extent of progress in levelling up of wages rates in the depressed sectors--these do not suggest that trade unions can relent in their efforts, even in the traditional role. In addition, they are likely to face a more demanding, or even indifferent, younger, more educated, and relatively affluent group of clients. They will need considerable fresh methods to deal with this new generation of workers, in newer kinds of less satisfying, more grievance-generating jobs. Both their domestic housekeeping and job-related service tasks will become difficult and complex.

(9) Lastly, the society itself will apply a much more rigorous test to union contribution and activity before granting the pro-

tection of social, political and economic approval. Unions cannot survive long unless they are sensitive to the emerging problems and related concerns of the society. A thorough reappraisal will certainly invigorate the movement.

Notes

1. For further discussion, see A.M. Kruger, "The Direction of Unionism in Canada", in *Canadian Labour in Transition,* ed. Miller and Isbester (Prentice-Hall, 1971). See also S.M. Jamieson, *Times of Trouble: Labour Unrest and Industrial Conflict in Canada, 1900-66,* Task Force on Labour Relations, Study no. 22. and idem, *Industrial Relations in Canada* (Toronto: Macmillan, 1973).

2. See S.M.A. Hameed, "Canadian Collection Bargaining: Analysis and Prospect", in *Canadian Labour in Transition.*

3. See S.M. Jamieson, *Times of Trouble,* p. 39; and idem, *Industrial Relations,* chaps. 1 and 11.

12. Management Attitudes toward Management Associations, Unions and Strike*

by Laurent Belanger

In a study completed for the task force in 1967-68, we were asked to enquire into the evolution of management associations in the Province of Quebec and to assess the attitudes and practices of Quebec managers and/or owners in the area of labour-management relations. For this purpose we first collected information from documents published by various of these associations since the early forties. When we reached the area of attitudes and practices in the field of labour-management relations, we developed a questionnaire to be used in a series of interviews with top managers of twenty-five of the largest corporations and of an equal number of medium and small businesses.

The purpose of this chapter is to give a brief summary of the observations we made on three important issues: (1) the restructuring of management associations and the managers' attitudes toward this trend; (2) the role of the union at the firm level and managers' attitudes toward the degree of satisfaction they get from their dealings with the union; and (3) the strike and public interest.

(1) The Restructuring of Management Associations and Managers' Attitudes Toward This Trend

The multiplicity of management associations is a well-known fact in the Province of Quebec. However, when a distinction is made between management associations and all businessmen's associations, the number is lower than is usually believed. As a matter of fact, the figures we have calculated set the number of management associations at around 380 in 1966.

The multiplicity of these associations should not lead us to believe that there is no connection between them. Over the last ten years, we have observed a trend toward their regrouping into federations or provincial associations.

In the forest industry, only two associations are dominant: the Quebec Forest Industry Association and the Canadian Pulp and Paper Association. In the mining sector, we also found only two associations: Quebec Metal Mining Association and Quebec Asbestos Mining Association. In the milk production industry, the Quebec Industrial Milk Producers Association represents all the

---

*Reproduced by permission of Information Canada.

concerns operating in this sector. In the construction industry, the Quebec Constructor Association and the Montreal Building Association are very influential within the Quebec Construction Federation. In the trucking industry, one important association, the Quebec Truckers Association, claims a membership that owns the majority of the 30,320 delivery vehicles registered in 1966. In the retail business, *La Fédération du detail et des Service Inc.*, comprises eleven management associations.

In the gasoline retailing business, small "fraternities" of gas station owners are affiliated to the *Fédération des Fraternités des Détaillants d'Essence du Quebec*. These federations or provincial associations are formed within the limits of a profession or a sector of the economic activity.

Regardless of the specific sector of activity in which they work, a sufficiently imposing number of top managers are grouped within two associations usually regarded as the most important and the best heard: The Canadian Manufacturers' Association (Quebec branch), and the *Conseil du Patronat du Québec*.

The recent creation of the *Conseil du Patronat du Québec* remains a major change at the level of management structures. As a matter of fact, at the instigation of the *Centre des Dirigeants de l'Entreprise* and some English Canadian employers, the *Conseil du Patronat* was set up early in 1965. One of the council's objectives is "to assure a permanent liaison between management groups in the Province of Quebec, better coordination of their activities and interventions and, especially, to organize the dynamic contribution of management to the economic activity of the milieu."

Management Attitudes Toward the Unification Effort of Management Associations

Most of the business concerns are members of associations that represent management's views and interests on a professional basis. To belong to these associations is considered necessary. The managers in their respective sector have to deal with issues that have a direct impact on their business. They are also members of interprofessional associations such as the Canadian Manufacturers' Association, or the *Centre des Dirigeants de l'Entreprise*. The issues brought up at this level take a more general character. However, the people we have interviewed in the large-scale businesses think that none of these interprofessional associations could unify and represent adequately the managerial world in the Province of Quebec. Nevertheless, quite a few among them believed that the *Conseil du Patronat du Québec* could play the role of a unique representative of the managerial world. On this issue, the top managers of the twelve large-scale organizations out of twenty-one support the orientation of the C.P.Q., three are opposed, and six did not take a stand.

Those who stand behind the C.P.Q. look upon this organization as a necessary force to counterbalance trade unions and government power, to make their viewpoint known to the government in economic and social matters, and to dispensate management training in the managers' ranks.

Those who do not support the C.P.Q.'s orientation and effort believe that the organizing of management into associations goes against the concept of entrepreneurship and competition, and that the interests of the managerial world are so diversified that it is impossible to represent them all under the banner of a huge federation.

(2) Management Attitudes Toward the Union at the Firm Level

In the eyes of the population, management as a collectivity appears to be opposed to trade unions as institutions. However, the managers at the level of each particular business concern, while opposing trade unions in general, may maintain good labour-management relations within their firm. We asked the managers about the way they perceive the union in their plants and the amount of satisfaction they get from their dealings with each particular union. In the medium and small business, the following statements, in order of importance, are those most applicable to the ways in which unions are perceived:

(i) The union is a valuable means of communicating the workers' views to management;

(ii) The union cooperates with management on maintaining discipline;

(iii) The union reduces worker productivity;

(iv) The union helps management to run the plant more efficiently;

(v) The union promotes harmony between management and the workers.

In the large-scale business, managers tend to look upon the union in the following manner:

(i) The union is a valuable means of communicating the workers' views to management;

(ii) The union cooperates with management on maintaining discipline;

(iii) The union distorts the views of the workers to the management;

(iv) The union helps stabilize wages and competition in the industry;

(v) The union interferes with efficient management of the plant.

Comparing the small and medium businesses to the large ones, we observed that twelve out of twenty-one owners or managers of small and medium businesses consider the union as a precious link between management and the work force, whereas only seven of eighteen think that way in large-scale organizations. Eleven managers out of twenty-one in small and medium businesses think that the union helps in maintaining discipline, whereas six top managers in large concerns believe this to be the case.

Nine managers or owners of small and medium businesses believe that the union contributes to reduce worker productivity; seven believe that a union is a means to increasing it.

In large-scale businesses, six managers affirm that the union distorts the views of the workers and five out of eighteen think that the union helps stabilize wages and competition in the industry.

"That the union promotes harmony between management and labour" is a statement that six managers/owners are inclined to apply to the union. In the case of small and medium business managers this statement comes in the fifth position. In large-scale organizations, the statement in the fifth position is that "the union interferes with the efficient management of the plant". Five top managers think this way, while two more or less agree.

From all the opinions expressed above, it is possible to conclude that only two statements apply most clearly to the union: (i) it is a valuable means in communicating workers' viewpoints to management; and (ii) it helps in maintaining discipline.

The Degree of Satisfaction that the Managers Get from their Dealings with Unions

The managers of each concern were in a position to appreciate the amount of satisfaction they derived from their relationships with the union at the time of the study, since all enterprises visited had been unionized for many years.

In small and medium businesses, eighteen managers or owners out of twenty-five interviewed were satisfied with the relationships they maintained with the union; six were more or less satisfied. In spite of that, their attitudes toward the union's claims and requirements were quite divided. As a matter of fact, thirteen managers or owners thought that the union's demands were reasonable, whereas twelve did not. All of them believed that unions do not interfere with efficient management of the plant and fifteen looked upon the union as the only communication link between the management and the work force.

There are many explanations for this positive attitude on the part of the managers. In the course of the last two negotiations, thirteen businesses could reach an agreement without the services of a mediator, and six had to call for mediation only once. Nineteen considered the union honest in its claims and fifteen concerns could negotiate collectively without the threat of a strike or a production slowdown.

In large-scale businesses, nine top managers out of eighteen consider their relationship with the union satisfactory. The other half consider it more or less satisfactory. Fourteen think that trade-union demands are very reasonable, except in some cases where the union makes exaggerated demands as a matter of bargaining strategy.

Third-party intervention is more frequent in large businesses than in medium and small ones. In the last two contract negotiations, eleven companies out of eighteen had to use the services of a mediator twice, four companies had to use them once, and three could do without them.

Threats of strikes have been made in twelve concerns, but only in eight did strikes in fact occur.

(3) The Strike and Public Interest

Managers and owners of all medium and small businesses are opposed
to a strike in the public sector, because of moral, economic and
social consequences brought on by a work stoppage in that sector.
Compulsory arbitration is the only solution to labour-management
conflicts in that sector, even though all managers agree that it
is not the best answer.

Nineteen managers out of twenty-five believe that resorting to
strike is not a useful means in collective bargaining. For the
majority of them, conflicts must be settled at the workers' level:
harmony must be developed by open dialogue. Quite a few managers
look upon compulsory arbitration as a means of settling interest
disputes in the private sector, provided that "specialists" in
the labour-management field are informed adequately to deal with
bargaining issues.

Those who favour an open dialogue between the parties are also
those who believe the roots of disputes reside in the absence of
communication. They express their attitude in the following manner: "We do not listen to each other for two reasons: ignorance
and individualism. The union and the management adopt too rigid
a position and each party tries to outdo the other."

In large-scale concerns, attitudes are not so clear cut. Thirteen top managers believe that the right to strike should be withdrawn in the public sector when essential services are at stake,
since the community has a right to get those services. For nine
managers out of twenty, the right to strike should not be granted
in the public sector. However, these persons are quite vague
when it comes to defining what an essential service is.

To replace the right to strike in the public sector, those
managers would put forth a series of mechanisms, such as fact-
finding boards, penalty systems, enforcing the existing legislation, and compulsory arbitration.

To the question about the threat of a strike as a means to
settle disputes, the majority of top managers interviewed answered
that such a threat is a useful means of arriving at an agreement,
but the occurrence of the strike is in fact a disaster for both
parties. These same managers, however, cannot propose a substitute for the strike. A few would like to see a stronger union
leadership in the plant, the development of new bargaining techniques, and problem-solving mechanisms at the plant level.

When these people are asked to spell out the reasons why collective bargaining breaks down before reaching an agreement, they
come up with three main categories of breakdowns (figures in parentheses indicate the number of managers who mention the item).

(i) Behaviour of individuals at the bargaining table:
-negotiators are incompetent;   (3)
-negotiators are too rigid;   (6)
-lack of mutual understanding;   (5)
-personality clash;   (4)
-attitudes of parties between rounds of
 negotiation;   (2)
-lack of communication;   (1)

-trade union radicalism;   (2)
(ii) Technical matters:
-the necessity of having the labour
 contract ratified by the membership;   (1)
-foreign influence on the trade union's
 demands; and   (5)
(iii) Institutional issues:
-job security.   (1)

13. Managerial Job Satisfaction: A Comparison Between Anglophone and Francophone Managers

by Rabindra N. Kanungo

Satisfaction with one's own job depends primarily on the inter-action between the characteristics of the job and those of the employee. Job characteristics refer to the various outcomes or benefits that the job provides for the satisfaction of employee needs. Employee characteristics refer to the nature of employee expectations, values and perceptions regarding the job outcomes. Job satisfaction is basically determined by the difference be-tween an employee's perception of his existing job outcomes and his beliefs or expectations about what these job outcomes should be for him.[1] When he feels satisfied, his job expectations are in line with his perceived job outcomes. However, a state of dissatisfaction with the job indicates that the perceived job outcomes fall short of the employee's expectation. Since job satisfaction is partly a function of employee expectations or beliefs about job outcomes, it is quite conceivable that two groups of employees holding the same job within an organization may have different job expectations, and consequently will exper-ience different levels of job satisfaction. It must be empha-sized that the beliefs and expectations of employees regarding job outcomes and their feelings of job satisfaction are deter-mined through a social comparison process.[2] Employees form opin-ions about what they should get from their job and how they should feel about their job by comparing themselves with members of the group to which they belong. Hence, differences among em-ployees with respect to their job expectations and job satisfac-tions may primarily stem from the nature of their reference groups.[3]

In most large corporations in Quebec, one finds the existence of two culturally distinct groups of employees often holding similar jobs, one of English-Canadian origin and the other of French-Canadian origin. It is quite conceivable that these two groups of Anglophone and Francophone employees, due to differen-ces in their cultural background provided by their own reference groups, may differ with respect to the levels of their need sat-isfactions on the job, given the same levels of job outcomes. In the present study, this possibility was explored within the motivational framework of Maslow's five need categories.[4] The major question raised was what differences exist between Franco-phone and Anglophone managers in a large corporation with respect to the satisfaction of various needs on the job.

A second purpose of the study was to explore differences, if any, in the levels of job satisfaction among male and female managers belonging to each of the sociolinguistic groups. Several

145

earlier studies have shown that women employees in general feel
more satisfied with several of their job outcomes than men.[5]
The reason for this finding may stem from the facts that cultural
conditioning of male and female roles at work has created a lower
expectation of job outcomes among female employees, and that given
the same job outcomes as males, the females may find the outcomes
closer to their expectations than males. The present study attempted to find out if similar trends are noticed among the female
managerial employees.

The Job Opinion Questionnaire

A questionnaire that was written in both the French and English
language, and pretested and developed earlier (Kanungo, Misra,
and Dayal, 1975; Siok, 1971) was used in the study to collect information on employees' satisfaction with various job factors.[6]
The first part of the questionnaire was designed to provide personal demographic data from the respondent, such as the level of
his position within the organizational hierarchy, his language-
group affiliation, sex, age, levels of education and income,
years of experience both within the organization and in the present job. In the second part, the respondents were required to
indicate on a seven-point scale the present level of satisfaction
or dissatisfaction in their job with respect to fifteen job factors or outcomes. The fifteen factors were listed in the questionnaire in a random order. These job factors represented the
goals for the satisfaction of five need categories as proposed
by Maslow (1954). Five job factors--comfortable working conditions, adequate earnings, fair pay, attractive fringe benefits,
and restricted hours of work--represented the "physiological"
need category. Two job factors--job security, and sound company
policy and practices--represented the "safety" need category.
The "social" need category was represented by three job factors--
good interpersonal peer relations on the job, considerate supervision, and technically competent supervision. The "ego" need
category included two factors--recognition, and responsibility
on the job. Finally, the "self-actualization" need category
included three factors--opportunity for advancement, achievement,
and interesting nature of work.
    Besides the fifteen job factors, the respondents were also
asked to indicate their overall job satisfaction on a similar
seven-point scale. For the purpose of scoring the responses,
ordinal weights of one to seven were assigned respectively to
the seven verbal levels on the scale: extremely satisfied, moderately satisfied, mildly satisfied, neutral, mildly dissatisfied,
moderately dissatisfied, and extremely dissatisfied.

Sample and Procedure

With the help of the questionnaire, data were collected from
lower-to middle-level management personnel of a large public

service organization in Montreal. The questionnaire was distributed by mail to a matched sample of 300 employees that included
an approximately equal number of Francophones (52 female and 97
male) and Anglophones (54 female and 97 male) holding the same-
level jobs within the organizational hierarchy.

Out of 300 employees who received the questionnaires, 216 (72
per cent) returned the completed questionnaire by mail. Nineteen
of these completed questionnaires indicated that the respondents
used both French and English as their mother tongue. Due to the
difficulty of classifying these 19 respondents in either Francophone or Anglophone categories, they were eliminated from the
analysis. Thus, a total of 197 respondents were included in the
sample. There were 82 Francophone (25 female and 57 male) and
115 Anglophone (43 female and 72 male) managers in the sample.
A breakdown of the sample with respect to various demographic
characteristics is presented in table 13.1. The last column of
table 13.1 reveals that the sample was composed of two-thirds
male and one-third female. Most of them belonged to adult and
middle-age categories. Approximately half of the sample had
college degrees and the other half were high school graduates.
More than 90 per cent of the sample belonged to the middle-class
income category. Although approximately three-fourths of the
sample were working for the organization for more than ten years,
the same proportion had less than five years' experience with
their present job. The above demographic characteristics of the
present sample resemble very closely what one usually finds in
lower to middle levels of management in large corporations.

Results

The main purpose of the study was to compare the job satisfactions of Francophone and Anglophone employees matched as far as
possible with respect to other demographic characteristics. The
characteristics of the two groups are presented in table 13.1.
Chi-square tests on the frequency data for each of the demographic
variables revealed significant relation in three cases. The
Francophone sample tended to have a greater number of respondents
who were younger (X^2 = 14.39, p < .01), had less experience with
the organization (X^2 = 10.81, p < .05), and had higher levels of
education (X^2 = 7.06, p < .05). These sample differences stem
from the fact that the organization under study, like many other
corporations in Montreal, considered English more suitable for
managerial jobs and a decade or two ago had mainly recruited
Anglophones for these jobs. The report of the Royal Commission
on Bilingualism and Biculturalism (1969) reveals this fact more
clearly for the Montreal area.[7] Recently, however, Francophones
coming out of universities with a good knowledge of English have
been recruited more and more to share these jobs with the Anglophones. This pattern of recruitment creates a condition where,
managerial job level held constant, one finds younger Francophone managers with less organizational experience but with
higher levels of education.

TABLE 13.1

Demographic Characteristics of the Sample, Expressed in
Percentages

	Franco-phone (N-82)	Anglo-phone (N-115)	Total (N-197)
Sex			
Male	69.51	62.61	65.48
Female	30.49	37.39	34.52
Age			
20-35 years	40.24	26.96	32.49
36-50 years	57.32	53.04	54.82
51-65 years	2.44	20.00	12.69
Education			
Less than high school	1.22	2.61	2.03
High school graduate	35.37	53.04	45.69
College graduate	63.41	44.35	52.28
Income level			
Below $10,000	23.17	14.78	18.27
$10,000-20,000	71.95	78.26	75.63
Above $20,000	4.88	6.69	6.10
Experience with present job			
Less than 5 years	78.05	68.69	72.59
5-10 years	18.29	27.83	23.86
More than 10 years	3.66	3.48	3.55
Experience with the organization			
Less than 5 years	15.85	9.57	12.18
5-10 years	18.29	13.04	15.23
11-20 years	32.93	20.87	25.89
More than 20 years	32.93	56.52	46.70

Job Satisfaction of Anglophone and Francophone Managers

Levels of actual satisfaction derived from the job with respect
to each of the five sets of job factors corresponding to the five
Maslow need categories were calculated for each respondent from
his responses to the second part of the questionnaire. A 2 x 5
analysis of variance on repeated measures was performed on the
satisfaction scores. There were two groups of Anglophone and
Francophone employees, and five need categories. The results of
the analysis revealed that only the main effect of linguistic
affiliation (F (1,195) = 22.79, $p <$ .01) was significant. Neither

FIGURE 13.1

Anglophone and Francophone Job Satisfaction Profile

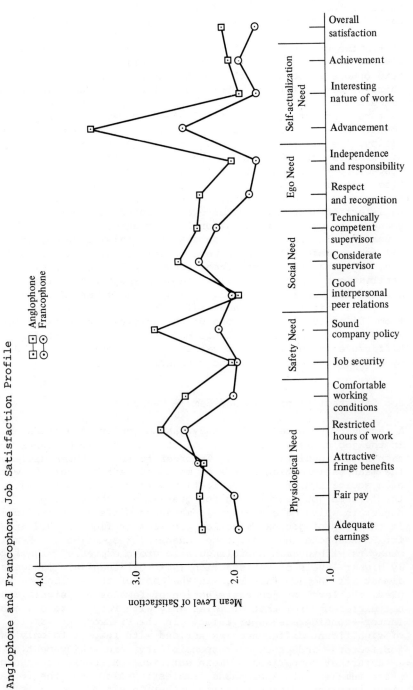

the need category effect nor the interaction effect was found to be significant. This suggested that the two groups of managers systematically differed with respect to their levels of satisfactions on the job. The manner in which the two groups differed can be seen from the satisfaction profiles presented in figure 13.1. The profiles present the mean satisfaction scores of each of the two groups for each job factor. Inspection of figure 13.1 clearly shows a higher level of satisfaction experienced by the Francophone respondents than by the Anglophone respondents. In thirteen out of fifteen job factors, the Francophone means indicated higher levels of satisfaction, and in the case of six job factors (adequate earning, $t = 2.95$; fair pay, $t = 2.63$; working conditions, $t = 2.63$; company policy, $t = 3.37$; respect and recognition, $t = 3.14$; advancement, $t = 4.01$) statistically significant differences were obtained at the .01 level of confidence. With respect to the overall job satisfaction, Francophone respondents also felt significantly more satisfied ($t = 2.96$, $p < .01$) than Anglophones. One might wonder whether the higher levels of job satisfaction among Francophones are related to their being younger in age and organizational experience, and more highly educated. In order to find an answer to this question, the overall job satisfaction scores were correlated with the respondent's age, organizational experience, educational level, and linguistic affiliation. Results revealed that, except for the linguistic affiliation variable ($r = .25$, $p < .01$), no other variable correlated significantly with overall job satisfaction (the rs ranged from .06 to .08). Thus, none of the demographic variables on which the two samples could not be matched can account for the difference in the levels of satisfaction experienced on the job by Francophone and Anglophone managers.

Job Satisfaction of Male and Female Managers

A secondary purpose of the study was to explore the differences in the job satisfaction levels of male and female managers within each sociolinguistic group. In order to reveal these differences, the mean satisfaction scores of male and female subgroups within each sociolinguistic classification were calculated for each of the fifteen job factors and for overall job satisfaction. The manner in which male and female managers differed is presented in the form of job satisfaction profiles in figures 13.2 and 13.3 for Francophone and Anglophone managers, respectively. Female managers within each sociolinguistic group expressed significantly higher levels of satisfaction ($p < .01$) than male managers on almost all the job factors. In the case of the Anglophone samples, the level of job satisfaction of females was significantly not different from that of males only with respect to one job factor--considerate supervision. In the Francophone sample, lack of significant difference was noticed with respect to only two job factors--independence-responsibility, and achievement.

    A further comparison of mean satisfaction scores of Francophone females with Anglophone females revealed that the former group experienced significantly higher levels of job satisfaction

FIGURE 13.2

Francophone Male and Female Job Satisfaction Profile

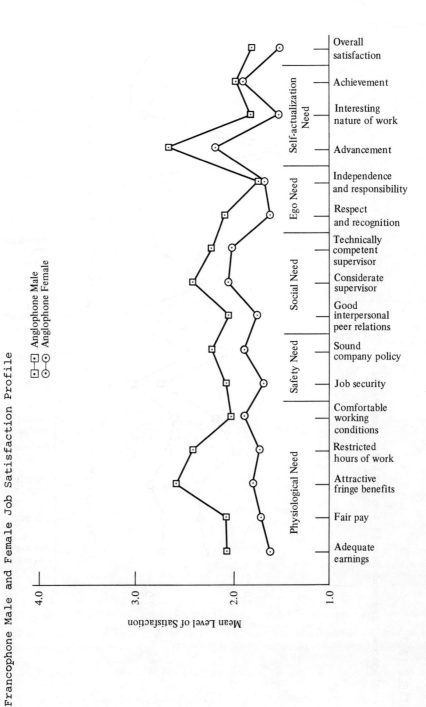

□—□ Anglophone Male
⊙—⊙ Anglophone Female

TABLE 13.3

Anglophone Male and Female Job Satisfaction Profile

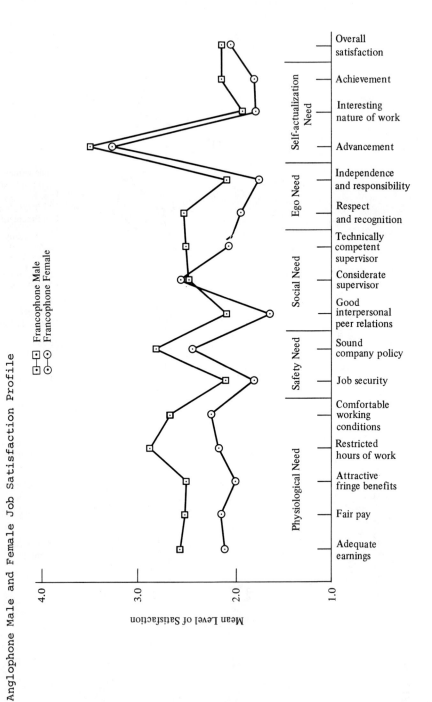

(p < .01) than the latter group. Only with respect to achievement, independence-responsibility, and technically competent supervision were the satisfaction levels of the two groups the same. Similar comparisons of Francophone and Anglophone males revealed significantly higher levels of satisfaction (p < .05) experienced by Francophone males in every case except security, fringe benefits, and considerate supervision. In the case of fringe benefits, Anglophone males showed a higher level of satisfaction than Francophone males.

Discussion and Conclusion

The results of the study reveal some interesting differences between Francophone and Anglophone, and between male and female managers with respect to levels of need satisfaction experienced on the job. Given similar job outcomes, Francophone managers seem to derive greater satisfaction on the job than Anglophone managers. Likewise, female managers seem to feel more contented on the job than male managers.

The male-female differences can be explained in terms of the cultural norms and sex-role prescriptions that have existed within the organizations for a long time. Until recently, the organizational norm has been to employ only males in supervisory positions. Women have been perceived as less aggressive, less forceful and less concerned with deriving their identity from their work. Hence they have been considered as less suitable for managerial jobs. As a result of such sex-related stereotypes, female managers may believe that they provide lower job input than men, and consequently may have developed lower levels of expectations for job outcomes. Their lower expectations, coupled with the perception that they are being equally treated with males in managerial positions, may have caused the greater job satisfaction among female managers noticed in this study.

The Francophone-Anglophone differences in job satisfaction can again be explained in terms of distinct cultural differences between the two groups. Anglophones are more likely to be products of the Protestant ethic type of socialization process that places greater emphasis on constantly striving for more than is currently possessed. This may be reflected in less satisfaction with the current job outcomes for the Anglophone managers. The Francophone manager's Catholic ethic and family-oriented training, on the other hand, emphasize enjoyment of and contentment with whatever one has. This may be reflected in a higher level of job satisfaction.

The differences between the two groups in the levels of job satisfaction can also be explained in terms of different levels of expected job outcomes. If satisfaction with job outcomes is a function of what one expects and what he actually gets,[8] the present results suggest that Francophone managers would expect lower job outcomes than Anglophone managers. Several reasons may account for the Francophone manager's expectation of lower outcomes. First, it may be a reflection of low need for achievement

Low-need achievers are known to look for either very easy or very difficult goals for themselves, and the case of Francophone managers could be an instance of setting easy goals or low aspiration levels. In fact, McClelland (1961) has reported lower levels of need for achievement among Francophone compared to Anglophone children.[9]   Secondly, it must be emphasized that the differences in job satisfaction observed in this study have to be understood within the larger context of the history of industrial development in the Province of Quebec. Industry in the province has been established and controlled primarily by Anglophone-dominated organizations; the Francophone's experience with managerial professions is somewhat more recent. English is still used as the primary business language and this has hindered Francophones in functioning more effectively in managerial jobs. Also, whereas the Anglophones placed a high priority on success in the managerial world, it was not long ago that Francophones frowned on this occupation[10]   and their elite tended to move away from any kind of commercial life.[11]   Above all, the Francophone education system was not geared, until recently, toward providing adequate management training.

These historical forces have shaped the psychological profiles of Francophone and Anglophone managers as revealed in this study. If Francophone managers have lower expectations of job outcomes, the reason may lie partly in the fact that they never perceived these outcomes as attainable goals for them within the organizational context.

Notes

1. See E.E. Lawler, *Pay and Organizational Effectiveness* (New York: McGraw-Hill, 1971). See also I.W. Porter, "A Study of Perceived Need Satisfactions in Bottom and Middle Management Jobs", *Journal of Applied Psychology* 45 (1961), pp. 1-10.

2. L. Festinger, "A Theory of Social Comparison Processes", *Human Relations* 7 (1954), pp. 117-140. See also E.E. Lawler, *Pay and Organizational Effectiveness*.

3. A.R. Korman, *Industrial and Organizational Psychology* (Englewood Cliffs, N.J.: Prentice-Hall, 1971).

4. A.H. Maslow, *Motivation and Personality* (New York: Harper, 1954).

5. See C.L. Hulin and P.C. Smith, "Sex Differences in Job Satisfaction", *Journal of Applied Psychology* 48 (1964), pp. 88-92. See also N.C. Morse, *Satisfactions in the White-Collar Job* (Ann Arbor: University of Michigan, Institute for Social Research, Survey Research Centre, 1953).

6. See R.N. Kanungo, S. Misra, and I. Dayal, "Relations of Job Involvement to Perceived Importance and Satisfaction of Employee Needs", *International Review of Applied Psychology*, 1975 (in

press).   See also R.B. Siok, "Job Motivation: An Eclectic Approach", M.B.A. thesis, Faculty of Management, McGill University, 1971.

7.   Report of the Royal Commission on Bilingualism and Biculturalism, *111 The Work World* (Ottawa: Queen's Printer, 1969).

8.   See A.J. Spector, "Expectations, Fulfillment, and Morale", *Journal of Abnormal and Social Psychology* 52 (1956), pp. 51-56.

9.   D.C. McClelland, *The Achieving Society* (New York: Irvington Books, 1961).

10. K. Parenteau, "The Impact of Industrialization in Quebec", in *Marketing: Canada,* ed. I. Litvak and B. Mallen (Toronto: McGraw-Hill, 1964).

11. S.M. Jamieson, "French and English in the Institutional Structure of Montreal: A Study of the Social and Economic Division of Labor" (M.A. thesis, McGill University, 1938).

14. Certification of Bargaining Units*

by E.E. Herman

"The Bargaining Units" study prepared for the Task Force on Labour Relations had the following objectives: (1) to evaluate the
effect of public policy on the determination of appropriateness
of bargaining units; (2) to analyze the legislative framework
within which the Canadian boards operate, particularly the division of jurisdiction among eleven different boards; (3) to investigate the impact of the Canadian constitutional allocation of
legislative powers on the natural evolution of bargaining units;
(4) to review recent developments in the area of collective bargaining structures; (5) to evaluate Canadian public policy toward
multiemployer bargaining units; (6) to examine public policy toward craft employees and to consider alternative bargaining units
for crafts within the collective bargaining framework; and (7)
to supplement the bargaining unit data published by this author
and contained in the book *The Determination of the Appropriate
Bargaining Unit by Labour Relations Boards in Canada*.[1]
   For all the diversity in structure, content and practice of
labour relations laws within Canada, there is a common problem
confronting all the different administrative agencies involved in
administrating the law. This problem is the determination of appropriateness of collective bargaining units. In view of this,
it is important to understand just what the term *appropriate bargaining unit* means and how such units can be chosen or identified
by the boards responsible for administrating labour legislation.
   Canadian labour relations acts do not specifically define the
work *appropriate* as it is to be applied in a particular law.
Webster's Third International Dictionary defines the word as
'especially suitable', 'fit', and 'proper'. It suggests *fit* as
a synonym and defines it as 'adapted to an end, object or design'.
Thus, the appropriate bargaining unit can vary according to what
objects one may have in mind. To use an extreme example, if one
wished to promote freedom of choice and self-determination, an
appropriate unit might be determined by allowing each worker to
choose his own representative. Thus, the role of the word *appropriate* is being strongly influenced by objectives sought. The
criteria employed by labour relations boards in determining appropriate bargaining units are those that, in the judgement of
the boards, best serve the policies and principles of the societies writing the laws. The different public policy objectives
examined in this part of the study were: laissez-faire, maximum
freedom of choice, stability of collective bargaining relation-

---

*Reproduced by permission of Information Canada.

ships, minimization of disturbance of existing institutions, maximization of national economic performance, and protection of the public interest. In a pluralistic society, these objectives may be followed concurrently; however, too much weight given to one objective could easily lead to conflict with another. For instance, stressing freedom of choice could lead to many small bargaining units, this in turn contributing to industrial strife and possibly disturbing the stability of collective bargaining relationships. Although criteria could be incorporated in legislation to realize the above objectives, it was concluded that the administrators of the legislation would still require broad discretionary powers in the exercise of their duties. To a significant extent they would still have to be given the authority to make value judgements in reaching their decisions.

In this study, an appropriate bargaining unit has been defined as one that best accomplishes chosen public economic and social objectives. The nature of society, in both Canada and the United States, suggests that the most effective goals of public policy should be to determine bargaining units that would reflect as much as possible the desire of the private parties without significantly disregarding national objectives.

The key term for board certification practices in determining appropriateness of bargaining units is *flexibility*. In view of the dynamic nature of the economy, no set rules can be established for the determination of appropriateness. The unit that was appropriate a year ago may be inappropriate today. Thus, the boards, in discharging their duties, must be willing to review on a continuous basis the application of criteria for the determination of appropriate bargaining units.

In conclusion, it was suggested that the desired social and economic objectives can be furthered by permitting the parties a considerable degree of freedom to experiment with bargaining units that at times may depart from the structure of certified units.

In another chapter of the study it was indicated that divided jurisdiction among eleven boards, and compulsory conciliation are deterrents to the natural evolution of bargaining units.

It was concluded that provisions for compulsory conciliation, together with the existence of provincial jurisdictions, create another impediment to the rationalization of Canada's bargaining structure. Such arrangements hamper the formation of actual interprovincial multiplant and multiemployer bargaining units and may also interfere with the development of various types of informal relationships on an interprovincial basis, relationships that could result in the extension of informal bargaining units across provincial boundaries. It was recommended that compulsory conciliation provisions should either be removed or, at the minimum, legislative arrangements should be made for conciliation on an interprovincial basis. The following statement by Woods rationalizes very well the compulsory conciliation conclusions contained in this chapter.

If compulsory conciliation were dropped from Canadian policy, even with provincial certification the parties would be free to merge bargaining units and to negotiate, engage in work stoppage and sign agreements without too much concern for the demands of the law. If we insist, however, on provincial jurisdiction and retain the present system of compulsory conciliation with its suspension of the work stoppage, part of the natural evolution of collective bargaining institutions will be prevented and much ingenuity will be displayed in attempts to evade the law.[2]

Also, in this part of the study the absence in Canada of a centralized labour relations board with the authority over companies with interprovincial industrial relations interests has been critically evaluated. It was suggested that the creation of such a national board would be a move toward the elimination of industrial relations conflict revolving around the issue of interprovincial bargaining units. Also, such a board would be more in step with the dynamic forces existing in the economic and industrial relations environment. Some of the forces are: changing technology, an expanding area of competition, interdependence of local markets through pressures for wage uniformity, company-wide contracts for firms operating in heterogeneous markets, and better coordination of bargaining by unions and employers.

It was pointed out, however, that centralization of labour relations in one national board has its drawbacks and that there are some benefits in decentralization. For instance, under provincial jurisdiction cases can be processed faster, the boards are more aware of the circumstances surrounding each case, and there can be more initiative for experimentation. Also, centralization implies local authority, whereas decentralization draws us nearer to the edeal of self-determination.

Although the arguments for provincial autonomy in industrial relations have some merits for smaller local firms, these would not necessarily be applicable to larger firms with interprovincial industrial relations interests. Heterogeneous jurisdiction may complicate and confuse collective bargaining in such firms.

Decentralization of industrial relations may also have economic consequences, encouraging location of industry on the basis of favourable labour legislation rather than on economic grounds. Decentralization can probably be viewed as a roadblock to the movement of dynamic elements in the economy. In view of this it was suggested that firms with interprovincial industrial relations interests be located under the jurisdiction of one centralized national labour relations board. This, however, raised the question of the means to be used toward the achievement of this objective. A number of alternatives were contemplated.

One possibility suggested was to bring industrial relations disputes under section 91 of the BNA act. Section 91 embraces areas under the exclusive powers of the Parliament of Canada.

Another alternative that was considered would be for Parliament to designate some of the industries "...to be for the general advantage of Canada or two or more provinces".[3] This would locate such industries under federal jurisdiction. The short-coming of this solution is the placing of a total industry, embracing both large and small firms, under a national board. Another drawback is that a parliamentary declaration takes over much more than industrial relations.

Still another choice considered was to locate industrial relations under concurrent powers. This would permit both the federal and provincial legislatures to assume responsibility, although the federal law under such a system would be supreme. There are a number of disadvantages to the concurrent power approach. Archibald Cox states that there is some justification for local control,[4] but on the basis of U.S. experience he prefers exclusive over concurrent powers, nevertheless. He cites the following reasons for his preference:

(1)   There would be interference with collective bargaining as "envisaged by national law if the states are permitted to impose additional obligations upon employees in labor unions".[5]
(2)   In some cases it would be too difficult to make a distinction between concurrent local laws which affect the implication and purposes of national law. Decisions on these matters could lead to lengthy litigations. Meanwhile the parties "would be left to build a highly delicate relationship upon shifting sands".[6]
(3)   The operation of local labour statutes affecting industries subject to national law "would destroy the uniformity and convenience which are part of the justification for federal legislation".[7]
(4)   Such systems could encourage interprovincial competition, "in deciding cases and writing statutes most attractive to the migration of industry".[8]
(5)   Labour legislation "lacks the degree of precision which is necessary before anyone can say whether the provincial and national policies are the same. Too much administrative discretion is required,"[9] which in turn would lead to many different interpretations.

Centralization and expansion of national authority in the field of industrial relations could take place through another method. The common-law provinces could assign to the Parliament of Canada authority in the area of industrial relations. This could be accomplished under section 94 of the BNA act. Since Quebec does not have the constitutional authority or the desire to give up any of its labour relations responsibilities, and the other large Canadian provinces share Quebec's sentiment on this subject, this solution is not very meaningful.

Still another avenue of action that could be utilized for the centralization of industrial relations is the court system. In order to take this particular approach one of the following procedures would be necessary: (1) a lawsuit challenging provincial jurisdiction; (2) federal legislation; or (3) "a constitutional reference framed to illicit opinions about federal authority over labour relations in interprovincial industries".[10]

The major obstacles to the implementation of any of the suggested approaches are not the legal barriers (which nevertheless are significant), but the difficulties in obtaining consent of the provinces for any of the above proposals.

It was suggested that the provinces could be persuaded to support the concept of centralization and the formation of a national board if they were invited to participate actively in the creation and operation of such a board. Also, an extensive public relations and education campaign would be necessary to acquaint the public and provincial officials with the advantages of centralization for the provincial jurisdictions and for Canada.

To conclude, the dynamic pressures in the industrial relations environment, outlined in the task force report, make a strong case for centralization of industrial relations under the auspices of a national board.

Another part of the study examined North American trends in the field of collective bargaining structures. In general, the analysis indicated a trend toward larger bargaining units and the increasing centralization of decision making among both unions and management. These trends in the structure of collective bargaining stem, to a large extent, from the attempts of the private parties, unions, and management, to adjust to a changing economic and technological environment and to either initiate or respond to changes in the realm of industrial relations. The growth of large, diversified corporations through mergers and acquisitions increased the number of unions dealing with the corporate centre and this tends to reduce the relative bargaining power of each union. The unions respond by creating alliances and cooperating in their bargaining efforts. Unions increase their bargaining power by using whipsawing tactics and selective strikes. Employers respond by forming alliances of their own and assisting the victims of selective strikes. The growing complexity of collective bargaining issues puts the effective dealing with many conflict situations beyond the ability of part-time local union officials. As a result, a large part of the bargaining function is shifted from the local to the national headquarters. All of these developments are a part of the dynamics of collective bargaining. Furthermore, all of them are related to the structure of bargaining.

The "bargaining structure" has been considered, in its broad sense, as including various types of informal as well as formal relationships. Thus, many of the structural changes examined involved the creation of larger and informal bargaining units, even though the structure of certified units remained unchanged. From this, it follows that while the certification decisions of labour relations boards can affect the structure of bargaining, the boards do not exercise complete control over this emerging structure. Certified bargaining units may constitute the basic "building blocks", out of which the structure of bargaining is built, but there remains much leeway for unions and employers to alter the structure by agreeing to establish bargaining units different than those certified.

Another chapter of the task force study examined the objectives of public policy toward multiemployer bargaining. It was concluded that in order to preserve the advantages of multiemployer bargaining for the bargaining parties and the economy, while protecting the public against its potential cost, it is necessary to have flexibility in both the statutory framework and decision making by administrative agencies. Legislation banning multi-employer bargaining is to be avoided, as is a general bias for or against certification of such units either through statutory provisions or the policies of labour relations boards. Public policy should encourage experimentation by private parties in the establishment of bargaining structures best suited for their needs, and this freedom to experiment should extend to multi-employer units. Only if it is likely that multiemployer bargain-ing units will adversely affect the public interest and the ad-verse effects are judged to outweigh the potential benefits to the bargaining parties, should certification of such units be denied. Moreover, if multiemployer bargaining units are likely to have an adverse effect on the public interest, it is worth asking whether this undesirable effect can be controlled by policy measures other than maintaining a fragmented bargaining structure.

At the time that this task force report was being prepared for submission, Canadian public policy regarding the certification of multiemployer bargaining units was in need of extensive reevalu-ation. While there was some variation in legislation and in the certification practices by the different boards, in general the boards displayed too little flexibility and had too much of a predisposition to deny certification of multiemployer bargaining units. In view of the available evidence, it was concluded that future legislation should vest in the boards broader discretion-ary authority regarding certification of multiemployer units. Furthermore, the boards should effectively utilize these powers, judge petitions for multiemployer certifications on a case by case basis, and renounce their bias against the certification of this type of bargaining unit. Finally, there should be adequate legal procedure for modifying the multiemployer bargaining unit after it has been certified. Absence of legislative authority for changes in the status of multiemployer units following their certification can partly explain the reluctance of Canadian boards to certify them.

Still another part of this study addressed itself to the various issues related to craft bargaining units. The interests and attitudes of the public, the industrial craft unions, and the employer with respect to craft bargaining units were evalu-ated. A complete section was devoted to legislation governing craft certification and to the process utilized by labour rela-tions boards in determining the appropriateness of craft bar-gaining units. The willingness of the boards to carve craft units out of industrial units was also examined. Another section of this particular chapter of the report reviewed craft certifi-cation criteria applied by labour boards. Various craft certi-fication options available to the boards were also evaluated. Finally, a new approach toward the craft issue in the form of certification of multi-craft bargaining units was considered.

The certification of multicraft bargaining units as an alternative to the certification of single-craft units has a number of
advantages, in that it would permit craft certification without
the costs presently associated with the emergence of such units.
Some of these costs can be identified as hostility of crafts
toward technological change, narrow seniority units, restriction
of interfirm mobility of labour, and jurisdictional conflicts.

However, the multicraft unit would also have some drawbacks.
Under such a unit, jurisdictional conflict that previously took
place outside the unit would probably be transferred into the
unit. Also, the problem of transition from the present structure
into the new structure would be enormous. Hostility of existing
crafts toward such units would also have to be taken into account.
Although initially craft unions would probably oppose a proposal
that would alter their status quo, in the long run the crafts
could benefit from this particular approach.

Certification of multicraft units would pose a new set of
difficulties for labour relations boards in terms of definition
of a craft and the determination of appropriateness of craft
bargaining units. These problems, however, are not insurmountable.

To conclude, the multicraft approach does not suggest a drastic break with the past. There are situations where a single-
craft unit or the inclusion of craft employees in an industrial
unit may be more appropriate than the determination of a multicraft unit, but there may be many other cases where the formation
of the multicraft unit is the most appropriate approach for the
bargaining parties and the economy.

In conclusion, flexibility, innovation, creativity, and experimentation should be reflected by labour relations boards in the
area of certification of bargaining units.

Notes

1. E.E. Herman, *The Determination of the Appropriate Bargaining
Unit by Labour Relations Boards in Canada* (Ottawa: Department of
Labour, 1966).

2. A.D. Woods and S. Ostry, *Labour Policy and Labour Economics
in Canada* (Toronto: Macmillan, 1962), p. 20.

3. F. Scott, *Federal Jurisdiction over Labour Relations,* paper
delivered to the 11th Annual Conference of the McGill University
Industrial Relations Centre (Montreal, September 1959), p. 44.

4. Archibald Cox, address given at the 7th Annual Meeting of the
National Academy of Arbitration (Washington, D.C., 22 January
1954), and reprinted in *Professional Labor Arbitration, 1948-1954,*
ed. Jean T. McKelvey, pp. 106-118.

5. *Ibid.*, p. 115.

6. *Ibid*.

7. *Ibid*.

8. *Ibid*.

9. *Ibid*.

10. F. Scott, *Federal Jurisdiction*, p. 46.

15. Compulsory Boards of Conciliation*

by W.B. Cunningham

Introduction

Since 1907, compulsory conciliation boards have been a feature of
Canadian public policy. Commonly, legislation has prohibited a
work stoppage until after a tripartite board has investigated,
conciliated, and reported its recommended terms of settlement.
By 1950, these compulsory boards had become the second stage,
after a conciliation officer, in a rather rigid two-stage compulsory procedure.
   During the 1950s a growing number of critics directed their
attacks on the compulsory board stage, and in the following decade, several provinces substantially altered their policy in the
direction of deemphasizing the role of compulsory boards.
   Some provinces made formal legislative changes; others changed
their administrative practices. In the first category were British Columbia, Quebec, and Nova Scotia. British Columbia established a new form of government intervention; Quebec abolished
compulsory boards; and Nova Scotia made them available only at
the request of both parties. In the second category were New
Brunswick, Ontario, and Manitoba, where the exercise of administrative discretion made conciliation boards much less common than
in earlier years.
   Critics of the compulsory boards had stressed, among other
things, that the second compulsory stage reduced the effectiveness of the conciliation officers at the first stage of compulsory intervention. Such officers functioned, the critics argued,
in a situation in which neither party to a dispute felt the pressure of an impending strike, since the worst that could follow a
failure to agree was the second-stage compulsory board. Defend-
ers of the conciliation boards feared that their elimination
might increase the number of strikes, and pointed to specific
instances in which boards had brought about agreements, directly
or on the basis of board recommendations. Studies of the conciliation experience were scarce.
   The legislative changes in some provinces during the 1960s
make it possible to compare the conciliation results before the
changes and after them. There are two obvious questions to ask
about the effects of the reduced reliance upon the traditional
compulsory boards: (1) What was the result on the number of
disputes settled by conciliation officers? and (2) What was the
result on the number, duration, and size of strikes?

---

*Reproduced by permission of Information Canada.

Answers to such questions are never fully satisfactory and require personal judgements with which all persons may not fully agree. A lack of coordination in the recording of strike statistics and conciliation results makes the second question particularly difficult. And differences in record keeping, definitions, legislation, and administrative policies require much caution in any attempt to draw interprovincial comparisons.

The next sections of this chapter will discuss some results for Nova Scotia, New Brunswick, and Ontario respectively. For Ontario the results are presented in a somewhat different form and in more detail than for the two smaller provinces.

Nova Scotia

In 1964, Nova Scotia amended its Trade Union Act to make the appointment of conciliation boards conditional upon the request of both parties to a dispute. If there was no such request and thus no board, the legal restraint on a work stoppage ceased twenty-one days after the conciliation officer made his report to the minister. After 1964, the compulsory second stage did not exist. In the seven years before the change, the province appointed an average of sixteen boards annually, whereas only half this number were appointed in total during the next three years.

What was the effect on the number of settlements achieved by conciliation officers? In the seven years prior to March 1964, when boards were compulsory, the disputing parties reached agreements with the help of officers in 65.2 per cent of the disputes that went to conciliation. In the following three years, when boards were no longer compulsory, there was an 83.8 per cent settlement rate with no intervention beyond the conciliation officer. The Nova Scotia experience was consistent with the criticism that the boards impeded the effectiveness of the officers.

This sharp increase in the settlement rate does not necessarily mean that the officers were more directly effective than when they had functioned within the impending shadow of a conciliation board. Some of the settlements were obtained after the officer had withdrawn his services, and a few were obtained after a legal strike. But if the average pre-1964 settlement rate had applied to the 173 disputes after 1964, there would have been about another thirty-two boards appointed in those three years. Assuming that the purpose of the boards is to obtain agreements and lessen the number of strikes, the absence of these boards that otherwise would have been appointed had no noticeable adverse impact in Nova Scotia. Without the boards the parties reached settlements either with the help of officers or by themselves after the officers withdrew.

In the three years after the change, there were twenty-eight disputes not reported as settled at the officer stage. Of these, fifteen lapsed, about double the number at this stage for any previous three-year period. This suggests that the compulsory boards may have prolonged the existence of some bargaining relationships

that could not be sustained apart from the formal board requirements. In the remaining thirteen disputes the officer had withdrawn his services, the bargaining relationship continued, but
no agreement had been reached by the end of the reporting year.
In general, the eventual outcome of such disputes, unless a strike
results, goes unrecorded in official government records.

What about the effect of the change on the number of strikes
that followed conciliation?

TABLE 15.1

Strike Activity in Nova Scotia Before and After Reduction in
Number of Conciliation Boards

Years	Total Disputes	Number of Boards	Number of Strikes (conciliation completed)
1961-63	171	63	11
1965-67	173	8	13

Source: *Annual Reports*, Department of Labour, Nova Scotia.

Table 15.1 summarized the results for two three-year periods, one
before and one after the 1964 change. One of the thirteen strikes
in the latter period occurred after a conciliation board had reported; thus only twelve strikes followed directly after the
efforts of a conciliation officer. It is abundantly clear that
the sharp reduction in the number of boards did not lead to any
surge in strike activity.

New Brunswick

A departure from the traditional two stages of compulsory conciliation occurred first in New Brunswick. Without formally amending
its Labour Relations Act, a significant change in administrative
policy became effective early in 1962. For a short period, the
Minister of Labour followed a policy of refusing all requests for
boards. This was changed after a few months to a policy that
could be called "no boards except..." The exceptions were not
explicitly formulated. In general, if both parties requested a
board, or if there was a request by one party in a dispute of
more than ordinary public interest, a board was more likely to be
appointed. The parties did not know beforehand whether or not
the minister would grant a request. The fiscal year ending 31
March 1963 was the first full year of experience with the new
policy.

New Brunswick had never appointed many boards but the change
in policy after 1962 is obvious. Comparing the five years before
and after the change shows a drop from thirty-nine boards to only
five. The percentage of settlements reached without the disputes'

going to the board stage increased from 65.9 per cent to 80.2 per cent, about the same as in Nova Scotia. Thus, the New Brunswick experience was also consistent with the criticism that the boards impeded the effectiveness of the officers.

There are three further comments to make about these results.

(1)   The increase in the settlement rate after the change in policy is less if agreements reached after a strike are excluded. This calculation would show an average settlement rate of about 77.5 per cent for Nova Scotia and 75.1 per cent for New Brunswick. These still represent increases of about nine to twelve percentage points.

(2)   Reported figures on conciliation results must be treated with much caution. The general point may be illustrated with reference to the forty-eight disputes reported for New Brunswick in 1967. Seven of these referred to one union's seeking a contract with seven garages in one city, and were dealt with unsuccessfully by one officer. In reality it was one dispute. If recorded as one dispute, the settlement rate for that year would have been 81.0 per cent instead of 70.8 per cent, and the five-year average rate would have been 82.7 per cent instead of the 80.2 per cent stated above.

(3)   An earlier study of the New Brunswick experience, covering nearly ten years prior to 1957, showed an average settlement rate of only 45.3 per cent at the officer stage.   This suggests that the parties and the conciliation officers have developed, through experience, a greater maturity and skill in collective bargaining.

TABLE 15.2

Strike Activity in New Brunswick Before and After Reduction in Number of Conciliation Boards

Years	Total Disputes	Number of Boards	Number of Strikes (conciliation completed)
1958-1962	138	39	8
1962-1967	197	5	13

Source: *Annual Reports*, Department of Labour, New Brunswick.

Table 15.2 summarized the New Brunswick experience with strikes following completion of the compulsory conciliation stages. From the thirteen strikes in the period following the change in policy on appointing boards, it is necessary to subtract three disputes that went to boards (or enquiry commissions) after the conciliation officer's report. There were only ten strikes following the officer stage only. Since the total number of disputes in the second period was about 41 per cent higher than in the first period, it is again clear that the change in policy

did not generate more strikes. As in Nova Scotia, the parties
continued to reach agreements in the relative absence of compulsory conciliation boards and without any significant change in
work stoppages.

Ontario

Between 1958 and 1967, Ontario made two major changes in its reliance upon compulsory boards. The first was a result of unrest
in the construction industry. An amendment to the Labour Relations Act in 1962, following recommendations in the Goldenberg
Report, eliminated the compulsory board stage in the construction industry. Since October 1962, boards have been appointed
only when requested by both parties.

In February 1966, a change in administrative policy moved
Ontario practices in the direction of those introduced earlier
in New Brunswick and Manitoba. The minister began to make much
more use of his discretionary power to refuse requests for boards.
There was no explicit criterion for determining in which disputes to appoint a board. In general, they were more likely to
be appointed in public interest disputes such as those in utilities and municipalities; in pattern-setting disputes; and in
some disputes where the parties were seeking a first agreement.
But in none of these was it certain that the minister would
appoint a board.

Ontario changed its policy because of a developing disenchantment with the usefulness of conciliation boards. The delays implicit in the procedures frequently irritated the parties,
particularly the unions. There was a growing belief that the
easy availability of boards reduced the prestige and influence
of the officers, that the two-tier conciliation requirement had
become too rigid and formal, and that too often the parties used
the procedures in an effort to obtain a bargaining advantage
rather than a settlement.

In Ontario there was an increasing number of so-called wash-
out reports, ones that contained no recommended terms of settlement. The usefulness of a report with recommendations is an
open question. There is no question, however, that it is much
easier to write a report that makes no judgement about the issues. By making specific recommendations, a board chairman runs
the high risk of eventually antagonizing one of the parties and
of becoming unacceptable as a chairman of future boards. When
fees from board appointments become a significant income supplement, as they had become for some chairmen of boards in
Ontario, writing wash-out reports reduces the risk of future
unacceptability and the consequent loss of income from this
source. Furthermore, if a chairman does not write recommendations, neither party nominee is under any pressure to write a
dissenting minority report, as he would be if a board made recommendations that were unacceptable to the party he represented.
Whatever the reasons may have been, and it appears that the
above influences were operative, wash-out reports had become

common in Ontario. No accurate data on their number were available, but estimates place them at more than 50 per cent in some years. The Department of Labour saw no value in such reports. Their frequency added to the disenchantment with conciliation boards.

When an officer was unable to settle a dispute, the Minister of Labour had to decide for or against the appointment of a board (except for a small number of disputes that lapsed, usually less than 1 per cent). In 1959, the minister referred 86 per cent of such active disputes to boards; by 1967, only about 14 per cent went to boards. In total there were only 102 board dispositions in 1967, whereas the annual average for 1958-1962 was 372 boards. These figures reflect the significant change in the use of ministerial discretion.

An examination of the Ontario experience for the ten-year period up to 1968 showed that conciliation officers reported settlements in slightly more than 50 per cent of the disputes. Apart from 1961, their settlement rate showed a surprisingly small variation: 46.6 per cent in 1965 and 54.7 per cent in 1959 was the range. (There was doubt about the reliability of the 1961 figures.) Despite the major reductions in the number of disputes legally required to go to boards, first in the construction industry (1962) and then generally (1966), the results showed no noticeable effect on the ability of officers to achieve direct settlements. In this respect the Ontario experience, contrary to that of Nova Scotia and New Brunswick, does not provide empirical support for the criticism that compulsory boards adversely affected the success rate of conciliation officers.

Table 15.3 is relevant to the question of the extent to which work stoppages reflected the reduction in compulsory boards. In 1966, the department began its new policy of ministerial discretion. In that year, the number of strikes and the number of employees involved were much higher than in the preceding years. Except for 1958, the duration in man days was also much higher. In 1967, although the first two measures declined, all three measures remained high relative to previous years. Thus during the first two years following the new policy, Ontario had more work stoppages, involving more workers and a greater time loss, than in any previous two-year period.

There are many possible explanations for these results apart from the reduction in the general availability of conciliation boards. The table clearly indicates that the Ontario results in 1966 and 1967, when expressed as a percentage of the totals for all Canada, were usually a smaller proportion than previously.

With the exception of 1959, the number of stoppages in Ontario was a smaller percentage of total stoppages in Canada in 1966 and 1967 than in earlier years. The same is true for the number of employees involved. Indeed, in 1967 the 64,357 employees involved, while constituting the third highest number for the period, represented only 15.6 per cent of the Canadian total, a much smaller percentage than found in any previous year. An inspection of the third measure, duration in man days, shows that the time lost in 1966, as a percentage of the Canadian total, was the second lowest,

TABLE 15.3

Work Stoppages Calculated for Ontario and Canada, from 1958 to 1967

Years	Number			Employees Involved		Duration in Man Days	
	Canada (1)	Ontario (2)	2—1	Ontario	% of All in Canada	Ontario	% in All in Canada
1958	259	132	51.0	58,467	53.2	1,918,030	67.9
1959	216	104	48.1	25,540	27.4	267,730	12.6
1960	274	156	56.9	24,085	49.0	337,370	45.9
1961	287	166	57.8	39,817	40.8	644,770	47.8
1962	311	172	55.3	32,985	44.6	424,590	29.6
1963	332	181	54.5	37,744	45.8	364,190	39.7
1964	343	188	54.8	52,442	51.5	712,095	44.9
1965	501	269	53.4	92,633	54.1	1,343,001	57.0
1966	617	299	48.5	123,450	30.0	1,428,098	27.6
1967	438	220	50.2	64,357	15.6	1,631,260	40.6

Sources: For 1958 to 1965 the *Carrothers-Palmer Report*, table 37, p. 228; for 1966 to 1967, the Ontario Department of Labour. Figures for Canada, and the calculation of Ontario percentages, are based on figures reported monthly in the *Labour Gazette*.

and in 1967 the fifth lowest, of the ten years covered. Obviously the increases in the absolute values of the Ontario measures during 1966 and 1967 were part of the national pattern of increased stoppages, but relatively, the Ontario increases were smaller.

To what extent the new policy on conciliation boards was responsible for the lower relative increase is an open question. What can be stated positively is that the evidence does not indicate any relative increase in the number and degree of work stoppages in the two years after the minister severely reduced the number of disputes referred to boards.

Construction: Ontario

Usually there is not enough information to classify conciliation results by industry. The Carrothers-Palmer *Report of a Study on the Labour Injunction in Ontario* (vol. 1) provided detailed information for the 1958-1965 calendar years, permitting the selection and rearrangement of the data that follows.

Following the abolition of compulsory boards in 1962, there was a decline in the proportion of direct settlements achieved by conciliation officers. Prior to 1963, they obtained settlements in about 45 per cent to 55 per cent of the construction industry disputes. In 1963 and 1964, this rate fell to about 32 per cent, then rose again in 1965 to its earlier level.

There is no obvious explanation for this drop in the officer settlement rate. It does not appear to be the result of either the two-year bargaining pattern or economic trends in the industry. With their newly won freedom from compulsory boards, the parties had to readjust their bargaining tactics. Prior to the change a failure to agree at the officer stage meant the likely appointment of a board with its inherent time-consuming procedures and the uncertain timing and content of its report. After the change a failure to agree meant the prospect of a work stoppage. An agreement requires the consent of two parties; one party alone can prevent an agreement. It appears that at least one party, perhaps the unions, feared a possible work stoppage less than it feared a conciliation board.

In 1965, the officers again achieved settlements at about the rate obtained before boards were abolished. The two previous years may have been merely a transition period during which the parties were experimenting within the new, less restrictive legal framework.

There were few boards in the construction industry after they became voluntary (see table 15.4). The ones appointed in 1964 and 1965 were successful in reaching agreements.

Work Stoppages: Construction

It has already been pointed out that after compulsory boards were abolished in late 1962, conciliation officers were less successful in directly settling disputes in this industry. This means that in 1963 and 1964, a larger proportion of disputes reached

TABLE 15.4

Board Dispositions in the Construction Industry
in Ontario, from 1958 to 1965

Year	Number of Boards	% of All Ont. Boards	% Settled
1958	41	7.9	46.3
1959	33	6.4	48.5
1960	20	4.4	40.0
1961	43	13.3	44.2
1962	25	3.8	44.0
1963	8	0.5	25.0
1964	5	0.7	100.0
1965	1	0.1	100.0

Source: *Carrothers-Palmer Report*, tables 30 and 32.

the stage where work stoppages were no longer unlawful. An obvious question is whether there was any substantial change in the
number and size of stoppages in the construction industry in
these two years.

Table 15.5 shows that the absolute number of stoppages in construction in 1963 remained the same as in the previous year, and
in 1964 the number was slightly lower. In these two years,
these stoppages were a falling proportion of all stoppages.

TABLE 15.5

Work Stoppages in the Construction Industry
in Ontario, from 1958 to 1967

Year	Stoppages	% of Ontario Total	Employees Involved % of Ont. Total	Duration in in Man Days % of Ontario Total
1958	37	28.0	40.1	26.7
1959	27	26.0	13.1	20.0
1960	69	44.2	45.5	50.0
1961	62	37.4	33.7	49.5
1962	63	36.6	26.6	11.4
1963	63	34.8	31.0	40.4
1964	58	30.9	12.3	8.5
1965	85	31.7	14.0	14.2
1966	75	25.1	14.2	7.8
1967	64	29.1	36.6	45.8

Source: For 1958 to 1965, *Carrothers-Palmer Report*; for 1966 to
1967, Ontario Department of Labour.

Employees involved, as a proportion of those in all stoppages, rose in 1963 and then fell in 1964 to the lowest ratio in any of the ten years. Although having risen in 1963, the ratio was much lower (31 per cent) than it was in 1958 (40.1 per cent) or in 1960 (45.5 per cent). The duration in man days showed a similar pattern. In 1963, the ratio rose very sharply in construction, but not as high as it had been in 1960 and 1961; then it fell even more sharply in 1964 to less than 10 per cent, much lower than in any earlier year.

This record suggests two conclusions. First, the abolition of compulsory boards did not lead to an increase in the number or size of strikes in the construction industry during the two years that followed the change. The increase that occurred in 1963 in two of the measures was a normal result of the concentration of bargaining for major agreements in that year, and the ratios were not as high as in some earlier years. In 1964, the two measures were lower than in any earlier year.

Second, the parties themselves were reaching a larger proportion of agreements after the officers had completed their conciliation efforts. This conclusion necessarily follows because the number of work stoppages did not increase even though the officer's direct settlement rate was substanitally lower.

For the five-year period after 1962, stoppages in construction were 29.8 per cent of all stoppages, compared to 35.3 per cent in the earlier five-year period. This reinforces the previous conclusion that the change in the legislation did not increase the number of stoppages relative to those in other industries. The number in construction rose about 50 per cent in 1965 over 1964, but the other measures indicate that in a year of major bargaining, stoppages in construction accounted for a surprisingly low proportion of employees involved and of the duration in man days in all disputes. If the results in 1965 had followed the 1961 and 1963 pattern (a two-year pattern that reappeared in 1967) the ratio of employees involved would have been at least double, and the ratio of duration in man days about triple, the actual 1965 figures.

In 1966, all three ratios remained low. Stoppages in construction were about one-quarter of total stoppages (the lowest ratio for the ten years), involved 14.2 per cent of all employees (one of the four ratios below 26 per cent), and contributed only 7.8 per cent of the total duration in man days (again the lowest ratio for the ten years).

These favourable results did not continue in the last year of the period. Although the proportion of stoppages in construction to total stoppages in 1967 remained below 30 per cent, lower than in most years, there were only two earlier years in which the other two ratios were higher. These earlier years, however, were ones before 1962. Thus there is no reason to attribute the 1967 results to the absence of a compulsory second stage of conciliation.

In summary, the two general conclusions for Ontario are as follows.

(1)   The sharp reduction in the number of disputes going to conciliation boards did not increase the proportion of settlements
reached by the officers. In the construction industry the proportion of direct settlements by officers fell during the two years
after the elimination of compulsory boards.

(2)   The elimination of boards as a compulsory second stage in
the construction industry, and their later reduction in all industries, did not lead to greater strike activity relative to the
experience for all of Canada. The available evidence on work
stippages gives no reason to think that their number or size was
any greater than it would otherwise have been if the boards had
remained compulsory.

One caution is in order. The reported experience for Ontario
is limited to slightly less than two years after the general
policy change. A longer experience would be preferable before
drawing firm conclusions.

Conclusion

Beginning in the 1960s, Canadian public policy for the settlement
of labour disputes has deemphasized the role of compulsory boards
of conciliation. Those provinces that have abolished them or
sharply reduced the numbers appointed are satisfied that the
benefits to collective bargaining have been desirable and that
the changes have not increased the incidence or magnitude of
strikes. The experience reported above supports this opinion.
The parties were able to reach agreements without the assistance
of conciliation boards and without any adverse results in the
experience with work stoppages. There may be some nostalgic
regrets for the fate of this old, well-known, and distinctively
Canadian procedure. But not many.

Note

1.   See W.B. Cunningham, *Compulsory Conciliation and Collective
Bargaining: The New Brunswick Experience* (Montreal: McGill
University Industrial Relations Centre, 1958), pp. 22-23.

16. Multinational Corporations and International Unions*

by John Crispo

Canada might be said to have more than its share of multinational corporations, especially of those headquartered in the United States. Differentiating the Canadian case even more obviously is the additional presence of so many international unions also head-quartered in the United States, and perhaps therefore more appropriately termed American or, at best, binational unions. The presence of these twin phenomena makes Canada a particularly striking illustration of what may lie ahead if and when collective bargaining becomes truly international.

The limitations of this chapter reflect the research methodology that has been employed. Aside from the author's own earlier works on international unionism,[1] major reliance has been placed on a limited number of related studies,[2] and on a continuing series of interviews with leading corporate, government, and trade union representatives familiar with the impact of foreign institutional forces on Canadian industrial relations.

After providing some background data, this chapter will highlight several generalizations about the conduct in Canada of both multinational corporations and international unions. This will be followed by a section on their impact on Canadian collective bargaining, which, in turn, will lead into a discussion of selected issues and problems growing out of their presence.

Background Data

To set the stage for what follows, it is useful to have on overview of the current situation in Canada with respect to the presence of both multinational corporations and international unions. This can be accomplished most easily by citing a brief passage from a recent article on this same general subject matter.

A statistical basis for concern about the impact of foreign institutions and pressures on Canadian industrial relations is

---

*Reproduced by permission of Gerard Dion, Editor, *Industrial Relations Quarterly Review*.

*not hard to come by. On both the corporation and trade union
sides there is ample evidence to indicate just how pervasive the
potential for foreign influences already is in Canada.*

*On the corporate side, foreign firms continue to play an in-
creasingly dominant part in Canadian industry. Aggregate figures
show that over 35 per cent of Canadian industry is owned outside
the country. For particular industries, including oil and gas,
mining, and selected parts of manufacturing such as automobile,
chemical, and rubber, foreign ownership accounts for over 70 per
cent of the activity. Thus, in many industries where collective
bargaining is well established, the possible scope for foreign
intervention on the management side is great indeed. Unlike the
situation on the union side, however, not all of this potential
influence flows from the United States, since between 15 and 20
per cent of foreign ownership in Canada is held in countries
other than the United States.*

*As for the union side, the historical situation is somewhat
different, in that the proportion of Canadian workers belonging to
international, or, better still, binational, or American unions
has been diminishing over the past few decades. None the less,
the figures for foreign--that is, international, binational, or
American--union penetration into Canada are still very impressive.
Although the Canadian members of international unions in Canada
make up only about 7 or 8 per cent of those unions' total membership, they represent more than 60 per cent of the organized labour movement in Canada. Moreover, these unions represent eight
of the ten largest unions in Canada and are dominant in many of
the industries mentioned above in connection with foreign ownership. Except for Quebec, where a somewhat divided and dismem-
bered Confederation of National Trade Unions represents between
one hundred and one hundred and fifty thousand workers in a
number of industires, the bulk of the significant national union
membership is to be found in the public and quasi-public sectors
of the economy.*[3]

Multinational Corporations and International Unions:
Their Conduct in Canada

An attempt to summarize the behaviour of both multinational corporations and international unions[4] in Canada presents many problems, aside from the complex diversity of their performance in
different situations. In the first place, it is important to try
to distinguish between actual and potential involvement by the
headquarters of these institutions in the affairs of their Canadian offshoots. Equally important is the challenge of ascertain-
ing their indirect as well as their direct influences in the
Canadian setting. This reflects the fact that any existing inter-
ference--if that is the appropriate term--is not always as overt
as one might hope from a research point of view.

There are many common variables that help to explain the conduct of both multinational corporations and international unions
in Canada--for example, the history and traditions of the organ-

ization in question, which can vary on both sides from almost
complete centralization to the virtual granting of autonomy in
most areas. On the corporate side, there are centrally controlled,
totally integrated operations at one end of the spectrum, and
quite independent profit-centred operations at the other. On the
union side, the spectrum is not as broad, especially at the centralized control end, for reasons that will be dealt with later.
Nonetheless, there is also a range of behaviour among the international unions, as best illustrated by the tendency for industrial unions to grant more autonomy to their Canadian sections
than has been the case with the craft unions.

The personalities and styles of the leaders of multinational
corporations and international unions also tend to have a bearing
on their handling of the Canadian situation (as they do, of course,
on their handling of their other foreign operations). Here again,
there is more potential for decisive foreign intervention in the
Canadian industrial relations scene on the corporate, as distinct
from the union, side, if only because of more authoritarian and
hierarchical forms of organization in the former.

A third set of variables that are particularly pertinent to
the Canadian scene involve the common cultural, linguistic and
social character of the country (with the exception of Quebec) in
relation to its American neighbour, which is the base of most of
the multinational corporations and all of the international unions.
This, along with all that characterizes the common continental
heritage of the two countries, can give rise to the temptation to
treat much of Canada as if it were no different from any part of
the United States. Standing against this temptation, however,
are not only the distinctive nature of the Province of Quebec,
but the differing federal-provincial arrangements in the two
countries as they apply to the field of industrial relations, and
the spirit of nationalism that is abroad in Canada today.

A more prosaic set of characteristics that affect the handling
of industrial relations in Canada by multinational corporations
and international unions includes the size of the Canadian operation, both in absolute and relative terms, and the degree of
penetration of the United States market by Canadian-produced goods.
On the corporate side, the more important the Canadian operation
in terms of overall production and penetration of the American
market, the more disposed the American headquarters will be to
keep a watchful eye on the total operation in Canada. In the
collective bargaining arena, this watchfulness will be more pronounced, the more likely Canadian developments are to have an
impact south of the border.

On the union side, the absolute and relative size of the Canadian operation is of great significance, if only in terms of the
necessary base membership required to run a reasonably viable
operation in Canada without continuing subsidization from south
of the border. Assuming that base to be present, an autonomously
minded leadership and membership in Canada has a much greater
chance of realizing its wished. Even then, however, the international union in question cannot be expected to ignore the

Canadian situation if its members in Canada are producing goods
and services, many of which find their way into the United States.
This can lead to some interesting contrasts. One can be seen in
the United Automobile Workers, which are party to increasingly
continental negotiations, at least with the "Big Three" of the
automobile manufacturers, even though, as international unions go,
the Canadian section of this union has a great deal of autonomy,
which it is apparently more than willing to compromise when it
comes to these particular corporate relations.

This illustration brings out another factor that can have a
major impact on the way in which multinational corporations and
international unions treat their Canadian operations. Where both
are headquartered in the United States, it stands to reason that
each will tend to keep a sharper watch on Canadian developments,
simply because both are, in most instances, leery of the tail
wagging the dog, so to speak.

Finally, it is to be expected that both institutions will take
a closer look at Canadian developments if and when their offshoots
in Canada become embroiled in strikes or lockouts, especially protracted ones. In this event, multinational corporations will
become more concerned, the more integrated their North American
or world operations; and international unions will become more
concerned, the more liable they are for strike benefits.

When one examines the comparative record of multinational corporations and international unions in Canada from the point of
view of the amount of autonomy and independence granted their
Canadian wings, it is not surprising to find that on balance,
international unions have been more responsive to outcries for
such autonomy and independence. This follows from the basic
nature of unions, which is democratic, as distinct from that of
the corporation, which, as already mentioned, tends to be more
authoritarian and hierarchical.

There are both advantages and disadvantages to the respective
postures of these two institutions in relation to the question
of Canadian autonomy and independence. On the corporate side is
the danger that the pressures for such autonomy and independence
may be unwisely ignored because of the corporations' essentially
autocratic structure; but there is also the compensating ability
to respond quickly once a decision to do so is made. Because of
their inherently more participatory and grassroots structure,
unions are usually in a better position to cope with nationalis-
tic fervours of one kind or another, but are at a consequent disadvantage when such phenomena run counter to the need for an
effective international response to the multinational corporation.

Finally, to conclude this section, it should be stressed that
despite the impression that may have been conveyed above, and
subject to the qualifications that follow in the next section,
many, if not most, multinational corporations and international
unions have a fairly consistent record, in the field of industrial
relations, of leaving matters in the hands of their Canadian operations until there is a crisis of some kind. One of those interviewed for this study referred to this trait as "management by
exception", which is to imply that, by and large, both the

institutions in question leave their Canadian operations to run
their own shows, unless there is a major reason for intervention.

Impact on Canadian Collective Bargaining

The impact of multinational corporations and international unions
on Canadian collective bargaining varies immensely for reasons
already cited in the foregoing section, as well as for others
less important and too numerous to mention. The results, in
terms of collective bargaining practices and procedures in Canada,
range from what might best be described as continental negotiations
to virtually independent negotiations in Canada.

Continental bargaining is really bargaining controlled south
of the border and applies only in situations where both the multinational corporation and international union involved are headquartered in the United States. Examples of such bargaining are
few and far between. Initially, such bargaining appears to have
begun in a few companies such as the American and the Continental
Can companies, the Marmoraton mine of the Bethlehem Steel Corporation, and the Union Drawn subsidiary of Republic Steel, where
highly centralized management was the order of the day, or the
Canadian operation was so small and insignificant that for collective bargaining purposes it was decided simply to deal with
it in the United States negotiations. More recently, a much more
significant case has been added to those now subject to continental negotiations in Canada. This is the Chrysler case, where
negotiations with the United Automobile Workers were fully integrated, after the Canadian-United States Automobile Trades Agreement was enacted between the two countries, thereby creating a
modified common market for automobiles and their parts, and thus
an incentive on both sides to move toward a more joint approach
to bargaining.

Closely related to continental bargaining, at least in terms
of impact on comparative conditions of employment in the two
countries, are situations where there is a fairly close following in Canada of the corresponding American contracts. This
appears to be the case with Ford and General Motors, largely
because they cannot expect to treat Canadian workers any less
generously, relatively speaking, than does Chrysler. This is
the general policy that the United Automobile Workers in Canada
pursues, with varying degrees of success, with all American
subsidiaries over which it has some influence. How widespread
American pattern-following is in Canada is difficult to discern,
but it is prevalent to some extent in almost every situation, if
only because of the general tendency in Canada to look to developments south of the border for precedents.

This latter observation must be qualified, however, by the
fact that in some ways, Canada has shown more independence in
the field of collective bargaining in recent years than in the
past. On the wage front, for example, Canada has generally out-
stripped the United States in a number of recent years, even
before phases 1, 2 and 3 of the American wage and price restraint

program were introduced. When it comes to fringe benefits, Canadian unions, including the Canadian sections of international
unions, have yet to do much pioneering, although they do not seem
as prone in some industries to follow American precedents as reli-
giously as they once did. Thus, for example, the Canadian section
of the United Steelworkers of America has not yet pursued sabbati-
cal leaves, though they have been in effect in basic steel in the
United States for some time.

To be differentiated from continental bargaining and close
pattern-following are situations where, at least on the corporate
side, the Canadian subsidiary handles its own industrial relations
within fairly broad guidelines set by the company headquarters.
Few such situations are to be found among international unions,
except insofar as the concept of "more,more, more" is a guideline.

Last, but far from least, are those situations where negotiations take place quite independently in Canada despite the presence
of multinational corporations and/or international unions, although
in these cases, either one or the other, but not both, is usually
present. All sorts of examples of this type of negotiation can
be found, in everything from airlines and railways to construction
and retailing.

Finally to be mentioned in this discussion of the impact of
multinational corporations and international unions on collective
bargaining practices and procedures in Canada is participation by
non-Canadians, and particularly Americans, in negotiations in this
country. This is more common on the corporate side, especially
where the Canadian operation is small, than on the union side.
However, on both sides it appears to be diminishing, largely
because of increasing sensitivity about such involvement. Today,
this kind of participation is being confined largely to crisis
situations. In these and other cases, outside involvement by one
side often invites similar involvement by the other. For the most
part, however, foreign involvement, with the exception of continental negotiations, makes itself felt more indirectly than directly.

Issues and Problems

The presence of foreign institutions on the Canadian industrial
relations scene has long been a source of controversy. Debate
began on the union side and on that front has covered every conceivable issue, from early opposition by Canadian management
spokesmen to the presence of alleged foreign union agitators in
Canada, to more recent allegations by some national union groups
concerning the supposed profiteering by international unions at
the expense of their Canadian members.

Criticism of multinational corporations in Canada has been extensive of late,[5] but little of this criticism has been directed
at their industrial relations practices. This is surprising,
given the importance of such corporations in industries where
collective bargaining is prevalent, and given the controversy that
has surrounded the international unions, which could be construed
in some ways as their counterparts. The explanation for this
disparity in the degree of controversy these two institutions

have generated may again be traced to the fact that one is essentially autocratic while the other is basically democratic.

Both multinational corporations and international unions should expect to be subjected to increasing scrutiny, given the nationalism present in Canada. If for no other reason, both these institutions are vulnerable to criticism by nationalists because of the dual loyalty to which their Canadian offshoots are subject. On the one hand, they are part of an international organization having its headquarters elsewhere; on the other, they are integral parts of a host country to which they also have some obligations.

In addition to the general question of dual authority, there are a number of more specific charges that can be levelled against multinational corporations and international unions in the field of industrial relations in Canada. Many of these criticisms are confined to the union side, where they pertain to the purported adverse impact of the American labour movement on its Canadian counterpart. Although the net effect of international unions on the Canadian labour movement and on Canadian workers has doubtless been positive, there have been some negative repercussions. International unionism has periodically contributed to disunity in the Canadian labour movement, has given it an unduly fragmented structure, and has tempered its philosophy in such a way as to make it more conservative.

Of more concern in some quarters has been the impact of multinational corporations and international unions on both the process and the results of collective bargaining. Procedurally, both institutions have probably tended to restrain industrial strife in Canada, although at times they are accused of just the reverse. Substantively, and probably with more validity, either or both could at times be charged with the imposition of inappropriate American precedents in Canada: for example, the granting of wage parity in the automobile industry. On this subject, the *New York Times* once editorialized, quite appropriately:

The bad part of it is that the decision was made, under coercion of a strike deadline, by American corporate and union leaders much more concerned with their own interests than the immediate consequences for Canada. This is a type of economic imperialism no country can welcome.

Finally to be mentioned in this brief catalogue of issues and problems is the mutual interdependence that can arise between multinational corporations and international unions. Although this is hard to document, there is probably something to the notion that these institutions would prefer to deal with each other in Canada, as well as in the United States, if only because they know one another. This could conceivably lead both to take steps to mutually reinforce their respective positions in Canada.

Summary and Conclusions

Canada still presents such a unique case of industrial relations, because of the presence of both multinational corporations and international unions, that it is hazardous to generalize from its experience. As unique as that experience is, however, it may well offer a preview of what is to come on a more worldwide basis, as production and trade become more international.

Both multinational corporations and international unions are going to have to find ways of operating that reflect both the trend toward internationalism in industrial relations and the nationalist sensitivities that are bound to remain operative in many countries. This means that both types of organization must come up with viable combinations of centralized operation where essential, and national autonomy and independence where desired and feasible.

This author's past studies of international unionism have revealed at least four steps they must be prepared to take to respond to the nationalist aspirations of their Canadian leaders and members. These are: (1) the establishment of separate and distinct Canadian districts or sections; (2) election by the Canadian membership of the Canadian officers; (3) the convening of Canadian policy conferences to deal with Canadian matters; and (4) the establishment of effective Canadian staffs to service the Canadian membership. On the corporate side, there are no doubt parallel steps that should be taken by multinational corporations.

Changes are clearly taking place in Canada in terms of the way in which both multinational corporations and international unions conduct themselves in the country. Although some of these changes, such as continental bargaining, are hardly in the direction of more autonomy and independence for the Canadian sections of these organizations, the net effect of the changes they are introducing would seem to be in that direction. In that sense, these two important types of international institution may be learning in Canada to reconcile their dual loyalties and the potential conflicts of interest growing out of them. This challenge must be met both in Canada and elsewhere if the world wide trend toward more internationalism in the industrial relations sphere is to continue.

Notes

1. John Crispo, *International Unionism--A Study in Canadian-American Relations* (Toronto: McGraw-Hill, 1967); and idem, *The Role of International Unionism* (Washington: Canadian-American Committee, 1967).

2. See Bryan M. Downie, *Relationships between Canadian-American Wage Settlements: An Empirical Study of Five Industries* (Kingston, Ontario: Queen's University, Industrial Relations Centre, 1970); and idem, "Centralized Collective Bargaining: U.S.-Canadian Experience", in *Industrial Relations Quarterly Review*, vol. 26, no. 1 (Quebec: Laval University Press, 1971). See also David H. Blake, "Multinational Corporation, International Union, and

International Collective Bargaining", in *Transnational Industrial Relations,* ed. Hans Gunter (The International Institute for Labour Studies, 1972); and Duane Kujawa, *International Relations Management in the Automobile Industry: A Comparative Study of Chrysler, Ford and General Motors* (New York: Praeger, 1971).

3.   John Crispo, "Multi-National Corporations and International Unions: Their Impact on Canadian Industrial Relations", prepared for a conference on Industrial Relations and the Multi-National Corporation, sponsored by the University of Chicago Graduate School of Business, May 1973 (to be published by the University of Chicago Press).

4.   From this point onward in the chapter, the term *international union* is used, if only because of the long-standing convention and tradition of so referring to such unions, even though they are at best binational and, in many cases, essentially American.

5.   The Hon. Herb Gray, P.C., *Special Report on Foreign Direct Investment in Canada* (Ottawa: Government of Canada, 1972).

PART V: MECHANISMS FOR CONVERTING INPUTS TO OUTPUTS

17. The Structure of Collective Bargaining*

by Robert J. Christy

The growing complexity of industrial relations in general, and
collective bargaining in particular, resulted, during the 1950s
and 1960s, in an interest in collective bargaining structure or
what Arnold Weber described as the size and scope of the bargaining unit; the distribution of decision-making power within bargaining agencies and the relationships between bargaining units.[1]
Weber suggests that this interest is directly resultant upon the
size and scope of bargaining units, which have become such that
effective collective bargaining, including the right to strike
and to resist demands, is made difficult by social and economic
consequences. Furthermore, he argues that the scope of bargaining
units now encompasses so many interests that bargaining agents
cannot accurately present needs and interests of constituents.
In line with this latter point, centralized decision making has
displaced, from the local to the plant or industry level, those
things best agreed upon at the former level. Lastly, suggests
Weber, talk of renewed "labour monopoly" via pattern agreements,
rapid growth in technology, and a concern for the preservation of
democratic values in industrial society have also helped to create
this interest.[2]

   Thus, during the previous two decades, several studies dealing
with some of the aspects of collective bargaining structure were
conducted in the United States and Canada. Chamberlain,[3] and
later, Livernash,[4] have found that in the United States, bargaining is decentralized, conducted by single employer structures,
located in the north-central region of the country. Multi employer structures were more prevalent, however, in the Pacific region
and in industries where the union focussed its attention on the
product or labour markets, rather than on individual companies.

Mr. Christy, an economist with the federal government and formerly
on staff with the Canada Department of Labour, wishes to thank Dr.
G. Clack, Dr. P. MaCarthy, and Dr. A. Craig for welcomed advice
throughout the course of the study. However, the opinions expressed in this paper are those of the author and do not necessarily reflect the opinions of the above individuals, the Canada
Department of Labour or other federal government agencies.

*Reproduced by permission of Information Canada.

In Canada, work in the area of collective bargaining structure was initiated jointly in 1965-66 by the Economic Council of Canada and the Canada Department of Labour for the former's federal government reference on prices. From this initial work, findings of which appear in the *Third Annual Review*,[5] several papers and studies have emerged. Craig and Waisglass, in 1968, published national aggregate data which explored, for the years 1953-66, the structure of actual bargaining units, the stage at which negotiations ended, the duration of collective agreements, and wage changes resulting from collective bargaining.[6] Later, the prime minister's Task Force on Labour Relations commissioned three studies dealing with bargaining structure. Besides requesting an updating of the original 1965-66 study, the task force also commissioned a study to examine the problems and issues facing labour relations boards vis-a-vis the appropriateness of bargaining units,[7] and another to examine the status and trends in poliparty negotiations.[8]

Methodology and Format of the Chapter

This chapter, a summary of the findings of the task force study of a similar name, draws on and extends the 1965-66 study initiated by the Economic Council and the Canada Department of Labour. It examines, for the selected years 1953-1968, basic collective bargaining information[9]--the structure of negotiating units (to be distinguished from bargaining units in the section below), the stage at which negotiations ended, and duration of collective agreements on a national, a regional and an industrial basis. This basic data was obtained from negotiating units which negotiated for 500 or more employees and come from all major industries except railway transportation and construction, for which reliable data was unavailable. The concluding section of the chapter suggests plausible, though inconclusive, reasons for the structural features of the Canadian collective bargaining process.

Negotiating Unit Structure

Within the field of industrial relations, some confusion has resulted because the term *bargaining unit* has acquired several meanings. As Herman points out, the term has been attributed to three situations. In the legal sense, it refers to a particular labour organization certified, by a labour relations board, as the exclusive bargaining agent for a group of employees. The term is also used when referring to a group of employees, represented by one or more organizations, in which the composition of the group is determined voluntarily by the bargaining parties without assistance from a labour relations board. Lastly, the term refers to the actual group of employees and employers who meet to negotiate or renegotiate the terms of a collective agreement and may thus be composed of one or more certified or voluntary bargaining units.[10]

Because the composition of units conducting negotiation is a vital aspect of collective bargaining structure, it was Herman's third concept of the bargaining unit (the group of employees and employers that meets to negotiate, i.e., the actual bargaining unit) that held the greatest relevance for this study. However, to eliminate confusion that possibly might arise, the term *actual bargaining unit* was substituted in this chapter by the term *negotiating unit*.

Table 17.1 presents, nationally and regionally for the selected years 1963 to 1968, statistics on: (1) the number of negotiating units that both fulfilled the employment criteria of 500 or more employees and had a collective agreement in force on December 31 of the indicated year; (2) the corresponding number of employees; and (3) the proportion of negotiating units (and employees) falling into each category of an eight-part typology used to analyze negotiating unit structure. The table indicates, nationally and regionally, that the number of negotiating units fulfilling the employment criteria, and the corresponding number of employees, increased during the 1953-1968 period.

The national aggregate data shows that 80 per cent of the negotiating units, representing over 70 per cent of the employees in the study, were classified as single corporate structures, of which 60 per cent were single establishment and 20 per cent were multiestablishment units. Of the remaining 20 per cent, 7 per cent were classified as multicompany units (units informally created by several companies for collective bargaining purposes) and 13 per cent were classified as employer associations where the association negotiated for its members. The table also shows that most negotiating units, approximately 90 per cent, negotiated with one union.

The regional data in table 17.1 show that most negotiating units (representing the majority of employees) located in the Atlantic Provinces, Quebec, Ontario and the Prairie Provinces and most units negotiating in more than one province were single corporate structures. However, a higher proportion of multiestablishment, single corporate structures were found in the Atlantic Provinces, in the Prairie Provinces and, as would be expected, in the multiprovincial group than in Ontario and Quebec. The table also shows that a larger proportion of multiunion structures were found in the Atlantic Provinces than in the other regions, and that many of the units negotiating multiprovincially were also multiunion. British Columbia, on the other hand, had a high proportion of multicorporate negotiating units, of which employer associations formed a large group. However, single-union structures were more prominent in British Columbia than multiunion ones.

Structural shifts during the 1953-68 period were not prominent nationally or regionally with the exception of the Prairie Provinces and British Columbia. In the prairie region, there were increases in single establishment, single corporate and in multicompany structures, with corresponding declines in other categories. In British Columbia, the proportion of single corporate structures declined, while multicorporate structures increased correspondingly.

TABLE 17.1

Percentage Distribution of Negotiating Units and of Corresponding Employees Classified According to Type of Negotiating Structure, Selected Years 1953-1968[a]

Type of Negotiating Unit	Canada				Atlantic Provinces				Quebec				Ontario			
	1953	1958	1963	1968	1953	1958	1963	1968	1953	1958	1963	1968	1953	1958	1963	1968
Single establishment																
Single union	52[b]	56	55	56	25	33	32	29	63	66	63	61	65	66	66	70
	(29)[c]	(39)	(38)	(36)	(9)	(30)	(20)	(20)	(53)	(58)	(49)	(47)	(41)	(49)	(52)	(53)
Multiunion	3	5	4	5	17	17	12	13	6	3	4	6	2	6	5	5
	(2)	(3)	(3)	(2)	(8)	(14)	(10)	(8)	(3)	(2)	(2)	(4)	(1)	(3)	(3)	(3)
Multiestablishment																
Single union	24	20	19	17	50	33	36	29	19	11	12	11	20	15	15	12
	(35)	(32)	(31)	(28)	(40)	(44)	(35)	(39)	(34)	(17)	(20)	(21)	(46)	(34)	(31)	(31)
Multiunion	2	2	3	2	0[f]	0	4	4	0	3	4	3	2	1	1	1
	(2)	(3)	(3)	(2)	(0)	(0)	(1)	(2)	(0)	(3)	(4)	(2)	(1)	(1)	(1)	(1)
Multicorporation																
Multicompany																
-single union	4	5	6	6	0	0	4	4	4	4	4	3	3	2	4	5
	(2)	(4)	(6)	(5)	(0)	(0)	(24)	(10)	(3)	(6)	(4)	(5)	(3)	(2)	(2)	(5)
-multiunion	2	1	0	1	8	0	0	0	0	0	0	0	0	1	1	1
	(9)	(1)	(0)	(1)	(43)	(0)	(0)	(0)	(0)	(0)	(0)	(0)	(0)	(1)	(1)	(1)
Employer association																
-single union	11	11	12	13	0	17	12	21	6	11	13	16	9	9	8	7
	(19)	(17)	(18)	(23)	(0)	(12)	(9)	(21)	(6)	(14)	(20)	(20)	(9)	(10)	(9)	(9)
-multiunion	2	1	1	1	-[g]	-	-	-	2	1	1	1	-	-	-	-
	(2)	(2)	(2)	(2)	(-)	(-)	(-)	(-)	(1)	(1)	(0)[h]	(1)	(-)	(-)	(-)	(-)
Total																
Negotiating units	189[d]	343	419	367	12	18	25	24	52	117	142	120	66	121	142	128
Employees	3738[e]	5641	6606	6671	347	306	433	292	801	1587	1910	1923	1056	1747	1981	1950

TABLE 17.1 (cont'd)

Type of Negotiating Unit	Prairie Provinces				British Columbia				Multi provincial			
	1953	1958	1963	1968	1953	1958	1963	1968	1953	1958	1963	1968
Single corporation												
Single establishment	48	50	59	65	38	33	28	24	-	-	-	-
	(45)	(50)	(59)	(70)	(12)	(14)	(13)	(16)	(-)	(-)	(-)	(-)
Multiunion	0	5	4	5	-	-	-	-	-	-	-	-
	(0)	(7)	(6)	(3)	(-)	(-)	(-)	(-)	(-)	(-)	(-)	(-)
Multiestablishment												
Single union	35	26	20	16	8	20	15	18	58	79	79	79
	(24)	(24)	(20)	(15)	(5)	(16)	(14)	(11)	(59)	(80)	(80)	(79)
Multiunion	-	-	-	-	4	3	3	0	8	11	8	11
	(-)	(-)	(-)	(-)	(3)	(1)	(2)	(0)	(10)	(13)	(12)	(13)
Multicorporation												
Multicompany												
-single union	4	8	9	5	8	17	25	21	-	-	-	-
	(2)	(6)	(7)	(3)	(2)	(5)	(15)	(8)	(-)	(-)	(-)	(-)
multiunion	-	-	-	-	4	3	0	3	17	0	0	0
	(-)	(-)	(-)	(-)	(5)	(6)	(0)	(4)	(26)	(0)	(0)	(0)
Employer association												
-single union	13	11	9	9	33	20	28	30	8	5	8	5
	(29)	(14)	(9)	(9)	(68)	(53)	(51)	(66)	(2)	(2)	(3)	(3)
-multiunion	-	-	-	-	4	3	3	3	8	5	4	5
	(-)	(-)	(-)	(-)	(4)	(4)	(6)	(5)	(6)	(5)	(5)	(5)
Total												
Negotiating units	234[d]	38	46	43	24	30	40	33	12	19	24	19
Employees	2695[e]	413	514	507	705	854	960	1331	560	734	808	669

Notes to Table 17.1

a   Figures outside the parentheses are percentages referring to
negotiating units. Percentage figures in parentheses refer to
employees.
b   Columns outside the parentheses may not total to 100% due to
rounding.
c   Columns inside the parentheses may not total to 100% due to
rounding.
d   Total negotiating units are expressed as absolute figures.
e   Total employee figures are expressed as hundreds. Read 373,000
for 1953.
f   Zeros indicate that for the year in question, there were no
negotiating units or employees falling within the classification.
g   Dashes indicate that units of the designated type were not
observed in the geographic region.
h   Less than 1/2%.

Table 17.2 presents, on an industrial basis, 1953-1968 negoti-
ating-unit-structure mean averages. Three features are immediately
apparent from the table. First, the majority of employees in most
industries negotiate in single corporate negotiating units. Second, multicorporate structures are prominent in transportation and
storage, trade, and personal services industries, and to a lesser
extent in manufacturing and public utilities. Third, while single
corporate negotiating units are prominent in many industries, a
high proportion of these units were multiestablishment structures.

Stage at which Negotiations End

One of the foundation stones of Canadian industrial relations, and
an inherent part of collective bargaining structure, has been the
conciliation process in collective bargaining. Initiated, on a
localized basis, during the early years of this century, the process, with its clearly defined steps, gained prominence during the
post-1945 era both federally and provincially. In general, 1950-
1968 legislation, in all jurisdictions, provided for bipartite negotiations with a two-stage compulsory conciliation process prior
to strike action. Because of the existence of the concept throughout the country and because major legislative changes were not
introduced until the 1970s, it was possible to develop, for analytical purposes, the following typology of stages of completed negotiations: (1) bargaining (bipartite negotiations); (2) conciliation officer (settlements brought about by a conciliation officer);
(3) conciliation board (settlements brought about by a conciliation
board; (4) postconciliation bargaining (negotiations, with or without a third party, following conciliation but prior to strike);
(5) strike (settlement during or following a strike).
Table 17.3 shows, nationally and regionally for selected years
1953-1968, the proportion of negotiating units, covering 500 or
more employees, that completed negotiations at one of the above

TABLE 17.2

Percentage Distributions of Negotiating Units and Corresponding Employees Classified According to Type of Negotiating Structure and Industry, (1953-1968 Mean Averages)

Major Industry	Single Corporation		Multicorporation	
	Single Establishment	Multi-Establishment	Multicompany	Employer Association
Mining	76 (48)	13 (34)	5 (9)	6 (9)
Manufacturing	65 (42)	20 (26)	3 (6)	13 (25)
Transport and storage	35 (33)	33 (18)	4 (3)	39 (46)
Communication	30 (13)	70 (87)	- (-)	- (-)
Public utilities	5 (2)	82 (93)	13 (5)	- (-)
Trade	32 (30)	5 (5)	51 (45)	12 (20)
Community services	61 (42)	36 (57)	3 (1)	- (-)
Personal services	55 (56)	2 (2)	10 (10)	32 (33)

Notes

a Percentage figures outside the parentheses refer to negotiating units, while those inside the parentheses refer to employees.

b Rows of figures outside the parentheses may not total to 100% due to rounding.

c Rows of figures inside the parentheses may not total to 100% due to rounding.

d Dashes indicate that structures of the designated type (for the given data) were not observed in the industry.

TABLE 17.3

Percentage Distributions of Negotiating Units and of Corresponding Employees Classified According to the Stage at Which Negotiations Ended, Selected Years 1953-1968a

Type of Negotiating Unit	Canada				Atlantic Provinces				Quebec				Ontario			
	1953	1958	1963	1968	1953	1958	1963	1968	1953	1958	1963	1968	1953	1958	1963	1968
Bargaining	74b (64)c	58 (47)	55 (67)	42 (36)	100 (100)	78 (72)	83 (64)	67 (78)	82 (80)	67 (66)	66 (62)	56 (49)	60 (56)	54 (35)	50 (46)	26 (20)
Conciliation officer	3 (3)	17 (14)	12 (9)	35 (21)	0 (0)	11 (16)	6 (3)	25 (15)	0 (0)	14 (13)	10 (8)	25 (23)	4 (7)	15 (15)	18 (20)	43 (25)
Conciliation board	18 (24)	18 (27)	10 (19)	8 (16)	0 (0)	0 (0)	11 (33)	8 (7)	18 (20)	11 (14)	12 (8)	4 (15)	28 (29)	22 (21)	11 (10)	7 (8)
Postconciliation bargaining	2 (5)	1 (5)	7 (11)	3 (11)	0 (0)	0 (0)	0 (0)	0 (0)	0 (0)	0 (0)	5 (14)	0 (0)	2 (1)	1 (16)	14 (19)	5 (12)
Strike	2 (2)	5f (7)g	3 (3)	12 (15)	0 (0)	11 (12)	0 (0)	0 (0)	0 (0)	6k (4)g	6 (7)	15 (13)	7 (7)	7f (12)g	4 (13)	19 (33)
Other	1 (2)	2 (0)	1 (1)	0 (0)	0 (0)	0 (0)	0 (0)	0 (0)	4 (3)	4 (3)	0 (0)	0 (0)	0 (0)	0 (0)	4 (3)	0 (0)
Total Negotiating units	164d	196	215	208	11	9	18	12	45	57	77	52	57	67	56	87
Employees	3246e	3360	3072	3921	328	86	269	182	655	681	1164	614	872	920	467	1447

TABLE 17.3 (cont'd)

Type of Negotiating Unit	Prairie Provinces				British Columbia				Multiprovincial			
	1953	1958	1963	1968	1953	1958	1963	1968	1953	1958	1963	1968
Bargaining	91 (73)	70 (63)	93 (93)	61 (71)	61 (23)	26 (16)	45 (48)	16 (6)	73 (73)	54 (69)	85 (94)	70 (78)
Conciliation officer	5 (3)	11 (19)	3 (5)	29 (22)	11 (5)	43 (20)	23 (11)	53 (22)	0 (0)	8 (5)	8 (4)	10 (4)
Conciliation board	0 (0)	15 (15)	0 (0)	7 (5)	17 (62)	22 (55)	14 (11)	21 (37)	18 (18)	38 (27)	8 (3)	20 (18)
Postconciliation bargaining	0 (0)	0 (0)	3 (2)	4 (2)	11 (10)	8 (1)	14 (28)	5 (30)	9 (19)	0 (0)	0 (0)	0 (0)
Strike	0^m (0)	0 (0)	0 (0)	0 (0)	0 (0)	8 (7)	0 (0)	5 (5)	0 (0)	0 (0)	0 (0)	0 (0)
Other	5 (24)	4 (2)	0 (0)	0 (0)	0 (0)	0 (0)	5 (0)^h	0 (0)	0 (0)	0 (0)	0 (0)	0 (0)
Total Negotiating Units	22	27	29	28	18	23	22	19	11	13	13	10
Employees	263	294	309	358	587	725	296	838	540	654	567	483

Notes to Table 17.3

a Percentage figures outside parentheses refer to negotiating units while percentage figures inside the parentheses refer to employees.
b Columns outside the parentheses may not total to 100% due to rounding.
c Columns inside the parentheses may not total to 100% due to rounding.
d Total negotiating units are expressed as absolute figures.
e Total employee figures are expressed as hundreds. Read 324,000 for 1953.
f One per cent of the negotiating units settled this dispute after returning to work.
g One per cent of the employee units settled this dispute after returning to work.
h Less than 1/2%.
k Two per cent of the negotiating units settled their dispute after returning to work.
m Strike data were recorded for the Prairie Provinces during years other than those selected.

---

stages. The table also shows that while strike activity increased on a national level during the 1950s and again during the 1960s, a majority of negotiations, involving the majority of the employees, were settled before a strike. It also shows that during this period, the proportion of negotiations terminating at the bargaining stage, i.e., before conciliation, and at the conciliation board stage declined, while the proportion of negotiations settled by a conciliation officer or, to a lesser extent, through postconciliation bargaining increased.

The regional data in table 17.3 show that a higher proportion of negotiating units and a corresponding higher proportion of employees in the Atlantic and Prairie Provinces settled interest disputes without third-party intervention than was the case in other regions. In British Columbia, on the other hand, a small proportion of negotiating units and their employees settled without third-party intervention. However, in all regions except Quebec and Ontario in 1968, the proportion of settlements achieved either during or following a strike did not exceed 12 per cent, suggesting, especially for Quebec, Ontario and British Columbia, that negotiators relied heavily on government conciliatory services or postconciliation negotiations. Similarly, like the national data, the regional statistics indicate that during this period there was a shift away from settlements achieved without third-party intervention to ones that relied on conciliation, specifically the conciliation officer.

Aggregate figures (1953-1968) for negotiations conducted by the negotiating units in the study were generated on an industrial basis and distributed proportionally by stage of settlement. The results of this exercise, found in table 17.4, show that with the exception of the textile, transportation equipment, and transportation and storage industries, 90 per cent of the negotiations,

involving over 90 per cent of the employees, were concluded prior
to strikes. Many industries--for example, clothing in the manufacturing sector, communications, public utilities, and community
services--settled over 70 per cent of their negotiations (involving
over 73 per cent of their employees) without third-party intervention. Other industries, such as mining, textiles, transportation
equipment, electrical apparatus, nonmetallic mineral products, and
transportation and storage, settled fewer than 50 per cent of their
disputes at the bargaining stage, thus relying on conciliation or
postconciliation to achieve an agreement prior to strike action.

Duration of Collective Agreements

Collective agreement duration, the third aspect of collective bargaining structure examined in this study, has an important effect
on collective bargaining for two major reasons. First, agreement
duration establishes, with the exception of reopened agreements,
the timing of the subsequent round of negotiations, by locking in
both parties to an agreement for a fixed period of time, usually
not less than one year. Second, in arriving at a mutually agreed
upon duration, the parties must weigh the costs and benefits, both
explicit and implicit, that result from long-or short-term collective agreements--management often trading off deferred wage increases and front-end loaded wage bills for long-term agreements
and labour peace; unions accepting long-term agreements with substantial benefits but foregoing the opportunity to frequently renegotiate benefits as economic changes occur.

Table 17.5 shows, both nationally and regionally for the select
years 1953-1968, the proportion of negotiating units and correspondingly, the proportion of employees, that negotiated collective
agreements of varying durations. The table shows that in 1953
over 50 per cent of the negotiating units, both nationally and
regionally (with the exception of Quebec), signed collective agreements with a duration of less than fourteen months, and that in
all geographic areas, over 50 per cent of the employees were
covered by these agreements. At the same time the proportion of
negotiating units and employees negotiating twenty-three-to twenty-
five-month agreements varied geographically. In Western Canada,
this proportion was low, ranging from 0 to 11 per cent (0 to 7
per cent of the employees), while in the eastern regions, specifically the Atlantic Provinces and Quebec, it was higher. Negotiations for thirty-five-to thirty-seven-month agreements were
not common. However, the popularity of short-term agreements decreased during the 1950s and 1960s, as the data in table 17.5
bear out. The table shows a steady decline in the proportion of
negotiating units that bargained for agreements of less than fourteen months. Correspondingly, negotiating units, especially those
in Quebec and Ontario, shifted to twenty-three-to twenty-five- and
thirty-five- to thirty-seven-month agreements. In the Atlantic
Provinces, in the Prairie Provinces and in British Columbia, however, thirty-five- to thirty-seven-month agreements were not popular.

TABLE 17.4

Percentage Distributions of Negotiating Units and Corresponding Employees Classified According to Industry and the Stage at which their Negotiations Ended, 1953-1968[a]

Industry	Bargaining	Conciliation Officer	Conciliation Board	Post Conciliation Bargaining	Strike	Other	Absolute Number of Negotiations 1953-1968	Absolute Number of Employees 1953-1968 ('00)
Mining	49[b] (52)[c]	8 (6)	21 (20)	13 (8)	8 (8)	2 (6)	156	2470
Manufacturing	57 (46)	16 (16)	15 (22)	5 (7)	6 (8)	- (-)	1831	30247
Food & beverages	60 (48)	16 (19)	12 (16)	6 (10)	5 (7)	1 (0)	205	2649
Textiles	41 (40)	26 (21)	14 (13)	5 (5)	15 (22)	- (-)[e]	74	1069
Clothing	72 (81)	5 (5)	12 (7)	3 (3)	8 (5)	- (-)	74	1320
Logging & sawmilling	56 (30)	23 (24)	15 (36)	2 (4)	2 (7)	2 (0)[e]	184	7436
Pulp & paper	64 (64)	21 (19)	7 (7)	6 (8)	2 (2)	- (-)	284	4201
Printing	65 (59)	10 (11)	19 (26)	5 (4)	- (-)	- (-)	77	685
Iron & steel products	50 (38)	13 (10)	23 (34)	6 (8)	7 (9)	2 (1)	236	3522
Transportation equipment	45 (38)	15 (11)	17 (18)	10 (14)	14 (18)	1 (0)[e]	199	3359
Nonferous metal products	50 (38)	18 (20)	18 (20)	8 (15)	6 (8)	- (-)	72	1391
Electrical apparatus	48 (54)	15 (10)	18 (24)	4 (7)	5 (5)	- (-)	125	2040

TABLE 17.4 (cont'd)

Nonmetallic mineral prod.	44	(44)	11	(11)	32	(29)	3	(5)	5	(11)	5	(0)^e	64	523
Petroleum & chemical prod.	67	(64)	8	(8)	15	(19)	5	(4)	5	(5)	–	(–)	147	1127
Transportation & storage	47	(41)	23	(21)	12	(13)	7	(8)	10	(16)	2	(0)^e	184	3446
Communications	88	(92)	7	(6)	2	(1)	2	(1)	–	(–)^d	–	(–)	189	6166
Public utilities	78	(73)	9	(9)	9	(11)	–	(–)	1	(0)^e	3	(6)	100	1868
Trade	55	(50)	20	(23)	13	(15)	6	(4)	7	(8)	–	(–)	169	2251
Community services	71	(78)	10	(8)	17	(13)	1	(1)	–	(–)	1	(1)	136	1539
Government services	54	(61)	13	(12)	20	(16)	5	(4)	3	(4)	4	(3)	269	3854
Personal services	59	(55)	23	(25)	11	(13)	3	(4)	4	(4)	–	(–)	80	600

Notes

a Percentage figures outside the parentheses refer to negotiating units, while those within the parentheses refer to employees.

b Rows outside the parentheses may not total to 100% due to rounding.

c Rows inside the parentheses may not total to 100% due to rounding.

d Dashes indicate that negotiations, for the given data, did not end at the designated stage.

e Less than 1/2%.

TABLE 17.5

Percentage Distributions of Negotiating Units and Corresponding Employees Classified According to the Duration of their Negotiated Collective Agreement, Selected Years 1953-1968[a]

Duration of Agreement	Canada				Atlantic Provinces				Quebec				Ontario			
	1953	1958	1963	1968	1953	1958	1963	1968	1953	1958	1963	1968	1953	1958	1963	1968
Less than 14 months	64[b] (68)[c]	35 (35)	18 (20)	13 (15)	55 (56)	22 (15)	22 (9)	25 (51)	46 (60)	34 (33)	14 (11)	10 (10)	65 (65)	27 (17)	13 (12)	4 (3)
14-22 months	11 (8)	8 (14)	6 (5)	7 (6)	0 (0)	0 (0)	6 (3)	0 (0)	16 (16)	4 (3)	5 (3)	10 (18)	16 (14)	9 (6)	5 (3)	9 (5)
23-25 months	21 (21)	45 (33)	51 (45)	49 (46)	45 (44)	67 (73)	56 (60)	42 (30)	33 (21)	47 (43)	49 (40)	38 (26)	18 (20)	49 (33)	52 (50)	53 (35)
26-34 months	1 (2)	4 (3)	4 (2)	10 (17)	0 (0)	11 (12)	0 (0)	25 (17)	2 (2)	2 (3)	4 (2)	4 (9)	2 (5)	4 (3)	7 (5)	15 (36)
35-37 months	1 (1)	7 (12)	20 (26)	20 (15)	0 (0)	0 (0)	17 (29)	8 (3)	2 (1)	14 (17)	27 (44)	35 (31)	0 (0)	7 (33)	21 (24)	18 (20)
Greater than 37 months	1 (0)[d]	1 (2)	2 (2)	1 (1)	0 (0)[g]	0 (0)	0 (0)	0 (0)	0 (0)	0 (0)	0 (0)	4 (6)	0 (0)	3 (8)	2 (5)	0 (0)
Total																
Negotiating units	164[e]	196	215	208	11	9	18	12	45	57	77	52	57	67	56	87
Employees	3246[f]	3360	3072	3921	328	86	269	182	655	681	1164	614	872	920	467	1447

TABLE 17.5 (cont'd)

Duration of Agreement	Prairie Provinces				British Columbia				Multiprovincial			
	1953	1958	1963	1968	1953	1958	1963	1968	1953	1958	1963	1968
Less than 14 months	95 (97)	63 (64)	21 (19)	29 (25)	72 (85)	43 (71)	36 (56)	21 (7)	73 (65)	15 (12)	15 (32)	30 (58)
14–22 months	0 (0)	7 (5)	7 (4)	4 (2)	11 (5)	9 (3)	5 (2)	0 (0)	0 (0)	31 (57)	8 (15)	10 (6)
23–25 months	0 (0)	30 (31)	62 (68)	50 (54)	11 (7)	39 (22)	32 (19)	68 (87)	27 (35)	46 (29)	54 (44)	40 (29)
26–34 months	0 (0)	0 (0)	0 (0)	4 (3)	0 (0)	9 (4)	5 (4)	5 (5)	0 (0)	8 (12)	0 (0)	0 (0)
35–37 months	0 (0)	0 (0)	3 (3)	11 (15)	6 (2)	0 (0)	18 (12)	5 (1)	0 (0)	0 (0)	23 (10)	20 (7)
Greater than 37 months	5 (3)	0 (0)	7 (6)	4 (2)	0 (0)	0 (0)	5 (7)	0 (0)	0 (0)g	0 (0)	0 (0)	0 (0)
Total Negotiating units	22	27	29	28	18	23	22	19	11	13	13	10
Employees	263	294	309	358	587	725	296	838	540	654	567	483

Notes to Table 17.5

a Percentage figures outside parentheses refer to negotiating units, while figures inside the parentheses refer to employees.
b Columns outside the parentheses may not total to 100% due to rounding.
c Columns inside the parentheses may not total to 100% due to rounding.
d Less than 1/2%.
e Total negotiating units are expressed as absolute figures.
f Total employee figures are expressed as hundreds. Read 324,600 for 1953.
g Duration data were recorded in this category for the indicated regions during years other than those selected.

TABLE 17.6

Mean Average Duration of Collective Agreements Classified by Industry, Selected Years 1953-1968

Industry	1953	1958	1963	1968	Mean Average for 1953-1968
Mining	18	25	28	22	23
Manufacturing	16	20	25	27	23
Transportation and storage	19	27	32	24	26
Communication	12	14	15	14	14
Public utilities	14	21	24	23	21
Trade	15	21	31	26	23
Community services	17	22	22	21	23
Government services	13	18	22	18	19
Personal services	16	21	31	31	28

Note

All figures, expressed as months, are mean averages weighted by the number of employees in each negotiation unit examined.

Collective agreement duration varied from industry to industry as shown by table 17.6, a presentation, for selected years 1953-1968, of mean average durations of collective agreements, weighted by the number of employees in each negotiating unit. The table shows that negotiating units in some industries--such as transportation and storage, and personal services--tended throughout the period to negotiate long-term agreements. On the other hand, negotiating units in other industries--for example, communications, government services, and public utilities--negotiated short-term agreements.

Conclusions

It is impossible, on the basis of the statistical presentation given above, to draw definitive causal conclusions about Canadian collective bargaining structure. For instance, the negotiating unit structure data show regional variations, with British Columbia and, to a lesser extent, the Atlantic Provinces having a higher proportion of centralized negotiating units (multiestablishment or multicorporate) than other regions. The best one can do is suggest that in general, negotiating unit structure is probably resultant upon the dictates of labour relations boards, the geographic locations of employees in a negotiating unit, intracommunication problems of the parties, industry characteristics, and expediency. The plausibility of these factors is enhanced when one remembers that industries such as fishing, logging, and pulp and paper, important components of the economies of British Columbia and the Atlantic Provinces, are scattered over wide, isolated areas, suggesting a need for centralized negotiations. Furthermore, excluding the self-evident centralized nature of multiprovincial negotiations, there are grounds for suggesting that the factors of geography, communication, industry characteristics and expediency offer partial explanations for multiprovincial negotiating units.

A similar rationalization process can be employed when discussing plausible causal factors for the stage of settlement. First, there can be little doubt, for instance, that short-term economic fluctuations will have a decided impact on settlement stages. One need only examine recent negotiations to note the effects of inflation on settlement stage. Second, the shift away from using conciliation boards as a settlement technique is probably partially explained by a refusal, on the part of some provincial governments after the mid-1960s, to appoint such boards. Third, one can plausibly suggest that as issues in collective bargaining become more complex, the parties go to later stages of negotiation to give some appearance of "progress" while complicated decisions are reached by, and among the members of each side. Such a supposition could be especially true in multicorporate or multiunion structures.

Lastly, the shift from short-to-long-term collective agreements may be plausibly, although partially, explained by two important variables--economic fluctuations in the short run and expediency in the long run. It seems reasonable to suggest that during periods of relative economic stability, negotiators would strive for a long-term agreement, while during periods of economic instability, shorter-term agreements would result. A comparison of agreement duration data on a year-by-year basis tends to substantiate this suggestion. In the long run, however, as negotiations and the issues negotiated become more complex, it becomes expedient-- probably imperative--for long-term agreements to be negotiated.

While shedding some light on collective bargaining, this chapter indicates that researchers must quantify more industrial relations and collective bargaining information. Furthermore, they must also create and conduct viable tests and testing methods to which the quantified data may be applied. Only then, it would seem, could supposition, still a vital part of collective bargaining and industrial relations, give way to definitive answers.

Notes

1.   For a fuller explanation of the term *collective bargaining structure,* see Arnold Weber, ed., *The Structure of Collective Bargaining* (New York: Free Press, 1961), pp. XV-VI; Neil Chamberlain, "Determinants of Collective Bargaining Structure", in *Challenges to Collective Bargaining,* ed. Lloyd Ulman (Englewood Cliffs, N.J.: Prentice-Hall, 1967), p. 14; and E. Robert Livernash, "New Developments in Bargaining Structure", in *Trade Union Government and Collective Bargaining: Some Critical Issues,* ed. Joel Seidman (New York: Praeger, 1970).

2.   A. Weber, *The Structure of Collective Bargaining,* pp. XVI-XVII.

3.   Neil Chamberlain, "The Structure of Bargaining Units in the United States", in *Industrial and Labour Relations Review,* vol. 10, no. 1 (October 1956).

4.   E. Robert Livernash, "The Relation of Power to the Structure and Process of Collective Bargaining", in *The Journal of Law and Economics* VI (October 1963).

5.   Economic Council of Canada, *Third Annual Review: Prices, Productivity and Employment* (Ottawa: Queen's Printer, 1966), pp. 128-130.

6.   Alton Craig and Harry Waisglass, "Collective Bargaining Perspectives", in *Relations Industries,* vol.23, no. 4 (October 1968).

7.   E.E. Herman, G.S. Skinner, and H.M. Leftwich, "The Bargaining Unit", study for the Task Force on Labour Relations, Ottawa, 1968.

8.   C. Gordon Simmons, "Co-ordinated Bargainings by Unions and Employers", study for the Task Force on Labour Relations, Ottawa, 1968.

9.   The data presented in the chapter were gathered in two parts. First, in 1966, collective bargaining information for 1953 to the second quarter of 1966 was gathered and computerized.   Then, in early 1969, the data for the remainder of 1966, along with 1967-68 information for those negotiating units which, in 1966 fulfilled the employment criteria, were collected.   Thus, new negotiating units that fulfilled the employment criteria and began negotiating in 1967-68, or began in 1967 with retroactive provisions, are excluded.   This includes many public service units.

10. Edward E. Herman, *Determination of the Appropriate Bargaining by Labour Relations Boards in Canada* (Ottawa: Queen's Printer, 1966), p. 1.

18. Supervisory Collective Bargaining*

by Robert Rogow

This brief examination of the supervisor as trade unionist begins with an explanation of the underlying environmental circumstances that may move supervisors toward collective bargaining. The chapter will also deal with public policy toward supervisory bargaining, and examine some instances of viable supervisory bargaining in the absence of public policy support. Concluding will be some summary remarks.

The Changing Role and Status of the Supervisory Employee in Modern Industry

Profound changes in the position of the first-line supervisor have resulted from technological modernization, managerial rationalization, and the expansion of rank-and-file unionism. These changes, on balance, have been destabilizing. Older supervisory perceptions of career opportunities, of status relative to people supervised and relative to staff technologists, of acceptance by and loyalty to top management, have been shaken by these changes. Managerial slowness in recognizing and adapting policies to these changes has been an important contributor to past instances of supervisory discontent.

Over the past quarter century a substantial literature on the status of the first-line supervisor or foreman has appeared. Despite differences in conceptualization, approach, and research design, a remarkable degree of agreement emerges on one point: the foreman is in trouble.

This common theme, that the first-line supervisor faces an unusually stressful situation, is expressed in many ways, some mutually contradictory. But whether he is seen as "the man in the middle", or as "a member of two organizational families" with inconsistent values, as "master and victim of double talk", as facing a secular decline in his status and authority and a simultaneous rise in his responsibilities, or as facing increasingly successful competition from the university-trained supervisor and

This chapter represents, primarily, a summary and updating of the author's larger study on the supervisory employee and collective bargaining. For further detail and citation of all sources, see Robert Rogow, *Supervisors and Collective Bargaining*, Task Force on Labour Relations, Project no. 42, June 1968.
*Reproduced by permission of Information Canada.

staff man, he is seen as a man under pressure--pressure in some
sense greater than that facing other ranks in the industrial
hierarchy.

From a position at an earlier stage of industrialization that
was quasi-independent (with something approaching "independent
contractor" status within the plant) the foreman has been trans-
formed not only into dependent employee, but into dependent employee under conditions of considerable uncertainty. The modern
foreman often does not even know precisely who his boss is; he
is confronted with a multiplicity of line and staff people, each
of them with conflicting priorities, whose displeasure he must
avoid.

Studies in the U.S. and the U.K. point to "a barrage of complaint and criticism" forthcoming from foremen because of confusion over their actual position. With an extended management
hierarchy and the growth of specialist departments, many matters
affecting the work of their departments are settled with little
participation by or even consultation with the foremen. They
often lack authority to settle worker problems and are therefore
bypassed by the shop steward. As a result, the steward's authority in the eyes of the work force often exceeds that of the
foreman, who is seen as a mere figurehead.

Technology, work flow, and the sequencing and nature of tasks
performed by work groups all shape the role and behaviour of
foremen. Supervisory responsibilities vary enormously with the
technical conditions of production--the degree of planned variation in product, the complexity of production stages, the variations among unit, batch, and continuous-flow operations. These
determine whether the foreman's primary job is surveillance,
instruction, liason, quality control, discipline, coordination,
consinsus building, buffering, foreign affairs, or....

In the automobile assembly plant, for example, the assembly
line itself takes over many of the control functions that a supervisor would perform in other technological settings. Foremen in
auto, freed from the need of pressuring workers, can concentrate
on manning problems, bottlenecks, relations with other foremen
whose work groups are "upstream" or "downstream" in the production
sequence, and personal relationships with the work group. The
line itself receives some of the hostility that in other industries might be directed toward the foreman.

Not only technology but culture causes great variability in
the nature of the foreman's role and status. National differences
in value systems, in social structure, in managerial recruitment
patterns, in social distances among differing occupational groups,
in composition of elites leading developmental processes, in size
of typical firm, in insulation of firm and industry from competitive pressures--all these differences affect the position of the
supervisor. (These differences can and do exist within countries
--especially those as regionally and culturally differentiated as
Canada--as well as among countries.)

National differences in culture and in socio-economic conditions
influence how the supervisor is perceived , and how he perceives
himself. In the large majority of industrialized countries, for

example, the foreman is not seen by management or by himself as a part of management, but is seen instead as a senior member of the work force--a view with obvious implications for supervisory unionism. Management in Canada and the U.S., on the other hand, vigorously maintains that foremen *are* part of the management "team".

Despite a desire to identify with management and an agreement with the often-repeated slogan that they are indeed management, foremen frequently express doubts about their acceptance into managerial ranks. Complaints that they receive inadequate training, inadequate authority to meet their responsibilities, even inadequate explanation of the reasons for decisions affecting them, are common. Because they want to be considered part of management rather than part of the work force, North American supervisors' discontents over compensation and indicia of status are more often over relative than over absolute standings. Students of the explosive, though abortive, growth of foremen's unions during World War II in the U.S. and Canada frequently pointed out that absolute levels of supervisory compensation were reasonable, but that resentment against narrowing of margins *vis-a-vis* rank-and-file workers was intense.

The Legal Status of Supervisory Collective Bargaining

Public policy in Canada, as exemplified by labour codes, court decisions, and decisions of labour relations boards, has been fairly consistent in the past in denying the same legal protection from employer reprisal and the same support for collective bargaining to supervisory employees that was extended to rank-and-file workers. Some recent evidence of a modification of this position exists, however.

Established Policy

Canadian public policy has traditionally been unsympathetic to the idea of supervisory unionization. This lack of sympathy has not gone to the extreme of illegalizing supervisory unionization, supervisory collective bargaining, or even supervisory strikes. Rather, it has taken the milder form of excluding supervisory and managerial employees from the protection of provincial and federal labour codes.

Coverage by protective legislation, or the absence of coverage, strongly affects the fortunes of most employee groups seeking self-organization. For a country like Canada, exclusion of a group from the basic labour laws' definition of "employee" and/or from the bargaining unit means that employers are not under a legal compulsion to bargain, and may mean that employer self-help weapons against employee organizing that are otherwise barred by law are permitted.

Canadian labour codes, in excluding managerial and supervisory employees from the protected "employee" category, have generally refrained from specifying, defining, or identifying those to be excluded.[1] Canadian public policy has left to the labour relations

boards the task of defining, in a host of differing institutional
and technical settings, the proper boundaries for managerial and
supervisory exclusion. Case by case, board enquiries into the
exact nature of managerial responsibilities have been painstaking
and detailed. That this task has been an unusually difficult one
is suggested by the record. Many senior rank-and-file employees,
for example, possess minor or partial supervisory responsibilities,
varying from situation to situation in degree and in kind. This
poses complex investigatory problems to the boards, which have
generally attempted to avoid excluding employees whose supervisory
responsibilities have been very limited or purely formal or peripheral to their normal responsibilities.

Different industries and occupations have their own supervisory
peculiarities. The problem of the managerial and supervisory cutoff is particularly complex where professional or artistic employees
are involved, as past controversies over radio and T V producers
and producer-directors suggest. In over-the-road trucking, dock
foremen in truck terminals are sometimes included in teamsters'
bargaining units. Owner-operators have sometimes been held to be
employees by the federal board, but excluded because they perform
managerial functions in relation to their driver helpers, who were
held to be employees of the company rather than of the owner-operators.

The superviosry picture in maritime employment (where much supervisory unionism antedates Canadian legislation compelling employers to bargain with employee-selected unions) is complex.
There is, for example, a wide range of decisions, from a 1946 case
in which a rank-and-file seamen's union received certification for
a unit of licensed supervisory personnel to a 1966 case excluding
captains of two-man vessels from a rank-and-file unit.

In railroading, with a tradition of managerial unionism, the
board would seem to have modified its usual criteria at times to
conform somewhat to customary practice. Thus in 1958, railway
yardmasters were held to be nonmanagerial, despite their "authority
to control and direct the movement of cars, engines and trains
within the yard", and despite the fact that they had switch crews,
yard clerks, and cleaners working under them. The board's reasoning, that the yardmaster worked under the supervision of a
general yardmaster, would seem, if applied to other industries,
to shift the managerial cutoff point much higher in the command
structure than it now is. The board noted in this decision that
the railroad had treated yardmasters as employees in concluding
collective bargaining agreements with them in the same manner as
with other employees.

As these examples suggest, Canadian boards have found it difficult to adapt the laws' blanket exclusions in a consistent way
to the extremely varied character of the supervisory function in
different industrial and occupational settings.

Recent Modifications of Established Policy

A tendency to modify the earlier restrictions on supervisory collective bargaining appears to be emerging in Canadian jurisdic-

tions. This tendency may be in part a response to the liberalizing
recommendation of the Task Force on Labour Relations of the late
1960s, a response to an increasing interest in collective bargaining on the part of private-sector supervisors (causing, for example, a decade of unrest in the west coast stevedoring industry),
a response to the rapid emergence of public-sector collective bargaining (where supervisory and even managerial employees have
engaged in bargaining without apparent harmful consequences), or
perhaps a response to the reduced power of the traditional ideological dichotomy between labour and management in the thinking
of the Canadian public.

One example of the liberalization trend was the 1972 amendment
to the federal labour code. While retaining the earlier exclusion
of "persons performing management functions", it permitted the
Canada Labour Relations Board to certify bargaining units comprised
in whole or in part of supervisory employees. The amendments appear to leave to the board the task of distinguishing between
"managerial" and "supervisory" employees and functions. Manitoba,
in 1972, also narrowed the exclusion of managerial and supervisory
employees.

The British Columbia 1973 labour code, like the federal amendments, gave its board the power to include supervisory employees
in either separate units or units shared with other employees.
The federal changes appear responsible for the successful 1974
culmination of the west coast longshoreman's union's long campaign
to bargain for dock foremen. A significant increase in supervisory
unionization appears to be taking place in B.C. as a result of its
liberalized provincial legislation.

Traditional Areas of Supervisory Unionism

In spite of the importance of inclusion or exclusion by protective
legislation, supervisory unionism is something more than a creature
of such protection. Occupations and industries exist in which it
has proved viable and even vigorous without protective legislation,
and there are national settings within which it has experienced a
much more luxuriant growth than in North America, even in the absence of protective legislation.

Foremen as Members of Rank-and-File Unions

In printing and construction, in railroading, and a few other
industries, foremen have long been members of the same internationals and even the same locals as the workers they supervise. A
1943 tabulation of U.S. unions admitting both foremen and production workers to membership showed twenty to be affiliates of the
American Federation of Labor, three to be affiliates of the Congress of Industrial Organizations, and five to be unaffiliated.
(Most of these unions had, and still have, Canadian membership).
As the breakdown by affiliation suggests, and examination of
names of individual unions supports, supervisory membership is
strongly correlated with craft unionism.

(1) The Printing Industry. Incorporation of foremen into rank-and-file unions has been developed further in the printing industry than in any other. From its earliest days, employers and supervisors in the industry have been ex-craftsmen. Ease of entry into business, probability of ultimate return to union craftsman status in the event of business failure, and attractiveness of maintaining welfare benefits of craftsmens' organizations all contributed to this vertical fluidity. Supervision of craftsmen has traditionally been performed by unionized foremen, to the exclusion of the employer or senior managers. Foremen were prominent in the union affairs from the earliest beginnings of unionization.

The union foreman has been a strategic figure in the process of craft differentiation in the printing industry. As technology differentiated skills strongly enough so that a compositor-trained foreman could no longer effectively supervise the new crafts, splitoffs from the International Typographical Union occurred (pressmen, photoengravers, stereotypers). The pressmen early discovered that they could throw off ITU domination only by requiring that press foremen be members of their union. Their 1889 secession from the ITU was caused partly by the performing of press work by compositors, abetted by foremen who were nearly always compositors.

Its long history in printing suggests the industry's experience with supervisory unionism might provide a useful test of managerial claims that labour-management cooperation, managerial authority, and labour discipline are adversely affected by supervisory unionism. Little reference to such harmful effects can be found in studies of the industry, partly because of lack of scholarly attention to the question, but partly also because these problems have not proved to be as serious as the antiunion argument would have predicted.

Unfortunately for the purpose of examining the viability of supervisory unionism throughout the economy, the relatively good record of supervisory unionism in printing may be the result of conditions--historical, technological, and sociological--peculiar to printing and a handful of other industries. The high rate of upward and downward mobility already referred to, the internalized self-discipline and concern for quality of work of the skilled printing craftsman, and the limitations on supervisory discretion imposed by the unusually complex work rules of the trade, are examples of conditions that limit the transferability of the printing experience to many other industries.

(2) The Construction Industry. Almost all construction unions require the foreman to be a member. The usual explanation for this practice is twofold: first, that the construction foreman is primarily a working foreman; and second, that foreman membership is necessary to enforce the many working rules in the trade. In addition, the "rule-lessness" of the industry, the pragmatic, *ad hoc,* informal, favour-trading, power-responsive nature of industrial relations in construction, the strong industry identification, the narrow class lines between employer and employee, the common social and psychological outlook, and the relatively high mobility among rank-and-file, foreman, and managerial statuses, are important explanations of the prevalence of supervisory inclusion in rank-and-file unions.

(3)   The Railroad Industry. Despite the existence of separate
unions of supervisory personnel in railroading, the majority of
organized supervisors in railroading are members of rank-and-file
unions.   An estimated 80 per cent of supervisory and managerial
employees on U.S. railroads are union members, a percentage equal
to that among rank-and-file employees.   This includes some middle-
management employees as well as first-line supervisors.   To some
extent, the unusually high degree of supervisory unionization may
be an accidental historical by-product of the American Railway
Labor Acts of 1926 and 1934.   Another pro-unionization influence
somewhat peculiar to the industry has been the traditionally high
income and high status, relative to that of lower-level supervisors
and managers, of unionized rank-and-file employees such as railway
engineers and conductors.

Foremen as Members of Exclusively Supervisory Unions

The 1943 enumeration referred to earlier listed nine unions of
exclusively supervisory or managerial employees.   Three were unions of licensed maritime personnel, three of supervisory personnel in the postal and railway mail service, two were of railway yardmasters and supervisors, and one represented navy yard
foremen.   This concentration on government employment and heavy
transport with its quasi-governmental size and organizational
characteristics is of interest.   British experience also suggests
that supervisory unions are more likely to be found among government employees or employees of nationalized industries.   Of interest is the unusually early date of origin of the nine unions;
the median date of origin was 1908.
     Where numbers are large enough to make it practicable, there
appears to be some present-day tendency for supervisory and managerial employees in education and local government to attempt to
engage in separate bargaining with their employers, either within
or outside of rank.

Professionalism and Supervisory Unionism

The professional as employee has always posed some special problems in supervisor-supervised relationships.   Professionalism as
imputed status, labour supply characteristic, occupational mys-
tique, or ideology is far too complex a phenomenon to be treated
satisfactorily here, but a few relevant observations are possible.
     The rank-and-file professional employee is something of an
anomaly.   Compared to the usual nonsupervisory employee he pos-
sesses an internalized "managerial" set of controls, identifica-
tions with the stated objectives of the employing enterprise, and
self-disciplines.   (Some of the blue-collar crafts reflect similar, but weaker, value systems.)   Thus, direct and heavy-handed
supervision is less necessary and more resented.   Relationships
with organizational seniors are seen as colleague relationships
where the seniors share a common training and experience, or as
clientele relationships where the seniors lack this common background.   High proportions of professional employees have managerial responsibilities, either over fellow professionals or over

technicians and subtechnical workers, making the usual legal managerial cutoff a particularly onerous one to the professional employee organization. Further, the nature of professionalism makes the demand for sharing in managerial decision making far more intense than it is from blue-collar unions. In the latter case it is normally a defensive mechanism attempting to minimize harmful effects on preexisting relationships arising from technological and organizational innovation; in the former it is inherent in the notions of competence and responsibility of the professional ideology itself.

Supervisory Unionism Under Different National Industrial Relations Systems

That the extent and character of supervisory unionism varies sharply from country to country is clear. That such unionism is regarded by, for example, Western European top managements as less of a threat to managerial control than it is by their North American counterparts is also clear.

Much less clear, however, is the case for the transferability or relevance to North American industrial relations settings of European supervisory unionism experiences. Sharper European differentiations among, and lesser career movements among, the varying strata of supervision and management provide one of the more important reasons for this nontransferability. It is not merely that most European management regards the first-line supervisor as a part of the work force rather than as part of management. Even more significant a difference is the gulf separating middle-management and staff-specialist groups from top management, a gulf widened by the relatively greater importance of family ownership as opposed to professional management and of authoritarian as opposed to participative management philosophies. The greater relative weight of government employment in European industrial relations, the more active economic planning and coordination role of government, and the much greater incidence of bargaining by multiemployer organizations are also relevant differences.

Continental managerial unionism is primarily an associational form for people above the status of first-line supervision. Since it is the first-line supervisor who is primarily significant for self-organization questions in North America, the relevance of this fascinating organizational development to our enquiry is quite limited.

Predictably, Sweden provides examples of vigorous first-line supervisory unionism. About 90 per cent of blue-collar foremen belong to the Foremen's Union, which has been in existence for half a century. Legislation permits employers to require their foremen to refrain from membership in rank-and-file unions, and almost all collective bargaining agreements so provide. Unlike traditional North American public policy, however, Sweden does give legal protection to the foremen-only union. Performance of the Foremen's Union would appear to be quite responsible, with little employer complaint of noncooperation or impairment of foremen's responsibilities to management. Interestingly, clerical

supervisors are not in the Foremen's Union, but are often members
of the Union of Salaried Employees (SIF). Here membership in the
same union as their subordinates is common, but has not given rise
to serious problems. Opportunities for movement upward from foremen's positions in Swedish industry are described as more limited
than they are in the United States. The Salaried Workers' Federation (TCO) includes a number of additional supervisory unions.

Conclusion

Supervisory unionism has proved viable over long periods in a
somewhat limited number of areas. Characteristics more or less
unique and nontransferable explain such incidence.

Experience outside the traditional areas (especially the brief
and turbulent history of the Foreman's Association of America in
the 1940s) suggests that supervisory unionism has great difficulty
in establishing itself in the absence of supportive legislation,
favourable environmental circumstances (for example, government
concern over interruptions of wartime production of crucial products), or support from powerful rank-and-file unions. A managerial opposition to supervisory bargaining that appears much stronger
than its opposition to rank-and-file bargaining is one explanation
of that difficulty. Support from rank-and-file unions raises problems as well as opportunities for supervisory unionists. Some dependency relations, and some subordination of supervisory to rank-
and-file interests, may result.

In general, supervisory bargaining appears to be something of
a derived phenomenon, a secondary relationship. Just as the
supervisor is himself marginal in the work relationship to two
more powerful groups, so is supervisory bargaining reflective of
and dependent on the employer-employee relation in general. The
data suggest other dependencies as well: dependency on work flow
and technological characteristics, dependency on past bargaining
histories, dependency on internal political stresses in other
employee organizations, dependency on managerial sensitivity to
the supervisor's Janus-like position, dependency on ease of perceived movement upward in the administrative hierarchy, dependency
on commonalties of craft or professional identification between
supervisor and supervised, dependency on senior management's
insecurities *vis-a-vis* union encroachments into sensitive areas
of decision making, etc. The moral to all this seems to be the
avoidance of public policy making by abstract and universal principles, and the substitution of a more flexible adaptability to
the realities of supervision in specific industries, occupational
settings, and environments. This appears to be a direction in
which Canadian public policy is moving.

Note

1. As an interesting contrast to prevailing Canadian practice, the

amended labour relations act (Taft-Hartley Act) in the U.S. attempted to define a supervisor as:

...any individual having authority, in the interest of the employer, to hire, transfer, suspend, lay off, recall, promote, discharge, assign, reward, or discipline other employees, or responsibility to direct them or to adjust their grievances, or effectively to recommend such action, if in connection with the foregoing the exercise of such authority is not of a merely routine or clerical nature, but requires the use of independent judgment.

19. Professional Workers and Collective Bargaining*

by Shirley B. Goldenberg

The Controversy over Professional Bargaining

Although it has long been an accepted practice for professional
associations to engage in collective economic action--fee setting,
for example--on behalf of their self-employed members, these same
professional associations as well as employers and the general
public have frequently shown considerable resistance to the idea
of collective bargaining on the industrial pattern by salaried
professional workers. Some students and observers of labour
relations, on the other hand, regard collective bargaining as a
logical response to the employment problems of professional workers. Labour organizations are also looking to the rapidly growing
white-collar and professional segment of the labour force as a
potential source of future union membership.

As for the salaried professionals themselves, members of the
"closed" or traditional professional occupations, such as medicine,
dentistry, law, engineering, and architecture, have usually been
strongly opposed to collective bargaining, although even in these
professions there have been some significant exceptions.[1] Occupational groups, such as teachers and nurses, on the other hand,
have shown a growing propensity to bargain collectively in recent
years,[2] as have some university graduates with specialized degrees,
such as library science, social work, economics, etc., particularly when employed in government service.[3] For whereas the management orientation of the traditional professions in particular and
the generally responsible nature of professional functions and
duties have, by and large, precluded the identification of professional employees with nonprofessional workers in the labour
force, some of the problems faced by professionals in large scale
organizations are similar to those of their nonprofessional confreres. In addition, professional employees may have particular
problems of their own, such as the loss of control over standards
of professional performance in bureaucratic and profit-oriented
enterprises. The growing inability of many professional workers
to solve their employment problems on an individual basis, combined with the demonstration effect of successfully negotiated
settlements for nonprofessional employees, has stimulated the
pressure for collective action, at least in some professional
groups.

The form this action takes has varied considerably, both between and within professional groups and in different geographic
locations. For example, while groups of teachers and nurses are

---

*Reproduced by permission of Information Canada.

now employing increasingly militant tactics in many parts of the country, strike action by professional engineers who bargain collectively, as well as by professionals in government employment, has been virtually limited to Quebec. Quebec is also the only jurisdiction in which unions of professional workers have affiliated with a central labour organization.[4] This is in contrast to experience in the United States in recent years, where professional membership in AFL-CIO unions seems to have grown significantly.[5]

Professional workers face particular problems when they wish to bargain collectively--the problem of the appropriate bargaining agent, the method for the resolution of interest disputes, the protection of certain professional prerogatives, etc. In addition, there may be serious legal constraints both on the right to bargain collectively and on the formation of viable bargaining units. This chapter will deal with the major legal impediments to professional organization for the purpose of collective bargaining, using the case of the engineers as an example.

The Legal Right to Bargain Collectively

Because of the constitutional division of powers under our federal system, there is no uniform Canadian legislation affecting collective bargaining rights for professional workers. The legal status of collective bargaining for professionals, as for other workers, is determined by separate legislation in each of the provinces and at the federal level. There may even be different provisions in the same jurisdiction, depending on whether the professionals concerned are employed in the private or public sector.

The most blatant of the legal impediments to collective bargaining has been the practice of excluding the members of specific professional occupations from the definition of "employee" under labour legislation. Such exclusions have usually applied to the "closed" professions, such as medicine, dentistry, law, engineering, and architecture, although a few jurisdictions have also excluded teachers.[6] While experience shows that the exclusion of a professional group from labour legislation does not necessarily preclude collective bargaining under voluntary recognition procedures--the Ontario teachers are a case in point--there can be little doubt that an adverse public policy can reinforce employer resistance. Thus there has been considerable pressure by interested groups in recent years to abolish the professional exclusions. Others, notably the professional associations, have been equally insistent that the exclusions be maintained.

While considerably more professional workers in Canada now enjoy the legal right to bargain collectively than was the case a decade ago, labour relations acts in five provinces, Alberta, British Columbia, Newfoundland, Nova Scotia, and Prince Edward Island, still exclude the members of a number of the traditional professional occupations from collective bargaining in the private sector. Ontario labour legislation covers professional engineers but excludes the members of other traditional professions. There are no professional exclusions from labour relations acts in the remaining provinces or at the federal level.

With the notable exception of Saskatchewan, jurisdictions that grant professional workers bargaining rights under labour legislation also allow them the special protection of bargaining in a separate unit. Professional workers in Manitoba and New Brunswick and the engineers in Ontario may opt for separate bargaining units if they object to being included in units with nonprofessional employees. The federal Labour Code allows for separate bargaining units of one or more professional categories but the professionals may, if they wish, include in such units persons performing the functions but lacking the formal qualifications of a professional employee. This flexibility is absent in Quebec, where the legislation requires that bargaining units be limited to members of the same profession.

Only three jurisdictions deny collective bargaining rights to professionals in the civil service. Manitoba and Ontario still exclude all the traditional professions from their civil service legislation, although new legislation expected imminently in Manitoba could well make a change in this respect. British Columbia excludes only members of the legal profession. The public service legislation at the federal level and in Quebec, New Brunswick, and British Columbia provides for separate professional bargaining units, though not necessarily confined to members of a single profession. The remaining provinces have no professional exclusions; neither do they provide for separate professional bargaining units.

The Problem of Viable Bargaining Units

Even where professional workers have legal bargaining rights, certain groups complain that they are prevented from establishing satisfactory bargaining units by restrictive provisions in the law. While some frustration has arisen from statutory restrictions on the professional composition of bargaining units, most of the complaints have been based on the provisions for managerial exclusions. These exclusions have been the most serious impediment to the formation of viable professional bargaining units, particularly when the workers concerned are employed in an industrial context.

All collective bargaining legislation in Canada, whether or not it applies to professional workers, is predicated on a clear-cut differentiation between labour and management functions. This excludes from the definition of employee, and consequently from the bargaining unit, anyone performing "management functions" or employed in a confidential capacity. It is hardly surprising that the establishment of the demarcation line between labour and management functions would present more serious problems for professional workers than for the mass of nonprofessional employees for whom the legislation was originally envisaged. In view of the generally responsible nature of professional services and duties, as well as the obvious cases where professional and management functions are fused, a relatively high proportion of salaried professionals are, by legal definition and by decisions of labour relations boards, excluded from bargaining rights. While professional workers claim that the rigid definition of employee status

under existing legislation restricts their bargaining unit and
weakens their bargaining strength, management spokesmen have
pointed out the conflicts of interest that could result if professional workers with supervisory functions sat on the employee
side of the bargaining table.

The problem of managerial exclusions, with the corollary restriction of the size of the bargaining unit, is not equally serious for
all professional employees. In the case of teachers, for example,
it has been easily resolved, by simply excluding the principals.
Much depends on the nature of the professional role, the degree of
responsibility entailed, as well as the different circumstances of
employment that may exist in government, industry and other institutions. The problem of managerial exclusions has been most acute
in the case of the engineers and is dramatically illustrated by
their experience in Quebec and Ontario.

The Case of the Engineers

All professional exclusions were removed from Quebec labour legislation in 1964; the engineering exclusion was abolished in Ontario
in 1970. As groups of engineers had led the battle for professional bargaining rights in both these provinces, it was logical
to expect them to apply for certification once these rights became
available. In practice, however, engineers wishing to bargain
collectively have been reluctant to use the provisions of the law
because of their fear of managerial exclusions.

Quebec

The problem in Quebec is illustrated by the experience of professional engineers at the City of Montreal and Hydro Quebec. Incorporated under the Professional Syndicates Act,[7] and affiliated with
the CNTU, they chose to rely on power relationships to define their
bargaining units rather than submit to the provisions of the code
and risk a narrow interpretation of employee status (and consequently a high proportion of managerial exclusions) by the Labour
Relations Board.

An engineers' union was formed at the City of Montreal in October 1963, having enrolled 255 out of a possible 290 city engineers. But it took the threat of a strike in July of the following
year before the city would recognize the union and agree to bargain
with it. The first collective agreement was signed in May 1965,
after protracted negotiations and conciliation and another threat
of a strike. Union jurisdiction (the area of the bargaining unit)
had been one of the major issues in the negotiations. The recommendations of the conciliator in the matter of union jurisdiction
were virtually identical with the original union position and were
included in the agreement. The bargaining unit, as finally defined, did not conform to the requirement of the Labour Code to
exclude all persons exercising supervisory authority. Instead
it excluded only those engineers *exercising hiring and firing authority over other engineers* or employed in a confidential capacity.

The professional engineers at Hydro Quebec, like those at the City of Montreal, decided to force "voluntary" recognition on their employer. But it took two recognition strikes before their first collective agreement was signed. The union approached the Hydro Commission for recognition in January 1965, demanding a broad "professional" bargaining unit on the pattern established by the engineers at the City of Montreal. Hydro, on the other hand, insisted that the bargaining unit be based on the provisions of the Labour Code and wanted the Labour Relations Board to determine the managerial exclusions.

The first recognition strike began in May 1965 and lasted for five weeks. A noted expert on professional bargaining has commented on the results as follows:

Of the 555 engineers at Quebec Hydro, 440 were finally recognized as being acceptable for representation through the syndicate, whereas, if certification under the Code had been required, only about 280 would have been in fact covered by the eventual agreement. This was a true victory for "cadre" (supervisory) unionism.[8]

A letter of agreement defining the bargaining unit (June 1965) was followed by contract negotiations. But the bargaining broke down when Hydro implemented administrative changes that had the effect of increasing the number of managerial exclusions from the bargaining unit. This led to a second recognition strike beginning in April 1966 and lasting for eleven weeks. This strike resulted in a new settlement which respected the *principle* established in the first agreement, namely the exclusion from the bargaining unit of any engineer whose position carried authority over the *career* of other engineers or professionals.

The substantial salary increases and significant professional benefits in the first engineers' agreements at the City of Montreal and Hydro Quebec are unlikely to have been achieved if these groups had allowed their bargaining strength to be weakened by all the managerial exclusions required by the Labour Code.

It is interesting to note that the engineers' units that were established by "voluntary" recognition were subsequently recognized in the law. Special amendments to the Labour Code in 1969 recognized as certified associations the unions signatory to the engineers' agreements at the City of Montreal and Hydro Quebec. Their experience had proved that a workable policy of exclusions need only affect those with authority over engineers or other professionals with respect to promotion, salary, work assessment, and disciplinary matters.

Ontario

While fewer engineers in Ontario have been interested in bargaining collectively than was the case in Quebec, those wishing to do so have faced similar problems. The removal of the engineering exclusion clause from Ontario labour legislation marked the culmination of a protracted struggle by a determined group of employee

engineers wanting legal bargaining rights. The Society of Ontario
Hydro Professional Engineers and Associates (SOHPEA) had taken the
lead in this battle. However, the members of SOHPEA and other
groups of employee engineers, like their confreres in Quebec, have
been reluctant to use the labour legislation as a vehicle for collective bargaining, fearing the erosion of their bargaining strength
by the provision for managerial exclusions.

SOHPEA was considered the group most likely to make the first
application for certification after the removal of the engineering
exclusion form the Labour Relations Act. But this did not occur.
In January 1973, SOHPEA signed a voluntary Master Agreement and
Redress Procedure with its employer rather than go before the Labour Relations Board for certification under the act.

SOHPEA already had a form of voluntary collective agreement
with Ontario Hydro by virtue of a Letter of Understanding signed
in September 1961. This letter contained a recognition clause and
a system of joint consultation on working conditions through the
medium of a Joint Society-Management Committee. However, it differed from a standard collective agreement in it provision for continuous negotiations and had no termination date. It also covered
employees performing supervisory functions apart from those employed
in a confidential capacity.

Although SOHPEA had not been certified, it applied to the Labour
Relations Board, under section 13(3) of the Labour Relations Act,
for conciliation of a dispute arising out of the joint consultation
system. But the board refused to grant conciliation services,
noting that SOHPEA did not meet the definition of a trade union
because of its managerial inclusions. SOHPEA then proceeded to
negotiate the Master Agreement and Redress Procedure referred to
above.

Like the Letter of Understanding of 1961, the present Master
Agreement is not a collective labour agreement as the term is generally understood. In a sense it is a voluntary agreement as to
the procedure to be followed in negotiating a collective agreement
in the future. It deals with the composition of the bargaining
unit, the recognition of SOHPEA as the bargaining agent, union
security, the terms of the agreement, a mediation/arbitration
mechanism for the settlement of interest disputes, and a redress
procedure for rights disputes culminating in final and binding
arbitration.

The inclusion of managerial employees was crucial for SOHPEA,
whose membership of some 14,000 is drawn from Ontario Hydro Management and Professional grades, including about 75 on the top
executive payroll. As the act specifically excludes both those
exercising managerial functions and those employed in a confidential capacity in labour matters, several hundred SOHPEA members
could have been deprived of bargaining rights under regular certification procedures. The Master Agreement only excluded those
employed in a confidential capacity, which in practice resulted
in no exclusions at all.

SOHPEA was also concerned about special professional provisions,
particularly a provision for the resolution of disputes without
resort to a strike. The Master Agreement satisfied these desires,

along with the desire for a broad interpretation of employee status for eligibility to the bargaining unit.

The experience of the Quebec and Ontario engineers obviously differs considerably. More than half the professional engineers in Quebec have chosen to bargain collectively; about 10 per cent have done so in Ontario. Quebec engineers are affiliated with a central labour organization, the CNTU, and consider the strike an important bargaining weapon. Ontario engineers have not joined unions and are strongly opposed to the strike. But on one point both groups are in complete agreement. A more flexible definition of employee status under labour legislation, corresponding to the realities of professional employment, could do much to relieve the current anxiety with respect to managerial exclusions. While other professional groups may face fewer problems than the engineers in defining their bargaining units, they are unlikely to disagree with them on this point.

Notes

1. Note the groups of engineers in Quebec and Ontario who are actively engaged in collective bargaining. (Their case is described later in the chapter.) There are even some unions of lawyers in Quebec, and also doctors' syndicates for negotiations under medicare legislation. Interns and residents on hospital staffs bargain collectively as well. So do several groups of university teachers.

2. Teachers and nurses now bargain collectively in virtually all jurisdictions, although legislation in some of the provinces restricts their right to strike.

3. University graduates with specialized degrees as well as members of the traditional professional occupations are already covered by collective agreements in the federal public service and in the public service of Quebec and New Brunswick.

4. Engineers at the City of Montreal, Hydro Quebec and the government of Quebec, other professional employees at the City of Montreal and the government of Quebec, some groups of nurses and junior college and university professors are affiliated with the Confederation of National Trade Unions (CNTU). The majority of teachers in the province are affiliated with the *Centrale des enseignants du Québec* (CEQ), which recently adopted union status.

5. *The seven-year old Council of American Federation of Labor and Congress of Industrial Organizations Unions for Professional Employees now represents more than 1,000,000 members. And according to the Department of Labor, this year about 3,000,000 professional and technical people, including such unlikely unionists as lawyers and architects, are working under collectively negotiated contracts....A.F.L.-C.I.O. officials calculate that this fig-*

*ure represents about half of all the professional and technical
workers who are "organizable", or employed in groups large enough
to make collective bargaining feasible.* (Rafael Steinberg, "Professionals in Unions Cite Old Reasons: Pay, Security", *New York
Times,* 28 July 1974.)

6. Although teachers are excluded from the labour relations acts
of Prince Edward Island, British Columbia and Manitoba, there is
provision for them to bargain collectively under separate public
schools acts. Teachers are not excluded from the Trade Union Act
of Saskatchewan, but they bargain under different legislation, the
Teacher Salary Agreement Act. Teachers are excluded from labour
legislation in Ontario, but bargain under a system of voluntary
recognition by their employers. Collective bargaining legislation
for teachers is imminent in Ontario.

7. A 1924 statute whose general purpose was to permit the association, under certain conditions, of persons "engaged in the same
profession, the same employment or in similar trades, or doing
correlated work having as an object the establishment of a determined product". Some groups incorporated under this statute
entered into voluntary bargaining relationships with their employers. The act did not compel the employers to bargain collectively.

8. Jean-Réal Cardin, "Collective Bargaining and the Professional
Employee in Quebec", in *Collective Bargaining and the Professional
Employee,* (Toronto: Industrial Relations Centre, University of
Toronto, 1966), p. 92.

20. Collective Bargaining in the Railway Industry*

by Stephen G. Peitchinis

Introduction

Among the many factors that have influenced collective bargaining
in the railway industry over time, there are four whose influence
has been pervasive. The first is the involvement of government
in the development of railways. The relatively heavy financial
burden incurred by the government, and the generous contributions
made by it in the form of land, created the impression among the
people that the government was, or should be, an active partner
in the industry. This is the basis on which successive governments
justified their interference in the operations of the industry,
and railway workers opposed consideration of the ability to pay
as a criterion in the determination of their wages and conditions
of work. The second concerns the government's concept of the
industry's role in the development of the Canadian economy from
coast to coast, and its attempt to give expression to that concept in legislation relating to the physical structure, operations,
and charges of the industry. No other industry, whether privately
or publicly owned, has been subjected to as many rigid regulations
as have the railways. They were compelled to maintain unremuner-
ative lines, and stations which were virtually empty monuments to
an era that had long gone; and some of their charges were fixed
at levels that had no relation to the actual cost of conveyance.
In short, the railways were used as instruments of economic policy,
without compensatory payments for services rendered in the national interest. The effect of this on collective bargaining in the
industry was to virtually destroy it: the railways refused to
enter into any negotiations whose ultimate effect was likely to
cause increases in labour costs, without prior commitment by the
government that compensatory adjustments in charges would be
allowed. The third factor is the consistent failure on the part
of the government to require compliance by the parties with the
provision of the Industrial Relations Disputes Investigation Act,
that they bargain collectively and in good faith. It is worth
speculating what would have happened if the Minister of Labour
had refused to establish conciliation boards until the parties
demonstrated that they did in fact negotiate. The fourth factor
is the continuing reliance on the conciliation process, long
after it became evident that it was being used as a substitute
for, instead of a supplement to, the collective bargaining process.

---

*Reproduced by permission of Information Canada.

The Collective Bargaining Process

It should be stated at the outset that there is no alternative to the process of free collective bargaining. Therefore, when the process is terminated, or its progress is impeded, or artificial constraints are imposed on it, it is not the process of free collective bargaining that must be defended and justified, but rather the necessity for the imposition of impediments. For example, if it is deemed necessary that a time period be introduced on the process--from the commencement of negotiations to their conclusion --not only the time period itself must be justified, but also the measures that would become necessary to cope with the possible consequences.

There has been no real collective bargaining on the railways. It takes two to bargain and railway management has refused to participate. Their usual response to the demands of unions has been either outright rejection, on the ground that the existing rates of pay and condition of employment are "fair and reasonable", or a request that the unions indicate "what they would consider a fair settlement". There is no evidence of any effort on their part to present and attempt to justify bases for settlement alternative to those presented by the unions. Occasionally they have suggested possible alternatives, but invariably these were rejected by both the unions and conciliation boards, for being either irrelevant or not constituting a basis for negotiation. Indeed, many of their so-called counterproposals were so obviously designed to be rejected that they could have constituted valid grounds for charging the railways with failure to bargain in good faith.

Instead of presenting alternative proposals and arguing their merits, the representatives of the railways usually concentrated their efforts on finding weaknesses in the formulation and presentation of the union proposals. In this they were assisted by the court-like proceedings of conciliation boards. There is general consensus among persons well acquainted with the proceedings that more satisfactory results would have been obtained, and the collective bargaining process would have suffered less damage, if conciliation boards: (1) refused to commence proceedings until the railways presented genuine counterproposals; (2) refused to conclude the proceedings until the parties demonstrated readiness and willingness to negotiate; (3) refused to submit recommendations for settlement until the parties demonstrated that they made some effort to narrow their differences; and (4) conducted the proceedings on a round-table discussion basis.

The refusal of the railways to commit themselves voluntarily to any cost-raising adjustments in their employment contracts, and their virtual refusal to engage in collective bargaining either prior to or during conciliation proceedings, has been explained on the ground that restrictive legislation prevented the undertaking of cost-offsetting adjustments in operations and charges. Management was concerned lest offers to increase wages and benefits, however small, were interpreted by the government and the Board of Transport Commissioners to mean ability to offset cost without increases in charges. Even if increases in charges were not

necessary or possible, management did not wish to convey such an
impression. Since the railways were fighting for greater freedom
from government regulation and control, it was in their interest
to perpetuate the notion that as long as regulations and controls
remained in effect, the burden of increases in wages and benefits
would be borne by the public, either in the form of increases in
charges or in subsidies. On many occasions it was quite evident
that the "crises" in labour-management relations had nothing to do
with labour-management relations. Rather, they were conflicts
between the government and the railways regarding the nature and
degree of controls imposed on the operations of the industry.
Therefore, from the standpoint of the application of continuous
pressure on the government to review and relax the rigid regulations, it was to the industry's advantage to create a crisis situation out of every contract renewal, thereby forcing an examination by the Cabinet of the whole railway problem. The result is
reflected in the number of times that unions found it necessary
to prepare for strike action, and in the number of times that the
government found it necessary to pass emergency antistrike legislation.

   In the period 1946-1968, the unions prepared for strike action
on six occasions (1947, 1948, 1954, 1958, 1960, 1961) and went on
strike twice--in 1950 and 1966. In 1950, the workers were ordered
back to work by an act of Parliament--the Maintenance of Railway
Operations Act--and compulsory arbitration was imposed; in 1960,
they were forbidden to go on strike by an act of Parliament--the
Railway Operations Continuation Act; and in 1966 Parliament was
recalled from its summer recess and enacted the Maintenance of
Railway Operations Act, which provided for the resumption of railway operations and the settlement of the dispute through mediation.

Government Involvement in Disputes

Government intervention to prevent a strike from taking place
constitutes, in effect, intervention with the process of free collective bargaining. The fact that the government finds it necessary to intervene beyond the legally instituted intervention, as
provided in the Industrial Relations Disputes Investigation Act,
may be construed as evidence of the inadequacy of existing legislation.

   Under the Industrial Relations Disputes Investigation Act,
railway workers are given the legal right to take strike action;
nevertheless, the federal government has demonstrated repeatedly
that it will not tolerate strikes on the railways. This is analo-
gous to giving the people a legal right to carry arms in order to
defend their properties and the nation, and at the same time
legislating compliance with the Sixth Commandment--thou shalt not
kill.

   The justification for government intervention beyond the machinery provided in the Industrial Relations Disputes Investigation Act
has been founded on "the national interest". But since the intent
of this act was to safeguard the national interest, the necessity

for direct government intervention implies that the act has failed to provide effective protection. The question arises, therefore, where has it failed?

It has failed because the parties did not find it possible or elected not to abide by one of its main provisions, namely, to bargain in good faith. The consistent failure of the railways to make counterproposals to the demands of the unions precluded the possibility of bargaining either prior to, or during, conciliation proceedings. Indeed, even the conciliation proceedings themselves have come to be regarded as a burdensome and costly ritual, and have been treated as a forum for the presentation of the parties' respective views on the issues under examination and on related problems.

One can only speculate whether disputes would have been allowed to go to the brink, had the government resolved not to interfere, and demonstrated such a policy. It is doubtful that the railways would have gone to the eleventh hour as frequently as has been the case, had work stoppages been a distinct possibility. As one union official put it: "We and the railways would have been forced to find some way to resolve our problems." He regarded both the conciliation process and the prospect of government intervention as impediments to the search for more efficient alternatives.

However, although free collective bargaining must continue to be the ideal ultimate objective, in the context of existing economic and political reality some form of government involvement is inevitable. The people regard the railways as a public utility that provides an essential service; they will not tolerate the interruption of that service because of labour-management disputes. Under such circumstances, no government can afford to remain passive when a work stoppage becomes a distinct possibility. Therefore, the objective should be to devise a more effective bargaining process, and thus reduce the need for frequent government involvement.

The involvement of the political process in the determination of railway charges and its bearing on the collective bargaining process is demonstrated clearly by events in the period 1958-1961.

On 29 July 1958, a conciliation board under the chairmanship of Mr. Justice Thompson recommended certain increases in wages over a period of two years, retroactive to 1 January 1958. Although agreeing that the recommended wage increases were reasonable,[1] the railways informed the Minister of Labour that they could "neither accept nor reject" the report until the sources of the necessary revenue were determined. Clearly, the dispute that followed--the taking of a strike vote, the setting of a strike date, and the general crisis atmosphere that prevailed to November 27 when an agreement was reached--was not a dispute between management and the unions, but rather a conflict between the railways and the government. The absence of government policy and indecision in high places were largely responsible for the state of confusion that prevailed.

On 17 November 1958, the Board of Transport Commissioners granted the railways authority to raise freight rates by 17 per cent effective 1 December 1958. But protests from eight provinces

alleging that general increases in freight rates were discriminatory and caused inequities in the freight rate structure, resulted
first in a government announcement in March 1959 that no further
general increases would be permitted until a royal commission[2]
investigated and reported on the problem, and then, in the enactment of the Freight Rates Reduction Act, effective 1 August 1959,
which provided for a rollback of the 17 per cent increase to 10
per cent and the payment of $20 million per annum to compensate
the railways for loss in revenue. Thus the dependence of the
railways on the government for revenue was increased, raising the
prospect of further direct government involvement in labour-management relations. On 2 May 1960, the Board of Transport Commissioners ordered a further rollback of the authorized increase in
rates to 8 per cent.

The provinces also questioned "the propriety of the action of
the Board of Transport Commissioners in basing an increase in
freight rates on an anticipated wage increase which had not been
unconditionally agreed upon by the railways and their employees".
In agreeing with this criticism of the board, the government
declared:

*We consider that in future the railways and their employees must
come to a definite agreement before a wage increase should be
accepted by the Board of Transport Commissioners as the basis for
an increase in freight rates; otherwise the Board as it foresaw
itself, is apt to be forced into making judgements about wage
settlements which are not its proper responsibility.*[3]

This statement implied recognition of wage settlements as a basis
for the determination of increases in freight rates. But subsequent developments do not support such an interpretation: the
17 per cent increase in rates was authorized on 17 November 1958;
the government statement was issued on November 26; and a labour-
management agreement was concluded on November 27.   However, as
indicated above, in March 1959 the government declared that no
further general increases in rates would be permitted, and ordered
a rollback of the 17 per cent authorized increase to 10 per cent.
Under such circumstances, it is hardly possible for labour and
management to enter into serious and conclusive negotiations.
This is reflected in the events of the subsequent process of
contract renewal.

In August 1960, a conciliation board under the chairmanship of
Mr. Justice J.V. Milvain recommended wage increases totalling about
14 cents per hour to be granted over a period of two years retroactive to 1 January 1960. The railways took the stand that under
the existing government policy regarding increases in freight
rates they could not accept the report. The conflict that followed, which culminated in the setting of 3 December 1960 for
strike action and in the enactment of the Railway Operations Continuation Act on 2 December 1960 prohibiting the strike, was
really a conflict between the railways and the government, as
were so many of the other "labour-management conflicts" on the
railways. For the railways, the issue was not whether the

recommended increase in wages was justified, but rather whether
they should operate under a government policy that prohibited
adjustments in operations and charges designed to offset the
resulting increases in operating costs. In rejecting the report
even though they may have agreed with its recommendations, railway management were in effect inviting the unions to do what they
themselves would have liked to do, namely, stop operations.

In early May 1961, an agreement was concluded on the basis of
the conciliation board's recommendations, but after the government
had accepted a recommendation of the Royal Commission on Transportation to pay the railways $50 million per annum for services
rendered in the national interest. Thus, another labour-management conflict was settled without settling the main source of the
conflict--the unduly restrictive rules and regulations relating
to railway charges and operations.

The problem arose again in 1964, when a conciliation board
recommendation for an increase in wages was rejected by the railways. In a letter to the prime minister dated 22 June 1964, the
presidents of the Canadian National and Canadian Pacific railways
declared:

*The Railways find themselves deprived of authority to raise added
revenues to meet increased costs and circumscribed in their ability to effect economies through the discontinuance of unremunera-
tive operations. Under these conditions, they cannot undertake
the responsibility of assuming added costs of the magnitude implicit in the majority report of the Monroe Conciliation Board.
Even though rejection of the report may inevitably lead to a railway strike, existing circumstances leave us no alternative.
Before taking this action, however, we felt the matter should be
placed before you.*

Evidently, the dispute was not between the railways and the
unions, but rather between the railways and the government. By
implication, removal of the restrictive regulations under which
they operated would have made the railways more responsive to
union demands and recommendations of conciliation boards.

If the main impediment to the establishment of an effective
process of collective bargaining in the industry was the restrictive legal framework within which the railways operated, then the
considerable liberalization of the regulations under the National
Transportation Act of 1967 should become reflected in the commencement of genuine collective bargaining. The general consensus
among persons knowledgeable of the situation is that this will not
take place in the short run, despite the recent success in negotiations. It is suggested that the removal of legislative obstacles merely opens the road to free access; whether the road will
be used, how it will be used, and the extent to which it will be
used, depends upon how accustomed the parties have become to the
use of alternative roads. Although the successful negotiation of
the last contract has generated some optimism among participants
and observers, it takes time to become accustomed to the arduous
process of collective bargaining.

In addition to the attitudes of the two parties, the attitude
of the government will be of paramount importance in the evolution of collective bargaining in the industry. Much will depend
on what role the government conceives for itself in the new setting. If it wishes to assist in the development of free collective bargaining on the railways, then it must demonstrate to the
parties that it will not interfere in the determination of terms
and conditions of employment beyond the provisions of the Industrial Relations Disputes Investigation Act. However, to make
certain that it will not falter under provocations and pressures,
the government must convince itself first that it would be in the
national interest to permit the parties to settle their differences through the free process of collective bargaining, even
though this may entail the interruption of railway services. Only
when the government demonstrates its resolve not to interfere
will the railways abandon the convenience of conciliation and begin serious bargaining.

The Conciliation Process and the Collective Bargaining Process

It was stated, at the beginning of this chapter, that conciliation
proceedings involving labour-management disputes on the railways
have usually assumed the form of an imperfect substitute for the
collective bargaining process, and as such have been an impediment
to the development of genuine collective bargaining in the industry. Instead of creating and maintaining an environment conducive to negotiation, and conducting the proceedings as a continuation of the negotiation process, most proceedings had been conducted in a court-like setting in which the onus was put on the
representatives of labour (1) to prove that existing rates of pay
and other conditions of employment were not "fair and reasonable";
and (2) to justify the contractual changes sought by the unions.
The procedure enabled the railways to concentrate their efforts on
the presentation of general arguments relating to the operational
and cost implications of meeting the union demands in total, on the
legislative restrictions under which they operated, and on the
cross-examination of the representatives of unions. At the end,
faced with demands but without offers, the boards assumed the
onerous task of determining the bases for "just", "honourable",
"equitable", "fair and reasonable" settlements.
    Some boards made a serious effort to get the parties to nego-
tiate; and some, those chaired by Mr. Justice F. Craig Munroe
being a good example, made an effort to find rational criteria
for the determination of revised terms of employment. Regret-
tably, the majority made no such effort: they held hearings
rather than negotiations; permitted cross-examinations designed
to misinform rather than inform; they adjudicated instead of
conciliating; and they handed down judicial judgements instead
of bases for possible settlement.
    A good example of proceedings that have resulted in alienation
rather than conciliation is the 1966 dispute involving the Canadian Brotherhood of Railway, Transport and General Workers, and
the Canadian National Railways. The Brotherhood asked for an

increase in wages proportionate to the increase in productivity. In his report, the Chairman of the Conciliation Board rejected the Brotherhood's demand on the ground that an increase in wages proportionate to the increase in productivity would leave nothing for the other factors that contributed toward the increase in productivity! To quote from his report:

It is a fallacy to suggest that all of the actual increased productivity should be allotted to labour, and be reflected entirely in increased wages....It is practically self-evident that other factors should be taken into consideration, such as increases of capital, new equipment and managerial ability.

This report contains all the elements that a conciliation report should not contain: it reflects deficient and inaccurate knowledge of the subject matter; in both tone and approach it is biased in favour of one of the parties; and it fails to examine issues on the ground that they were already examined in relation to some other dispute. Such a report is more likely to alienate than to conciliate. Every reference to the proceedings of this board, and to the Chairman's Report, particularly from the participants on the labour side, has been extremely critical. One union participant commented:

From the outset it became evident that he (the chairman) was biased in favour of the railways, and incompetent respecting the subject matter. So, we decided to shorten the presentation and arguments in order to get a report out as fast as possible. We knew what kind of a report will come out of him, and we did not give a darn.

When one of the parties assumes, or circumstances compel it to assume, such an attitude, conciliation becomes just another fruitless stage of the bargaining process that preceded it.

The Need for a Conciliation Commission

It is suggested that the existing ad hoc conciliation machinery should be replaced by a permanent Essential Services Conciliation and Arbitration Commission. The structure and powers of the commission, as well as its relationship to government and government departments, should be of the same nature as those of the Board of Transport Commissioners, the Tariff Board, and the Combines Investigation Commission.

Although the primary function of the commission would be to provide conciliation services, a function of equal importance would be the establishment of research facilities, which would supply the supporting evidence for the settlement of disputes. It is also envisaged that the commission would employ competent research staff, train conciliation and arbitration officers, hear appeals on issues of contract interpretation, and possess the same quasi-judicial powers as the agencies referred to above.

The proposal is based on five premises.

(1) The most serious imperfection in labour-management relations is the lack or inadequacy of information relating to employment security. When information regarding prospective changes in processes of production, anticipated changes in skill requirements, and anticipated changes in the nature of employment generally, is not made available to employees, or is conveyed vaguely, inadequately, or inaccurately, it becomes a source of uncertainty and distrust, increases the risk in employment, and becomes a serious impediment to progress in negotiations. There cannot be perfect relations under conditions of imperfect knowledge. It is suggested that the commission could become a source of reliable information, and reduce this serious obstacle in the collective bargaining process.

(2) A serious weakness in the existing system of conciliation is the fact that it is a government service. It is suggested that as long as it remains under the control and direction of a government department, a just basis exists for suspecting that conciliators have been influenced by the government's economic policy. Although there is no evidence of direct government interference during conciliation and arbitration proceedings, ministerial public pronouncements urging consideration of the economic situation cannot pass unnoticed by those adjudicating on wage claims. It is hardly possible for arbitrators to consider questions of wage increases "in a vacuum"; consideration will inevitably be given to the consequences of their decisions. The relevant question is whether government-appointed or government-employed conciliators are influenced unduly by the prevailing economic policy. The greater the suspicion that they have been so influenced, and that they have shown bias toward government policy, the less likely it is that their decisions will be accepted by the parties.

(3) The government will continue to regard interruptions in railway services consequent on labour-management disputes contrary to the national interest.

(4) As long as railway services continue to be regarded by the people as essential public services, the nature and manner of public involvement in the settlement of disputes between railways and their employees should be somewhat different from the system applicable to industries not so regarded.

(5) The existence of a public agency with authority over railway operations and charges, and the fact that the supply and pricing of certain railway services are fixed by special legislation, are a recognition of the industry's special position in the economy.

To ensure that the existence of a conciliation service does not induce the parties to forego negotiations prior to the institution of conciliation proceedings--as has been the case heretofore--it is also proposed that bargaining sessions be chaired by a member of the commission, and that his consent be required for the institution of conciliation proceedings. This proposition is based on the assumption that neither party would wish to be accused by an official body of not bargaining or bargaining in bad faith; and that the commissioner would withhold his permission to refer issues to conciliation until he became firmly convinced that phase one of the bargaining process had run its full course.

Phase two would commence with the referral of the issues to the Conciliation Commission. In addition to its efforts at conciliation, the commission would utilize its specialized resources and experience in the search for a mutually acceptable settlement. Also, it is anticipated that there would be either a formal legislative link, or an informal liaison between the Conciliation Commission and the Transportation Commission. The ad hoc nature of conciliation boards precluded the possibility of such a link.

Failure to arrive at an agreement during the conciliation phase (phase two) would bring conciliation proceedings to an end. Phase three would involve an examination of the outstanding issues by the commission itself, which in consultation with the Transportation Commission and the government would issue a report setting out the basis on which a settlement must be concluded. In essence, this phase of the process would be one of compulsory arbitration. But, unlike the compulsory arbitration system used generally, this one would have the advantage of being integrated into the collective bargaining and conciliation process. The fact that the basis for settlement would be formulated by individuals who had participated in the proceedings from the beginning, is the best guarantee that the award would be based on the most comprehensive knowledge of the situation and the issues involved.

It is to be hoped, of course, that resort to phase three would be infrequent: the presence of a commission member during the initial phase of negotiations should compel the parties to bargain, and should also prove a deterrent to delaying tactics by either party; whereas the existence of a permanent Conciliation Commission, with expert staff and research facilities, should reduce substantially the time taken under current proceedings, introduce impartiality in the process, and provide greater certainty that the conciliators and adjudicators know what it is all about.

It is also envisaged that the commission would maintain continuous contact with both labour and management; would be consulted on all matters relating to the employment of labour and union-management relations; and would participate in the formulation of solutions to actual or potential problems. For example, whenever management contemplated the implementation of measures which, directly or indirectly, would affect a group of employees, it should be required that the commission be notified. It would then convene the representatives of the parties for a conference, in an effort to make certain that both understood the nature of the changes, and the magnitude and nature of the effect that they would have on the employees. After accomplishing this, and getting a consensus that the change is desirable and necessary from the standpoint of efficiency, the commission, together with the parties would then be required to search for a basis on which the adverse effect on employees could be minimized.

Some have suggested that such semicoercive mediation will destroy whatever chance there might exist for the development of collective bargaining in the industry, following the elimination of restrictions on railway rates and operations. There are others, however, who suggest that the dislike of compulsory arbitration by both unions and management will be an incentive to them to leave nothing to arbitration. The fact is that, inasmuch as those concerned with industrial relations abhor compulsory arbitration, the compulsory prevention of strikes in key industries and vital services appears to have widespread public support. The government cannot ignore this fact.

In the context of the vital role attributed to the railways in the economy, the only way to avoid the imposition of compulsory arbitration is not to allow labour-management relations to reach that stage. The proposed Conciliation and Arbitration Commission is intended to provide some direction in this regard. Also, there should exist a joint labour-management committee at the highest level, to discuss negotiable issues as they arise, to commission studies on issues that require careful and detailed examination, and to keep under review matters that enter into the domain of collective bargaining. The existence of such a committee would reduce both the fanfare associated with annual and biennial negotiating sessions, and the countdown pressures involved in attempting to reach agreements on numerous difficult issues, within relatively short periods of time.

The leaders of certain unions have indicated their willingness to participate in such a committee. In their opinion, an arrangement of this nature can do much for the evolvement of an environment conducive to effective collective bargaining. They have conveyed the impression that they are so eager to eliminate the justification for government involvement, and to get out from under government guardianship, that they are willing to experiment with any alternative that would strengthen the process of free collective bargaining.

Because of certain well-known developments in the industrial relations scene in recent months, the illusion has been created that alternative arrangements are no longer urgent, and perhaps not even necessary. This is an unfortunate and dangerous conclusion. Reliance on ministerial involvement to prevent strikes, or shorten their duration, will erode the effectiveness of the collective bargaining process. As stated elsewhere in this chapter, one of the aims of the Industrial Relations Disputes Investigation Act is to protect the public interest against the consequences of labour-management disputes. If it is determined that the act no longer fulfils that function adequately or effectively, then it should be changed. Ministerial involvement as the final arbiter is no substitute for effective legislation.

Reflections of the Failure of Collective Bargaining--
The Firemen's and "Run-Through" Issues

The issues referred to here have been widely publicized, and hence they are sufficiently well known not to require a detailed examination in this chapter. The main purpose in dealing with them is to isolate those aspects of the conflicts that manifest the state of labour-management relations in the industry. The Firemen's Dispute, or the so-called Diesel Issue, concerned the Canadian

Pacific Railway's 1956 proposal to remove firemen from freight and yard diesels, whereas the "Run-Through" Issue concerned the 1964 decision of the Canadian National Railways to eliminate the train stops and crew changes at the Nakina and Wainwright terminals.

Both problems were mainly the result of the same technological change--the diesel locomotive. Its introduction eliminated the traditional functions performed by firemen, and also facilitated longer runs without having to change train crews. It is natural, then, that the railways should have wished to dispense with the services of firemen, and to run through those terminals at which it was no longer necessary to stop. However, their attempts to put these changes into effect resulted in conflict--two strikes by firemen, and a wildcat strike by the employees who were to be dislocated from the Nakina and Wainwright terminals.

The labour-management conflicts on these two issues are manifest examples of what is most likely to happen when one of the parties declares that a given issue is not subject to negotiation, regardless of how important it might be to the other; and when technological changes are implemented without prior consultation regarding possible adverse effects on employees and the introduction of measures to offset or reduce those effects. Therefore, although the direct source of the problems was change in technology, the primary cause of the conflicts is found in the failure of the collective bargaining process.

In neither case was the right of the companies to institute the technological changes challenged. What was challenged was their right to institute the changes without prior or adequate consultation with representatives of the workers affected, and in the absence of any definite plans regarding the employment of those who were expected to be affected adversely. Even on the diesel issue, which not only involved the employment of firemen but also the termination of their craft, and hence the destruction of their organization, the spokesman for the Brotherhood of Locomotive Firemen and Enginemen declared:

If the company had seen fit to accompany its proposal on the diesel issue with a concrete blueprint, spelling out in detail what provisions it was willing to make for the 1,000-odd firemen who would be immediately cut off the payroll, and not inconsiderable number of other firemen who would ultimately lose their employment if the company request were granted, the no-compromise position which the union throughout maintained might have been at least in some respects relaxed or modified.[4]

In the run-through conflict, the CNR argued that under the provisions of collective agreements, management had the right to make unilateral changes in working conditions during the contract period. Given this right, however, the question arises whether it should be exercised without prior consultation with union officers, and without adequate provisions to offset or reduce the adverse consequences. It is suggested that the residual rights argument is but an excuse for mismanagement in the sphere of industrial relations. A statement by Mr. Donald Gordon at the Economic

Council of Canada Conference on Labour-Management Relations to
the effect that management is action oriented, and by implication
does not have time to engage in consultation and negotiation with
labour representatives prior to technological and operational
changes, reveals an approach to industrial relations that cannot
be regarded as conducive to labour-management cooperation.

When the time interval between the initiation of organizational
or technological changes in the planning department and their implementation is relatively short, and for reasons of competitive
advantage sudden and unpublicized action is necessary, the argument against procedures causing undue delays may have some validity. But most changes that have become a source of labour-management dispute have been of a nature requiring rather extensive
planning and careful study. Hence, time does not appear to have
been an obstacle to consultation. The run-through conflict is a
case in point: the decision to institute the run-through plan
had been preceded by rather detailed studies relating to every
aspect of the change; yet its announcement was delayed to zero
hour, and presented to the workers, their unions and the communities affected in its final form. Not only were the unions not
consulted, but also their accredited representatives in the area
were not given advance notice of a meeting called by the company
at Nakina on 30 September 1964 to announce its decision to purchase the homes of workers who were to be dislocated.

In his report on the conflict, Mr. Justice Freedman[5] castigated
the company for the manner in which it called and conducted the
meetings at Nakina, and commented that while the company's decision
to purchase the homes of dislocated men was commendable, its decision not to inform union representatives that a meeting was being
called could not but impair labour-management relations. Indeed,
the manner in which the company handled the plan, from its conception to its attempted application, appeared designed to discredit
union leaders in the eyes of those whom they were supposed to protect against arbitrary measures. According to Mr. Justice Freedman,
the employees who booked sick to protest the plan's implementation
were protesting not only the run-through but also the arbitrary
manner in which the company attempted to institute it. They were
protesting as well against their union leaders, who failed to
secure protection against unilateral changes in working conditions
during the existence of a contract.

In retrospect, a number of management representatives have
recognized and admitted that the company erred in taking the stand
that run-throughs were a nonnegotiable issue falling within the
domain of managerial prerogatives. Evidently, they did not anticipate the consequences (and Mr. Justice Freedman least of all).
As a result, all railways are now contractually committed:[6] (1) not
to put into effect any technological, operational and organizational change that is likely to be permanent and that may effect a
material change in working conditions with adverse effects on employees, without giving advance notice of not less than ninety days
if a relocation of employees is involved, and sixty days in other
cases; (2) to negotiate with the unions measures to minimize the
adverse effects of proposed changes on employees; (3) to refer to

mediation by a board of review--composed of equal representatives from both parties--all matters on which agreement can not be reached; and (4) to refer to compulsory arbitration all matters on which the board's recommendations are unacceptable to either party.

Thus, although the companies retain the right to determine and make technological, operational and organizational changes, they cannot put these changes into effect without a prior agreement or decision on measures designed to offset or reduce their adverse effect on employees.

Had a similar agreement existed between the railways and the Brotherhood of Locomotive Firemen and Enginemen, the conflict relating to the removal of firemen from freight and yard diesels may not have arisen. But the problem in this case was considerably more complex: it involved not only the displacement of firemen, but also the end of their craft and the disappearance of their union organization. Under the circumstances, it is understandable why the Brotherhood would not have entered into a contract that recognized management's right to make technological, operational and organizational changes, and that limited negotiations regarding the consequences of those changes to measures designed to minimize their adverse effects on workers.

This suggests that there arise issues in labour-management relations that connot be resolved through the process of collective bargaining. The question is whether labour relations legislation should stipulate that when one of the parties refuses to negotiate on an issue, the problem be referred to an impartial tribunal for a ruling.

Notes

1. Statement issued by the government, 26 November 1958.

2. On 13 May 1959, the MacPherson Royal Commission on Transportation was appointed, under terms set forth in Order in Council P.C. 1959-577.

3. Statement issued by the government, 26 November 1958.

4. Mr. W.E. Gamble, speaking on behalf of the Brotherhood of Locomotive Firemen and Enginemen, *The Labour Gazette,* February 1957, pp. 178-179.

5. Report of the Industrial Enquiry Commission Relating to CNR "Run-Throughs", Mr. Justice Samuel Freedman, Commissioner.

6. Article VII of Master Agreement between CNR, CPR and Other Railways and the Associated Railway Unions of Nonoperating Employees, 14 March 1967.

21. Collective Bargaining in the Chemical Industry*

by G.E. Eaton

Delimitation of Study

The Chemical industry per se is not really an industry in the usually accepted sense of the word, but rather a convenient term for a conglomeration of industries or product systems with different motives....[1]

For purposes of this study, "chemical industry" was restricted to the product groupings and industries included in the Standard Industrial Classification (SIC) used by the (then) Dominion Bureau of Statistics,[2] or to what might be described as the "core" of the industry, that is, companies producing industrial chemicals which, in turn, are the raw materials used in producing "consumer chemicals".

The so-called petrochemicals, an ever widening range of refined petroleum products, were excluded from the scope of the study. Field work was confined to Ontario and Quebec, as these two provinces alone accounted for about 80 per cent of the establishments and value of factory shipments and about 80 per cent of employment in the industry. Again, much of the field work done and generalizations made relate primarily to industrial chemicals and primary plastics, although in the case of plastics the study was extended to cover plastic fabrications, so that at least one finished or consumer chemical could be examined in depth.

On the employer side, officials of all but one of the principal producers of industrial chemicals and primary plastics were interviewed, while on the trade union side, largely because of availability (and nonavailability) as well as the time factor, interviews were held with Ontario-based executive and staff officers at the international, national and local levels in respect of three of the major unions involved in the industry. However, a significant number of collective agreements drawn from Ontario and Quebec were examined.

This chapter constitutes a summary of a preliminary study on industrial relations in the chemical industry in Canada, undertaken as a limited research project for the Task Force on Industrial Relations (Privy Council Office) during 1967.

*Reproduced by permission of Information Canada.

The Industrial Relations System and Collective Bargaining Relationships

The system of industrial relations[3] in the chemical industry does not appear to present any special or unique characteristics not duplicated in some other industry. The economic environment has been the least restrictive in impact on the parties in the deter- mination or allocation of rewards, which is the primary function of an industrial relations system.

Since World War II, expanding markets, providing a growth median much higher than the average for all manufacturing; high capital content or technologically oriented production processes with a high rate of capital investment per worker (in excess of $25,000); corresponding low labour content; interrelatedness with other buoyant and capital intensive operations such as petrochemicals; and relatively skilled occupational categories all helped to cre- ate a climate in which employees can and have enjoyed relatively high levels of rewards. The average weekly wages and salaries (earnings) in chemicals thus tended to be well above the indus- trial composite for manufacturing generally.

In the circumstances of a high-growth, high employee-compensa- tion industry, trade unions are probably able to achieve changes in the levels of rewards more easily than would be the case in other industries. What is surprising, however, is that the indus- try is not more extensively organized for collective bargaining purposes. As we shall see, a number of fairly large companies have been able to avoid collective wage determination except for small pockets of unionized employees in some areas. This has been possible largely because certain companies have been willing to pay wages at least as high and even higher than what would be obtained through collective bargaining.

Bargaining Structures and Relationships

The typical unit of bargaining in the chemicals and chemical pro- ducts industry is the plant or single establishment. This is true whether the typology is multiunion--single company or multi- establishment--single union.

Two major considerations appear to be: (1) the strong asser- tion of local autonomy in some international unions such as the International Chemical Workers Union (ICWU) and the Oil Chemical and Atomic Workers Union (OCAWU); and (2) union rivalry and frag- mentation of representation. A third factor is employer resis- tance to coordinated bargaining.

International Unionism and Local Autonomy

There is some evidence to suggest that the dominance of the inter- national union in Canada may be a factor contributing to the mea- sure of local autonomy in some unions. Certainly it appeared to be a factor contributing to union militancy in some locals. In one particular local, restiveness developed on the eve of negotiations held during 1966 as the rank and file felt that the local was not functioning effectively. They threatened and actually began an "independence movement" which would lead to disengagement of the local from the international and establish it as an independent Canadian union. The local executive insisted that the issue be handled without outside (i.e., international representatives) intervention. It was resolved when new officers were elected to the local executive as well as to the Bargaining and Grievance Committee, and the local adopted an extremely militant attitude in negotiations.

Coordinated Bargaining Through Cooperation at the International (and National) Union Level

Given the strong tradition of local autonomy in particular unions in the chemical industry, the most practical technique available to the international is to become a party to each plant agreement and to try to standardize claims and conditions of employment where possible.

In certain areas in Ontario, officers of locals have attempted to coordinate bargaining, but rival unionism has been a serious constraint. For instance, the president of Local 536 ICWU in Maitland, Ontario, attempted to coordinate claims and tactics with the UMW District 50, which represents workers at the Chemical Industries Limited (CIL) plant nearby in Kingston. However, he found that the UMW felt itself precluded from cooperating, on the grounds that it could not agree to coordinate tactics with international unions that regarded it as fair game for raiding. It is, of course, possible for rationalization to take place in the union structure where a single union, or for that matter a single local, deals with a number of employers in interrelated product markets, and yet coordinated bargaining remains a distant ideal. This was the situation in Sarnia where four of five locals of the OCAW merged into a composite Local No. 914.

Union officials expressed the view, however, that a master agreement would be extremely difficult to achieve in view of the diversity of products made by companies with which the composite local bargained.

U.S. Technique of Coordinated Bargaining

The OCAWU developed a technique in the oil industry in the United States which might have possibilities for Canada. In 1965, the OCAWU enunciated a national policy for bargaining in terms of conditions and objectives which it would seek to incorporate into a two-year contract. Each local was then given the opportunity to opt for the national programme, and in so doing, it was deemed to have given a mandate to the district director to carry through the national programme. The vote for the national programme was regarded as tantamount to a strike vote, authorizing the district officers to settle for no less.

In Canada, jurisdictional disputes among the trade unions in the chemical industry have been quite acute. The ICWU, with 15,000 members in Canada (11,000 in Ontario, 3,000 in Quebec, 1,000 in Alberta), regards the OCAWU as its chief competitor for worker allegiance. The OCAWU has an estimated 14,000 members, with about 4,000 in oil, 2,000 in gas, and 8,000 in petrochemicals and chemicals.

Product diversification on the part of large companies makes jurisdictional conflict almost inevitable. The development of synthetic fibres brought conflict for the textile unions. Plastics fabrication impinged on glass workers, since plastic substitutes are fast displacing glass (e.g., bottles and other containers). Automobile companies are using an increasing quantity of plastics to replace metal and are undertaking their own plastics fabrication.

Coordination and Merger Proposals

After nearly two years of discussion, a number of the international unions that were experiencing acute jurisdictional problems were able to establish a formal link through a chemicals, petrochemicals and synthetics committee, to try and coordinate their activities and to explore the possibilities of mergers or joint bargaining. The unions involved included the OCAWU, ICUW, Textile Workers Union, Rubber Workers Union, and Glass and Ceramic Workers Union. The major obstacles standing in the way of the coordinated bargaining are: (1) different contract expiry dates; (2) the constitutional limitations (labour relations are predominantly a matter of provincial jurisdiction and governed by provincial labour relations acts); (3) union rivalry; and (4) employer resistance.

The Employer's Point of View

To the employer, jurisdictional disputes and rival unionism can lead to competitive wage bidding and to increasing emphasis on union security clauses, such as maintenance of membership. These disadvantages are likely to be outweighed, however, by the benefits that employees feel accrue from wage flexibility. Employers, without exception, stated that the significant criterion for them in wage negotiations is community or area or prevailing rate. Thus, although some employers (e.g., Domtar) have experimented with centralized control of collective bargaining, involving multiplant--multiunion representation, they would not be anxious to promote coordinated bargaining for wage purposes if this meant single agreements covering workers in a number of product markets or in the same product market.

Domtar, incidentally, negotiates 150 collective agreements with 37 international and national unions. All negotiations are centralized in the head office, and 6 full-time negotiators negotiate about 8 agreements monthly. Claims submitted by unions to plant executives are forwarded by them with appropriate comments.

The company has also experimented for some years with annual conferences at which senior officials of the unions involved as well as of the federations (CLC and CNTU) meet management officials, with a view to promoting better understanding and mutual trust.

Attempts at uniformity have included also a uniform, company-wide pension plan, as well as a reciprocal transfer plan. Under the latter, it was proposed that, subject to ratification by employees and unions, an employee in a given union and plant could transfer to a plant where there was another union and apply for seniority on the basis of a formula--one year's seniority for each five years of service.

The Pattern of Wage Settlements--Community or Area Rates

The most significant factor to emerge from discussions with unions and management was the importance of community or area rates in the chemicals industry. This means that many union-management negotiations are conducted within guidelines established or partly established outside of their industry. In Amherstburg, near Windsor, wage rates in chemicals are influenced by the presence of the automobile workers. In Montreal, wage rates paid by chemical firms appear to be influenced by the concentrations of petrochemical firms in Montreal East.

In towns close to Toronto--Ajax, for example--area rates appear also to be significant. Perhaps the most striking example of the influence of a community or area rate is found in Sarnia, where chemicals and petrochemical activities are highly concentrated. The average weekly earnings are higher in Sarnia than anywhere else in the country and higher also than the average for the manufacturing industry generally. The wage structure in chemicals is directly geared to petrochemicals and the pacesetter is a non-unionized company, Imperial Oil Limited. In a number of negotiations in Sarnia, unions have made an attempt to achieve a "union rate" that is a differential between the unionized rate(s) and the nonunionized "adjusted rates", but in each case, adjustments have been made by Imperial Oil to re-establish leadership as the pacesetter for the area.

The other wage criterion stressed in wage negotiations, from the trade union side, is the cost of living or trend in rising prices, particularly in housing. This appears to be of greater concern to younger members of the labour force and to younger union officials.

Important Issues in Bargaining

In addition to wages, other major issues of importance appear to be shift work, safety and health, seniority, technological displacement, and retraining programmes.

Automation and resulting displacement of labour were not at the time of the study a serious issue in collective bargaining. The industry was expanding and creating new jobs so rapidly, that

it was possible to reabsorb workers and recruit new job seekers.
A policy of attrition rather than displacement was also followed.
Where problems did arise, the real issue was not displacement per
se, but its impact on the bargaining unit.

The Tenor of Labour-Management Relations

The number of work stoppages in the chemical industry has not been
significant. Causes of strikes, as reported, were wage and fringe
benefits, work scheduling, reduction of the work force on specific
tasks, disciplinary issues, union security, and in one particular
case, union certification.

Attitudes of the Parties in Bargaining Relationships

Union attitudes

Most striking was the awareness shown by union officials engaged
in negotiations of the importance of power or the threat of economic sanctions in effecting settlements. Younger officials in
the unions apparently felt that rational argument merely represented part of the preliminary skirmish and that in the final analysis, they must be prepared to take the strike vote and get
tough. This firmer attitude on the part of the younger union officials was confirmed by management officials.

All union officials interviewed felt that unions were accepted
by management as necessary evils and that the general approach by
management to contract administration reflected a preoccupation
with management rights. It was evident in strict interpretations
of the collective agreements and of grievances by management.

Management attitudes

No resistance to trade unionism, in principle, was voiced by management officials, but reference was made repeatedly to the "residual" or "sovereignty" theory of management authority. Management officials also conceded that they tended to adopt a strict
or legalistic approach to grievances and administration, but that
this was consistent with preserving managerial authority.

Company officials also confirmed that from management's point
of view, a new note of unreasonableness had become evident among
union officials, particularly in the younger age group. Impa-
tience and militancy seemed to be consistent with the outlook--
"the future will not wait".

A number of company officials inferred, however, that while the
attitudes of the unions had not changed, the tactics might have.

Third-Party Intervention--Conciliation Officers, Boards and Arbitration Boards

Union officials at the local level appeared highly critical of conciliation officers and arbitrators. The allegation was that conciliation officers did not seem to have sufficient expertise in what was a highly specialized field; and much criticism was directed at ad hoc arbitrators for the irregular quality of their awards. The inference appeared to be that a panel of permanent arbitrators skilled in labour relations might be a distinct improvement, but union leaders (and employers) reacted negatively to this proposal when it was put specifically to them.

The management reaction generally was that the third-party intervention system worked as well as could be expected, and that there appeared to be an inescapable element of delay, due sometimes to the self-interest of both parties. Trade union officials at the local level expressed strong disenchantment, however, with the two-stage conciliation process, which they felt gave rise to dilatory tactics on the part of management. Data available from the Canada Department of Labour from 1953 to 1967 seemed to confirm that the conciliation officer stage had come to be almost completely by-passed in the chemicals industry.

Plastics as a Subindustry within the Chemical Industry

The plastics industry can be differentiated on the basis of: (1) the chemically oriented production of plastic compounds with polymers; and (2) the substitute or synthetic industry, which involves the replacement of traditional materials with high polymers by plastics. Incidentally, the plastics industry of the future is seen by some industry spokesmen, not as a mere extension of the chemical industry, bridging the gap between it and the product producer, but rather as an integral part of the industry in a broader sense. That is to say, instead of plastic manufacturers, there will be product manufacturers who will use plastics as one of their essential materials. The implication is that there will be a shift to large-scale enterprises, with increasing concentration of capital and ownership. More immediately, however, the industry is structured into producers of basic raw materials-- for example, basic resins--which in turn are used by processors or fabricators to make finished plastic products. The raw materials or chemical constituents segment is dominated by relatively large chemical firms and constitutes the high-wage and high-earnings sector of the plastics industry.

The processing and fabricating segment, on the other hand, is dominated by a large number of small operations and may be characterized as the low-earnings sector. Not only are wage rates and earnings low, relative to the national manufacturing average, but there tend to be high rates of labour turnover, seasonality of employment, and relatively weak or unstable unionism. The picture is not markedly different where one finds large chemical producers or producers of raw materials engaged in fabricating

plastic products. Thus, while there are low-earnings and high-
earnings sectors within the industry itself, plastics as a whole
may be viewed as the low-earnings sector of the chemical industry.

The System of Industrial Relations in the Plastics Industry

Collective bargaining is not the predominant method of determining
wages and conditions of employment in the plastics industry. The
majority of firms are nonunionized, and of the inhibiting factors
the economic milieu (including product market, labour market,
financial structure, and level of technology) appears to be the
most significant, as well as the pattern of unionization itself.
The degree of union fragmentation and multiplicity of unions is
astonishing. The pattern of company diversification and/or inte-
gration, geographical spheres of union influence, and traditional
union rivalry have been among the contributing factors.

Collective Bargaining Relationships

The economic factors that have served as constraints on unionization have also influenced collective bargaining relationships.

Small Size of Firms and Establishments

Of a sample of sixty-three plastic processing firms, 65 per cent
had fewer than fifty employees, while 82 per cent had fewer than
one hundred employees.[4] Actually, only eleven had over one hundred employees.
    Generally it is much more difficult to organize small firms,
especially where the owners are actively engaged as operators
and managers. In the small enterprise, not only is the owner/
operator in direct contact with most of his employees, but he can
deal directly and promptly with grievances, even if not to the
full satisfaction of employees.

Financial Structure of Industry

The plastics industry as it presently operates lends itself to
small-scale operations. With a modest amount of capital an
operator can purchase of number of machines and produce a specialized product for a specific (custom) market. At the same
time, many operate marginally viable concerns.

Low Earnings

A relatively low earnings potential is aggravated by insecurity
of employment for all but the highly skilled toolhands, lead
hands and working foremen. Seasonal variations and consequent

layoffs are significant in some product lines. Christmas toys is
an obvious example.

Relatively High Incidence of Female Employment

Females constituted nearly one-third of the labour force of the
companies sampled. This was probably a factor contributing to
the relatively low incidence of unionization, since women, for a
variety of reasons (partial commitment to labour force, lower job
expectations, etc.) have been more difficult to organize into
stable union membership.

High Labour Turnover

The data obtained suggested that plastics processing establishments
experienced an almost unbelievably high rate of labour turnover.
Moreover, the companies seemed resigned to a fluctuating labour
force, provided they could retain a core of relatively skilled and
experienced employees.

Collective Bargaining Approaches and Procedures

Perhaps the most interesting feature was the conduct of negotiations, on behalf of a number of firms in the industry, by professional mediators associated with the Central Ontario Institute of
Labour Relations (COILR). Employers explained that their foremost
concern was to manage their businesses, of which they knew something. In fact, though, they were likely to be bogged down in
union meetings and to be pressured by career union negotiators,
hence reliance on COILR.
    Under this "arms-length" bargaining technique, employers did
not participate directly with union negotiators and negotiations
were never held on company premises. Employees were thus "insul-
ated" against the drama and tension of negotiations. Professional
negotiators, supplied by the COILR, performed in the role of
mediators. When they thought a settlement could be reached, the
proposal was taken to the employer for final approval. The business agent of the union involved was doing the same thing--attempt-
ing to sell the "package" to members of the union.
    Whatever the advantages to the employer, arm's-length and off-
site bargaining constitutes a watered version of unionism for
employees. The union is providing a purely mechanical function,
without some of the important psychological and social benefits
which unionism can and does offer.
    Moreover, this type of arrangement lends itself readily to the
suspicion that the two professional negotiators have struck their
own deal and are united in purpose in terms of selling the agreement to their respective principals.
    If trade unionism is to become a more potent agency for raising
the earnings of workers in plastics relative to their better-paid

brethren in chemicals, two major developments would seem necessary: (1) a greater degree of interunion cooperation and larger bargaining units, or put another way, less fragmented representation; and (2) coordination of industrial relations policies on the part of employers. Machinery for this purpose already exists in the Society of Plastics Industry of Canada, but like its counterpart in chemicals, the Canadian Chemical Producers Association, it does not involve itself in collective bargaining as such, but conducts surveys and makes the findings available to members.

In closing, it might be noted that the plastics industry provided the Canadian Labour Movement with its *cause célèbre* during 1966 and for some time after. Tilco Plastics, located in Peterborough, Ontario, obtained an injunction to prevent picketing by the Textile Workers Union of America, which had struck the plant to back up contract claims. Massed picketers defied the injunction to protest against the use of this legal procedure and some were eventually tried for contempt of court, convicted, and given prison sentences. The resulting labour agitation led to the appointment of a one-man Royal Commission (Justice Ivan Rand) to investigate the use of the injunction and to review other aspects of the legal framework of labour relations in Ontario.

Notes

1. J.S. Dewar, at the convention of the Canadian Manufacturers Association, 29 May 1967.

2. Included: explosives and ammunition, mixed fertilizers, plastics and synthetic resins, pharmaceuticals and medicines, paints and varnish, soap and cleaning compounds, toilet preparations, industrial chemicals, printing inks, and others.

3. A common analytical model, developed by Dr. Alton Craig, then Chief, Industrial Relations Research Division, Economics and Research Branch, Canada Department of Labour, based on four basic components--(i) inputs; (ii) mechanism for converting inputs to outputs; (iii) outputs or rewards; and (iv) feedback loop--was proposed by the task force for all its research projects. See Report of the Task Force on Labour Relations.

4. Survey carried out by the Society of Plastics Industry of Canada, in 1967.

22. Joint Labour-Management Councils*

by Aranka E. Kovacs

Introduction

The discussion in this chapter will focus on the establishment of
provincial joint labour-management councils in Canada. The observations made are based on the author's study completed in 1968 for
the Task Force on Labour Relations in Canada (known also as the
Woods Commission), examining the establishment or intended establishment of joint councils in the ten provinces of Canada.[1] In
order to summarize the findings of the report made to the task
force, the author will discuss the subject matter in three parts.
Part 1 will examine the scope of joint councils; the goals, attitudes and future of joint committees; and the role of governments
in this area. Part 2 will summarize very briefly the structure
of existing provincial joint councils, and attempts to establish
them in other provinces of Canada. The situation in all ten provinces will also be viewed briefly. It should be noted that the
observations are based on the 1968 study; any current developments
since that time are not incorporated in this chapter. Part 3 will
present the author's recommendations based on the findings of this
study. The recommendation to establish a Canadian Industrial
Relations Council was incorporated into the final recommendations
made to the federal government in the Report of the Woods Commission, the Task Force on Labour Relations in Canada.

(1) Discussion of Principles

Scope

The scope of the provincial joint councils varies from province to
province, but generally all are concerned with legislation dealing
with industrial relations. Focussing on labour relations acts,
the aim is to review existing legislation in order to make joint
proposals for amendments. There are certain issues, such as injunctions, that are considered to be "hot and emotional" topics,
and joint councils steer away from such areas for examination.
Issues for joint consideration are selected where compromise appears possible after discussion. Automation, for example, has
been discussed by the Nova Scotia and British Columbia joint councils. In Manitoba, the conciliation procedure and unfair labour
practices have been examined jointly. In Ontario, manpower prob-

---

*Reproduced by permission of Information Canada.

lems and retraining have been considered. In Quebec, the Workmen's
Compensation Act, night work for female labour, and labour courts
were on the agenda for discussion. In Nova Scotia, in addition to
a model agreement on automation being jointly reached, the issue of
strikes was also reviewed. In Prince Edward Island, the areas of
communications between labour and management, and education were
subjects for joint examination.

Thus the scope of the committees is wide, and the topics selected for joint examination depend on the circumstances and events
surrounding the parties in each province. Generally, issues that
could generate too much heat are not handled, as it is believed
that less controversial matters bring greater cooperation. One can
speculate that as greater acceptance and a longer history of joint
consultation emerges, those areas too will be considered. Joint
councils, however, need clear terms of reference in order to give
these committees a sense of direction. While they work with current problems, the setting of long-range goals also gives the councils a course or vision. Defining such goals, however, becomes
difficult, as the tone and activities of joint councils are influenced by the government in power and the personalities in the top
echelons of government. Thus, in Canada, the existing joint councils have not, with the exception of Nova Scotia, set any long-
run objectives. They have taken a step-by-step approach in handling topics.

Goals, Attitudes, and the Future

The most illusive achievement of joint councils lies in the area
of communications between labour and management. All persons interviewed stressed better understanding of mutual problems, improved relations, clearer view of each party's position in relation to problem areas, and greater degree of harmony by minimizing
conflict. A series of continuous and regular meetings between the
two sides, resulting in discussion and dialogue, tends to open
minds, thereby moderating extreme positions. It was pointed out
that maturity in viewpoint and respect of opinions of others also
results. It was maintained that while friction in industrial
relations is not eliminated, the chief aim of joint consultation
is to provide a channel of continuing dialogue for management and
labour representatives away from the drama of the bargaining sessions. These matters are not measurable in monetary terms, but
it is very apparent that industrial relations is also human relations, which involves "people and emotions".

Leadership in connection with the effective functioning of the
joint councils becomes very important. It was pointed out by both
labour and management members that, first, the chairman must be
chosen with care. The chairman must be a dynamic individual who
is close to and familiar with the industrial relations scene in
the province, but who can remain impartial and neutral in order
to promote mutual understanding and cooperation and general good
will among the members of the joint committee. The chairman must
have a great deal of time to give to such an endeavour and must
possess a dynamic quality in order to keep the committee continu-

ously active. The characteristics favoured for membership on joint
committees include those cited for the chairman, plus the willingness to actively participate and the ability to work with people
who hold contrary views. Members must also be experienced and
knowledgeable in the labour-management field.

Of importance to joint councils is that their status and the
role of the individuals contained in them be made clear. The purpose of the joint councils in relation to the government and in
relation to the people concerned must be clarified. The objective
of joint consultation is not to mould the two sides to similar
viewpoints but to give both, through a formal structure and channel of communication, an opportunity to jointly study subjects that
have an impact on the parties and the public interest. The question of prime importance is whether any good will that is generated
at the provincial level filters down to lower levels of management
and labour. It was pointed out that on the labour side, organization is more formal but on the management side, the structure is
more fragmented. While employers belong to the Canadian Manufacturing Association or to the Chamber of Commerce, no federation of
employers exists in Canada, along lines similar to the Swedish group
for example. The employers' group does not have an organizational
structure for committing them to provincial policy, and industrial
relations is only one area among many to occupy the attention of
management. Therefore, only by example will any experience gained
through joint provincial councils filter through to individual
employers. It was pointed out that labour has a more structured
organization and since representatives are elected officials in
most instances, the possibility of influencing rank-and-file members is greater. However, it was also recognized that union leadership must be responsive to members' wishes and the main concern
of labour in supporting joint councils becomes a political one.
Not only is it a political problem for union leadership, but it
also raises the question of whether support of a joint committee
will blunt the labour union's role in the political arena. Will
the effectiveness of political action be minimized if, by supporting joint action, labour unions are not able to pressure governments separately on issues which are eventually discussed in the
joint councils and agreed to by a joint committee? Understandably
this is a crucial concern for labour unions represented on joint
committees at the provincial level.

What is the future of provincial joint councils that appeared
to be popular in the 1960s in Canada? In discussing this problem
with labour and management representatives, it became clear that
some accomplishment must be evident to the members if the joint
committees were to continue meeting. The focus in Canada has been
on neutral subjects and when dissatisfaction is eliminated by
joint proposals, a sense of accomplishment is present. But it was
pointed out that although the joint committees have taken a step-
by-step approach, it also becomes necessary to plot a course for
the future as long-range objectives give to the committees a direction for their continued existence. It was suggested that
original goals need re-examination in order to maintain a dynamic
atmosphere to carry and sustain the joint committee on its future
course. Perhaps a built-in system of assessment and evaluation

is needed to appraise the work of the committees. In most instances, it was believed that the second structural level in the form of a joint conference was necessary, not only to broaden the contact of the two parties but also to give them a feel for the broader industrial relations problems in the province.

Role of Governments

The provincial governments' role in the promotion and sponsorship of joint councils in Canada is an interesting one. While governments are often instrumental in establishing the joint committee, it appears that such a move is only feasible after labour and management have shown an interest and willingness to meet in order to jointly discuss problems affecting both sides. While labour and management representatives accept government sponsorship financially, both sides express a wish for the least government intervention in the work of the joint councils.

The idea for joint meetings sometimes stems from certain industrial relations crises in the province, that is, a strike causing a serious impact provincially or locally. The idea for a joint committee may also stem from dissatisfaction with labour legislation, causing both sides to examine existing labour relations acts. In some provinces, as in Nova Scotia, for example, ad hoc labour-management conferences were held frequently prior to the formal establishment of a joint council. In some instances, provincial economic councils have also been interested in labour-management affairs, and while it has been only one of other areas of concern to such bodies, nevertheless groundwork was laid. Still another experience that brings labour and management groups together is participation on community boards, as in the case of Manitoba. That, too, lays the foundation that makes both sides more receptive to joint meetings on a more focussed level. Sometimes, too, concerned individuals hold the belief that labour and management should meet outside of the bargaining rounds to discuss mutual problems. In other instances, universities take the lead in promoting and sponsoring labour-management cooperation.

Although joint councils have not received a great deal of publicity, still there must be a formal announcement of their formation. Members feel that while they do not wish to be in the public attention constantly, they must be given recognition formally if they are to function as a body with some voice even in an advisory capacity. While members of certain joint councils (as in Ontario) met behind closed doors in the early formative stages, a formal public announcement of the existence of the committee becomes necessary in order to lend support to the effectiveness of the council. In time, reports appear on the activities of joint councils in the Department of Labour's annual reports, labour representatives make reports to their federation or congress conventions, and management members report to the employer or business associations on the work of these committees.

Thus, while provincial governments, through the respective departments of labour, have been instrumental in supporting joint councils in Canada, their involvement remains as a backdrop once the committees are formally established. Although governments

have taken the lead in some provinces (for example, Manitoba) to
set up joint councils, it is a strongly held belief that governments should remain in the background, allowing the joint committees to charter their own course and direction once they are
formed.

The interesting question is, why do the provincial governments
find it worthwhile to sponsor joint councils? This is a query
that both labour and management leaders ask. It was pointed out
by representatives interviewed from both sides for the task force
report in 1968[2] that there are various reasons for government support. It is in the interests of governments to provide an "out"
for professional politicians. Joint councils ease the strain and
pressure on the Minister of Labour when joint recommendations are
made to amend the Labour Relations Act, for example. The government then is not subjected to criticism from either side when
recommendations for amendments are made jointly. However, it was
maintained that the government must also be responsive to the
public interest and must take the initiative in decisions on its
own. While joint councils make the political positions of the
Minister of Labour more comfortable, it should be remembered that
in some provinces--Ontario, for example--both sides represent big
business and big unions, and governments must take into account
the interest of the citizen at large, since they have a responsibility wider than to the parties involved in the joint council.

It was also observed by those interviewed that joint councils
provide the Minister of Labour with an avenue of communication
with labour and management. While government interference usually
ends when the joint council is established, whether by an act
(as in Quebec), or by an announcement in the provincial legislature, the secretary of the joint council is in most cases an administrative member of the Department of Labour, and thus the joint
council also acts as a forum to which governments can bring a
problem. Governments hope to create a "climate" for impending
changes in legislation when joint recommendations are received.
Another point made was the possibility of establishing a joint
council to act as a smoke screen for government inaction, especially when a moratorium on changes to an act is used before the
joint committee makes a report. But the general consensus was
that the joint committee is not an arm of government, although
supported financially and indirectly by the provincial governments.
Government cooperation and assistance are necessary if the committee is to function with an effective voice in the industrial
relations scene.

Another point of concern raised the question of how much research can be done by joint council members. While emphasis in
some provinces (Nova Scotia, for example) is on joint study, it
is obvious that the members themselves do not have the facilities
or the time and qualifications, in some instances, to carry out
research. The provincial governments or the universities, therefore, provide the initiative and the facilities for research in
all instances. The problem is to clarify the role of joint councils in this area, since government control of subject matter for
discussion and research by the joint councils is not wanted.

At the same time, financing of joint council activities comes mainly from the governments and there is reliance on research staff in
the departments of labour for information and data. The joint councils are not staffed by full-time persons, even where there is
university connection, and thus the joint committee must rely on
outside research assistance. The extent to which they can initiate
their own research areas will depend on the relationship with government, on conditions in the industrial relations scene in the
provinces, as well as on the personalities involved in active participation on the joint councils.

(2) Summary of Provincial Experiences

British Columbia

The B.C. Labour-Management Committee was formally announced in the
B.C. legislature in February 1966. The committee was set up with
five representatives from the management side, five representatives
from labour, a chairman, who was the Deputy-Minister of Labour, and
a vice-chairman, who was the director of the Institute of Industrial Relations at the University of British Columbia. An administrative officer from the Department of Labour acts as secretary.
The members are government appointed after consultation with both
labour and management.

Alberta

In Alberta, there exists no joint labour-management consultation
committee. An informal channel of communication exists which the
government encourages as a means of keeping in contact with labour
and management in the province. At the time the study was conducted for the task force, the view was expressed by management
representatives that they preferred to approach industrial relations at the grass roots level and there did not appear to be a
need for joint consultation at the provincial level. Labour representatives maintained that the government should create a climate for improved industrial relations through legislation, and
that there was a need for some structural communication system
with both management and government.

Saskatchewan

There is no permanent joint labour-management committee at the provincial level in Saskatchewan. But in 1965 an ad hoc Labour-Management Legislative Review Committee was set up to study the Trade
Union Act, and to report to the government with respect to amendments to the act. The committee consisted of a chairman, vice-
chairman, three management representatives, three labour representatives, and a secretary. One government official pointed out
that there appeared to be no need at the time for a permanent joint
council, since the province did not experience severe industrial
relations problems: Saskatchewan was still primarily an agricultural province, with relatively little industrialization.

Manitoba

The provincial Department of Labour in Manitoba took the initiative, in 1964, in establishing a permanent Labour-Management Review Committee. The committee is composed of an equal representation of twelve members from labour and twelve members from management. In addition to the twenty-four members, there is a secretary, assistant secretary, as well as the chairman and vice-chairman. The members were selected by the Minister of Labour after recommendations of names were submitted by both sides. The secretary and assistant secretary are civil servants in the Department of Labour, but have no vote on the committee. The chairman was appointed from outside the province with the belief that a greater degree of impartiality would result.

A second level in the structure of the Manitoba Labour-Management Review Committee is made up of a subcommittee of five representatives each from labour and management, with an alternating chairman from each side. This working subcommittee reports to the general committee. A third structural level was also formed, with a smaller working subgroup of four members, and there were six smaller study subgroups examining specific issues. Although the province lends financial support, there is no direct government interference with the work of the committee. It makes an annual report to the Minister of Labour.

Ontario

In Ontario, the first attempt at joint consultation came with the formation by the Minister of Labour of a Joint Labour-Management Committee. Four employer representatives and four labour representatives were invited to participate, in addition to a chairman and secretary. The original committee met privately and behind closed doors until it was decided to publicly announce and acknowledge the establishment of the joint committee. The formal announcement of a permanent joint council was made by the Minister of Labour in April 1967. The permanent joint council, called the Union-Management Council, was a new committee composed of five representatives from labour and five representatives from the management side. The original committee was dissolved, although some of the members remain on the permanent council. The director of the Industrial Relations Centre at the University of Toronto was appointed chairman. At the time of its establishment, the Minister of Labour stated: "The Council will give labour and management an opportunity of working together to develop new means of accommodating their varied interests." But he also added that, "...it is definitely not a short-run panacea for labour and management difficulties. Its real impact...may not be felt for some time."

Quebec

The idea of a joint labour-management council in Quebec originated in the late 1930s when a former Deputy Minister of Labour was in-

strumental in its promotion. It was in 1941 that the Quebec government passed an act of Parliament establishing the Superior Labour
Council. Since the tone and activities of the council are strongly
influenced by the government in power, the Superior Labour Council
has had its periods of activity, as well as times of dormancy.

The act establishing the council states that the council is a
consultative body and is composed of twenty-four members appointed
formally by the Lieutenant-Governor in Council, upon the recommendations of the Minister of Labour. The minister receives suggested
names of eight persons representing labour and eight persons representing management. The remaining eight members are appointed
from people in the Province of Quebec who are knowledgeable about
social and economic problems. These eight members are lawyers, or
academicians such as sociologists or economists. According to the
1941 act, there may also be six associate members, but they have
no voting power. These associate members comprise three representatives from the Department of Labour, and three from the Department of Municipal Affairs, Trade and Commerce.

The twenty-four-member council is appointed for a three-year
term, but members are eligible for reappointment. The act also
provides that a secretary, who is a civil servant, be appointed.
The secretary has no voting power. The president of the Superior
Labour Council and two vice-presidents are elected from the group
at large.

The act further stipulates that a Permanent Board of nine members be set up, composed of members of the Superior Labour Council.
This consists of a president, two vice-presidents, and six other
members--two persons each from labour, management, and the third
group. In addition, the Department of Labour, and the Department
of Municipal Affairs, Trade and Commerce may also appoint one
associate member each, without voting power. Members of the Permanent Board hold office for a one-year term and are eligible for
reappointment. The associate members on the Superior Labour Council and the Permanent Board are appointed without term. The Permanent Board is a working board and submits its report to the
Superior Labour Council.

There were several weak spots in the Superior Labour Council
discussed by those who were interviewed for the task force report.
The large size of the Superior Labour Council--twenty-four members
plus the associate members--makes it unwieldy as an effective operative body. The value of the Permanent Board to function as an
executive group within the Superior Labour Council structure was
also questioned. The third group of academicians on the council
found their role and purpose unclearly defined.

It appears that a re-examination of the objectives of the Superior Labour Council, as well as its structural organization,
is forthcoming in the near future if the council is to serve a
beneficial role and purpose in the industrial relations scene in
Quebec.

New Brunswick

At the time of the task force study, moves were under way for the

establishment of a joint committee in New Brunswick. Even as early as ten years before, efforts were made to set up a tripartite
committee of representatives of labour, management, and government.
Other attempts were made by the Minister of Labour, as well as by
a local committee of interested labour and management representatives in Saint John. The Saint John committee, consisting of four
management and four labour members, felt that a neutral body or
institution should be the sponsoring agent of such a joint council
rather than the government. Thus the University of New Brunswick
was approached, and since interest was shown, a subcommittee
formed to look at the experience of the Nova Scotia Joint Study
Committee and its relations with Dalhousie University. At this
time too, a Select Committee of the New Brunswick Legislature was
studying the Labour Relations Act and in its recommendations suggested that the government provide financial assistance to the
University of New Brunswick in order to establish a permanent
Labour-Management Study Committee.

When the task force study was made by the author, there were
strong indications of a keen willingness and interest on the part
of the labour and management representatives to participate in
joint consultation, and of the university to act as the coordinating agent.

Nova Scotia

The Nova Scotia Joint Study Committee was formed in 1962, and more
words have been published and spoken about it than any other joint
venture in Canada. The impetus for establishing the permanent Nova
Scotia Joint Study Committee was channelled through the Institute
of Public Affairs at Dalhousie University.

Both labour and management were involved in the gradual opening
up of a joint communications channel. The groundwork was therefore
laid for a receptiveness to the idea of forming a permanent joint
council. The leadership given by the Institute of Public Affairs,
the Dalhousie Bureau of Industrial Relations, the Dalhousie Labour-
University Committee, various studies of joint committees in Europe,
the recommendation of the McKinnon report for joint consultation,
a public address by the Swedish Labour Attache on labour-management
cooperation--all these events and circumstances paved the way for
the formation of a permanent joint study committee in Nova Scotia
in 1962.

When the committee was first set up it consisted of four labour
union representatives, four management representatives, and two
members from the Dalhousie Institute of Public Affairs. In its
second year of operations the committee was enlarged to sixteen
members, seven members from the labour side and seven members from
the management side, plus two people from the Institute of Public
Affairs.

The committee consists of three levels. At one level is the
Joint Study Committee, representing the policy-making area. The
second level is represented by the Joint Study Conference which
is held annually, in which a wider delegation of interested parties becomes involved. The discussion flowing from the study
groups at the conference gives direction to the Joint Study

Committee for the coming year. There are also subcommittees set up to study specific issues. The emphasis of the Nova Scotia Committee is joint study of mutual problems, and a great deal of pride was expressed by those interviewed with respect to the accomplishments of the Joint Study Committee.

Prince Edward Island

The P.E.I. Labour-Management Relations Council was established by the Minister of Labour in 1966. It consists of three management and three labour representatives, plus a chairman and a secretary, who is the Administrative Secretary to the Minister of Labour. The P.E.I. joint council represents the first level in the structure. An annual conference with a wider representation of interested delegates represents the second level, similar to the structure in Nova Scotia. The objective of the two-level system is that from the delegates attending the conference, the joint council will receive a feedback and therefore some guidance as to the problem areas that the council should be concerned about in the coming year. Subcommittees to study specific topics are also set up by the P.E.I. joint council, in order to facilitate its work.

Newfoundland

Although the idea of a joint labour-management committee was not new to the labour and management representatives interviewed, a joint council has not yet been established in Newfoundland. The main reason is that the relationship between the government and labour has been strained in the past. In addition, the seasonal nature of industry, a weak labour movement, restrictive labour legislation, and inadequate educational and manpower training facilities were cited by those interviewed as further obstacles, up to that time, to the formation of a joint labour-management council in Newfoundland. However, a breakthrough occurred in November 1967, when a joint labour-management conference was called in Corner Brook. Optimism was expressed that from that conference a permanent provincial joint committee would be established in the near future.

(3) Conclusion

Having examined joint labour-management councils at the provincial level in the provinces of Canada, the author believes that there is an important role for joint councils in the Canadian industrial relations scene. From observations made and information received on the role and functioning of joint committees, the author recommends the establishment at the federal level of (1) an Industrial Relations Council of Canada; and (2) a Summit Conference of Provincial Joint Councils.

The task force, in its report to the government, incorporated the author's recommendation to establish a permanent body known as the Canadian Industrial Relations Council.[3] It is the author's contention that the Industrial Relations Council would constitute a task force on labour-management relations. The chairman would also be the research director of the council. His double role and title of chairman and research director would tend to emphasize the research nature of the council, as well as its consultative aspects. Its broad terms of reference would be to establish a climate of mutual trust through organized and regular communications. The council would study and discuss problems of a socio-economic nature relating to industrial relations in Canada. It would examine labour legislation and make recommendations for amendments to outdated and ineffective laws regarding industrial relations at the federal level. It would, for example, study the problems confronting labour and management and the public when technological progress gives rise to dislocations and serious automation impacts on sectors of the economy.

The Canadian Industrial Relations Council would make annual reports to Parliament. Its studies and recommendations would serve as a source of continuous contact and information for the government on matters relating to the industrial relations scene.

It would provide a permanent body to review the problems confronting labour and management and government on a regular and rational basis, and not just "in the heat of the day", when crises develop. In this manner, a more solid and harmonious relationship will emerge, based on rational collaboration and self-regulated communications.

The Industrial Relations Council of Canada would be, in effect, a secretariat of experts and involved, responsible people, independent and free of political control, whose aim would be to overcome narrowness of interests. The ultimate objective of the council would be to involve labour and management in the socio-economic aspects of industrial relations problems, and through organized consultation and the use of documented information based on thorough research, to develop an awareness of the impact of their activities on the total society.

It was further proposed by the author that a summit conference be called by the Industrial Relations Council of Canada every second year. The summit conference would be a meeting of all the permanent joint labour-management committees that have been established at the provincial level in Canada. The summit conference would be attended by the permanent appointed members and the chairmen of the various provincial joint labour-management councils, plus the ministers of labour and the provincial deputy ministers of labour, in addition to the members of the Industrial Relations Council of Canada, and senior Canadian government officials.

On the programme of the summit conference would be a review of the activities of each provincial joint council, with discussion on its approach, accomplishments and objectives. The chief value derived from such a conference would be to help break down the provincial isolation that exists across Canada. A member of a joint labour-management committee in the West would know what is being done by joint committees in the eastern provinces. By comparing problems and discussing solutions, members would have some knowledge of how other provinces are utilizing the joint committees and for what purposes.

There would be benefits derived from association and contact with other members who serve on joint councils, and value in the exchange of ideas and experiences with regard to the activities of joint councils, and industrial relations in general. In addition, contact of joint-council members would provide them with some avenue for expressing pride in their own achievements and would give them an opportunity for assessing their activities and accomplishments. The Summit Conference on Industrial Relations would give them an opportunity for assessing their activities and accomplishments. The Summit Conference on Industrial Relations would provide members of joint councils with a challenge and stimulus to carry on with greater enthusiasm in the year ahead.

Thus, the Summit Conference on Industrial Relations would serve encouraging the continuation of provincial joint labour-management committees in Canada.

Notes

1. See A.E. Kovacs, "A Study of Joint Labour-Management Committees at the Provincial Level in the Provinces of Canada", Project no. 56, prepared for the Task Force on Labour Relations in Canada, (Ottawa, April 1968).

2. Over one hundred people were interviewed for the study, consisting of labour and management representatives, and Department of Labour officials, as well as interested or involved academicians. See A.E. Kovacs, "A Study of Joint Labour-Management Committees".

3. See the Report of the Task Force on Labour Relations, *Canadian Industrial Relations* (Ottawa: Privy Council Office, December 1968), pp. 214-15, for details on the structure of the Canadian Industrial Relations Council as recommended by the task force.

23. Compulsory Arbitration in Australia*

by J.E. Isaac

Historical Background

As Australia is one of the most highly unionized countries in the world, it might be supposed that "free" collective bargaining of one form or another would be the prevailing characteristic of industrial relations in that country. But the distinguishing feature of Australian industrial relations, in comparison with many other countries, is the elaborate provision of legally constituted tribunals to intervene in disputes by the processes of conciliation and compulsory arbitration.

There are two aspects to the Australian arbitration machinery. One aspect was by design: to be involved in settling "genuine" disputes on a whole variety of periodic and day-to-day problems. The other aspect evolved as a result of the interaction of social, economic, and institutional forces: under the guise of "paper" disputes to formulate national wage policy. The latter feature of the machinery was not envisaged by those who framed the federal constitution and set up the arbitration machinery. Indeed, the surprising thing is that, despite considerable legal obstacles, the arbitration system should have evolved into an agency for national wage policy.

The origin of Australian compulsory arbitration can be traced to a series of nation-wide stoppages in the 1890s. Following a period of rapid union growth and increased militancy in the preceding decade, the employers in a number of key industries (shipping, wool, coal) reacted strongly to union ascendancy. In the circumstances of a prolonged economic depression, they held out for "freedom of contract" and in effect successfully repudiated unionism and collective bargaining. The question of compulsory arbitration had been discussed and rejected by both employers and unions on a number of occasions prior to the 1890s. But with their

This chapter is an extract from Study no. 4, Task Force on Labour Relations (Ottawa, November 1968). Since it was written, changes have occurred in the Australian system. Inclusion of these changes will be found in D. Yerbury and J.E. Isaac, "Recent Trends in Collective Bargaining in Australia", *International Labour Review*, vol. 103, no. 5 (May 1971); and J.E. Isaac, "Compulsory Arbitration and Collective Bargaining Reconsidered", *Journal of Industrial Relations*, vol. 16, no. 1 (March 1974).

power squashed and their survival threatened, the unions reversed their stand on compulsory arbitration, seeing in it a source of support and protection. The general public and governments, disturbed at the industrial upheavals and the absence of adequate machinery to deal with large-scale stoppages, began to give serious thought to legal provisions for settling industrial disputes.

In the context of employer rejection of collective bargaining in the key areas of employment, the Australian governments could have prescribed an arrangement for compulsory collective bargaining ("duty to bargain"), as did the United States and Canadian governments many years later. Or they could have prescribed something like the Canadian compulsory conciliation arrangement as a means of bringing unions and employers together to the bargaining table. Instead, they embraced compulsory arbitration, an alternative that a number of notable political leaders were advocating as a means of replacing the "law of the jungle", with its "barbarous expedient" of strike action that threatened to dominate industrial relations. The concept of the "rule of law", which compulsory arbitration was expected to provide, had a considerable popular appeal and by the early years of the 1900s, compulsory arbitration became the basis of industrial legislation in the newly established federal government and in most of the states.

Only two states chose the tripartite wages board system on the industry lines, the original concept of this system being to prevent "sweating" in those areas of employment that were not effectively unionized. However, of those who work under the award or determination of statutory authorities (and these make up 90 per cent of employees), only 10 per cent now come within the wages board system, the rest being subject to compulsory arbitration. It is reasonable, therefore, to represent compulsory arbitration as the characteristic feature of Australian regulation.

The object of this brief historical excursion is to emphasize three things:

(1) The introduction of compulsory arbitration following the "accident" of large scale stoppages in the 1890s. If these stoppages had not occurred, it is reasonable to suppose that Australia would have continued to follow the English practice of "free" collective bargaining.

(2) The faith of large numbers of Australians at the time and even today in the wisdom of the "rule of law" concept of industrial relations. The persistence of this faith is somewhat surprising because in other parts of the world, most of the important issues in industrial relations that lead to disputes are regarded as matters involving *conflict of interest*. These matters are not amenable to the "rule of law" for judicial solution, but must be settled ultimately by compromise. The fact that compulsory arbitration has not worked with textbook purity has given the system a desirable and necessary degree of elasticity in coping with situations requiring concession to economic power, even if under the guise of "doing justice".

(3) The long time that has elapsed since compulsory arbitration was first introduced. Every country is saddled with its history; and in industrial relations, history bites deeply into the minds, attitudes, and preferences of the present community. Three

generations have now grown up on this system and despite strong
resentment from employers in the early days, it has become part
of the accepted way of industrial life. Employers, unions, and
governments have adapted their form, procedure, and personnel on
industrial relations matters to the existence of compulsory arbitration. There has, of course, been a core of chronic dissatisfaction with the arbitration system; but this dissatisfaction has
been not so much with the system as such as with some of the features of its operation.

Evaluation

An evaluation of any industrial relations system would be mislead-
ing if it did not emphasize the importance of those historical
factors that have established certain norms, institutional structures, and public attitudes. Weaknesses in particular arrangements
for settling industrial disputes that emerge purely from theoretical analysis may turn out to be less significant and less persuasive if projected realistically into the historical context of
the country in question. So it is with Australian compulsory arbitration. A cautious evaluation of the Australian system would
be that despite many of its weaknesses, on the whole, it has worked
reasonably well and that, given the historical background, a forced
move to an alternative system would not necessarily be more successful. For the present, at any rate, there is no strong feeling on
the part of unions or management for an alternative system, to an
important extent because they have adjusted themselves comfortably
to an arrangement that enables a third party to shoulder the burden
of much decision making in industrial relations.

However, if Australia were starting afresh, it would not necessarily choose the arrangements that have evolved. And for those
countries desiring to adopt compulsory arbitration as a *standing
arrangement* for settling industrial disputes and looking to Australian experience as an object lesson, it may be useful to set
down some of the credits and debits of compulsory arbitration as
it appears to have worked in Australia, discounting as far as possible the effects of the peculiar circumstances of the Australian
constitutional problems on the workings of compulsory arbitration.

On the credit side, four points should be noted. First, the
institution of conciliation and compulsory arbitration has provided, early in the history of industrial relations, a device for
a *speedy* settlement of industrial disputes of all kinds, in private and in public employment. Secondly, the pervasiveness of
compulsory arbitration in the economy has produced a greater degree of uniformity in the standards of wages and working conditions
than might be expected to prevail in a country with such a wide
geographical spread and diversity of union size and power. The
standards achieved by the strong unions have tended to be applied
generally to workers with weaker bargaining power. Thirdly, in
giving registered unions legal status and security, compulsory
arbitration removed much industrial unrest associated with union
organizational drives and established the basis for stable unionism. It has also provided elaborate legislation for the protection

of the rights of individual union members against oppressive and unreasonable practices of union leadership. Fourthly, the existence of penal sanctions, particularly when used discriminately, has reduced the loss from long, drawn-out stoppages and has often provided the means for strengthening the hand of union leadership against fruitless strike action. The comprehensive scope of the arbitration machinery is, of course, a reflection of the full acceptance of public responsibility for industrial relations.

Against these credit points, the question may be asked: Once trade unions are well established, protected and accepted (and this could be done without compulsory arbitration), is there a strong case for a degree of public responsibility that freely intervenes in disputes, prescribes the terms of employment and imposes restrictions on strike action even when the public interest at large is not in jeopardy? Should public responsibility only be exerted in this manner when the public interest is threatened in a meaningful way? In answer to these questions it should be emphasized again that compulsory arbitration in Australia does not work with textbook purity. Much of what formally goes for "compulsory" is not such but voluntary; much of "arbitration" is negotiation and accommodation to the power positions of the parties; penal sanctions are frequently not sought or applied. These qualifications in themselves show the limits to which compulsory arbitration can be pushed.

Nevertheless, the existence of efficient facilities for compulsory arbitration must be assumed to play an important part in any process of "voluntary" negotiation between unions and employers, such as to distinguish it from the negotiating processes in the United States and Canada. Reference has been made to the "stultifying" effects of the ready availability of compulsory arbitration and the possible use of penal sanctions on the conciliation phase; on the readiness of the disputing parties to exchange concessions with each other; and on the degree of self-reliance of unions and management in fixing the terms of employment and, even more importantly, in the application of these terms. To those who admit these stultifying effects but retort "so what", the answer appears to be evident in the large number of short-lived stoppages, which reflect, in good part at least, the inadequacy of union-management leadership in attending to claims and grievances and its tendency to farm these matters out to the arbitrator. If a judgement is to be made (and it cannot be a positive proof) this is the outstanding difference between North American and Australian industrial relations. A further judgement, of course, is required as to whether, on balance, this is a small price to pay for the virtual elimination of protracted strikes. Unfortunately, there is so far no work on which such a judgement can reasonably be made. There is also the financial cost of running the arbitration machinery, but this should not be exaggerated. In cost comparisons with the United States and Canada, the expense involved in mediation and conciliation services, as well as the additional staffing that unions and management in these countries provide for industrial relations, must be set off against the cost of compulsory arbitration.

In the same way, in comparing the operation of collective bargaining in Canada, with its compulsory conciliation provisions, with the comparatively "free" collective bargaining system of the United States, a judgement must be entered on what net contribution the strike-delaying process of compulsory conciliation, particularly in the normative phase, makes to industrial relations. If, as is often likely to be the case, true negotiations on contract are deferred until the "ritual" of compulsory conciliation has been worked through, the question arises whether delaying strike action in disputes that are not reasonably put in the national emergency class is of any real value to industrial relations. True, the recommendations of the conciliation board may influence the ultimate terms of settlement. But it does not follow invariably that these recommendations are more just, fairer, or economically more commendable than the terms that the disputing parties would have reached independently.

Of course, under national emergency conditions the urgency of a settlement calls for a degree of public intervention that puts aside as a secondary consideration the effect of such intervention on union and management self-reliance. Could it be that the Canadian provisions, particularly those of Alberta and British Columbia and, even more so, the provisions of Australian compulsory arbitration, are more appropriate for emergency situations? Certainly, the notions of compulsory arbitration found fertile soil in the circumstances of the Great Strikes of the 1890s. When compulsory arbitration legislation was brought down soon after, the justification was put in terms of the experiences of the 1890s. But once the machinery was set up and made freely available, time made habit of this machinery despite the avowed objective of the legislation to encourage the development of collective bargaining. The wisdom of the much espoused American concept of the "arsenal" approach is seen clearly in this light. The only condition that would encourage "free" collective bargaining in Australia is a more tardy and uncertain application of compulsory arbitration and a willingness on the part of tribunals to suffer protracted strikes without making available either awards or sanctions.

However, this approach has not been attempted seriously in Australia, partly because of a morbid fear of long strikes and partly because of the general acceptance of the "rule of law" in industrial disputes--on interests and on rights.

Thus, the choice in favour of compulsory arbitration, or any arrangement interposing third-party "settlements" in industrial disputes, must be based on the relative social value of the force of public regulation in some sense or another, as against the value of industrial settlements arrived at largely by the disputing parties themselves on the basis of their respective self-interest. True, this self-interest, as any sophisticated employer and union leader knows, must be exercised to a greater or lesser degree in the context of public reaction and the public interest: there is no such thing as *absolute freedom* in negotiations! But there is surely a difference between, on the one hand, the negotiation and acceptance by the employer and the union of the limits to which they will *agree* to advance their respective self-interest in the face of likely public opposition and, on the other, the *dictation* of these limits by a public tribunal. That the first situation calls for sophisticated and responsible union and management behaviour goes without saying. But it is only by applying pressures for greater sophistication and self-reliance that these qualities will develop; not by persistent public regulation of the terms of employment. It may be idealistic and unrealistic that, even given self-reliance, we should expect much concern for that vague entity, the "public interest", from individual unions and employers under conditions of full employment. This is a valid doubt, but in Australia neither union nor management has been exposed sufficiently to the pressure for self-reliance.

It should be understood that whatever doubts have been expressed about the wisdom of compulsory arbitration on interest matters apply largely to private employment. In public employment, there is a strong case for keeping political influences at bay in determining the terms of employment. On balance, the recommendations of a nonpartisan committee of enquiry or of a compulsory arbitration tribunal might be expedient arrangements.

Finally, a word about the contribution that Australian compulsory arbitration has made to the evolution of a national wage policy machinery. Leaving aside the question of whether Australian national wage policy has contributed to economic stability and a socially desirable distribution of income, the main requirements of a national wage policy machinery are not contingent on the existence of compulsory arbitration. This is supported at least by the experience of the Netherlands and Sweden. The development of compulsory arbitration in Australia into, among other things, an instrument of national wage policy was the result of the peculiar constitutional, institutional and economic circumstances of Australian history. The case for compulsory arbitration in general cannot fairly rest on this aspect of the Australian system.

Note

Dean H.D. Woods of McGill University has made a useful distinction between "accommodative" and "normative" conciliation in the Canadian system, and no doubt this distinction applies, to a greater or lesser degree, to the conciliation process under collective bargaining in other countries. The same distinction may be made usefully in compulsory arbitration. Accommodative arbitration results in an award that embodies, substantially, the terms that the parties themselves would have reached, bearing in mind their bargaining powers. The "rules of evidence" of a purely judicial procedure, if not abandoned, are diluted and the main objective of arbitration is to find something close to a mutually acceptable solution. The award is thus a pragmatic attempt to resolve the dispute, to avoid a strike, or to induce a return to work. Normative arbitration, on the other hand, attempts to impose a "just" solution on the parties, taking into account the merits of the case rather than the power situations of the parties or the accept-

ability of the terms to both sides. The difficulties of deriving
a formula for a "just" settlement, particularly in interest disputes, and the general desire of the arbitrator to avoid a strike
or a prolongation of a strike, tend to encourage accommodative
arbitration.

24. A Collective Bargaining Simulation

by J. Lewiski and G. Swimmer

Introduction and Ground Rules

The following exercise is designed to give the student some feeling for the process of union-management negotiations.

The periodic negotiation of the terms of reference of employment is a fundamental part of the Canadian industrial relations system. To simplify the scope of this exercise, the negotiations will involve amending an existing collective agreement.

(1) Students will be divided into groups, which in turn will be subdivided equally into a management and union negotiation team. Team members will be assigned roles to help clarify their tasks and areas of special interest in the coming negotiations. For instance, the personnel manager of the company is concerned with management's unrestricted right to hire and fire workers. It may be his task to answer union charges of management abuse of this right. It is important that *all team members stick to their roles* during the entire simulation.

(2) When the teams are formed, each team will hold sessions to determine their negotiation positions.

(3) The preliminary strategy sessions will develop an initial position, which will be documented and presented to the instructor. The paper should consider original demands, fallback demands, expected gains, and an evaluation of the opposing team. In addition, all documentary evidence that will be used to strengthen the union's or management's case in the coming negotiations should be included. Each team is free to obtain whatever evidence from outside sources it wishes. *Half* of the grade on this simulation will depend upon this paper.

(4) All wage demands must be defined in terms of a *cents (¢) per hour across-the-board increase*. A cost of living clause, if any, should be considered in terms of the number of *cents per hour* increase per worker for a one percentage point increase in the consumer price index. Pension demands should be framed in terms of employers' contribution. For instance, the union might demand that management contribute 1 per cent of all workers' wages to the pension fund. Framing demands in this way will enable both sides to establish the monetary cost of the proposed contract. See page 282 for costing formulas.

(5) The legal environment for the simulation is determined by the relevant provincial labour act.

(6) The teams will meet three times, in rooms designated by the instructor, to negotiate a new contract. The first session will set the groundwork for future meetings. At session 1, each team will present the opposing team a list of demands and clauses it wishes to see incorporated into the new contract.

(7) Sessions 2 and 3 will be held in the rooms and at the hours
designated by the instructor. Further meetings must be arranged
by the teams.

(8) Total time in negotiations is limited to one week from the
date of the first meeting. At this time the teams have either
decided to go to conciliation or have settled upon a new contract.
Neither team may stop negotiating before the conclusion of session 3. In the event of an impasse, both teams involved must submit final reports to the instructor analyzing why and on which
issues the bargaining failed. Those teams that reach agreement
must submit a copy of all changes and additions included in the
new contract.

(9) All strategy and negotiation sessions are in the *strictest
confidence*.

(10) All teams will present a three-to five-minute report to the
entire class, summarizing the strategies and results of their
negotiations.

(11) The timing and procedures of this simulation may be changed
at the discretion of the instructor.

The Company

J.A. Atchinson is a manufacturing company located in the north-
eastern industrial area of the city. The company manufactures
house trailers and portable buildings for construction, oilfield
and survey crews. The company also undertakes specialty manufacturing. The arctic oil exploration has proven a real boom to
the company's business. The firm has three revolving shifts.

The company was started in 1952 by J.A. Atchinson, who is the
president of the company. In order to expand in 1960, 1,000,000
shares were offered at a par value of $5.00 each. J.A. Atchinson
retains control of the company. The expansion plan has led to
the formation of branch plants in Manitoba and acquisition of a
sheet-metal fabrication firm in Saskatchewan. The most ambitious
project under way is the construction of a vacation trailer manufacturing plant in Nova Scotia. The expected contribution to the
company's overall financial earnings of this city's plant with
the completion of the Nova Scotia plant will be reduced to 55 per
cent by the fall of 1975.

The company enjoys a good reputation for quality with its customers. Few changes have been initiated in the production process
and the company can still be described as labour intensive.

In recent years, the company has encountered stiff competition
from new modern entries into the manufacturing field. It has
maintained its leadership position largely because of the president's personal dynamism and charisma. Nonetheless, the need for
more automation and prefabrication in the company's production
process has become clear to management.

The Union

The workers of J.A. Atchinson Enterprises came together and formed
Local 122 of the Canadian Constructionists Union in May of 1957.
The national union is a member of the CLC.

Recently, international unions have won large pay increases in
similar industries in the local area. In the past, Atchinson
Enterprises' wage increases have only kept up with the cost of
living. Because of this there is considerable organizational activity by one particular international union at this plant.

Constructionist Union officials are concerned about the ability
to maintain their membership. In the entire bargaining history
of the company, the union has never called a strike. In the seven
times the union has gone to grievance arbitration the decision has
been in favour of the company. This is largely due to the fact
that the contract is not comprehensive in defining many areas of
labour activity.

At the present time, the union operates under an agency shop
arrangement. The union does have 200 card-carrying members from
the 300 employees contained in the collective bargaining unit.
There are an additional 50 nonunion office workers who are not
part of the unit.

Union-management relations have been good in the past. This
has led to charges of "coziness" between management and top union
officials by many in the rank and file. Recently, three old-time
shop stewards were rejected in an election in favour of younger,
more militant candidates. A concerted attempt is being made to
get rid of the president and vice-president of the union. Elections are to be held in six months' time. In a response to these
efforts, the president and vice-president have pledged to take a
much harder line toward management in the next negotiations.
Specifically, they have vowed to introduce a jointly sponsored
pension plan into the next contract. The younger stewards also
want to see more holidays, paid education leaves, higher wages,
provisions for maternity leaves for female employees, and a medical care plan.

The present contract is considered to have good grievance and
arbitration procedures, but many other clauses are considered
inadequate by the rank and file. It is felt that much of the
residual power not spelled out in the contract and granted to management leaves many important areas to management's sole discretion. Some shop stewards believe that "management discretion"
has allowed the personnel manager to fire militant unionists.

There is also a lot of talk in the shop about job security.
Rumours are spreading that management may buy prefabricated
sheet metal from its new Saskatchewan subsidiary. Extensive layoffs could result.

Most of the workers have less than five years' seniority with
the company. Only about 25 per cent of the workers have over ten
years' seniority. Of the latter, the majority have been with the
company since the early 1950s.

The union is very militant with respect to pension plans. It
would like to see major concessions made by the company to the

older workers to provide for a better retirement, as well as introduction of a pension plan for all workers. The company has operated a pension plan for its office staff for the past fifteen years.

Management and Union Representatives

(Detailed role profiles will be distributed by the instructor.)

Management

(1)   Director of Production
(2)   Personnel Manager
(3)   Vice-President in charge of Finance
(4)   Assistant General Manager
(5)   Director of Salary Administration
(6)   Assistant Director, All Operations

Union

(1)   Local Union President
(2)   Vice-President
(3)   Secretary-Treasurer
(4)   Shop Steward--Construction
(5)   Shop Steward--Shipping and Receiving
(6)   National Union Representative

The Contract

ARTICLE 1

Intent and Purpose

The purpose of this agreement is to maintain a harmonious relationship between the Company and its employees; to provide an
amicable method of settling any grievances or differences that
might arise; and to promote the mutual interests of the employer
and the employees.

ARTICLE 2

Recognition

(1) The Company recognizes Local 122 of the Union as exclusive
bargaining agency for its plant in this city, save and except
all office staff, salesmen, salaried foremen and those above
salaried foremen, security guards, and salaried inspectors.

(2) The Union recognizes the sole right of the Company to manage
the plant and direct the work of the employees, including the
right: to hire, promote, demote, suspend, discharge for cause,
lay off, assign to jobs and shifts, or transfer from department
to department; to increase or decrease the working forces; to

determine the products to be handled, processed or manufactured;
and to determine the schedule of production, the methods, processes,
and means of production, and the handling of same.

ARTICLE 3

Union Security

(1) The Company and Union agree that any present employee of the
Company or any new employee hired by the Company shall not be required to be a member of the Union.

(2) The Company agrees that all employees are required to pay an
amount equal to the monthly dues of a member in good standing of
the Canadian Constructionist Workers.

ARTICLE 4

Checkoff

(1) The Company agrees to deduct the monthly Union dues from each
employee's pay on his first payday in each calendar month during
the term of this agreement, and in the case of a newly hired employee, on the first payday in the month next following date of
hire. The total so deducted, with an itemized statement of same,
in duplicate, shall be forwarded to the Union prior to the end of
the month in which said deductions apply.

(2) It is agreed that the president of the Union will be allowed
reasonable time to interview new employees at the beginning of
their first shifts.

ARTICLE 5

Hours of Work and Overtime

(1) This article is intended to define the normal hours of work,
and shall not be construed as any guarantee of work or pay, or of
hours of work per day or per week, or of days of work per week.

(2) The normal hours of work for all employees shall be eight
(8) hours per day. A day is defined as the twenty-four (24)-hour
period beginning with the time the employee commences work.

(3) The normal work schedule for other than seven (7) consecutive
day operations shall be five (5) consecutive days, forty (40) hours
except in cases of breakdown, emergencies and holidays.

(4) The work week shall be a period of seven (7) days beginning
at 12:01 A.M., Monday.

(5) Schedules of work shall be posted or otherwise made known to
employees by 2:00 P.M., Thursday of the preceding week. Schedules
of work shall not be changed to avoid the payment of overtime.

ARTICLE 5 (Cont'd)

(6)   For the purpose of calculating, if overtime is payable, the Company at each plant shall set out the hours of work in Schedule A, which may vary from department to department and between employees within a department. The hours set out shall total not more than eight (8) in any day or forty (40) for any payroll week, unless mutually agreed. The schedule of hours may be changed from time to time by the Company as required.

(7)   The Company and the Union recognize that it may be necessary for employees to work in excess of their regular number of hours. The Company will limit the hours of work beyond such regular number of hours to what is reasonable.

(8)   For all hours worked in excess of the number of hours set out in Schedule A, an hourly paid employee, other than a continuous shift operator, shall be paid overtime at one and one-half (1½) times his regular hourly rate or temporary rate, whichever is being paid when overtime commences. For all hours in excess of thirteen (13) continuous hours, twice such rate shall replace one and one-half (1½). After thirteen (13) hours of continuous work, a second meal will be furnished by the Company to be eaten on Company time not to exceed twenty (20) minutes.

(9)   An employee who has left the Company's premises, and is specially called outside his scheduled hours for emergency work, shall be paid four (4) hours at his job rate or for the hours actually worked at the overtime rate, whichever is greater.

(10) Sunday Work: Double the regular hourly rate shall be paid to hourly paid employees for work performed on Sunday, except where the work regularly falls on Sunday, in which case the employee shall be paid double the regular hourly rate if he works on his day off in lieu of Sunday.

ARTICLE 6

Seniority

(1)   Seniority is defined as the length of an employee's service with the Company in any of the plants, determined by inclusion on plant payroll, and referred to herein as "plant work". Such service shall be calculated as the elapsed time from the date he was first employed on plant work, unless his seniority was broken, in which event the calculation shall be from the date that he returned to plant work following the last break in his seniority, subject to the following:

(i)   Service in the capacity of foreman or assistant foreman will not be considered in determining an employee's seniority.

(ii)   An employee returning to plant work from another part of the Company's service will be credited with his previous service in plant work.

ARTICLE 6 (Cont'd)

   (iii) An employee's seniority rights shall become effective nine (9) months from the date of hiring.

   (iv) Seniority shall be on a divisional basis until an employee has completed eighteen (18) months of seniority service.

(2) The seniority of an employee shall be considered broken, all rights considered forfeited, and there is no obligation to rehire when he:

   (i) voluntarily leaves the service of the Company or is discharged for cause;

   (ii) fails to return to work when called or cannot be located after a reasonable effort on the part of the Company.

ARTICLE 7

Paid Holidays

(1) Six (6) paid holidays shall be recognized, as follows:

New Years' Day	Dominion Day
Christmas Day	Thanksgiving Day
Good Friday	Remembrance Day

(2) For each paid holiday, eight (8) hours holiday pay at his job rate sahll be paid to a regular employee.

ARTICLE 8

Vacations

(1) The vacation year is the period from June 1 to May 31, inclusive.

(2) An employee shall be entitled to an annual vacation with pay, in accordance with the following schedule, on the basis of his service as of June 1 in each year.

Length of Seniority	Length of Vacation
1 year and less than 5 years	2 weeks
5 years and less than 12 years	2½ weeks
12 years and less than 18 years	3 weeks
18 years and less than 25 years	4 weeks
25 years and over	5 weeks

ARTICLE 9

Wages

(1) Each job shall be described and classified and a rate of pay applied to each employee on such job, in accordance with the

ARTICLE 9 (Cont'd)

provisions of the agreement.

(2)   Job description and classification is the joint responsibility of the plant foreman acting on behalf of the Company, and the union vice-president acting on behalf of the employees.

(3)   The job description and classification and the standard hourly wage scale are incorporated into this agreement as appendix A, and govern the wage schedule and dates of implementation of changes in the wage scale.

(4)   As of the date each standard hourly wage scale becomes effective, the standard hourly rate for each job class shall be the standard hourly rate for all jobs classified within such job classes.

(5)   Except as otherwise provided by this agreement, the established rate of pay for a trade or craft apprenticeship job shall apply to any employee during the time such employee is assigned to the respective rate of classification.

ARTICLE 10

Grievance Procedure

If a grievance arises in the plant, an honest effort shall be made to settle the difference in the following manner.

(1)   There shall be a grievance committee consisting of four (4) employees selected by the Union, who have at least six (6) month's service with the Company. The Union agrees to advise the Company, in writing, of the names of the members of the grievance committee, and also of any change that may occur.

(2)   In addition to any special meetings of the grievance committee and the Company, there shall be a regular meeting of the grievance committee and the Company to be held on the third Thursday of each month.

   Members of the grievance committee will not suffer any loss of pay for attending regular meetings for processing grievances through steps 3 and 4, provided that the total number of hours lost does not exceed six (6) hours for all committee members attending such meetings in any calendar month. No remuneration shall be paid for lost time exceeding six (6) hours.
   A representative of the Union shall obtain the permission of his foreman before leaving his work to deal with a grievance. Such permission shall not be unreasonably withheld.

   Step 1. Any employee who believes that he has a justifiable grievance shall take up the matter with his foreman with or without his grievance committeeman's being present, or the grievance

ARTICLE 10 (Cont'd)

committeeman may take up the matter with the foreman, as the
employee elects. Grievances not adjusted in this way within one
(1) full working day are eligible to be brought forward to step 2.

Step 2. The grievance will be put in writing and shall be submitted to the superintendent by the grievance committeeman within
six (6) full working days after the employee has received the verbal decision of the foreman. The written grievance will contain
particulars of the incident giving rise to the grievance and will
be signed by the aggrieved employee and dated as of the date of
its submission. The superintendent shall give his answer in writing to the grievance committeeman within six (6) full working days
after the date of the presentation. Grievances not adjusted in
step 2 are eligible to be brought forward to step 3.

Step 3. In the case of an appeal from such decision, notice of
the appeal must be given within seven (7) days of the date of the
superintendent's written decision. Notification of such appeal
shall be made in writing to the plant superintendent or his representative. The grievance committee of the Union and representatives of the Company shall attempt to settle the grievance at the
regular meeting, or if the grievance is of an urgent nature, at a
special meeting at a time mutually arranged. The plant superintendent or his representative shall give his decision in writing
to the chairman of the grievance committee within five (5) working
days of the date of such meeting. Grievances not adjusted under
step 3 are eligible to be brought forward to step 4.

Step 4. In case of appeal from such decision, notice of the
appeal must be given in writing to the general superintendent or
his representative within seven (7) working days of the date of
the written decision of the plant superintendent or his representative. The general superintendent or his representative shall
meet with the grievance committee and a representative of the
International Union within ten (10) working days, in an attempt
to arrive at a settlement. The general superintendent or his
representative shall submit his answer in writing within five (5)
working days.

A grievance must be presented within fifteen (15) days of occurrence unless it concerns discharge, to which the paragraph below
is applicable. Grievances not presented within the time provided
will not normally be considered and, in any event, are not subject to arbitration. As well, a grievance not referred to the
next step within the time allowed will be considered settled.
When an employee has been discharged the Company will notify
the grievance committeeman concerned within forty-eight (48) hours.
A discharged employee may appeal the discharge to the plant superintendent within three (3) working days. If a settlement is not
reached a grievance may be presented at step 4 within five (5)
working days.

ARTICLE 10 (Cont'd)

(1)   In the event that more than one employee is directly affected by one specific incident and each such employee would be entitled to process a grievance, the chief steward may sign the statement of the grievance on behalf of the aggrieved employees, and shall identify the grievance as a "Group Grievance". Where retroactive wages are claimed, the names of such employees shall be attached to the grievance.

(2)   If the Company is alleged to have violated any provisions of this agreement and such violation affects the interests of the Union as a party to the agreement, the Union may file a grievance, beginning at step 2, which shall be signed on behalf of the Union by the chairman of the grievance committee and shall be identified as a "Union Policy Grievance".

(3)   Grievances that concern the interpretation, application, or administration of the manual may be initiated by the Union and shall be resolved in accordance with the provisions of this section beginning at step 3.

    The grievance and arbitration procedure may be invoked by the Company. Such grievances may be initiated by the Company at step 3 of the grievance procedure by filing with the chairman of the grievance committee. For such purposes the provisions of this Article 10 shall be read and construed with the necessary changes.

ARTICLE 11

Arbitration

Grievances concerning the interpretation, application, operation, or alleged violation of this agreement that are not settled in step 4 of the grievance procedure, may be referred to an arbitration board by notice in writing to the Company within fifteen (15) days from expiry of the time limits for settlement under step 4. Such notice shall indicate the agreement clauses relied upon.
    The Union shall, within five (5) days thereafter, appoint its representatives on the arbitration board and the Company within five (5) days thereafter shall appoint its representatives.
    If the two (2) representatives fail to settle the grievance within a further period of seven (7) days, they shall jointly appoint a third impartial member who shall be chairman of the arbitration board. If the representatives fail to agree upon a chairman, then he shall be appointed by the Deputy Minister of Labour upon the request of either party.
    The decision of a majority of the board shall be final and binding upon both parties, but the board shall not have jurisdiction to change, amend, add to or subtract from any of the provisions of this agreement. However, if the agreement has been violated by the Company and disciplinary action resulting in loss of wages is involved, the board may decide whether the disciplinary

ARTICLE 11 (Cont'd)

action should be modified if, in its opinion, the extent of the
discipline is unreasonable in relation to the offence. Where there
is no majority decision, the decision of the chairman shall be the
decision of the board.

The parties will each bear one-half (½) of the expenses and remuneration of the chairman and his secretarial expenses and rent,
but all other expenses shall be borne by the party incurring them.

ARTICLE 12

Duration of Agreement

(1) This agreement shall be effective from 1 December 1972 until
1 December 1974 and shall continue in force after 1 December 1974
on a yearly basis, which in each instance of renewal shall be regarded as the term of the agreement until terminated by either
party, giving the other party not more than sixty (60) days', and
not less than thirty (30) days' notice in writing prior to the ex-
piration date. If amendments are contemplated by either party to
become effective in the ensuing term, the party proposing such
amendments shall give notice in writing thereof to the other party
not more than ninety (90) days and not less than sixty (60) days
prior to 1 December 1974. During the period of negotiations, this
agreement shall continue in full force and effect.

(2) No provision of this agreement shall be applied retroactively
from the date of signing except as specifically provided.

APPENDIX A

Job Classification

(1)	Janitor
(2)	General Labourer
	Forklift Helper
	Shipping and Receiving Labourer
(3)	Fabrication Helper
	Truck Swamper
	Yard Labourer
(4)	Furniture Assembler
	Carpet Layer
(5)	Mill Utility Man
	Yard Runner
(6)	Forklift Operator
	Crane Operator
(7)	Welder
	Crewleader
	Steelcutter
(8)	Millwright
	Blacksmith Mechanic

APPENDIX A (Cont'd)

(9)   Machinist
               Carpenter
               Electrician
               Plumber
(10)   Group Leader, Maintenance

Standard Hourly Wage Scale

Job Class	Appendix B Effective 1 Dec. 1972	Appendix C Effective 1 Dec. 1973
1	2.91	3.46
2	3.15	3.71
3	3.22	3.78
4	3.27	3.83
5	3.36	3.93
6	3.61	4.19
7	3.83	4.42
8	3.97	4.57
9	4.31	4.93
10	4.57	5.20

Financial Data

Sales

For the last five years, the plant's sales and net earnings were:

		Sales	Earnings
	1969	$ 8,263,000	$ 657,000
	1970	10,512,000	663,000
	1971	10,989,000	540,000
	1972	14,038,000	770,000
	1973	15,067,000	978,500
Projected	1974	16,000,000	1,300,000[a]
	1975	16,500,000	1,500,000[a]

Note

a Assumes substantial subcontracting.

The company expects that sales should remain at the high levels due to exploration work being carried out in the Canadian arctic regions. They have already received orders for $2.5 million in specialized equipment.

Dividends

In the last three years, the company has paid no dividends, preferring to reinvest its earnings in new projects. However, it has decided on a dividend payment in the current fiscal year which will amount to 25 per cent of the yearly earnings' being distributed as dividends.

Economic Strategy

The company has been investigating the use of the Saskatchewan acquisition to fabricate some of the standard components in its trailers. The company estimates that a prefabrication plant would reduce labour force requirements by thirty to forty workers in the construction department of its present plant.

TABLE 24.1   J.A. Atchinson Enterprises Ltd.
        Local Plant Balance Sheet as at 15 July 1974

                (End of 1973 Fiscal Year)

Assets

Cash and bank balances	$2,729,000	
Accounts receivable	5,485,000	
Marketable securities, at cost	849,000	
Inventories of goods, including work in progress	6,125,000[a]	
Prepaid expenses	63,000	$15,251,000
Investment in affiliated companies	$3,763,000[b]	3,763,000
Fixed Assets		
Buildings, less depreciation	$2,375,000	
Equipment, less depreciation	1,950,000	4,325,000
Total Assets		$23,339,000

Liabilities

Bank notes payable	$2,500,000	
Accounts payable and interest	1,529,000	
Accrued wages	145,000	
Reserve for dividends	250,000	
Income taxes, accrued	782,000	
Contractual advances	1,048,000	
Liabilities, current		$ 6,254,000
Bond payable, due 1979		2,000,000
Total Liabilities		$ 8,254,000

Net Worth

Common stock, 1,000,000 shares par $5		$ 5,000,000
Reserve for expansion		6,000,000
Retained earnings		4,085,000

Notes

a   Finished inventories = $3,000,000

b   Common stock held in Prairie Fabrication Ltd.

TABLE 24.2   J.A. Atchinson Enterprises Ltd.
                 Local Plant Income Statement as at 15 July 1974

(End of 1973 Fiscal Year)

Net Sales		$15,067,000
Cost of Goods sold		
Materials and overhead	$8,506,000	
Labour	3,458,000[a]	
Selling and administration expenses	1,007,000	
Other expenses	139,000	$13,110,000
Earnings before taxes		1,957,000
Taxes		978,500
Net Earnings		$ 978,500

Note

a   Includes $500,000 for office workers.

TABLE 24.3   Payroll of the Edmonton
                        Plant of J.A. Atchinson

Job Class	No. of Workers in Each Class	Wages Per Hour[a]
1	10	3.46
2	20	3.71
3	20	3.78
4	20	3.83
5	50	3.93
6	60	4.19
7	50	4.42
8	30	4.57
9	20	4.93
10	20	5.20

Note

a   Average wage = $4.21 per hour.

TABLE 24.4   Selected Financial Ratios,
                 Trailer Manufacturing Industry Averages

Payroll/Total employment   9,190

Payroll/Total cost of goods sold   .28

Net earnings/Sales   .05

Net earnings/Net worth   .07

Costs of Various Contract Changes

(1) Annual cost of a one cent (1¢) per hour across-the-board
wage increase:
    (40 hours) x (52 weeks) x (300 workers) x ($.01) = $6,240.

(2) Annual cost of a 1 per cent employer contribution to the
pension fund:
            (.01) x (300 workers) x (average hourly wage) x
                    (40 hours) x (52 weeks) =

(3) Annual cost of one extra holiday:
            (300 workers) x (8 hours) x (average hourly wage) =

References

*Agreement between Burns Foods Ltd. and Canadian Food and Allied
   Workers, 1 April 1969.*

*Basic Agreement, 16 September 1972, between Edmonton Steel Works
   (Steel Co. of Canada) and Local 5220 of the Steel Workers of
   America.*

Center for Labor and Management, University of Iowa, *Collective
   Bargaining Simulation.*

Van Horne, James. *Financial Management and Policy.* 2nd. ed.
   Englewood Cliffs, N.J.: Prentice-Hall, 1971.

Zif, Jay and Otlewski, Robert. *Contract Negotiations.*
   New York: Macmillan, 1971.

PART VI: OUTPUTS OF THE IR SYSTEM *

25. Union-Nonunion Wage Differentials in Ontario

by Gerald F. Starr

This chapter examines the role of unions in wage determination.
Three possible types of union effects on wages can be distinguished. First, unions may change the general level of money or
real wages throughout the economy. Second, they may influence
the rate at which general money wages are increasing over time.
Finally, they may alter the wages of unionized labour relative
to nonunionized labour. Each of these effects is quite distinct. In the present study the main concern is the last of
these, that is, the union role in shaping the wage structure.
As a by-product, the role of other factors in determining relative wages is considered as well.

Understandably, the techniques used to estimate the independent impact of unionism and other factors on wages are somewhat
complex. In this summary, only the substantive results of the
study are presented. The discussion of the analytical models
and difficulties in statistical interpretation is kept to a
minimum. Readers interested in a more detailed description of
the methodology and interpretations of the results should con-
sult the complete study.

The Data

A unique set of Canadian data permits a highly disaggregated
approach to analyzing union impact on wages. A tape from the
1969 Canada Department of Labour Occupational Wage Rate Survey
provides information on union status, wage rates, employment
location, industry, and other characteristics for individual
establishments.

Data on employment, wages, and union status for the selected
occupations and basic rates are provided in table 25.1. It can
be seen that, particularly for the blue-collar occupations,
there are a large number of reporting establishments in each of
the cells. Only in the case of unionized white-collar occupations are there fewer than one hundred observations. Moreover,
the coverage of the survey is quite high, being virtually complete for the larger establishments. The establishments
responding to the survey account for over 90 per cent of manu-

---

* Reproduced by permission of the author.

facturing employment in Ontario.

The Analytical Approach

As can be seen from table 25.1, average wage rates in union
establishments are typically higher than those in nonunion
establishments. For unskilled production workers, the difference
is approximately 20 per cent. But not all of this difference may
be attributable to unionism. Other factors that influence wage
rates (e.g., size of firm, capital intensity, etc.) may be of
different importance for union and nonunion establishments.
After these factors are taken into account, the remaining wage
differences attributable to unionism may be considerably
higher or lower than those indicated in table 25.1. Another
weakness in the comparisons embodied in this table is that, as
they are based on overall averages, no indication is given of
variations in union effects. In other words, from the table it
is impossible to discover the conditions favourable to relatively
large union effects on wage levels.

The technique used here for distinguishing the effects of
unionization from the influence of other factors that may contribute to wage differentials is multiple linear regression analysis.
The wage rate levels in individual establishments are related,
through an equation, to a number of wage-influencing factors.
These factors include the union status of the plant, for instance.
Under ideal conditions, the regression technique allows us to
identify the independent role that each of the factors plays in
influencing wages, after taking into account the influences
attributable to all other factors. More specifically, the coefficients in the regression equations, estimated from the data
at hand, can be used to calculate the changes in wages
associated with a given change in one of the factors or variables,
with the influence of all other factors being held constant. In
addition, calculated statistics indicate the level of confidence
that can be placed in the relationships appearing in the
equations.

The Variables

The factors or variables appearing in the equations fall into
two groups. The first set of variables captures some of the
variation in wage rates that would arise in the absence of
unionism. These are called control variables. The second set
relates to the conditions under which union effects on wages
will be large or small. These are called union impact
variables.

The union effect on wages is captured primarily by a variable
indicating the union status of the establishment, that is,
whether or not there exists a collective agreement covering

TABLE 25.1 Union and Nonunion Wage Rates in Manufacturing Industries in Ontario, 1969

Occupation	Union			Nonunion		
	Establishments	Employees	Average Wage Rate Rate	Establishments	Employees	Average Wage Rate Rate
			$ per hour			$ per hour
Basic Rates[a]						
Male	1,950	395,705[b]	2.54	1,798	111,960[b]	2.10
Female	1,950		2.18	1,798		1.78
Unskilled blue-collar						
Cleaner	970	4,477	2.70	547	1,054	2.29
Labourer, production	779	12,086	2.57	446	2,795	2.16
Labourer, non production	510	5,151	2.72	225	891	2.32
Semiskilled blue-collar						
Shipper	1,337	6,800	2.77	1,064	2,700	2.51
Industrial truck operator	822	6,261	2.98	325	837	2.69
Truck driver, heavy truck	483	2,761	3.20	339	1,144	2.73
Skilled blue-collar						
Electrician	708	3,829	3.78	187	526	3.71
Machinist	518	3,089	3.61	220	645	3.42
Mechanic (machine repair)	816	5,686	3.55	415	1,092	3.09
Welder	446	2,414	3.53	182	525	3.17
			$ per week			$ per week
White-collar female						
Bookkeeping machine operator	45	91	92.83	765	1,023	86.07
Junior typist	84	455	84.58	913	2,024	74.53
Senior secretary	125	385	122.02	1,358	3,053	107.83
White-collar male						
Senior accounting clerk	88	179	135.10	696	1,299	136.86
Order clerk	70	192	123.94	817	1,725	121.06
Senior clerk	85	421	137.73	589	2,106	147.04

Source: Canada Department of Labour, Occupational Wage Rate Survey.

a The basic rate is defined as the rate paid to labourers or equivalent unskilled employees after termination of a learning or probationary period, if any.

b Relates to total nonoffice employment in the establishment.

nonoffice employees. Additional union impact variables reflect the expected employment impact of a given wage change (the elasticity of demand for union labour), the product market structure of the industry, and profit levels.

Variations in the elasticity of demand for labour have been captured in part by using as variables the extent of union organization in the industry and the importance of labour costs (the proportion of wages in value-added). The product market structure has been quantified through a measure of the degree to which the industry's output is concentrated in the largest firms in the industry, the employee size of the establishment, and the average employee size of all establishments in the industry. Profits were measured alternatively by industry after-tax rates of return on equity assets, and by crude estimates of profits per production worker man-hour.

The Male Basic Labour Rate

The study singles out the male basic (unskilled) labour rate for extensive analysis, as this wage rate is available from all establishments responding to the survey and is often identified as a key bench mark rate in wage administration programmes. Under the assumption that the union effect is constant for all establishments, the linear regression equation indicates that the interestablishment union-nonunion wage differential averages 18 cents per hour for male unskilled labour. (In relative terms, the differential turns out to be 9 per cent.) Thus it appears that when factors other than unionism are taken into account, the differences between union and nonunion wages appearing in table 25.1 are reduced considerably (from 44 cents, or 21 per cent).

When union effects are allowed to vary, three union impact variables are found to be important. Union wage rates tend to be high in industries where wages are a small porportion of value-added, industry production is concentrated in a few firms, and there is a high degree of union organization in the industry. An increase in each of these variables over its predominant range (i.e., a range covering at least 80 per cent of the establishments in the sample) is associated with the following wage changes:

Source of Wage Variation	Wage Change (cents per hour)
Wages as a proportion of value added	37
Extent of union organization in the industry	22
Product market concentration	9

Notice the comparatively small role of the product market structure in wage determination. It would appear that many con-

centrated industries that pay high wages do so primarily because
they are often highly unionized and have relatively low wage costs.

The role of the other union impact variables is not as pronounced.
For example, wages rise somewhat faster in relation to plant
size in union as compared with nonunion plants. But this difference in behaviour is not exceptionally large and, in fact, is just
barely significant according to conventional statistical tests.
In other words, there is only weak support for the view that
unions are more successful in raising wages in large plants than
in small plants. However, it must be noted that unionism accounts
for at least part of the observed relationship between wages and
plant size. When the union impact variables are added, the independent effect of plant size on wages is perhaps one-half to one-
third smaller than indicated above.

The role of profits in wage determination does not appear to
be pronounced. It is true that more profitable industries do tend
to pay higher wages. But this relationship is substantially
weakened when other factors are considered in the wage determination equations and is not statistically significant judged by the
usual tests. Union wages appear to be high in profitable industries largely because these industries also tend to have a high
degree of union organization, a low proportion of wage costs in
value-added, and a concentrated market structure. Profitability
as such would appear to be less important, although again the
evidence does suggest at least some positive impact on wages.[1]

The analysis is quite clear with respect to average plant size
in an industry. This variable has virtually no effect on wages.
Either it is a poor proxy for barriers to entry into an industry
or this factor plays no role once other influences on wages are
taken into account.

In order to gain an impression on the extent of variation in
union effects, the regression equations were used to calculate
the distribution of union effects in terms of employees. This
distribution shows a substantial concentration about the mean
value of 27 cents per hour. About 50 per cent of the union
employees in the unskilled labour category receive wages that exceed those of comparable nonunion employees by 20 to 29 cents per
hour. On the other hand, just 12 per cent of unskilled union
members receive as much as 50 cents or more per hour in excess of
wages paid to comparable nonunion workers. Similarly, just 11
per cent of union members receive less than 10 cents per hour
above comparable nonunion workers.

The above distribution indicates also that the average union-
nonunion wage differential in terms of employees is somewhat
larger than the average interestablishment differential. The
relative differential in terms of employees is 14 per cent, compared with an interestablishment relative differential of under
10 per cent. This difference arises because the larger unionized

establishments are concentrated in those industries in which the union effect on wages is above average.

The Female Basic Labour Rate

In absolute terms, the average interestablishment union-nonunion wage differential for unskilled females is 13.5 cents per hour, noticeably below that for males. But the low wages of females result in the relative differential's being almost identical for both groups - 8.0 per cent for unskilled females and 9.0 per cent for unskilled males.

The similarity in results between males and females extends to the union impact variables. Again, a high degree of union organization in an industry, a concentrated product market structure, and a low proportion of wages in value-added are associated with high union wages. Also, the evidence does not indicate a strong impact of profits on female wages. The only differences are that for females, the proportion of wages in value added is not as dominant a factor as for males, and plant size has an appreciable and statistically significant effect on a union's wage gaining ability in the case of females.

The union impact on female wages does appear quite varied. The calculated distribution of union effects in terms of female union members is less concentrated about the mean than in the case of males. Union effects throughout the range of 0 to 40 cents per hour are quite common. On the other hand, the calculated distribution for female union members shows fewer extreme values. Fewer than 12 per cent of female union members are subject to effects outside the above range.

As in the case of males, the female union-nonunion wage differential in terms of employees is greater than the differential in terms of establishments. Taking account of the distribution of female union members raises the absolute differential to 20.0 cents per hour. In relative terms, the differential increases modestly to 12.2 per cent. In both cases, the estimated differentials turn out to be remarkably close to those found for males, although slightly smaller.

In addition to the similarity of union impact on both male and female unskilled wage rates documented throughout the study, about the same proportion of male and female production workers are union members.[2] Therefore, the implication of the findings is that unionism has not materially affected the degree of inequality between male and female wages in manufacturing.

Union-Nonunion Wage Differentials by Skill Level

There is no concensus on whether unions have widened or narrowed

wage inequalities among various grades of production workers.
For instance, evidence has been given to support the view that
unions, taking advantage of a comparatively inelastic demand,
have had a greater relative effect on the wages of skilled workers
than of the unskilled.[3]   But this is at odds with the arguments
of many who claim that unions are egalitarian institutions that
attempt to reduce or eliminate all types of differentials,
including those based on skill. The common conception is that
industrial unions tend to negotiate equal cents per hour increases for all workers in the bargaining unit, with special
skill adjustments or equal per cent increases, across the board,
being agreed to only reluctantly.[4] The result, of course, would
be a compression of relative skill differentials. Yet another
view arises from the belief that skilled workers have generally
been in short supply and that, consequently, their wages have
been determined largely through the operation of market forces.
In contrast, it is argued that the unskilled are typically in
abundant supply and therefore unions have an opportunity to
raise wages above market levels.[5] If this were the case, the
union impact on unskilled wages would be greater than that for
skilled, in absolute as well as relative terms. Indeed, the
union impact on skilled rates would be very small, if not zero.

A consideration of the union-nonunion wage differentials for
the occupations appearing in table 25.1 sheds light on these
various possibilities. The average interestablishment differentials for the three unskilled occupations range between 14 and
15 cents per hour -- just slightly below the estimate for male
basic labour. The differentials for the semiskilled occupations
are more varied, ranging from 8 to 16 cents per hour. Nonetheless, they remain substantial. In marked contrast, the
differentials for the highly skilled are small. For three of
the four skilled occupations, the differentials are less than
five cents per hour and are not statistically significant
according to the usual tests. The other skilled occupation
shows a modest differential of 11 cents per hour. These
findings suggest that the union impact on relative wages is
largely confined to the unskilled and semiskilled. For the
skilled worker, the union effects are small, although probably
positive. Overall, unionism in manufacturing has probably been
associated with a narrowing of both relative and absolute wage
inequalities between the highest- and lowest-paid categories of
production workers.

The examination of the wage variations for the specific
occupations appearing in table 25.1 provides also a convenient
opportunity to check the inferences drawn earlier in the analysis
of male and female basic wage rates. Although they involve substantially different and smaller samples of establishments, the
specific occupations do display wage patterns quite similar to
those reported previously. First, the approximate size of the
interestablishment union-nonunion wage differentials for the
unskilled and semiskilled occupations is only slightly smaller

than that for male basic labour. Second, three union impact
variables are again predominant. A high degree of union organization in an industry, a low proportion of wages in value-added,
and a concentrated product market structure are all associated
with high or union wages. Only one difference was apparent.
For these specific occupations, there was little evidence to
suggest that wages increase faster with plant size in union as
opposed to nonunion establishments.

The Union Impact on White-Collar Wages

Unionism may affect the wages of white-collar workers in two ways.
First, there may be a direct wage effect associated with the
unionization of these workers. Quantitatively, however, the
extent of such direct effects appears limited at the present time.
Despite a recent rapid expansion of white-collar unionization
among government workers and certain professions, inroads in
manufacturing have been few. In the survey used in this study,
under 5 per cent of the manufacturing establishments in Ontario
reported having a collective agreement covering any office
employees. In addition to the limited extent of unionization, it
is also not clear what power can be exercised by organized white-
collar workers in manufacturing.

    Second, there may be an indirect effect, as the unionization
of an employer's blue-collar workers may alter the wage decisions
he takes concerning his unorganized workers. Employers who grant
large increases to their blue-collar workers may feel compelled
to grant similar increases to their unorganized white-collar
workers. Employers may do this out of their sense of fairness
or to prevent discontent among white-collar workers caused by
an erosion of traditional wage differentials. Instances of
this type of behaviour abound in descriptions of employer wage-
setting practices. But the quantitative significance of such
indirect effects may be questioned. Although parallel increases
for white- and blue-collar workers may occur occasionally,
employers concerned with profit maximization may not follow
this practice when the result would be wages for office
employees that are far in excess of market rates.

    In the study, the magnitudes of both the direct and indirect
effects are estimated for the six white-collar occupations in
table 25.1. The few female white-collar workers who work in
union-organized offices have a considerable wage advantage.
The estimated interestablishment union-nonunion wage differential for these workers is about 10 per cent, or comparable to
that for unskilled blue-collar labour. But in the case of male
white-collar workers the effects are small. For two of the
three male white-collar occupations, the differentials, although
positive, are small and not statistically significant. For the
other occupation, the differential is negative. There is no
apparent reason for this difference by sex in union effects.

Perhaps it arises because the male jobs are more senior positions which sometimes do not come under the terms of collective agreements. It may in part reflect the previously noted tendency for the union-nonunion wage differential to decline with skill levels.

There is little evidence that indirect effects of unionism on white-collar wages are quantitatively significant for either males or females. In fact, having a union in the plant appears to slightly depress the wages of the associated white-collar workers.

Perhaps the most intriguing result is the limited role that the union impact variables play in explaining white-collar wages. Although the direction of the effects is often as expected, the relationships are typically quite weak and not statistically significant. A high degree of union organization in an industry, a concentrated product market structure, and a low proportion of wages in value-added, are conditions found to be clearly favourable to a high level for blue-collar wages. This is further evidence that indirect union effects on wages are weak, if not totally absent. The limited role of the union impact variables also sheds light on an important question of interpretation. Because no strong relationships with white-collar wages are apparent, we can be more confident that such factors as product market structure, degree of union organization in an industry, and labour costs as indicated by the proportion of wages in value-added are actually capturing variations in union effectiveness (the interpretation advanced throughout the study) rather than reflecting a more general causal factor, such as employer ability-to-pay, which presumably would affect the wages of all workers, white-collar and blue-collar alike.[6]

The Union Impact on Nonunion Employees

The estimates given above, as well as those made in other studies, fail to take account of the possibility that some non-union employers might raise their wages as a result of unionism. An attempt was made to measure the importance of such effects, based on the approach that nonunion employers might raise their wages in efforts to forestall union organization. If this kind of behaviour is important, nonunion wages would be high in situations where the union impact is potentially high and the probability of union organization is high. In the analysis, this latter probability was indexed by the size of the nonunion firms and the extent of union organization in the industry.

The results were not entirely satisfactory, as the estimates derived from the regression equations were not plausible in some respects. Further work would be necessary before calculations could be made of the difference in wages between union workers and those of comparable groups of nonunion workers totally

unaffected by unionism. But the analysis did yield indications
that in fact the threat of unionization does have at least some
effect on nonunion wages. Particularly for unskilled workers,
it was found that, all other things being equal: (1) increases
in the degree of union organization in an industry generally
are associated with increases in nonunion wages; (2) nonunion
wages increase more rapidly with plant size at high levels of
union organization in an industry than at low levels; and (3)
nonunion wages are high under circumstances that favour a
large union impact on wages. All these findings are consistent
with the view that, at least to some degree, nonunion employers
increase their wages in response to the threat of union organization.

Conclusion

Consistent with a number of United States studies, the study
found that for basic labour the union-nonunion wage differential
for females closely approximates that for males, but that the
differential for the skilled occupations, even in absolute
terms, is considerably smaller than the differential for the
unskilled and semiskilled occupations. In fact, the differential
for the highly skilled may be zero. However, the skilled occupations probably represent fewer than one-quarter of all
production workers. It would seem, then, that a global estimate
of the union-nonunion wage differential in terms of employees
for all production workers would be only slightly less than the
differential indicated for the unskilled. The assumption that
one-quarter of all production workers are skilled and receive
no wage advantage from unionism, while all the rest follow the
pattern of the basic male rate, yields a global estimate of the
differential of approximately 10 per cent.

Among the control variables, the ratio of males in a plant
has a surprisingly strong influence on wage rate levels. This
raised the question of whether or not a high proportion of
females in a plant is the result, rather than the cause, of low
wages. In other words, it may be that firms hire a high proportion of females because, for one reason or another, their wages
are low. If this is the case, the inclusion of this variable
in the regression equations would be wrong and could have the
effect of biasing the estimates of union effects downwards. As
a precaution, alternative calculations were made, taking into
account this possibility. Omitting the ratio of males from
the male basic rate regressions has the effect of only slightly
increasing the interestablishment union-nonunion wage differential to 10 per cent. But the size of the union impact variables
is increased substantially with the result that the differential in terms of employees rises to 22 per cent. Under these
assumptions, the global union-nonunion differential in terms of
employees was calculated to be approximately 17 per cent.

The two global estimates indicated above probably are extremes. The actual global differential more than likely falls in the range of 10 to 17 per cent. It should also be kept in mind that these estimates do not take into account the impact of unionism in nonunion firms. As the study suggests that such effects may be important, the above estimates understate to some extent the total impact of unionism.

Two additional points should be mentioned. First, the global estimates of the union-nonunion wage differential are actually quite close to those originally proposed by Lewis and those derived from a few recent United States studies using data for individual establishments or workers. It would appear that the union effects in Ontario manufacturing are not markedly different from those in the United States. In light of the findings of the study, the numerous estimates based on industry aggregated data, which are typically quite large, appear to be biased upwards because of their failure to take into account the strong positive associations that exist between, on the one hand, the degree of union organization in an industry and, on the other, union and nonunion wages.

Second, as well as significant average union effects, the study shows substantial variations in union wage levels. The interpretation of these variations given in the study is that they reflect differences in union effectiveness. This is not the only explanation. But regardless of the interpretation, there are strong empirical relationships that signify a highly structured labour market. Within a local labour market there are large differences in the wages paid to workers in a given occupational category. These differences, many of which appear inconsistent with traditional explanations of wage differentials, must be kept in mind when the relative roles of competitive market forces and institutional factors are being considered as determinants of the wage structure.

Notes

1. These findings of weak profit effects must be qualified. The data sources used to measure profits may be subject to considerable measurement error and this may bias results toward showing no relationship between profits and wages. It should also be mentioned that the analysis is based on the assumption that only a proportion and not all excess profits are absorbed in wages.

2. Females comprise 19 per cent of all union members and about 23 per cent of all production workers in Canadian manufacturing. See Statistics Canada, *Annual Report of the Minister of Industry, Trade and Commerce Under the Corporations and Labour Unions Return Act, 1969*, part II (Ottawa: Queen's Printer, 1971), p. 67.

3. Sherwin Rosen, "Unionism and the Occupational Wage Structure in the United States", *International Economic Review*, vol. III, no. 2 (June 1970), pp. 269-73.

4. For example, see Peitchinis, *The Economics of Labour*, pp. 335-36.

5. Pradeep Kumar, "Differentials in Wage Rates of Unskilled Labour in Manufacturing Industries", *Industrial and Labour Relations Review*, vol. 26, no. 1 (October 1972), pp. 631-46.

6. Of course, it would be desirable to have further support for the interpretation given in the study. In particular, it would be desirable to examine the relationships, if any, between production worker wages and union impact variables during the period prior to the spread of unionism in manufacturing.

26. Wage Adjustments in Canadian Industry, 1953-66*

by G. L. Reuber

Introduction

A central question in analyzing the determinants of wages is to
what extent the rate of change in wages is determined by the
level of aggregate demand and competitive market responses, and
to what extent it is determined by other influences, such as
bargaining power, institutional practices, and special factors
associated with particular industries. Although wages, like
other prices in the economy, are determined by supply and demand,
in order to devise an effective stabilization policy it is
important to understand not only this interaction but also the
effectiveness of various instruments of economic policy in
modifying supply and demand conditions, and the implications of
these instruments for the other goals of public policy.

This study focusses on only one important part of the first
aspect, namely, the determinants of wages in the Canadian manufacturing industry.[1] The research undertaken consists of two
related parts. The first is an examination of the determinants
of wages within major (two-digit) industrial classifications.
An attempt is made to bring together two independent lines of
research, that of assessing the determinants of wages at a
highly aggregative level by applying "Phillips-curve" analysis,
and that of studying the short-run relationship between
variations in output and employment in manufacturing. The second
part of the analysis focusses on the role of "key" industries and
"key" bargains in the determination of wages in Canada. Previous
research in Canada has suggested the interesting possibility that
insofar as key bargains play a role in determining wages in
Canada, these key bargains may originate in the United States.
Investigation of this hypothesis remains difficult because of
the lack of satisfactory statistical data.

A Model for Evaluating the Determinants of Wages in Manufacturing Industries

In order to examine the determinants of wage changes at the level
of individual industries, Phillips-curve-type wage adjustment
relationships such as those fitted by Bodkin, Bond, Reuber and
Robinson are not satisfactory.[2] Wages in one industry are likely
to be influenced by wages in another; unemployment in particular
industries has little meaning, especially among less-skilled
labourers. Further, both the level and the rate of change in
wages in a particular industry are likely to be influenced by

---

* Reproduced by permission of Information Canada.

that industry's own level of and changes in output, as well as by its profit position, trade union strength, and other factors peculiar to it.

In order to proceed, a model was developed to explain the rate of change in wages in particular industries in terms of the excess demand for labour -- the difference between the quantity demanded and supplied. It was estimated by a two-stage procedure. In stage one an estimate was made of industry i's demand function for labour, and in stage two this was combined with the supply function of labour confronting industry i to estimate the determinants of the rate of change in wages in industry i.

(1)   Industry Demand for Labour

Following the models developed by Brechling and O'Brien, and[3] Ball and St. Cyr,[4] short-run employment functions can be fitted for each industry i as follows:

$$MH_i = f_1(\overset{+}{Q_i}, \overset{-}{t}, \ \overset{+}{MH_i-1}, D) \tag{26.1}$$

Q_i = output in the ith industry;

t = time, numbering quarters consecutively;

D = seasonal dummy variables, one for each quarter.

The expected signs of each relationship are shown above the explanatory variables.

This relationship can be fitted in either log-linear (implying a constant elasticity of substitution production function) or linear form, with built-in adjustment factors in both cases. Both forms differ here from the usual demand relation because of the exclusion of prices (wages) as a determinant of demand, due to lack of statistical data. In the short run, relative price effects may be small, and a time trend has been included to reflect changes in technical progress and in relative supplies of labour inputs to reflect longer-term influences.

The demand for labour in this analysis is expressed in terms of man-hours, since the determinants of their price, expressed as average hourly earnings, is the concern of the study.

Setting $MH_{it} = MH_{it}-1$, the equilibrium level of labour inputs, MH^*, can be derived from equation 26.1. If actual employment in any quarter is MH_i, then $MH_i - MH_i^* = e_i$, representing the level of vacancies and redundancies expressed in terms of man-hours, in any industry in any given quarter. Therefore, e_i must be composed of a random element with an assumed mean of zero over time, and a lag element to provide for the adjustment of actual to desired labour inputs over time.

From equation 26.1, two estimates of "desired demand" can be derived. MH_i* is the amount of labour employers in an industry eventually wish to have, on average within a year, if everything else remains unchanged. MH_i, the level of labour inputs in any quarter from equation 26.1, is the amount of labour desired by employers at the end of the current quarter following an output change. Figure 26.1 assumes a given supply relationship as a function of wages paid in industry i. D_1 is the demand for labour in period one, equal to the supply ob, at the wage oa. Demand is completely inelastic with respect to W_i in accordance with the production function assumed in equation 26.1.

$MH_i = \hat{MH}_i + u_i$, where $\hat{MH}_i$ is estimated man-hours and u is the residual error term;

$MH_i* = \hat{MH}_i - MH_{i-1} + MH_i*$, where   is the estimated coefficient of MH_{i-1} in equation 26.1; $e_i = MH_i - MH_i*$ $= \mathcal{N}_i + \alpha(MH_{i-1} - MH_i*)$.

Figure 26.1

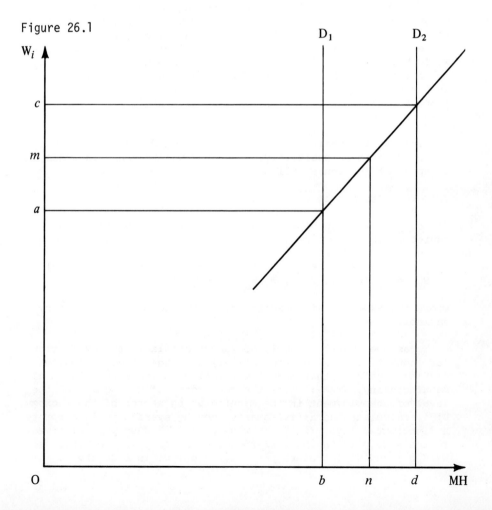

If demand increases to D_2, at the new equilibrium entre-
preneurs will wish to hire od man-hours at wage oc. In the
first quarter after the change, however, they may only hire on
man-hours at wage om, leaving nd vacancies still to be filled.
Thus, employers can choose to fill their vacancies slowly in
approaching the new equilibrium. Therefore, one would expect
MH_i to be significantly related to the change in wages. Alternatively, employers may immediately raise the wages to
approximately the new equilibrium level. In this case MH_i* would
be a "better" estimate of the demand for labour.

There are at least two a priori reasons for believing that
MH_i would perform better than MH_i* in explaining wage changes.
Moving to the new equilibrium position in the current quarter may
be costly, due to greater direct costs for recruitment, a prob-
able extra increase in wages to be paid out to both existing and
new employees, and the presence of uncertainty leading to
unnecessary adjustments to random disturbances.

The importance of allowing for the independent influence of
vacancies and redundancies has been emphasized in the context of
Phillips-curve analysis. However, in this model, random disturbances reflected in the variable e_i, if isolated by employers,
would have little influence, and the adjustment component of e_i
is reflected in MH_i and MH_i*, which indicate how far along the
supply curve employers move in any quarter. Thus there is no
scope for the independent influences of vacancies and redundancies on wages.

Finally, it remains to note that one would expect changes in
MH_i or MH_i* to be positively associated with changes in wages, as
is apparent in figure 26.1.

(2) Industry Supply of Labour

The supply relationship for each industry i can be formally
expressed as:

$$S_i = f_2 \ (\overset{+}{W_i/W_t}, \ \overset{-}{U*^{-2}}, \ \overset{+}{W_i/W_{usi}}, \overset{-}{\Psi^*_{i-2}}) \tag{26.2}$$

where the expected signs again are shown above the explanatory
variables.

We assume that the supply of labour available to any particular industry i is a function of: (i) the wage (average hourly
earnings) paid in that industry relative to the wage paid in all
manufacturing, W_i/W_I; (ii) the reciprocal of the square of the
level of unemployment in the manufacturing sector of the economy,
$U*^{-2}$, calculated as a five-quarter moving average to incorporate
a distributed lag; (iii) the wage paid in industry i relative
to the wage paid in the corresponding industry in the U.S.,
W_i/W_{usi}; and (iv) profits per unit of output in industry i,

calculated as a four-quarter moving average and lagged two quarters to allow for an information lag, π^*_{i-2}.

W_i/W_T is included on the assumption that the amount of labour supplied to an industry depends on the wage paid in that industry relative to wages in manufacturing generally. As W_i rises relative to W_T, the supply of labour can be expected to increase, and vice versa. With respect to the level of unemployment, with substantial unemployment little or no increase in wages may be required to hire more labour and vice versa. Thus S_i/ U^{*-2} O. Including the unemployment variable in the relationship in the form of the reciprocal of the square of the percentage level of unemployment allows for the changing importance of employment of the supply of labour as the percentage level of unemployment changes. U^{-2} implies that, for any given unit change in unemployment, the supply schedule shifts farther at low levels of unemployment than at high levels.

Because of the existence of collective bargaining, the labour market is not perfectly competitive and allowance must be made for the possibility that the supply of labour can be influenced by trade unions. Proxy variables that may be considered to represent union power are: W_T and the level of unemployment, reflecting the general economic environment; profits (in this model, profit per unit of output is included instead of per unit of invested capital, as it is a more reliable statistic and available on a quarterly basis); and the relationship between wages in the same industry in Canada and the United States, W_i/W_{us}.

The profits variable has both a distributed lag and a discrete lag of two quarters, thus ensuring that profits are at least partly predetermined in this model. As profit markups increase, unions may be expected to restrict the supply of labour.

The variable W_i/W_{us} was suggested by the aggregate wage-adjustment relationship by Bodkin et al. There are several ways in which the corresponding industry in the U.S. can influence wages in Canada. Many Canadian trade unions are affiliated with American unions. As well as sharing the same general policies, information, and bargaining expertise, they are likely to be based on U.S. conditions, with limited scope for adaptation. Also, many Canadian unions look to U.S. wages and wage changes for guidelines in framing their own demands, as in the recent demands for "wage parity" in the Canadian automobile industry. Thirdly, key groups of pacesetting wage bargains for Canada can be found in the United States, and wage changes there could have spillover effects on Canadian wages as well as on wages in other sectors of the U.S. economy. Fourthly, the close competition that exists in many product markets can also affect wage changes in Canada. Product competition acts as a constraint on Canadian wage demands due to the disparity in production size between the

two countries; however, with U.S. wage, and consequently price
increases, the opposite effect occurs. Finally, with large
labour mobility between the U.S. and Canada, W_i/W_{usi} may have
a direct influence on the supply of labour for particular
industries.

(3)   A Summary of the Model

Applying Walras's dynamic assumption, the rate of change in
wages per unit of time, dW_i/dt, in any industry may be assumed
proportional to the level of excess demand, XD_i, defined as the
difference between the quantity of man-hours demanded by and
that supplied to industry i at any given wage rate.

$$dW_i/dt = \lambda(XD_i) = \lambda(D_i - S_i) \qquad (26.3)$$

From this, equation 26.4 was derived:

$$\overset{+}{} \qquad \overset{-}{} \qquad \overset{+}{} \qquad (26.4)$$
$$\Delta W_i = \quad + \lambda MH_i + \beta_1 W_i/W_T + \beta_2 U^{*-2} +$$
$$\beta_3 W_i/W_{usi} + \beta_4{}^*{}_{i-2}$$

The role of productivity is implicitly allowed for in the production function, from which the demand for labour is derived;
and the role of profits is explicitly allowed for in the supply
relationship.

Empirical Estimates of Industry Wage-Change Relationships

Equation 26.4 is the basic relationship that has been estimated
for each two-digit manufacturing industry in Canada. In order
to estimate this relationship, a two-stage procedure was
followed, using multiple regression analysis. In stage one,
employment functions were fitted for individual two-digit
industries, from which values of MH_i and $MH_i{}^*$ were derived.
In stage two, equation 26.4 was fitted.

Estimates were made for the sample period from 1953 to 1966
inclusive, using both quarterly and annual data, the latter to
provide a check on the quarterly estimates. Overall, quarterly
observations are preferable because the number of observations
available on an annual basis is limited. Serious difficulties
arose, in the form of lack of data on earnings that incorporate
fringe benefits, the questionable quality of the profits data,
and the reclassification of industry data during the 1960s
which made it necessary to regroup the new classifications to
conform with the old. The industries for which the problems of
matching up data seemed particularly difficult are iron and
steel and nonferrous metals; these problems could lead to dis-
tortions in the estimates.

Estimated Employment Functions

Because of the simultaneous two-way relationship between employment and output, the employment functions for each industry were
fitted by two-stage least squares. Both linear and log-linear
employment functions were estimated. It was found that the
former performed as well as or better than the log-linear form
judged on the basis of the relative value of $\bar{R}^2$, which indicates
approximately the goodness of fit for the equation. Where there
was little difference between the two forms, in five industries
-- textiles, clothing, paper, printing, and iron and steel--on
the basis of $\bar{R}^2$, the values for $\widehat{MH}_i$ and MH_i* from both forms
were included in the estimated wage adjustment relations.
Further attention is given only to linear estimates.

All variables were included in the estimates, irrespective
of their statistical significance, as they were thought to represent the "best" point estimates of the relationships in
question even though these "best" estimates might not warrant
much confidence. If, as in a few cases, the estimated parameters
for variables had the wrong sign, they were dropped as incorrect
and the equation was re-estimated for greater accuracy.

Several points may be noted in connection with the estimated
employment functions.[5] Adjustment patterns seem to differ considerably from industry to industry; a long lag -- up to a year
-- is implied for textiles, paper, printing, iron and steel,
nonferrous metals, and electrical apparatus industries. However,
in the food and beverage industry, and in clothing, transportation equipment, nonmetallic mineral, and chemical industries,
most of the adjustment in employment will have occurred within
two quarters of the exogenous disturbance in output. Not
surprisingly, the significance shown by the t-ratios associated
with the coefficients for MH_{i-1} are generally higher where the
adjustment lag exceeds two quarters; where the lag is less than
two quarters the coefficient is frequently insignificant,
suggesting that there is considerable doubt about the short lag.
Secondly, the estimated coefficients for Q_i are statistically
significant for most equations, with the noteworthy exceptions
of the chemical and electrical apparatus industries; the former
is insignificant but has the correct sign, while the latter is
insignificant and has the wrong sign. When estimated by
ordinary least squares, the coefficients are significant and
have the correct sign. Most of the coefficients associated
with time are statistically significant but with greater variation than those of Q_i. Thirdly, the value of $\bar{R}^2$ in most cases
exceeds .70, indicating that the estimated relationships explain
quite a high percentage of the variation in labour inputs. In
three industries, however, on the basis of $\bar{R}^2$, the estimates
are unsatisfactory. For transportation equipment, nonmetallic
minerals, and chemicals, the estimated values of $\bar{R}^2$ range from
.61 to .27, with chemicals being the least satisfactory.

Estimated Wage-Change Relationships

Equation 26.4 was estimated by ordinary least squares.[6]   In
explaining the changes in wages from time t-4 to time t,[7]   one
must decide whether to date the relative wage variables at the
beginning or at the end of the period over which the wage
changes occur. Given that the assumed causal relationship runs
from relative wage levels to wage changes, most of the estimates
dated the relative wage variables at the beginning of the period.

Due to the short time span between observations, during which
variables can interact in making quarterly estimates, the question of lags becomes very important. Distributed lags were
built into the form of U^{*-2} and π_i^*, as well as a discrete lag
on $\hat{\pi}_i^*$. $\overline{MH}_i$ and MH_i^* were derived from employment functions
allowing for an adjustment lag, and thus were included without
one. To make further allowance for lagged reactions and the
conditioning effect of immediate past wage changes on current
changes, all estimates of equation 26.4 were rerun, including
lagged values of the dependent variable, $\Delta W_{-4} = (W_{t-4} - W_{t-8})$,
as an explanatory variable.

The main purpose of these estimates is to try to identify
empirically the factors that are particularly important in explaining wage changes in various industries from 1953 to 1966,
without being concerned about the size of the relationship
between the explanatory variables and wage changes. Table 26.1
presents a summary of the evidence of the influence of each of
these factors on wage changes in a particular industry. The
columns of table 26.1 have been ordered from left to right in
terms of the number of industries in which the explanatory
variable appears as a significant determinant of changes in
wages.

Proceeding on this basis, W_i/W_T shows more clearly, registering strongly in eight industries and more weakly in one of the
remaining four; unemployment is strong in seven industries,
weaker in one; labour demand shows up strongly in six cases,
more weakly in two and is not apparent in four. W_i/W_{usi} shows
through clearly in three industries, more weakly in one industry
and is not apparent in the remaining eight. Finally, profit
markups are significantly associated with wage changes in only
three industries and marginally in one; for eight there is no
significant association between profit markups and wage changes.

This evidence is generally consistent with the neoclassical
view that changes in wages primarily reflect market variables
(relative wages in Canada, the level of unemployment, and demand
for labour in particular industries) rather than union power
(wages relative to U.S. wages, and profit markups).

Two supplementary pieces of information can be briefly noted
in this connection. Evidence of a marginally significant

association between strikes and the percentage rate of change in wages of a sample of labourers covered by collective agreements was found in a paper by Sparks and Wilton.[8] This failure to uncover a *strongly* significant association with respect to a measure of union power may suggest that unions are limited in their ability to regulate wages. It is also interesting to observe that the simple correlation coefficient between the percentage rate change in wages in two-digit industries from 1961 to 1966 and the average percentage of employees in each industry belonging to a trade union is 0.04, which is insignificant statistically. The problem of measuring the relationship is worsened because reliable data on the degree of unionization in various industries in Canada are lacking.

Key Bargains and Key Groups

It is generally recognized that wage changes among industries are interrelated. One way is directly through the supply side of the market; a rise in industry j's wages is likely to induce a rise in industry i's wages, as the latter attempts to keep its workers from moving to industry j. This aspect is reflected in the supply equation.

Another channel through which wages are interrelated is via demand. If wages rise in industry j, which is important in the economy, and if the elasticity of demand with respect to income for the output of industry i is quite high, then the rise in industry j's wages is likely to stimulate significantly the output for industry i. This will in turn stimulate the demand for labour in industry i, leading to an increase in wages in this industry. Also, industries i and j may have direct input-output connections; thus a change in output in j inducing higher wages in j can also be expected to increase output in i, and may induce higher wages in i as well. These demand elements are allowed for in the demand equation 26.1.

Two ideas should be emphasized in relation to key bargains and key groups, as pointed out by the study of Eckstein and Wilson. The first is that wages in a key group of industries set the pace that wages in other industries tend to follow. The second is the importance of analyzing wage changes over bargaining periods to take account of a bargaining cycle for the key group, rather than mechanically on a quarterly or annual basis.

To test for the importance of key bargains and key groups in the determination of wages it is necessary first to identify the key group of industries and its bargaining cycle, and then to consider the interrelation between wage changes in the key group and the remainder of the economy.

For our purpose, three definitions of the key group have

TABLE 26.1 Summary of the Evidence Indicating a Statistically Significant Association Between Wage Changes and the Explanatory Variables Included in the Wage-Change Relationship, Quarterly Estimates, 1953-66

	Wage Relative to Canadian Wages	Unemployment	Labour Demand	Wage Relative to U.S. Wages	Profits
Food and beverages	*	X	?	?	*
Rubber	X	X	*	?	?
Textiles	X	X	?	?	?
Clothing	X	X	*	?	?
Paper	X	X	?	X	?
Printing	X	*	?	?	?
Iron and Steel	?	?	X	?	?
Transportation equipment	?	?	X	*	X
Electrical apparatus	X	X	?	X	X
Nonferrous metals	X	?	X	?	X
Chemicals	?	?	X	X	?
Nonmetallic minerals	X	X	X	?	?

Notes

X = significant association indicated;

* = marginally significant association indicated;

? = no significant association.

been employed. Key group 1 is that identified by Eckstein and
Wilson for the U.S. and confirmed by Ripley,[10] whose identifying
characteristics included the importance of high and volatile
profit rates in comparison with industries outside the key group,
aggregation in the form of interaction of the industries in the
key group, and the influence of profits on wage changes in the
bargaining process. After some adjustment, key group I for
Canada was defined to include rubber, iron and steel, transportation equipment, nonferrous metals, electrical apparatus and
nonmetallic minerals. The second key group, II, has been
defined in relation to certain characteristics of Canadian
industries: the strength of trade unions, the relative level of
wages and the rate at which wages have grown in the past, interdependence with other key industries, and the relative size of
the labour force. The selection on the basis of these criteria
resulted in a key group defined as follows: food and beverages,
printing, iron and steel, transportation equipment, nonferrous
metals, and electrical apparatus. Alternatively, the third key
group, III, was defined as the employees covered by a sample of
133 collective agreements for negotiating units of 500 or more
employees. This sample included 88 agreements in the manufacturing sector and 45 agreements in the primary and service sectors. The total sample covers about 225,000 employees, of whom
about 146,000 work in manufacturing industries, but in each
industry the sample covers only a small share of the total
employed, with a maximum of 8 per cent in wood products.

Neither definition I nor II of the key group stood up to
various tests of their validity.

In addition to emphasizing key industries and key bargains, the
concept of wage rounds for negotiating contractual wage agreements must be examined. Eckstein and Wilson identified a
bargaining cycle for the U.S. largely on the basis of evidence on
contract settlements provided by H.M. Levinson. Their view was
disputed by E. Kuh,[11] who examined data on wage settlements from
1955 to 1958 in the U.S. In Canada, data on collective bargaining
were examined following a similar procedure. No evidence of a
bargaining cycle was found, a conclusion consistent with earlier
findings of the Economic Council of Canada.[12]

Having failed to define and to identify key industries and
key bargains with any degree of assurance, and having failed to
find any creditable evidence of a bargaining cycle, there is
substantial doubt about two of the assumptions underlying the
Eckstein-Wilson hypothesis as far as Canada is concerned. Nevertheless, we proceeded with the next step, which was to test for
evidence of the influence of wage changes in the key group on
those outside the key group. Dummy variables identifying each
wage round were added to equation 26.4 and the equation was
refitted for various industries to test for the statistical
significance of the estimated coefficients of the dummy variables.
Most of the estimated coefficients were statistically insignificant.

Another test, while not conclusive, also failed to provide any reason for believing that wage changes in a key group of industries bear a stronger relationship to wage changes in particular industries than do wage changes generally in all manufacturing.

In order to test for the influence of wage changes for the third key group, which relates to employees covered by collective bargaining agreements, equation 26.4 was re-estimated, including the new variable $CB^* = \frac{1}{4}\sum_{j=0}^{3} CB_{t-j}$, where CB_t is the average annual percentage change in the base-rate wage rates over the life of the collective agreements for all negotiating units in the sample, completed in quarter t. The variable CB^* contains both a distributed lag, and a discrete lag of two quarters, to allow sufficiently for non-key-group wages to adjust to wage changes in the key group. The variable thus entered the equations as CB_{-2}^*.

Estimates using this equation proved more satisfactory. In addition, there is evidence that variations in CB_{-2}^* are significantly related to variations in W_i in seven industries and marginally in an eighth. Moreover, the inclusion of CB_{-2}^* has considerable impact on the statistical significance of other explanatory variables, especially U^{*-2}, the coefficients of which remain statistically significant in only four industries. This suggests that trade unions can exercise whatever control they may have over the supply of labour in an inverse relation to the level of unemployment in the economy. This interpretation is consistent with that of Sparks and Wilton. They also suggest that wage changes in the key group are themselves influenced by general labour market conditions. This result points up a major difficulty; the lack of a satisfactory method, with the data available, for testing the validity of the hypothesis that collective bargaining units serve as a pacesetting group in the explanations of changes in wages.

Conclusion

The evidence of this study is generally consistent with the view that in the majority of industries, wage changes are associated with changes in the relative wage and in the general level of unemployment. The influence of the demand for labour is also discernible, but the level of wages in the same industry in the United States and industry profits show through less clearly.

The estimates emphasize that general economic conditions have an important influence on wage changes in particular industries, in comparison with influences peculiar to particular industries.

There is little evidence of a significant association between strikes and the rate of change in wages negotiated under collective agreements. The degree of unionization is not significantly related to wage changes in Canada across industries from 1961 to 1966, nor does it seem to be related systematically to the role of profits and United States wages in influencing wage changes in Canadian manufacturing industries.

Little or no evidence has been found to support the key industry hypothesis for Canada. There is doubt concerning the identity of a Canadian key group, and about the existence of a bargaining cycle.

Something can be made of the key group hypothesis if the key group is redefined in terms of employees covered by collective bargaining units. The evidence is consistent with the view that the wage settlements arrived at by collective bargaining units for the economy generally are positively related to wage changes in many individual Canadian industries. However, it has not been possible to identify the separate influence of spillover effects of collective bargaining on wage changes in particular industries, and the influence of general labour market conditions.

Notes

1. G.L. Reuber, "Wage Adjustments in Canadian Industry 1953–66", *Review of Economic Studies* 37 (1970), pp. 449–468. See also idem, *Wage Determination in Canadian Manufacturing Industries*, Task Force on Labour Relations, Study no. 19 (Ottawa: Queen's Printer, 1970).

2. R.G. Bodkin, E.P. Bond, G.L. Reuber and T.R. Robinson, *Price Stability and High Employment: The Options for Canadian Economic Policy*, Special Study no. 5, prepared for the Economic Council of Canada (Ottawa: Queen's Printer, 1967).

3. F. Brechling and P. O'Brien, "Short-run Employment Functions in Manufacturing Industries: An International Comparison", *Review of Economics and Statistics* 49 (1967), pp. 277–287.

4. R.J. Ball and E.B.A. St.Cyr, "Short-term Employment Functions in British Manufacturing Industry", *Review of Economic Studies* 33 (1966), pp. 179–208.

5. See G.L. Reuber, "Wage Adjustments", p. 458.

6. For statistical definitions of the variables, see G.L. Reuber, "Wage Adjustments", pp. 458–59.

7. Wage-change relationships are presented in G.L. Reuber, "Wage Adjustments", pp. 460–61.

8. G.R. Sparks and D.A. Wilton, "Determinants of Negotiated Wage Increases: An Empirical Analysis", *Econometrica* 39 (1971), pp. 739–750.

9. O. Eckstein and T.A. Wilson, "The Determination of Money

Wages in American Industry", *Quarterly Journal of Economics* 74 (1962), pp. 379-414.

10. F.C. Ripley, "An Analysis of the Eckstein-Wilson Wage Determination Model", *Quarterly Journal of Economics* 80 (1966), pp. 121-136.

11. E. Kuh, "A Productivity Theory of Wage Levels -- An Alternative to the Phillips Curve", *Review of Economic Studies* 34 (1967), pp. 333-360.

12. Economic Council of Canada, *Third Annual Review: Prices, Productivity and Employment* (Ottawa: Queen's Printer, 1966).

27. Sex Discrimination in Wage Payment*

by Morley Gunderson

Sex discrimination in the labour market generally results in some combination of unequal pay for equal work and unequal employment (hiring, promotion) opportunities. Although both forms of discrimination are interrelated, it is sex discrimination in wage payments that is the focus of this chapter.

Some of the basic questions that we raise and attempt to partially answer are: What are the reasons for male-female wage differentials? What evidence do we have of the existence of such differentials? What legislative policies have been taken to combat sex discrimination in the labour market? Will discriminatory wage differentials persist in a free enterprise, capitalist economy with firms seeking to maximize profits? Would sex discrimination be any different under a different economic and industrial relations system? What is the foreign experience with sex discrimination in wage payments?

Reasons for Male-Female Wage Differentials

Male-female wage differentials occur because of male-female differences in such factors as productivity, absenteeism, turnover, and related labour market institutions. Wage and employment discrimination may also play a part.

Productivity differences between males and females may arise because females embody less human capital than males. Because of their dual role in the home as well as in the labour market, females tend to have a shorter expected length of stay in the labour force. In the terminology of human capital theory, females tend to have a shorter benefit period from which to recoup the costs of investment in human capital. Consequently, they are rationally (in the economic sense) reluctant to incur the costs of acquiring human capital in the form of training, technical education, labour market information or mobility. Discrimination may also play a part in this reluctance. Females may find it difficult to obtain loans to finance their education or training, and they may be excluded from the technical education and training that would improve their labour market position. In addition, wage and employment discrimination in the labour market may prevent them from recouping the full benefits of human capital formation. One empirical study of a Canadian training program, for example, found that although females improved their skills more as a result of training, they received smaller wage increases than males![1]

---

* Reproduced by permission of the author.

Male-female wage differentials may also arise because of differences in associated labour costs. To the extent that females have higher absenteeism and turnover, employers would be reluctant to hire them unless they worked for lower wages. Since turnover rates for men and women in the same occupations are not readily available, it is difficult to verify or contradict these allegations. The limited data that is available does suggest that turnover rates between males and females are not that different, and that the difference is narrowing over time as females tend to become more committed to the labour force.[2] In addition, the higher absenteeism and turnover among females may be largely due to their low-wage and dead-end occupations: which is the cause and which is the effect remains unclear.

Although differences in productivity, absenteeism and turnover may explain some of the difference between male and female wages within the same occupation, much of the wage differential occurs because females tend to be associated with labour market characteristics and institutions that yield low wages. They tend to be employed in what has been termed the secondary or peripheral labour market (nonunionized, highly competitive, low-profit, labour-intensive establishments);[3] whereas males are more often employed in the primary or core labour market (unionized, monopolistic, high-profit, capital-intensive establishments). Because females tend to be crowded or segregated into certain "female type" jobs[4] there is an abundance of supply in these occupations. Other things being equal, this abundance of labour supply will lower their marginal productivity and hence their wages. Thus, even if females are paid a wage equal to their marginal productivity, it will be less than the male wage, which tends not to be depressed by an excess supply. Ties to the household and to the husband's place of employment, as well as barriers (e.g., occupational licencing, discriminatory employment test, "protective labour legislation") designed to exclude low-wage competition -- all contribute, along with discrimination, to prevent the movement of females from the secondary to the primary labour market. Conditioning in a male-dominated labour market, and the education system also encourage females to underestimate their own capabilities and be more passive in accepting their labour market position.

In addition to the previously mentioned factors of productivity, absenteeism, turnover, and labour market segregation, both wage and employment discrimination may create male-female wage differentials within the same occupation. Employers discriminate because they have a preference for male rather than female labour, they have erroneous information concerning the labour market worth of females, or because of pressure from customers, coworkers or unions to hire males rather than females. In such circumstances, employers will hire females only if they can be paid a wage lower than equally productive males (wage discrimination). Or, if wages tend to be fixed, employers tend not to hire or promote females who are equally as productive as males (employment discrimination). Under employment discrimination the demand for female labour is reduced in high-wage occupations. Females are forced to seek employment in low-wage jobs, thereby creating an abundance of supply with its concomitant low marginal productivity and consequent low wages. Thus employment discrimination may also widen the wage gap between males and females.

Clearly, there are a variety of reasons for male-female wage differentials. Part of the wage differential may reflect differences in productivity and associated labour costs (absenteeism, turnover) as well as labour market segregation. Part of the male-female wage differential may also reflect wage and employment discrimination. What evidence do we have of the relative importance of the various factors influencing male-female wage differentials?

Evidence of Male-Female Wage Differentials in Canada

Based on the 1961 Canadian census, Ostry computes the unadjusted ratio of female to male earnings as .55. An adjustment for differences in such factors as hours worked, occupational distribution, age, and education raises this ratio to approximately .80, leading to the conclusion:

...*even after "accounting for" differences in the work year, occupational deployment and "quality" of labour between the sexes, there remained fairly sizeable pay gaps between male and female workers in Canada*.[5]

In a study based on the 1967 Survey of Consumer Finances, Holmes computes the ratio of female to male expected lifetime earnings as .41.[6] Thus, over their working lives females can expect to earn 41 per cent of what males earn. After accounting for male-female differences in such factors as age, education, weeks worked, occupation, marital status (to reflect absenteeism and turnover), class of worker, region, residence, and immigration status, the ratio of female to male earnings is approximately .56. Holmes implies that further adjustments for such factors as turnover, experience, and training would raise this ratio to about .75.

From Ontario data for the years 1968 and 1969, Gunderson estimates the ratio of female to male wages to be .82 within narrowly defined occupations in the same establishment.[7] The occupational job descriptions are *exactly* the same within each establishment for males and females, suggesting that the work is substantially similar. The study also shows that, other things being equal, unions tend to narrow the male-female wage gap by almost one-half. Whether they do so to ensure the minority rights of females or to protect males from low-wage female competition, they are nevertheless effective in narrowing the male-female wage gap. Similarly, when wages were paid according to an incentive pay system, the male-female wage differential was reduced by slightly over one-third. Because incentive pay tends to be based on objective criteria of performance rather than subjective criteria that allow for discrimination, the smaller male-female wage gap under an incentive pay system is not surprising. The study also tentatively concluded that equal pay for equal work legislation did not significantly narrow the male-female wage gap. This conclusion is tentative because establishments may not have had sufficient time to adjust to the equal pay legislation.

Studies of academic salaries and salaries in the public service also document considerable differences in the earnings of males and females in Canada. Robson and Lapointe found that the average female salary in Canadian universities during 1965-66 was about 80 per cent of the average male salary.[8] They attribute slightly over half of the gap to sex discrimination in wage payments, with the remainder due to differences in such factors as region, university size, degree, age, field, and rank. Most of the remaining gap was attributed to differences in rank, which may also reflect discrimination. In a study of wages in the public service, Judek also concluded that "almost invariably men were earning more than women with similar education and experience".[9]

Although their actual magnitudes differ concerning the extent of male-female wage differentials, the Canadian empirical studies clearly indicate that considerable differentials exist, even after controlling for the effect of intervening factors believed to influence wage payments. Sex discrimination in wage payments appears to be a fact in Canada. What has been done then, by way of legislation, to combat sex discrimination in the labour market?

Legislation to Combat Sex Discrimination in Wage Payments

With the exception of Quebec, all provinces and the federal government have adopted equal pay for equal work legislation. Since the vast majority of workers in Canada are under provincial jurisdiction, the federal legislation is mainly to serve as a model for the provinces.

Unfortunately, the equal pay legislation has been difficult to enforce, partly because of the problem of defining equal work. In general, equal work has been taken to mean substantially similar work rather than identically equal work. Yet comparison can only be made within the same establishment. There is also concern that equal pay laws may have an adverse employment effect on females, especially for those who would normally accept a lower wage to acquire on-the-job training and labour market experience. Faced with the prospect of equal pay, employers may simply not hire females or promote them to higher-wage jobs.

Partly to counteract such a possibility, fair employment laws (also termed "equal employment opportunity" laws), have been passed to prevent discrimination in recruiting, hiring, and promotion. All provinces in Canada have these laws, although in the Prince Edward Island and federal government legislation no explicit reference is made to discrimination on the basis of sex. By increasing the demand for female labour, fair employment laws may have the side effect of increasing female wages. In this sense, equal pay may be approached without the potential adverse employment effect inherent in equal pay laws.

Coexistence of Sex Discrimination and Profit Maximization

The existence of sex discrimination in wage payments proves some-what of an embarrassment to traditional economic theory. The dilemma is aptly stated by Stiglitz:

The central problem posed by the economics of discrimination is the following: Under what circumstances is it possible for groups with identical economic characteristics to receive different wages in a market equilibrium? If people of the same productivity receive different wages, then there are profits to be made by hiring the low-wage individual. If all firms are profit maximizers, then all will demand the services of low-wage individuals, bidding their wages up until the wage differential is eliminated. Why does this not occur? [10]

Stiglitz provides a variety of answers to this question, most of them based on the premise that wages are often set above the competitive wage. This may occur because of unions, minimum wages, or other wage-fixing legislation. Or it may occur because firms want to reduce absenteeism and turnover, improve their public image and the morale of their workforce, or have a queue of applicants from which to recruit. Whatever the reason for the higher than competitive wage, firms can pick and choose from the queue of applicants. This enables them to discriminate by hiring males for the high-wage jobs. Male-female wage differentials thereby persist in an economy with competitive forces subject to wage-fixing constraints, or when profit-maximizing firms set wages above the competitive level so as to have a queue of applicants.

The persistence of male-female wage differentials in the face of competitive forces has also been attributed to adjustment costs.[11]   It may simply be too costly to immediately replace males by equally productive females who would work at a lower wage. Even the slow replacement of only those males who quit or retire may be costly, in terms of morale, for the existing male work force that may also require a wage premium to work with females. Faced with these costly alternatives, even profit-maximizing firms may keep their high-wage male work force in spite of low-wage female competition.

Because information concerning the true productivity of workers is difficult and costly to obtain, employers may use a screening device, such as sex (or a university diploma), as an indicator of worker quality. Not only is such a screening device apt to foster erroneous information subject to prejudice, but it is also apt to give rise to preconceived notions that are slow to change. Worse, it may create a vicious self-fulfilling circle in the following manner: females are erroneously screened into low-productivity, low-wage jobs; given the dead-end nature of the job, they perform at its level and in fact they come to view themselves as suited for the job; in this fashion an initially incorrect signal becomes self-fulfilling and male-female productivity and wage differentials persist. Via the process of cognitive dissonance, employers readily accept subjective beliefs of differential abilities because this justifies their discriminatory behaviour. In this way discriminatory behaviour and beliefs in differential abilities come into equilibrium and become self-perpetrating: employers discriminate; to justify their actions they readily accept subjective beliefs of differential abilities; this enables them to discriminate further. In this manner, male-female (perceived) productivity differences and hence wages can persist even in the face of competitive pressures.

Others have argued that noncompetitive, non-labour market forces have served to maintain wage differentials between equally capable groups.[13]   Governments discriminate in the provision of education; both monopolies and governments discriminate in their employment policies, since they are not subject to competition pressures; and unions discriminate in training and apprenticeship programs. In addition, social pressures and extra market costs are placed on nondiscriminating employers, again enabling male-female wage differentials to persist, even in the face of competitive pressures that would normally have reduced them.

Although all of these factors -- wage fixing, adjustment costs, self-fulfilling erroneous beliefs, and noncompetitive, nonmarket forces -- may explain the persistence of discriminatory wage payments in the face of competitive forces, they are not completely persuasive arguments. Even if wages are fixed above the competitive level so that employers have a queue of applicants from which to hire, it would be more efficient to ration on the basis of desirable work traits rather than sex. Adjustment costs may explain why employers don't *immediately* replace their male work force with equally productive lower-wage females, but surely this process would occur in the long run. Erroneous beliefs concerning the labour market worth of females are probably prevalent, but surely capitalist enterprises would abandon these beliefs at the chance to make a profit by hiring

low-wage females. And although it is true that the noncompetitive sectors of the economy do not require profits to survive,
they are still under pressure to cut costs. And even if they
respond more to political rather than economic pressure it is not
clear what that implies about the persistence of discriminatory
male-female wage differentials. For these reasons, the coexis-
tence of sex discrimination in wage payments, and long-run
equilibrium in a competitive, profit-maximizing economy remains
somewhat of a paradox.

Sex Discrimination under Different Political-Economic Systems

As discussed previously, neoclassical economics would predict
that the forces of competition should remove any discriminatory
wage differentials. This suggests that a free enterprise,
capitalist economy should be relatively free of sex discrimination in wage payments. Only in noncompetitive sectors of the
economy would discriminatory wage differentials exist.

Marxist theory, on the other hand, suggests that sex discrimination is more likely under capitalism, with its class structures, private ownership of the means of production, and sex
roles designed to exploit workers. Discriminatory wage payments
are viewed as necessary to maintain a pool of cheap labour. The
belief is that under communism or socialism, with their dedica-
tion to egalitarianism and nonexploitation, discriminatory wage
payments would be nonexistent. Others would argue, however, that
under command economies with centralized control, discrimination
would be more prevalent. Because there is less pressure to show
profits, socialist employers could satisfy their desire to
discriminate and not hire females who are equally as productive
as males.

Obviously there is no concensus in theory as to which political
economic system is more likely to have discriminatory wage payments. Consequently, we must appeal to the empirical evidence.
Unfortunately, the data is rather fragmentary and difficult to
compare across countries. In addition, the political and
economic views of the analysts tend to be reflected in their
observations. Consequently, we are able to offer only
scattered evidence, and any conclusions derived should be
regarded as tentative.

As in Canada, discriminatory pay differentials seem to persist
in the U.S. In a review of six studies, Sawhill found that the
ratio of female to male wages, after adjusting for various
productivity differences, ranges from .63 to .88.[14]   In the
United Kingdom, women's hourly wages are around 80 per cent of
men's wages in the same occupation, with about 10 per cent
receiving equal pay.[15]   In Australia, where wages are determined
largely through judicial decree (i.e., an arbitration court in
consultation with union and employer associations), female basic

wages are 75 per cent of male wages.[16]   Only in a few occupations
and areas is equal pay a reality.

Because of their strong socialist parties and union movements
and their emphasis on egalitarianism, Scandinavian countries
mey be expected to have little sex discrimination in wage payments.   In Norway, where wages are generally determined by
collective agreements between trade unions and employers'
associations (subject to the scrutiny of an Equal Pay Council),
unequal pay for equal work still prevails.[17]   Female wages tend
to be about 85 per cent of male wages in the same job category
and are more in the neighbourhood of 90 per cent of male wages
when the comparison is made between homogeneous groups of the
same age and education.   In Sweden, the government has adopted
a conscious policy to alter sex roles in the school and home
so that women will have an equal chance to compete with men in
the labour market.   One report states:

*The division of functions as between the sexes must be
changed in such a way that both men and women in a family
are afforded the same practical opportunities of participating in both active parenthood and gainful employment
....Eventually to achieve complete equality... a radical
change in deep-rooted traditions and attitudes must be
brought about among both women and men, and active steps
must be taken by the community to encourage a change in
the roles played by both.   The view that women ought to
be economically supported by marriage... is a direct
obstacle to the economic independence of women and their
ability to compete on equal terms in the labour market.
Similarly, the husband's traditional obligation to support
his wife must be modified to constitute a responsibility,
shared with her, for the support of the children.... No
rapid advancement of women in employment and in the
professions, politics, trade union activity, etc., is
possible as long as men fail to assume that share of the
work of the home that falls to them as husbands and fathers.
The expression "male emancipation" has therefore been coined
in Sweden to denote the right of a husband to remain at
home while the children are small where it is found more
appropriate for the mother to devote herself to gainful
employment.*[18]

Measures that have been taken to implement this policy
include: the encouragement of girls to undertake education and
training in what have been traditional men's fields; labour
market policies to procure more jobs for women; the expansion
of child care facilities; the alteration of school curricula
to include compulsory courses for both sexes in child care,
metal work, woodwork, and needlework.   Although all sectors of
Swedish society do not necessarily support these changes, it
appears that equal pay for equal work is usual in Sweden.
However, reflecting the fact that women still predominate the

lower-pay job, the earnings of female industrial workers are about 80 per cent of men's. As one analyst states:

The statement of a revolutionary social position is quite a different matter from its adoption in practice.... A segregated labor market still persists in Sweden, and social attitudes on women's place remain fairly conservative.[19]

In the Soviet Union, where the female labour force participation rate is close to 80 per cent, women constitute about 80 per cent of the doctors and dentists and about 35 per cent of the lawyers and engineers.[20] They are also well represented in such traditionally male jobs as construction work and heavy equipment operators. According to one observer:

Soviet women earn the same pay as men for equal work. This is not only the law, but also the practice.... Because the USSR universalized equal pay to women for equal work, they earn 50 to 100% more than in any non-communist country relative to the general wage and salary in each. The increase in women's earnings since the Revolution has been at least twice as high as that of men.... None of this represents concessions to a women's liberation movement there. It constitutes implementation of a social outlook adopted before the Revolution by the party now in power, and carried out with high consistency for half a century.[21]

Others, however, have attributed the progress of Soviet women to industrialization rather than socialist egalitarianism:

Soviet women have achieved just about what might have happened anyway because of industrialization and urbanization.[22]

In spite of this obvious progress, considerable disparities still exist between the employment position of men and women in the Soviet Union. Women tend to be underrepresented in the higher-paying jobs within each occupation and they still tend to gravitate toward traditionally female roles. According to one observer:

Women do not reach the top in numbers anywhere near their ratio to the total employed in any occupation.... Even in the women's occupations, women are not often found in top jobs.[23]

Although it is hazardous to generalize from such an array of studies, the following conclusions appear to emerge. Sex discrimination in wage payments and segregation of females into low-wage, traditionally female occupations appear to exist under all industrial relations systems, regardless of their

political-economic affiliation. However, communist economies
and quasi-socialist economies dedicated to the principal of
egalitarianism seem to have done more to reduce such sex discrimination, especially unequal pay for equal work. Whether this
is due to the particular political-economic industrial relations
system, or to other factors, remains an open question.

Conclusion

Although its magnitude may vary across different countries, sex
discrimination in employment is clearly a prevailing phenomenon.
Will it persist over time? Will legislation be effective in
curbing it? What alternative and complementary policies would
be desirable in addition to, or in place of, legislation? These
are the pressing questions that must be answered before there
is any hope of removing sex discrimination in the labour market.

Notes

1. Morley Gunderson, "Determinants of Individual Success in On-
the-Job Training", *Journal of Human Resources*, vol. 8, no. 4
(Fall 1973), p. 480.

2. See, for example, *Women in the Labour Force: Facts and
Figures* (Ottawa: Information Canada, 1973), tables 21, 43, 61
and 69.

3. Peter Doeringer and Michael Piore, *Internal Labour Markets
and Manpower Analysis* (Lexington, Mass.: D.C. Heath, 1971).

4. This crowding hypothesis was given by M. Fawcett, "Equal Pay
for Equal Work", *Economic Journal* 28 (March 1918), pp. 1-6; and
F. Edgeworth, "Equal Pay to Men and Women for Equal Work",
Economic Journal 32 (December 1922), pp. 431-57. It has sub-
sequently been formalized in Barbara Bergmann, "The Effect on
White Incomes of Discrimination in Employment", *Journal of
Political Economy* 79 (March-April 1971), pp. 294-313.

5. Sylvia Ostry, *The Female Worker in Canada* (Ottawa: Information Canada, 1968), p. 45.

6. R. Holmes, "Male-Female Earnings Differentials in Canada",
Discussion Paper 74-5-2, Simon Fraser University Department of
Economics and Commerce, 1974.

7. Morley Gunderson, "Male-Female Wage Differentials and the
Impact of Equal Pay Legislation", *Review of Economics and
Statistics* (forthcoming).

8. R. Robson and M. Lapointe, A *Comparison of Men's and Women's
Salaries and Employment Fringe Benefits in the Academic Profession,*

Study no. 2 for the Royal Commission on the Status of Women in Canada (Ottawa: Information Canada, 1971).

9. S. Judek, *Women in the Public Service* (Ottawa: Economics and Research Branch, Canada Dept. of Labour, 1968), p. 49.

10. Joseph Stiglitz, "Approaches to the Economics of Discrimination", *American Economic Review Papers and Proceedings* 63 (May 1973), p. 287.

11. Kenneth Arrow, "The Theory of Discrimination", in *Discrimination in Labor Markets*, ed. O. Ashenfelter and A. Rees (Princeton: Princeton University Press, 1973), pp. 20-23.

12. See K. Arrow, "The Theory of Discrimination", pp. 23-26.

13. See, in particular, Richard Freeman, "Decline of Labour Market Discrimination and Economic Analysys", *American Economic Review Papers and Proceedings* 63 (May 1973), pp. 280-87; and Laster Thurow, *Poverty and Discrimination* (Washington: Brookings Institute, 1969).

14. E. Sawhill, "The Economics of Discrimination Against Women: Some New Findings", *Journal of Human Resources* 8 (Summer 1973), p. 386.

15. C. Larson, "Equal Pay for Women in the United Kingdom", *International Labour Review* 103 (January 1971), p. 1.

16. Richard Blandy, "Equal Pay in Australia", *Journal of Industrial Relations*, April 1963, pp. 19 and 24.

17. Kari Vangsness, "Equal Pay in Norway", *International Labour Review* 103 (April 1971), p. 382.

18. Cited in Marjorie Galenson, *Women and Work: An International Comparison* (Ithaca: New York State School of Industrial and Labour Relations, Cornell University, 1973), pp. 60-61.

19. Ibid., p. 106.

20. Ibid., p. 88.

21. William Mandel, "Soviet Women in the Work Force and Professions", in *Women in the Professions*, ed. Linda Fidell and John Dehamater (Beverly Hills: Sage Publications, 1971), pp. 100, 115 and 116.

22. B. Madison, "Women's Liberation and Social Welfare in the Soviet Union", *Social Service Review*, 1971, p. 24.

23. M. Galenson, *Women and Work*, pp. 81 and 97.

28. Four-Day, Thirty-Two-Hour Work Week*

by S. M. A. Hameed

Some men see things as they are and say: why?
I dream things that never were and say: why not?

G. B. Shaw

The purpose of this chapter is to suggest that a four-day,
thirty-two-hour work week is logically consistent with historical
development; it is inevitable, and coming earlier than generally
recognized. One of the most potent forces that will make this
a reality is the trade union movement. The long-term productivity trend and the recent innovation and experimentation with
a compressed work week will prove helpful in the realization of
this dream.

Historical Development

The innovative significance of a four-day, thirty-two-hour work
week in the history of management of time may be properly assessed
if we place it in a wider time perspective.

Historical trends in work and leisure indicate that sizable
gains have been made in reducing work hours since the turn of
this century. The developments of the past six decades are a
marked contrast to the uneventful history of the reduction of
hours of work going back to fifteenth century England.[1]

1495-1900

In the first recorded statutory regulation, Henry VII, in 1495,
"set the working day during summer from 5:00 A.M. to 7:00 or
8:00 P.M. with two hours of rest".[2] In the absence of any other
statute, this twelve- or thirteen-hour-long day decreed by Henry
VIII continued for a century and was reduced only by half an hour
by Queen Elizabeth I, who ordered a two-and-a-half-hour rest
instead of the earlier two-hour respite. The length of the work
day did not materially change until the end of the eighteenth
century,[3] although by the 1750s growth of a factory system had
begun in England, a predominantly agricultural and mercantile
society. The Industrial Revolution, signifying a drastic change
in production techniques, sent reverberating currents through all
facets of institutional living. The effect of this change on the
work day was negative, if any.

---

* This paper, with some modification, was published in S. M. A.
  Hameed and G. S. Paul, eds., *3 or 4 Day Work Week* (Edmonton:
  University of Alberta, 1974).

Wladimir Woytinsky reports that by 1800, "a working day of 14 hours was customary, one of 16 hours attracted little attention, and only a working day of 17 or 18 hours was considered an abuse".[4]   Thus, in the first 300 years (1495-1800) of the history of hours of work, economic factors were virtually dormant.   Production methods, technology, and market processes were undergoing very little change.   Reduction in hours of work was minimal and had its basis in custom and normal work practices.

The first legislative effort to regulate hours of work dates back to the Factory Act of 1833 in England, which applied to children in the textile industry and established a twelve-hour working day enforced by a system of inspectorate.   The law was subsequently amended in 1864 (The Factory Extension Act) to enlarge its coverage.   In Canada, the legislative phase began in the latter part of the nineteenth century,[5] whereas the U.S. federal government introduced a ten-hour day in 1868.   The Royal Commission on the Relations of Labour and Capital in Canada reported a ten-hour day for mechanics in 1889.   There were many exceptions to the ten-hour day, but it was considered widely prevalent throughout Canada.   Regional variations were observed, in that Ontario tended to have a work day shorter than ten hours while Nova Scotia and New Brunswick seldom exceeded the ten-hour limit.   The Province of Quebec showed evidence of much longer hours.[6]

Chart 28.1 indicates that the 400-year-long history of reduction in hours of work can be simply interpreted in the following terms: (1) throughout the period a six-day week prevailed; (2) a twelve-hour day was a predominant feature of almost the entire period, with the exception of a longer day associated with the early production requirements of the Industrial Revolution; and (3) a ten-hour day was established toward the close of the nineteenth century.

CHART 28.1 History of Workday Duration, 1495 to 1889

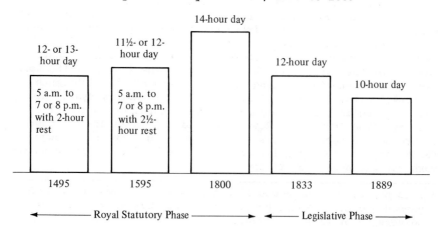

Post-1900

Since the turn of the twentieth century, standard hours have registered a steep decline in the first two decades, with an annual reduction of .63 per cent (see table 28.1). In the post-World War II period (1945-1956), the reduction was even greater, at 1.44 per cent per annum. The intervening span appears almost like a plateau, stretching over a period of twenty-five years (1920-1944) and registering a modest decline of .11 per cent per year. Since 1957, a second plateau seems to have developed, although productivity during this period has been such that reduction to a thirty-six-hour work week could have been possible. The potential of reduction that existed during this period is evidenced by the increase in hours paid for but not worked. To be more precise, fringe benefits, as a percentage of payroll, almost doubled during this period (from 16.2 per cent in 1957 to 28.15 per cent in 1969).

TABLE 28.1 Decline in Standard Work Hours, 1901-1969

	1901-1919	1920-1944	1945-1956	1957-1969
Average annual percentage reduction	0.63	0.11	1.44	0.14
Total percentage reduction	12.1	2.6	15.9	1.7

Trend comparison among the various types of hours of work is helpful in indicating the institutional arrangements, extent of manpower utilization in the economy, and the growing area of fringe benefits or paid leisure. Each of the three types of work (see chart 28.2) typifies certain economic or institutional characteristics of a society. For instance, standard hours are indicative of the structure of the provincial and federal labour legislation, labour's bargaining strength, and management's willingness to make concessions; hours paid for are representative of the labour cost and incidence of overtime; and actual hours worked show trends of economic activity. Thus the trend behaviour of these three types of hours of work in the Canadian situation has been different in a long-term perspective. It is precisely the difference in their inherent structure that makes it possible to make future projections.

Comparison between hours paid for and actual hours worked, as presented in table 28.2, shows the growing area of fringe benefits.

TABLE 28.2   Percentage Reduction in Hours Worked, 1949-1965

| | Percentage Reduction | | |
	1949- 1960	1960- 1965	1949- 1965
Standard hours	-7.55	-1.20	-8.67
Hours paid for	-5.31	+0.49	-4.85
Actual hours worked	-8.05	-3.0	-10.11

For example, during the postwar period (1949-1965), actual hours
worked declined faster (10.11 per cent) than hours paid for (4.85
per cent), thereby increasing the gap between the two series,
which is accounted for by the growing incidence of paid holidays,
paid vacations, and paid sick leave. This development may be
regarded as a major shift in the workers' outlook on work and
leisure. Previously their main emphasis was on reducing the
standard work week, which meant overtime earnings at the cost of
leisure, but it appears that in the sixties their efforts were
geared to reducing the effective work week. This implies a
reduction in actual hours worked, accompanied by a higher incidence of paid leisure.

CHART 28.2   Standard Hours, Hours Paid For, and Actual Hours,
             1920-1965

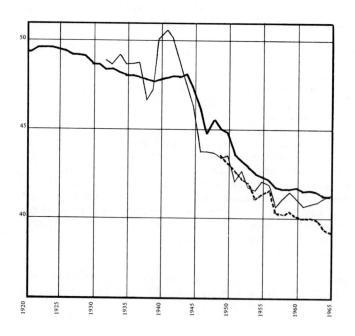

Innovations in Management of Time

In an interview with Samuel Crowthers in 1926, Henry Ford dec-
declared:

We have decided upon and at once put into effect through all the
branches of our industries the 5-day week. Hereafter there will
be no more work with us on Saturdays and Sundays. These will be
free days, but the men, according to merit, will receive the
same pay equivalent as for a full 6-day week.[7]

   In the history of management of time, this was the first
innovation of revolutionary proportions. An eight-hour day,
providing increased leisure, was considered healthy for stimula-
ting consumption. Other innovations appeared subsequently but
did not gain acceptance till very recently. Between 1971 and
1972, the number of companies introducing a compressed work week
in Canada and the United States increased approximately tenfold.[8]

   The newer concepts and their variations are too many to be
surveyed comprehensively, but in chart 28.3 an attempt is made
to show some of the popular forms.

CHART 28.3   Concepts and Practices in Work Schedules

Compressed Work Week				Flexible Work Week	Reduced and Rearranged Work Week		
4/40	8/80	3/40			3/36	4/36	4/32
Monday through Thursday, with a single daily shift of 10 hours	Tuesday through Friday, with a single daily shift of 10 hours	Thursday through Sunday, 4 shifts of 10 hours a day	Monday through Sunday, with 2 shifts working Sunday through Wednesday, and Wednesday through Saturday. The overlapping day is divided into a day shift and a night shift.	-Flexibility within the working day -Flexibility within the work week -Flexibility within the working month -Flexibility within the month with "banking" -Flexibility within the year			

New variations are being developed in the concept of the
compressed work week, creating new terms such as a modified or
rearranged work week, shortened work week, variable work week,
etc. A brief definition of the three basic concepts, identified
in chart 28.3, may help in establishing the distinction among
the subvariants.

Compressed Work Week. The number of working days in the
compressed work week is reduced from the standard five days to
three or four days. The number of hours per week remains unchanged, implying a proportionate increase in daily hours. This
could also involve a longer work cycle such as a fortnight or a
month; in this case, the term used is "compressed work schedule".

Flexible Work Week. In the flexible work week there is a
core period each day during which all the workers are required
to be on the job, but both in the morning and in the evening
there are flexible bands during which the workers have the freedom to come and go any time. If the flexibility is within the
working day only, there is no banking arrangement, but in longer
periods such as a month, debit balances can be carried over to
the next accounting period.

Reduced and Rearranged Work Week. A compressed work week has
fewer working days but the hours remain unchanged. In a reduced
and rearranged work week, the week is shortened and the daily
hours are also reduced. The reduction could range from thirty-
seven and a half to thirty-two hours, with a three- or four-day
work week.

Assessment and Projection

In this section, efforts will be made to evaluate the present
status and future acceptability of the compressed work week and
the reduced and rearranged work week.

Compressed Work Week. According to a preliminary survey conducted in May 1973 by the federal Department of Labour, there
are approximately 233 plants across the country that are
currently on a compressed work week. The majority of these
plants (116) are in Ontario,[9] but other provinces are represented as well: in Quebec there are 50 plants; in Manitoba,
17; Alberta, 16; New Brunswick, 10; B.C., 9; Saskatchewan, 9;
and Nova Scotia, 3.[10]   It is estimated that 30,712 workers are
currently on a compressed work week.

Another survey of 184 Canadian organizations, employing
493,061 workers, shows that the initiative in introducing a
compressed work week was taken primarily by management (59 per
cent), although in 25 per cent of the cases, the initiative
came from nonunionized employees.[11] It is interesting to note
that even unionized employees took an active part in establishing

a compressed work week, although in fewer cases (11 per cent).

A variety of reasons were given for implementing a compressed work week but the largest number of organizations (twenty-two) cited increase in leisure time as the prime reason, followed by an increase in efficiency and productivity (fifteen), increased utilization of equipment and facilities (eleven), and improved employee morale (nine).

Once implemented, 63 per cent of the organizations reported that the employees had very positive reactions. Among the factors that appealed to the employees, increased leisure, longer weekends and decreased travelling time and costs featured prominently. Table 28.3 shows that among seventy-six organizations that adopted the compressed work week, employee morale improved, absenteeism decreased, while turnover and earnings remained unchanged.

TABLE 28.3 Effects of Compressed Work Week in 76 Organizations on Employee Morale, Absenteeism, Turnover, and Earnings

Employee Morale

Improved	81.0%
Deteriorated	--
No change	15.7
Too early to assess	3.3
	100.0%

Absenteeism

Decreased	50.0%
Increased	1.3
No change	43.7
Too early to assess	5.0
	100.0%

Personnel Turnover

Increased	1.3%
Decreased	14.6
No change	80.5
Too early to assess	3.6
	100.0%

Earnings

Increased	8.3%
Decreased	3.8
No change	87.4
	100.0%

Source: *Report on the Compressed Work Week*, Samson Belair Riddell Stead, Inc., September 1972.

This survey result is one of many that indicates that the

employee and management response to a compressed work week is
overwhelmingly positive. Undoubtedly, the momentum has increased
in the last two years, but a significant underlying factor in
this overall development has been the adoption of a reduced and
rearranged work week. Thirteen of sixty-five reporting organizations (20 per cent) not only rearranged their work week but
actually reduced it from half an hour to as much as ten hours
per week (see table 28.4).

There are two factors that may slow down the momentum to some
extent, however. The first concerns problems such as fatigue,
difficulties in locating employees for overtime, for holiday
replacement, for sick replacements, and clients' irritability at
being short serviced.[12] Of sixty reporting organizations, thirty-
two mentioned some disadvantage resulting from the system.[13] In
some instances, the disadvantages became compelling and four of
the seventy-six organizations abandoned the compressed work week.
As a large number of organizations are still experimenting with
the compressed work week, it will have to be seen as to how many
do indeed make it a permanent arrangement. It may not be
unrealistic to predict that those organizations that *reduced and
rearranged* their work week have a better chance of retaining it.

The second factor affecting momentum is that the compressed
work week has so far spread only among the smaller, nonunionized
companies. Although we have seen that, in some instances,
unionized workers have been instrumental in instituting a compressed work week, existing labour contracts in many situations
will preclude the possibility of adopting it. Such arrangements
will have to be negotiated and it is more than likely that the
outcome will be a reduced and rearranged work week rather than
a compressed work week.

Reduced and Rearranged Work Week. The compressed work week
has a short-term attraction and the advantages attributed to it
are reminiscent of the "Hawthorne effect". Some of its disadvantages mentioned above diminish its long-term viability. In
contrast, a reduced and rearranged work week will likely suffer
from none of the disadvantages of a nonreduced compressed work
week and, therefore, has greater prospects of future acceptability. If the work week will be reduced and rearranged, what
exact form will it take? Two distinct possibilities exist:
(1) a four-day, thirty-six-hour work week; and (2) a four-day,
thirty-two-hour work week.

Four-Day, Thirty-six-hour Work Week. There are two distinct
trends in the establishment of a four-day, thirty-six-hour
work week: (1) a historical reduction in hours of work, discussed in an earlier section of this chapter, has resulted in
a standard work week of forty hours. In a parallel development,
the effective work week -- because of increasing vacations, paid
holidays, paid sick leave, and coffee breaks -- averaged over a
year, has come closer to thirty-six hours per week in 1973;[14]

TABLE 28.4   Nature of the Shortened and/or Rearranged Work Week

No. of Organizations	Now Working	Worked Before	Change in Hours
30	40 hours, 4 days/week	40 hours, 5 days/week	same
1	40 hours, 4½ days/week	40 hours, 5 days/week	same
1	40 hours, average 4 or 5 days/week	40 hours, 5 days/week	same
1	40 hours, average 3 or 4 days/week	40 hours, 5 days/week	same
3	37½ hours, 4 days/week	37½ hours, 5 days/week	same
3	37½ hours, 4½ days/week	37½ hours, 5 days/week	same
1	38 hours, 4 days/week	in effect since founding of the organization	
2	36 hours, 4 days/week	35 hours, 5 days/week	increased 1 hour
1	36 hours, 4½ days/week	35 hours, 5 days/week	increased 1 hour
7	35 hours, 4 days/week	35 hours, 5 days/week	same
1	35 hours, 4½ days/week	35 hours, 5 days/week	same
1	Average 33 3/4 hours, 3 or 4 days/week	33 3/4 hours, 5 days/week	same
1	40 hours, 4 days/week	50 hours, 5 days/week	decreased 10 hours
1	40 hours, 4 days/week	44 hours, 5½ days/week	decreased 4 hours
1	37 hours, 4 days/week	37½ hours, 5 days/week	decreased ½ hour
1	38 hours, 4 days/week	40 hours, 5 days/week	decreased 2 hours
2	36 hours, 4 days/week	37½ hours, 5 days/week	decreased 1½ hours
1	36 hours, 4 days/week	36½ hours, 4½ days/week	decreased 1½ hours
1	36½ hours, 4½ days/week	40 hours, 5 days/week	decreased 3½ hours
1	35 hours average, 4 or 5 days/week	37½ hours, 5 days/week	decreased 2½ hours
2	32 & 40 hours, 4 & 5 days/week	37½ hours, 5 days/week	decreased 1½ hours
1	34 hours, 4 days/week	37½ hours, 5 days/week	decreased 3½ hours
1	26 hours, 4 days/week	32½ hours, 5 days/week	decreased 6½ hours

Source: *Report on the Compressed Work Week*, Samson Belair Riddell Stead, Inc., September 1972.

and (2) the introduction of the rearranged work week, has not
only shortened the work week to four days, but also has
simultaneously reduced the number of hours per week to thirty-
six. Table 28.4 indicates that out of a total of thirty
organizations having less than a forty-hour work week, twenty-
one actually worked thirty-six hours or less per week. Thus,
there appears to be a large percentage of companies (46.1)
gravitating toward a four-day, thirty-six-hour work week. While
this seemed to be the trend among the companies that had already
switched to a compressed/rearranged and reduced work week, it
would be interesting to find out if companies on a regular work
week (five days, forty hours) are heading in this direction.

Survey Results

Three hundred and thirty-nine (339) companies, ranging in size
from 100 to over 10,000 employees, completed a questionnaire,
their regional distribution being: British Columbia, 25;
Alberta, 32; Saskatchewan, 3; Manitoba, 7; Quebec, 90; Ontario,
150; Maritimes, 13. A vast majority of them (270) worked a
forty-hour, five-day week. Smaller companies, employing between
100 and 499 workers (see table 28.5), were adequately represented
in the sample (35.4 per cent), as they are the ones more likely
to adopt a compressed work week. By the same token, the
representation of the larger companies, employing 10,000 or more
workers, was the lowest (2 per cent).

TABLE 28.5   Trend Toward Adopting Compressed Work Week, by Size
of Company

Number of Employees	Number of Participating Companies	Currently Work on Plan to Adopt a Compressed Work Week
100 - 499	120	13
500 - 999	94	6
1,000 - 4,999	102	11
5,000 - 9,999	14	3
10,000 - over	7	1

Only 34 companies indicated that they currently have or are
planning to introduce a compressed work week in the next two
years. Their distribution by the size of the company is vaguely
suggestive of two factors: (1) administrative problems associated with the introduction of a compressed work week in a larger
organization are very complex; and (2) the nature of existing
collective agreements prevents the introduction of a compressed
work week. The second significant factor is that the trade
union movement is opposed to a compressed work week (four days-
forty hours, for instance). The unions are more favourably
inclined toward a reduced and rearranged work week. It appears
that unions have a fairly good chance of obtaining a thirty-six-

hour, four-day work week, as 98 companies showed willingness to consider such a programme on the basis of its own strength. However, twice that number of companies (196) were not willing to consider a reduced and rearranged work week. One of the important reasons for the insistence on the reduced work week is the union claim that it will stimulate employment. Our survey ascertained the validity of this claim by asking the respondents: "If your work week is shortened to a *thirty-six-hour, four-day week,* what will your company have to do?" Table 28.6 indicates that a majority of companies (184) will have to expand their work force in order to reduce their work week to thirty-six hours. This supports the union claim. Undoubtedly this would amount to increased labour cost. Can the companies absorb it? One possible encouragement to the companies' adopting a reduced work week would be a government employment incentive programme tied in with a variable work schedule.

TABLE 28.6 Measures Taken by Companies to Enable Adoption of a Reduced Work Week

Measures to Allow 36-hour, 4-day Work Week	Number of Companies
Increased overtime	104
Expand work force	184
Absorb the change	59
Other measures (unspecified)	54

A government employment incentive programme to ease the transition toward a reduced work week and also obtain other benefits may be envisaged if the following stipulations are realistic: (1) employers will expand their work force in order to adopt a reduced and rearranged work week; (2) government will be prepared to give from the UIC funds an incentive payment to the employer for each additional worker hired; (3) the rate of government incentive per employee is not more than what is paid out in unemployment compensation. Our survey questionnaire queried the respondents regarding stipulations 1 and 3. As noted above, 184 companies (54 per cent of the respondents) indicated that they would have to expand their work force in order to adopt a thirty-six-hour, four day work week. Seventy-two (72) companies suggested an acceptable government participation rate, ranging from 0 to 50 per cent (see table 28.7).

TABLE 28.7 Acceptable Government Participation Rate

Range of Options	Number of Companies
0	2
10	25
25	26
50	19

A total of 96 companies said that they were prepared to initiate a thirty-six-hour, four-day work week if government gave an incentive payment for each additional worker hired, but only 72 of them indicated an acceptable rate of government participation, while the remaining 24 companies could not decide on the rate of participation. A few companies were strongly opposed to any form of government intervention in private business.

Four-day, Thirty-two-hour Work Week

It appears that a thirty-six-hour work week will be widely established, although it may not be a four-day week. In a number of instances, a compressed work week has meant an automatic reduction to thirty-six or thirty-seven hours a week. On the other hand, a long-term historical phenomenon has also reduced the effective work week (not the number of days per week) to around thirty-seven hours.[15] However, a little over two-thirds of our responding companies showed no willingness to consider a thirty-six-hour, four-day work week. Trade unions are not aiming at this either; they would prefer to skip this transitional phase and demand a thirty-two-hour, four-day week.

A brief submitted by the Canadian Labour Congress to the Commission of Enquiry into the modified or compressed work week reported the position of the CLC, which was resolved in its convention of May 1972:

BE IT RESOLVED that this convention urge all Canadian wage earners to resist pressures to accept changes in hours of work such as the four day forty hour week which restores the ten hour day and constitutes a serious danger to the eight hours or less per day already won by labour; and

BE IT FURTHER RESOLVED that the Canadian Labour Congress mount a campaign to urge all its affiliated organizations to press vigorously for a work week comprising 32 hours maximum with emphasis on a week of four days with eight hours or less per day, without loss of take home pay.

The position of the CLC is consistent with the role played by the trade union movement in the history of reduction of hours of work. From their agitation for a ten-hour day, launched in 1831 by the United Amicable Society of Bricklayers, Plasterers and Masons, to the present day, unions have taken a progressive attitude toward hours of work and have been successful in reducing them when aided by other factors such as (1) government encouragement; and (2) growing technology.

(1) *Government Encouragement.* Federal or provincial governments in Canada gave no legislative support or encouragement for reducing hours of work before the beginning of the twentieth century. In fact, at the federal level, there was no legislation to regulate hours of work till the passage of the Canada Labour Standards (Code) on 1 July 1965. Among the provinces, Ontario, British Columbia, and Alberta have laws that set daily and weekly

limits beyond which overtime may not be undertaken. In Manitoba
and Saskatchewan, any number of hours can be worked for at time-
and-a-half premium payment after the specified limit. These are
the provinces where permission is required to extend daily hours
for introducing a compressed work week without overtime. Such
permission has not been difficult to obtain. At the federal
level, the Johnstone Commission has recommended "that the Canada
Labour Code be amended to permit employees under federal jurisdiction to work longer but fewer days each week without overtime
pay".[16]

Individual government leaders have, in recent years, talked of
the possibility of a reduced and rearranged work week. Speaking
to the Niagara Falls Chamber of Commerce on 2 April 1971, Prime
Minister Trudeau said that "within less than a generation we will
be down to the thirty-two-hour week and perhaps eventually
less".[17]   Labour Minister John Munro has indicated a similar
trend, but made it clear that government legislation will have
to wait until collective agreements achieve such reductions.
(2) *Growing Technology*. The technological capacity in North
America is increasing at an astounding rate. A decade ago, the
capacity of computer technology doubled in seven or eight years;
now it doubles in half that time. The "doubling time" for other
types of technologies is also diminishing. The impact of such
fast-increasing technological capacity is evident in the doubling
rate of the GNP itself. For example, the United States took
forty years to double its GNP, from $250 billion to $500 billion,
whereas in one single decade, during the 1960s, the GNP almost
doubled again. Such unprecedented growth has become possible
through technological and scientific inventions, but unfortunately with no corresponding development in the social sciences to
cope with it.[18]   In the absence of a concerted social scheme for
translating technological development into institutional and
human development, one of the most potent instruments of change
in the North American society has been the trade union movement.

The long-term implications of growth in technology are: (i)
reduction in employment in the sector where productivity increases; (ii) decreasing capacity in the less productive sectors to
absorb displaced workers; (iii) increasing unemployment if hours
are not reduced; and (iv) growing need for preparing workers for
increased leisure.

(i) Over the last forty years, employment in Canada has
shifted from the goods-producing to the service-producing sector.
Between 1931 and 1968, employment declined in the goods sector,
from 60.9 per cent to 39.7 per cent; during the same period, it
increased in the service sector from 39.1 per cent to 60.3 per
cent. Undoubtedly, this trend is going to continue, although
service sector employment may not increase as fast as the reduction in the goods sector. The magnitude and degree of employment
shift between the two sectors will depend upon the relative
levels of productivity in the two sectors and government's
efforts to inaugurate employment-generating programmes.

(ii) Productivity in the goods sector has increased, in the
post-World War II period, at an annual average rate of 5.7 per

cent, which is three times the rate of increase in the service sector. But in the years ahead, computer technology and office automation will no doubt increase productivity in the service sector as well. As it did in the past, this will reduce the capacity to absorb additional workers.

(iii) As a result of growing technology and declining capacity of the service sector to absorb more and more workers, unemployment will become a serious problem. Therefore, Sar A. Levitan suggests that "as technology presses forward to generate possibly more serious unemployment difficulties, some experimentation with modest shortening of hours, while the economy is generally strong and prosperous, might well emerge in the years immediately ahead".[19] Increase in leisure, on the other hand, has the prospect of expanding the service sector, creating greater job opportunities.

(iv) There is no planned effort in the North American society to cope with the implication of the growing technology, that is, prospects of high unemployment, requiring a sudden reduction in hours of work, and lack of preparedness on the part of workers to adjust to increased leisure.

Given the past record of technology and productivity growth, when should Canadians expect a thirty-two-hour, four-day work week?

A Projection Using Labour Cost Estimates. The most important consideration in reducing the work week is increased labour cost that the management and the economy have to bear. A reduction from the present forty-hour standard work week to a thirty-two-hour week with the same take-home pay will amount to a 25 per cent increase in the labour cost. If overtime has to be paid at time-and-a-half to obtain the same forty-hour week, the labour cost will further increase to 37.5 per cent. How many years will the economy require to absorb this additional labour cost? Confining our analysis to the goods-producing sector, we find that average annual productivity increased in this sector by 5.7 per cent during the period 1946 to 1968. It may be expected that while productivity in the service-producing sector may not increase beyond 2 per cent annually in the next two decades, productivity in the goods-producing sector may average 5.7 per cent, if not better. If we assume that all the gains in productivity are devoted to reducing hours of work, maintaining current wages and providing for no other benefits, it will take 4.3 and 6.5 years respectively for absorbing a 25 per cent and 37.5 per cent increase in labour cost. However, it has been observed that productivity gains between 1830 and 1920 were divided in such a way that 50 per cent of them were devoted to a betterment in standard of living and higher wages and the other 50 per cent to reduced hours of work. The ratio has changed since 1920, as 60 per cent of the gains have gone to increasing income and 40 per cent to reducing hours of work.

The calculations in table 28.8 are based on 40 per cent of the productivity gains going toward reduced hours of work. It shows that a thirty-two-hour work week, incurring a 25 per cent increase in labour cost (with no overtime), is attainable in 1984.

If allowances are made for time-and-a-half overtime to make up to forty hours, incurring a 37.5 per cent increase in labour cost, a thirty-two-hour work week is attainable in 1989.

TABLE 28.8 Target Dates When Reduced Work Week May Be Attainable

1	2	3	4	5
Reduction from Standard 40-Hour Work Week to:	Increase in Labour Cost (with no overtime)	Attainable in: (year)	Increase in Labour Cost (with time-&-a-half overtime to make up to 40 hours)	Attainable in: (year)
39	2.6	1974	3.9	1975
38	5.3	1975	7.9	1976
37 1/2	6.7	1976	10.0	1977
36	11.1	1978	16.7	1980
35	14.3	1979	21.4	1982
32	25.0	1984	37.5	1989

Source: Based on a table in *A Shorter Work Week: Some Consequences for British Columbia*.

It is implicit in these calculations that companies with higher than the average productivity rates would obtain a thirty-two-hour work week earlier than the target dates. A beginning has occurred, as in 1971 there were 115,795 nonoffice employees working thirty-seven-and-a-half hours or less per week. According to our calculations, this level of reduction (i.e., thirty-seven-and a-half hours) is attainable by 1977 for all nonoffice employees.

Some of the factors that may further expedite the reduction process are as follows.

(1) The phenomenon of the rearranged or modified work week itself may create circumstances necessitating reduction. Companies switching to a three-day work week may automatically reduce the hours in that week from forty to thirty-six.[20]

(2) During the period 1949 to 1954, as the number of companies switching from six days to five days a week increased by 22 per cent, hours of work declined by 60 per cent. This pattern will repeat as the compressed work week gains momentum.

(3) There is always a small percentage of companies that can absorb a minor reduction without incurring overtime expense or the cost of hiring additional workers. Consequently, the target dates of these companies for attaining a reduced work week could be those in column 3 rather than those in column 5 of table 28.8.

Conclusion

A four-day, thirty-two-hour work week is a logical and practical extension of contemporary and historical developments. The compressed or rearranged work week is a modern innovation which can flourish only if it becomes consistent with the historical reduction process. A compressed four-day, forty-hour work week has short-term attraction for certain employees and management, but lacks long-term acceptability because: (1) in the coming years, the work week cannot stay at forty hours; it must be reduced in line with the historical reduction outlined in this chapter; (2) the element of fatigue and boredom will increase as the initial novelty wears off. There are already instances of dissatisfaction with a ten-hour day;[21] and (3) it does not have the support of the trade union movement.

A four-day, thirty-six-hour work week has relative advantages over a four-days, forty-hours arrangement. Therefore, a number of companies that adopted a rearranged work week did reduce it to approximately thirty-six hours. In our survey, ninety-eight companies (nearly one-third of the respondents) showed willingness to consider a thirty-six-hour work week. Undoubtedly, there would be a lesser incidence of fatigue and boredom. However, the trade union movement is not keen to negotiate for this level of reduction.

Having examined the limited viability of these two forms of modern innovation in the management of time, the study explored a projective technique to estimate the time it will take to usher in a thirty-two-hour, four-day work week. With the innovation of a three- or four-day work week at our threshold, it appears that in the seventies and eighties, the trade unions will devote their attention to obtaining a thirty-two-hour work week. Our projective technique, based on labour cost estimates, suggests that this is attainable within and during the next sixteen years. Needless to say, hours of work will continue to decline even below thirty-two hours per week. Among researchers and policy makers there is little or no communication on the future implications of this trend. Once leisure is recognized as a component of GNP, there will be little nervousness in reducing hours of work, and consequently, the trend in reduction may even be accelerated.

Notes

1. The history of hours can be stretched back to the fourth century Roman calendar, in which 175 days out of 355 were marked unlawful for business. See Erwin O. Smigel, "The Problem of Leisure Time in an Industrial Society", in *Computer Technology – Concepts for Management* (Industrial Relations Counselors, Inc., May 1964).

2. H. B. Shaffer, *Shorter Work Week*, Editorial Research Report, vol. 2, no. 22 (1954).

3. Strangely enough, there are accounts of much shorter work weeks in the U.S. as early as the fifteenth century. For instance, "Professor Rogers tells us that in the fifteenth century eight hours was the rule...." *Report of the Royal Commission on the Relations of Labour and Capital in Canada* (1889), p. 99.

4. Wladimir Woytinsky, "Hours of Labour", in *Encyclopedia of the Social Sciences* 7 (1937), pp. 479-80.

5. This section of the paper was previously published in S.M.A. Hameed, "Economic and Institutional Determinants of the Average Work Week in Canada", in *Work and Leisure in Canada*, ed. S.M.A. Hameed and D. Cullen (University of Alberta, 1971); see also W.R. Dymond and George Saunders, "Hours of Work in Canada", in *Hours of Work*, ed. Clyde E. Dankert, et al. (New York: Harper and Row, 1965), pp. 54-76.

6. *Report of the Royal Commission on the Relations of Labour and Capital in Canada* (1889), appendix F, p. 37.

7. Henry Ford, in an interview with Samuel Crowthers, appearing in *World's Work* for October 1926, as quoted in the *Monthly Labor Review*, December 1926, pp. 1162-65.

8. *Report on the Compressed Work Week*, Samson Belair Riddell Stead Inc., September 1972.

9. According to a report from the Ontario Ministry of Labour, "it is estimated that about 150 to 160 establishments are operating or have permission to operate on a compressed work schedule in Ontario". See *The Compressed Work Week in Ontario*, Research Branch, Ontario Ministry of Labour, September 1972.

10. Arthur Blakely, "Four-Day Work Week Liked", *Edmonton Journal* (Friday, 4 May 1973).

11. In reporting the results of this survey under the auspices of the compressed work week there is a definitional problem, as thirteen of the reporting organizations actually reduced the number of hours worked. See *Report on the Compressed Work Week*, Samson Belair Riddell Stead Inc., September 1972.

12. Ibid.

13. Ibid.

14. The concept of effective work week is different from actual hours worked. The source for the latter type of hours is *The Labour Force Survey*, which obtains information through a sample survey of households. Through door to door interviews of about 30,000 households, selected by the area sampling method across Canada, data on actual hours worked are collected as a response to the question, "How many hours did you work last week?" On the other hand, if paid vacations, paid holidays, paid sick leave, and

coffee breaks are averaged and subtracted from actual hours worked, we would obtain the effective work week.

The Commercial and Industrial Research Foundation has suggested that "increasing vacations, holidays, coffee breaks, etc., actually bring average hours worked per week closer to 36 than 40". See *A Shorter Work Week: Some Costs and Consequences for British Columbia,* Commercial and Industrial Research Foundation (Vancouver, 1967); also Peter Henle, "Recent Growth of Paid Leisure for U.S. Workers", *Monthly Labor Review,* 1962.

15. *The majority of unionized employees of the federal government and its Crown corporations, agencies and boards belong to the Public Service Alliance of Canada, and work a thirty-seven-and-a-half hour week.*

Evidence showed that the work week for 99.6 per cent of provincial government office employees is less than thirty-seven-and-a-half hours with almost one-third (32 per cent) of these same employees working thirty-five hours or less per week.

Figures from 1969 indicate that 40.1 per cent of office employees in private industry work less than thirty-seven-and-a-half hours per week, and 19 per cent work thirty-five hours and under. K.R. Robinson, "PSAC Priority - A Shorter Week", *Canadian Labour,* November 1971.

16. "The Canada Labour Code and the Shorter Work Week", *The Labour Gazette,* April 1973, p. 235.

17. Quoted in K. R. Robinson, "PSAC Priority".

18. *The Challenge of Growth and Change,* Fifth Annual Review, Economic Council of Canada (September 1968), p. 52.

19. Sar A. Levitan, "Can We Afford Not to Reduce Hours of Work?" *Challenge,* June 1965.

20. See David P. Ross, "Leisure as a Response to Technological Change in the Economic System", in *Work and Leisure in Canada,* ed. S. M. A. Hemeed and D. Cullen (Edmonton: University of Alberta, Faculty of Business Administration, 1971).

21. *After a three-month diagnosis, the nurses taking part in the volunteer pilot project found that their ten-hour days left them so worn out that they couldn't enjoy their three-day weekends. The experiment was to have lasted six months but the nurses unanimously requested an immediate return to the old five-day week routine. Canadian Hospital,* January 1972.

29. Patterns of Industrial Conflict[*]

by Stuart M. Jamieson

The magnitude and intensity of industrial conflict reached such
proportions in Canada during the mid-sixties as to be officially
deemed a "crisis" in industrial relations. The then Prime Minister, the late Rt. Hon. Lester Pearson, accordingly appointed a
special Task Force on Labour Relations to carry out a large-scale
programme of research and enquiry and submit a report with recommendations. As one contribution to this programme, the author
undertook a comprehensive historical and analytical survey of
labour unrest and industrial conflict in Canada since the turn of
the century.[1]
   This chapter is largely a summary of some of the major findings
and conclusions of that study. One central question was kept in
mind throughout, namely: Does the wave of labour unrest and strikes
during the later sixties and into the seventies, and the widespread violence and illegality that at times accompanied it, represent something new in the Canadian industrial relations scene,
a product of new and perhaps revolutionary developments of the
present era? Or is it merely the most recent manifestation of a
type of collective behaviour that for various reasons has occurred
on a broad scale on several occasions in the past?

Patterns

It is extremely difficult to present any sort of orderly picture
of industrial conflict in Canada. Strikes and other overt manifestations of labour unrest have numbered in the tens of thousands
in this country since the turn of the century. They have varied
in size and character from small, spontaneous "protest" or "wildcat" strikes of a few dozen men and a few hours' or days' duration, to large and prolonged shutdowns involving thousands of men
and millions of man-days lost from employment. They have occurred
at one time or another in every major region of the country, in
hundreds of different industries and thousands of different localities. A few significant patterns do seem to stand out, however.
   One outstanding characteristic of industrial relations in Canada, as A. M. Ross and P. Hartman brought out in their comparative survey of thirteen countries,[2] is that it broadly resembles
the United States in a generally similar and distinctly "North
American pattern of industrial conflict". This is to be expected,
of course, in view of the close economic and cultural ties of
Canada with the United States and, particularly, the dominant role
that subsidiary branches of American-controlled corporations and
"international" unions play on the Canadian industrial scene. The
main feature of this pattern, in which Canada ranks second only
to the United States, is and has been the unusually high "incidence" of strikes (as measured by man-days lost as a percentage

---

*Reproduced by permission of Information Canada.

of total employment), strikes of relatively high frequency, moderately large size and unusually long average duration, as compared to other comparably industrialized countries in Europe and Asia.

Canada has come second only to the United States (and over the past decade has surpassed it) in another aspect of industrial conflict, and one that Ross and Hartman did not deal with in their survey, namely, that of violence, illegality, and forceful intervention by the state in labour disputes. To judge from official records available, there have been hundreds of such disputes in Canada since the turn of the century, more than ninety of which occurred in the decade 1957-66 alone. They range from minor cases of arrests for picket-line violence to major riots involving thousands of people, and bringing widespread attacks on persons and property, personal injuries and deaths, and intervention by armed police and/or military forces.

Ross and Hartman, who published their survey in 1960, found that in all thirteen countries surveyed, including the United States and Canada, the incidence of industrial conflict had declined markedly in the post-World War II era, relative to the greatly expanded total work force and union membership. They predicted, prematurely as it turned out, a "withering away" of strikes in industrial society.[3]

Canada, however, proved to be an exception to this general pattern in two or three important respects. First, alone among the thirteen countries surveyed, the *average duration* of strikes in Canada had *increased* since the war, and remained substantially above that of the United States and other countries.[4] Violence, illegality and legal penalties arising out of labour disputes had likewise undergone a marked decline in most countries after World War II, including in Canada. Here again, there appeared to be a unique and marked reversal in this country during the 1960s, when industrial conflict appeared to be reverting to a pattern more characteristic of earlier decades. (However, in view of the events surrounding the general strike in France in 1968, and a number of large and frequently violent strikes in Italy, Great Britain and some other West European countries in recent years, Canada can no longer be considered unique in this regard.) Another related feature that stood out in the mid-1960s, and continues to do so, was the unusually large number and proportion of illegal "wildcat" strikes and picketing, and the frequency with which court injunctions were issued and stiff legal penalties imposed.

With the wisdom of hindsight, it now seems evident that Ross and Hartman, in their predictions, misinterpreted a low or declining stage of a *cycle* as a long-term or permanent *trend*. Historically, industrial conflict in Canada since the turn of the century has occurred in three long "waves" or "cycles". Each of these started in what might be described as a period of comparative quiescence. With relatively minor intervening fluctuations, labour unrest, overt protest, and conflict then rose in magnitude over a period of two to three decades, reaching a peak, in scope and intensity, that was widely interpreted as constituting a

crisis. This induced, or forced, various adjustments, compromises and changes in attitudes and policies among the major actors
on the industrial relations scene, bringing a new period of relative peace, followed by another mounting wave of conflict that
reached a new peak. And so on.

Chronologically, the first of these long waves in Canada started
in the mid-1890s, reaching a dramatic climax in 1919-20, with
the Winnipeg General Strike and its wide repercussions. The second encompassed the period from the early twenties to 1946-47, in
an unprecedented series of industry-wide strikes across the
country. The third wave covered the period from the late 1940s
to the mid-sixties and into the seventies, when industrial conflict in Canada reached new record levels of magnitude. (Here, it
is to be noted, industrial conflict appears to have remained on a
high plateau, rather than descending sharply from a peak as in
the previous cycles.) Within these long waves there were minor
cycles with minor peaks, as in 1912, 1923-24, 1937, 1943 and 1958.
Despite significant growth and major transformations in the Canadian economy over more than seven decades, the three major cycles
and peaks of industrial conflict appear to have had certain important characteristics in common, in causal factors and in out-
ward manifestations. This suggests that there are built-in characteristics or maladjustments, in the Canadian industrial relations
system and in the broader economic, social and political structure,
that generate class tension and conflict on a critical scale every
generation or so. From the vantage point of history, therefore,
the wave of strikes during 1965-66 and subsequent years and the
accompanying violence and illegality, though having certain unique
features peculiar to the present era, cannot realistically be
viewed as "unusual" or "unprecedented". Indeed, relative to the
much larger labour force and numbers and percentage of workers
unionized since World War II, the *incidence* of strikes was less
serious in 1966 (and in subsequent new record years of 1968 and
1972) than in the previous peak years of 1919 and 1946.

Interpretations

How is one to interpret this broad cyclical pattern of conflict?
A detailed examination and testing of the relevant statistics
since 1900 yielded some surprising results to the author and his
research associate, John Vanderkamp, insofar as they went counter
to a number of hypotheses or presuppositions that we had at the
outset.[5]

To begin with, one would have expected to find (as Albert Rees
did in a detailed statistical analysis in the United States),[6]
a close correspondence between cycles of industrial conflict and
business cycles. In virtually all cycles, Rees found that the
peak in strikes preceded the peak in the boom by several months.

In Canada, since the turn of the century, however, there
appeared to be no significant degree of correlation in this regard. Only during the 1960s and early 1970s, and to a much lesser
extent in the period from 1900 to 1912, were economic expansion

and price inflation accompanied at all closely by a mounting incidence of strikes.

For a number of reasons also - particularly the dependent organizational ties of most Canadian unions and unionized employers
with their parent bodies in the United States, and the similarities in union and employer ideologies, bargaining demands, and
objectives on both sides of the border - one would have expected
a close relationship of fluctuations in strike activity in Canada
with those in the United States. But here again, no significant
correlation was found, even when tested with one-year and two-
year lags.

The main reason for this lack of correlation appears to be the
fact that industrial conflict in Canada has been primarily a
regional phenomenon in most years since the turn of the century.
This is to be expected, of course, in a country with such wide
variations in resource endowments, industrial structures, occupational compositions, and per capita incomes among the different
regions. Such differences have been accentuated by the loose
confederal system of government with its high degree of provincial autonomy, the pronounced language and cultural divisions
(particularly between Ontario and Quebec, the most highly industrialized provinces containing a substantial majority of all
union members), and the very loose, decentralized structure of the
trade union movement in this country.

Regional differences have been so pronounced in most years that
"national patterns" of industrial conflict become an almost mean-
ingless abstraction in some respects. In most years since 1900,
for instance, strike behaviour in most provinces has diverged more
from the national average than the latter has from the national
patterns of the United States and some other countries. Only on
relatively rare occasions, under special combinations of circumstances, have various forces affected all regions in Canada more
or less simultaneously, such as to create, in character and scope,
truly nation-wide waves or patterns of industrial conflict. Such
were the three major and one or two minor peaks described earlier.

Much the same sort of generalization applies to industries.
Strikes in some industrial categories that are common to all parts
of the country have tended to concentrate in particular regions,
provinces, or localities. This has been notably true of public
utilities and the public service in Quebec in recent years, and of
construction in the three major metropolitan areas. However,
those industries which in various periods have accounted for a
disproportionate share of strikes and lockouts, and occasionally
widespread violence and illegality, are largely confined to certain regions or provinces. Thus, for instance, coal mining, which
dominated the strike scene until well into the 1930s, has been
confined largely to Nova Scotia, British Columbia and Southwestern
Alberta; centres of conflict in the lumber and fishing industries,
largely to the coast of British Columbia; steel, nickel mining and
smelting, and automobile manufacturing, largely to Ontario; and
textiles, boots and shoes, and asbestos mining, largely to Quebec.

An adequate analysis of the many and varied regional and industrial factors contributing to industrial conflict is beyond the

scope of this chapter. It would be more enlightening at this
point, rather, to focus on the broad features of the industrial
relations system itself in Canada, and some contributing economic,
political and social factors that have been more or less common
to all regions. Among these the following seem to stand out.

(1)   In common with the United States, the prevailing employer
ideology in Canada - even in highly monopolistic or oligopolistic
industries - has been one of aggressive and competitive "free
enterprise". It has generated, in previous decades, protracted
and at times violent resistance of many influential employer
groups, frequently supported by governments, to recognizing
unions or engaging in meaningful collective bargaining.

(2)   Related to this, in both cause and effect, has been a long-
established tradition of union militancy which has been frustrated
(and often exacerbated) by the fragmented and decentralized structure of the labour movement in Canada. As many critics have
pointed out, there are and have been too many unions in this country, most of them too small to function effectively on behalf of
their constituents. And in the aggregate they still represent a
relatively minor fraction (less than one-third) of the paid labour
force.

(3)   Deriving from the above two outstanding features has been
the prevalence of a highly fragmented (or segmented) and decentralized system of collective bargaining. Two-thirds or more of
all agreements in Canada are and have long been negotiated between local unions and individual companies or plants. Many employers, even more than unions, have been unable or unwilling to
organize effectively on a broader basis to engage in industry-
wide or market-wide bargaining on even a local or regional, let
alone nation-wide scale.

(4)   As a result of these weaknesses, both unions and employers
in Canada have, over the years, come to depend on governments to
an excessive degree, each party attempting to protect itself
against the other. In early decides, employers could in most
cases rely on governments to defend their legal right to refuse
recognition to unions or to protect their property, and their
strikebreakers, in situations of overt conflict. In view of prevailing employer attitudes and policies in most industries, many
unions, to achieve even bare survival, came to depend on governments to protect their rights to organize and to force employers
to recognize and bargain with them. With unions having won these
rights, employers since World War II have in turn come to depend
increasingly on governments to pass new legislation and on the
courts to enforce new and more severe restrictions on unions to
further protect their (the employers') property and prerogatives.

The result of all this for Canada is an interesting paradox.
In no country, with the possible exception of the United States,
have employers and unions proclaimed so vociferously the virtues
of freedom, of "free enterprise", "free" unionism, and "free" collective bargaining, including freedom to strike, picket and lock
out. Yet in no country, including the United States, have the two
parties become so enmeshed in such a detailed, complex, and on the
whole rigid web of legal regulations that sharply limit their freedom of action in such matters as: unfair labour practices; certifi-

cation of unions; collective bargaining, conciliation, and arbitration procedures; strikes, lockouts, picketing, and boycotting; issuance of injunctions; and the like. All these in turn generate - particularly among union members - widespread frustration, disenchantment with the law, resort to illegal actions, and consequent incurring of legal penalties.

The Task Force on Labour Relations, in its official report in 1968, submitted a number of recommendations for dealing with such weaknesses in Canada's industrial relations system, particularly the excessive legalism and rigidity that characterized much of the legislation then in force. Among such recommendations were: broadening the powers of the Labour Relations Board to enable it to consolidate bargaining units and to order multiunion, multiemployer and industry-wide bargaining for specific purposes; removing from the courts and vesting in the board the authority to issue injunctions governing labour disputes; and dismantling the cumbersome two-stage system of conciliation, to provide for more flexibility with greater emphasis on voluntary procedures. The federal and several provincial governments, notably British Columbia in its new Labour Code of 1973, passed new legislation in line with several task force recommendations.

Finally, there is and has been, overall, the unstable economic environment in which Canada's industrial relations system has had to operate. The Canadian economy, for a number of complex reasons, has been one that renders effective planning at the national or regional level exceedingly difficult to achieve. This was particularly apparent during the depression years and again in the postwar period. The result has been, as compared to most Western countries: a relatively slow rate of increase in productivity and per capita real income; a highly unstable pattern of growth in output and employment, with bursts of inflationary expansion followed by protracted recessions; erratic movements in wage and price levels; and, overall, a persistently high rate of unemployment in all but a few peak boom periods. Such developments have tended to exacerbate labour unrest and industrial conflict.

Such conditions have been integral to the industrial relations scene for many years. They help explain the relatively high incidence of industrial conflict and of violence and illegality in Canada as compared to most industrial countries. They do not in themselves, however, explain the long-prevailing cyclical pattern described earlier, nor the special features peculiar to each era, particularly the sixties and early seventies.

One obvious point of difference, of course, is that the two earlier major peaks of labour unrest, namely 1919-20 and 1946-47, occurred immediately following Canada's participation in world wars. In this country, as in the United States, wartime regulations served to restrict or contain overt conflict between organized workers and employers, but generated mounting tension that exploded in a wave of strikes when hostilities ceased. The strike wave of the later 1960s and early 1970s, by contrast, occurred long after Canada had been directly involved in any military venture.

Another difference in the nature and timing of the most recent wave of strikes, as compared to those in previous decades, is that it followed in close tandem with the underlying cycle of economic expansion and inflation of the 1960s and early 1970s.

The explanation for these differences would seem to lie mainly in a number of broad structural, legal, and institutional changes that have occurred in recent years. Many large and protracted strikes of earlier decades arose out of such phenomena as wage cuts and discriminatory layoffs or discharges imposed unilaterally by employers during periods of recession or depression; refusal of employers to recognize and negotiate with unions, accompanied sometimes by deliberate "union-busting" campaigns; and new and vigorous organizing compaigns by unions, leading to rapid growths in membership. Strikes arising from such issues had little direct relation to the ups and downs of the economy, so they did not tend to be concentrated at or near the peak of business cycles.

Such issues have, for the most part, ceased to be a cause of major strikes since World War II, due largely to changes in legislation and in employer policy. Therefore, strikes in recent decades, in the overwhelming majority of cases, have occurred in already unionized industries over the negotiation of new or revised agreements, or over disputes about the interpretation and application of agreements already in force. Issues arising from these would tend to be more economic in emphasis and more immediately responsive to cyclical changes in the economy and, in an age of greatly improved communication, to generate most pressure and conflict in peak periods of expansion and/or inflation.

There remains to be explained, finally, the unusual degree of turbulence of industrial relations in Canada over the past decade or more. This appears to have been mainly a by-product of large and comparatively rapid demographic and social changes. These included: the unprecedented influx of younger workers into the labour force during the 1960s, as a result of the very high birth rates of the immediate postwar years; the generally higher levels of education and aspiration, and the rapid and drastic changes in many attitudes and values that accompanied this major shift in age structure; and, particularly in an age of rapid and graphic communications, the impact upon labour relations in the late sixties and early seventies of the violent and highly publicized confrontations with "establishments" elsewhere, in other contexts and other countries: in universities, in civil rights campaigns, in mass demonstrations against the war in Viet Nam, and in the ghetto riots of blacks in the United States.

Notes

1.   See Stuart M. Jamieson, *Times of Trouble - Labour Unrest and Industrial Conflict in Canada 1900-66*, Task Force on Labour Relations, Study no. 22 (Ottawa: Privy Council Office, 1968).

2.   A. M. Ross and P. Hartman, *Changing Patterns of Industrial Conflict* (New York: Wiley, 1960).

3.   Ibid., chapter 5.

4.   In 1957, this author, in another publication, expressed the view that the long average duration of strikes in Canada during the postwar period could be attributed to the rather cumbersome system of compulsory two-stage conciliation of industrial disputes that was enforced by the federal and most provincial governments until well on into the 1960s. See also Stuart Jamieson, *Industrial Relations in Canada* (Ithaca, N.Y.: Cornell University Press, 1957), chapter 4.

5.   See John Vanderkamp, "The Time Pattern of Industrial Conflict in Canada, 1901-1966", Task Force on Labour Relations (Ottawa, 1968).

6. A. Rees, "Industrial Conflict and Business Fluctuations", *Journal of Political Economy* 60 (October 1952).

30. Work Stoppages: Should Authorization Be Mandatory?*

by F. R. Anton

The process of collective bargaining is now firmly established in
most industrial economies. Labour leaders maintain, and some
employers agree, that collective bargaining as practised today is
quite compatible with that form of "mixed" private enterprise
which prevails. Some even go so far as to say that collective
bargaining may well be essential to the system if it is to survive. If this is true, then we must try to understand the causes
of one increasingly disturbing aspect of collective bargaining--
namely, work stoppages--which, in general, are reluctantly
accepted as an important part of free collective bargaining
between labour and management.

During the past three decades, there has been a growing belief
in North America and Britain that a number of strikes have occurred
because union members were the helpless victims of their organizations and leaders. This belief is based partly on the growth
of large-scale trade unionism, the tendency toward the centralization of trade union organization, and the publicity given by
various sources to certain questionable union activities.[1]
Consequently, some government officials, employers and members of
the public appear to believe that some trade union members may
require protection from their representatives and from the usual
dangers of a centralized bureaucracy. One aspect of this general
belief is the notion that in the absence of some kind of control
over the calling of strikes, workers who do not wish to strike
are called out and strike frequency increases. Numerous proposals
have therefore been advanced that legislation should be enacted
prohibiting strikes, unless such strikes have been first approved
by secret ballot by a majority of the employees involved.[2]

At least three different approaches have been proposed: (1)
required supervision by a government authority; (2) a tripartite
supervisory committee composed of one union and one employer representative, with a third member approved by both; and (3) a mandatory clause in all union constitutions that no strike shall be
called unless approved by a majority of the employees involved in
a *union-conducted* vote. These ideas have already resulted in a
certain amount of legislation. For example, during World War II
the Government of Canada, under Order in Council P.C. 7307, required that a supervised strike vote be taken - after all steps
in conciliation had been exhausted - before a union might legally
call a strike in any industry coming under the jurisdiction of
the federal Parliament. Similar provisions were enacted in the
United States under the *War Labor Disputes Act* (Smith-Connally
Act); and currently the *Labor-Management Relations Act*, 1947
(Taft-Hartley Act) calls for a government-conducted strike vote
on an employer's last offer of settlement in national emergency
disputes that are still unsettled after an injunction against a
work stoppage has been in effect for sixty days. Since 1945, the

---

*Reproduced by permission of Information Canada.

Province of Alberta has required a majority vote before a strike can be called. Compulsory supervision of strike votes and majority authorization are required before any kind of a strike may legally take place. Until the beginning of 1969, British Columbia required a strike vote as well, which, if requested by either party to the dispute, could be supervised by an agent of the government. The State of Michigan also calls for a government-conducted vote before unions coming under state jurisdiction may strike. Likewise, a number of other states in the U.S.A. have legislated that it is an unfair labour practice for an employee, individually or in concert with others, to engage in a strike without authorization of the majority of the employees voting in a unit appropriate for collective bargaining.

Interest in strike voting was further stimulated early in 1954 when President Eisenhower, in his labour legislation recommendations to Congress, suggested:

There is nothing which so vitally affects the individual employee as the loss of his pay when he is called on strike. In such important decisions he should have an opportunity to express his free choice by secret ballot held under Government auspices.[3]

Debate on the issue of strike vote legislation is still active and widespread. For example, a number of witnesses appearing before the Donovan Commission urged the Labour Government in Britain to implement strike vote legislation for the specific purpose of reducing unofficial strikes, which at that time accounted for more than two-thirds of working days lost through industrial action, and for 95 per cent of all strikes.[4] Subsequently, legislation was introduced by the Conservatives with the passage of the Industrial Relations Act in 1971. The Trade Union Congress (TUC) responded to this with a declaration of all-out opposition and pledged itself to a policy of noncooperation. It asked all unions to refuse to register under the act, not to sign enforceable deals, not to attend the newly formed National Industrial Relations Court (NIRC), and not to allow their members to become members of the NIRC bench. The British act is about to be repealed by the Labour Government but a strike authorization requirement will probably be reintroduced despite the TUC's opposition to it. Thus an enquiry into some of the issues involved in such proposals is particularly relevant at the present time.

The purpose of this chapter is therefore: (1) to evaluate compulsory strike vote legislation in terms of wartime and recent experience; (2) to consider the arguments advanced by interested groups who favour such legislation; and (3) to evaluate these arguments from the point of view of labour leaders and others who oppose compulsory strike voting.

Results of Supervised Strike Voting in Four Jurisdictions

With the outbreak of World War II, steps were taken by the Gov-

ernment of Canada to improve the federal machinery for settling
the increased number of industrial disputes. On 7 November 1939,
under the powers conferred by Parliament by the War Measures Act
of 1917 and 1927, the scope of The Industrial Disputes Investigation Act[5] was broadened to include industries engaged in war production. Thus, many industries previously under provincial jurisdiction alone were brought within the scope of the federal act.

Among extensions of the act's provisions was a clause making
it unlawful for an employer to declare a lockout, or for employees
to go on strike, until a report had been submitted to the Minister
of Labour by a Board of Conciliation and Investigation. Further
powers were later granted to the minister to prohibit strikes until a secret ballot had been taken. It was required that before
employees could strike or take a strike vote they must notify the
minister of their intent. If the minister felt that a work stoppage would hinder war production, he could order that a strike
vote be taken under the supervision of his department. All employees who, in his opinion, were affected by the dispute were
entitled to vote and only where a majority of those entitled to
vote cast their ballots in favour of a strike could it take place.

The prohibition remained in force until September 1944, during
which period there were thirty-six applications for supervision
of strike votes. Sixteen of these disputes were resolved before
a strike vote was taken. In the remaining twenty disputes, involving 13,264 employees, fifteen decisions were given in favour
of strike action, five against it. Of the total number of employees participating in the twenty supervised elections, more
than 85 per cent favoured going on strike. Twelve strikes occurred after all the provisions had been met.[6]

In common with Canada, the American War Labor Disputes Act,
1943, also provided for taking strike votes.[7] The stated purpose
of the strike vote clause was to allow employees "an opportunity
to express themselves, free from restraint and coercion, as to
whether they will permit such interruption in wartime". The act
authorized the president to seize establishments interrupted by a
work stoppage where their operation was necessary to the war
effort and made it a criminal offence for a trade union to call a
strike in any plant seized by the government. Strikes were also
prohibited in privately operated establishments unless a thirty-
day strike notice had been filed, and if the dispute was not settled, the National Labor Relations Board (NLRB) was required to
conduct a secret-ballot vote to find out whether the employees
concerned wished to strike. The ballot contained a statement of
the major issues in dispute. The vote was conducted among those
employees who formed a unit considered appropriate for the purposes
of collective bargaining. No criminal penalties were imposed for
violating the strike vote provision of the act, but a civil suit
could be brought against violators by either the government or any
other party injured by the strike. This liability notwithstanding,
it was legal, if the government had not seized the plant, for the
union to strike after the thirty-day "cooling-off" period, irrespective of whether a majority of the employees involved had voted
against strike action.

During the two-and-a-half years that these provisions were in operation, the NLRB conducted over two thousand strike votes involving almost three million eligible voters. Eighty-two per cent of individual voters and 85 per cent of voting units authorized their leaders to call a strike.[8] Strikes occurred in some 15 per cent of the cases after all provisions of the act had been met.

Since 1945, the Province of Alberta has required a supervision on work stoppages. The current Alberta Labour Act requires that "no employee bargaining agent or employee on whose behalf the bargaining agent bargains collectively shall strike or cause a strike until a majority of the employees affected by a dispute ... vote to strike".[9] Similar provisions apply to lockouts where more than one employer is involved. The result of any vote is now determined on the basis of *a majority of those persons who actually vote*. In both cases balloting is supervised by the Board of Industrial Relations.

Reasons given by political leaders for introducing supervised strike and lockout voting may be summarized as follows.[10] Prewar legislation contained provisions for supervised voting by secret ballot on questions of acceptance or rejection of conciliation awards, and implicitly gave the Minister of Labour a degree of supervisory control over the certification of trade unions. Immediately after the war, when the province was faced with a spate of industrial disputes (of which some were thought to be communist inspired), it appeared logical to the authorities concerned to extend supervisory control to the even more significant issue of strikes. Moreover, the federal requirement of mandatory strike voting during the war had established a Canadian precedent. Additionally, senior members of the government believed that supervised strike vote legislation was desirable in order to guarantee and uphold the right of an employee (union member or not) to express his opinion without fear of censure, discrimination, or retribution. This right, it was asserted, could best be assured by protective legislation in the form of a supervised vote by secret ballot.

The recorded results of supervised strike votes conducted by the Alberta Board of Industrial Relations during the period 1954 to the end of March 1973 indicate that of 373 strike votes conducted (involving over 67,000 eligible voters and 863 bargaining units), more than 75 per cent of the valid votes cast favoured strike action.[11] A number of legal strikes occurred in the period under review. Previously, a majority of those *entitled to vote* in a bargaining unit had to vote in favour of a strike before it could legally occur. A majority of those casting valid ballots was not considered adequate. Employees at work who abstained from voting were regarded as having cast negative votes. Following decades of protest by organized labour and the defeat of the Social Credit government in 1971, the act was changed to permit a majority vote of those who *actually vote*. Moreover, unions are now allowed to conduct the ballot provided a supervisory officer is present. An analysis of the data for Alberta reveals that of the 373 strike votes conducted from 1954 to 1973, 83 per cent favoured strike action. Of the 863 collective bargaining units involved, more than 50 per cent consisted of small

firms employing less than 100 workers. In all but 15 per cent of
these cases majority approval for strike action was obtained.
Where strike votes were conducted in establishments employing more
than 500 unionized workers, in all cases the employees involved
voted overwhelmingly for strike action. (In the 21 strike votes
conducted in enterprises employing more than 500 workers, more
than 50 per cent were among teachers; the remainder involved
craftsmen, transit workers, and public employees.) Experience
elsewhere supports this finding--the larger the unit, the more
readily will employees vote affirmatively and by substantial
majorities for strike.

In common with Alberta, prewar labour legislation in British
Columbia required that on questions of acceptance or rejection of
conciliation awards, an award should be submitted to a secret ballot supervised by the minister.[12] There were no provisions at
that time for taking and supervising votes on strike issues.
After the war, when the province resumed its normal jurisdiction
over labour relations,[13] new legislation (based on the old) was
introduced containing innovations similar to those of the wartime
federal labour code. One such innovation was the compulsory,
supervised strike vote provision. In principle, the statute differed little from the Alberta Labour Act, particularly with regard
to the conciliation procedures to be followed by a union before
members could strike or any employer cause a lockout. One important difference was that to call a strike, British Columbia union
leaders required authorization only from the majority of employees
who voted, rather than from those *entitled to vote*, as in Alberta.

The reasons why British Columbia implemented strike vote legislation are broadly similar to those already given for Alberta. An
outbreak of strikes, both legal and illegal, followed in the wake
of World War II. It was alleged that several of these strikes
occurred because some major west-coast unions were influenced by
communists using unethical methods. To curb such influence and
to control the activities of radical elements among organized
labour, the public, members of the legislature, and employers'
associations all began to agitate for revised labour legislation.
Such control could be achieved, it was suggested, by requiring
that unions wishing to strike obtain majority approval through
secret ballots supervised by the government.[14]

During the periods 1952 to 1958 and 1964 to 1968, for which
data are available, strike ballots were taken among 184,268 eligible workers, of whom nearly 90 per cent cast valid votes. Of
these valid votes, 79 per cent favoured strike action. An average
of thirty-seven strikes occurred each year after the requirement
of the act had been met.

The State of Michigan requires, under its Labor Mediation Act,[15]
that when the parties to an industrial dispute are unable to resolve their differences they must submit the dispute to third-
party intervention by a tripartite mediation board. Failing settlement of the dispute, the Labor Mediation Board may conduct a
supervised strike vote by secret ballot among the employees in
the bargaining unit involved. Strikes are forbidden under the
act unless a majority of all employees casting valid ballots
authorizes strike action.

Arguments Supporting Extension of Strike Vote Legislation

In light of the foregoing experience with strike vote legislation
we are in a better position to consider the arguments advanced by
interested groups - who propose that similar legislation be enacted in other jurisdictions - and also to examine these arguments
from the standpoint of organized labour and others who oppose such
a requirement.

It is reasonable to assume that both the Canadian and United
States governments enacted strike vote legislation in wartime to
limit a union's right to strike, in the hope of minimizing the
number of strikes and thus enabling war production to be maxi-
mized. Official statements made at that time support this assumption. But no available evidence indicates that such legislation
reduced the number of work stoppages. For what it is worth, many
of those who administered the strike vote in the United States
held the view that such legislation tended to foster, rather than
discourage, strikes.[16] There were indications in Canada too that
in no important dispute did workers vote against strike action.
Moreover, the impression was gained that whenever strike votes
were conducted on federal authority, the public tended to regard
such supervised voting as carrying government sanction for a
strike.[17] It is therefore significant that in spite of substantial pressures, neither of the central governments saw fit to extend the strike vote requirement into postwar legislation. (However, it is true that the United States has a provision in its
Labor-Management Relations Act for employees to vote on their employer's final offer of settlement in a national emergency dispute,
after an injunction has permitted a cooling-off period of sixty
days.) The question remains, is mandatory authorization (whatever the method) of work stoppages worth the expense and effort
involved? To answer this question it is necessary to examine
more fully the main arguments in favour of *strike* authorization
rather than work stoppages generally, since lockouts are rare
events which, when they do occur, almost invariably represent
unanimous decisions on the part of employers.

Numerous proposals for the enactment or extension of a strike
vote requirement contain either or both of two assertions: (1)
that strike voting will tend to reduce the frequency of strikes;
and (2) only by means of a secret strike ballot can the employee
involved in a dispute express his "true feelings" about going on
strike.

The first assertion - that strike votes will tend to reduce
the number of strikes - is difficult to judge empirically. There
is little evidence available to show that such legislation is
effective in preventing strikes. British Columbia has a relatively higher incidence of strikes than Alberta,[18] although until recently both provinces had virtually the same legislation. The
fact that there were a number of cases where strike authorization
was withheld need not imply that strikes were avoided because of
a strike vote requirement. There is no way of knowing whether or
not strikes would have occurred in these instances had no strike
vote been taken, although it must be remembered that under existing

strike vote legislation in Canada, the strikes would have been illegal if they had occurred.

The second assertion, that only by means of a secret strike ballot can the workers involved in a dispute express their "true feelings" about going on strike, can also not be tested objectively. The evidence available in the United States concerning strike control provisions imposed on union locals by their international constitutions[19] suggests that most trade unions are obliged to follow procedures that are generally regarded as democratic. Yet this kind of evidence is unlikely to alter the opinion of those who favour supervision of strike voting held by secret ballot. The stand taken by an individual on such an issue depends to a large extent on his view of the function of trade unions in the so-called mixed free enterprise system, and the significance of collective bargaining in employer-employee relations. It may be true that in the absence of secret balloting some strikes are called that do not reflect the feelings of a majority of the employees, particularly if they are not members of the union concerned. Nevertheless, the data presented appear to substantiate the opinion held by antagonists of strike voting that, in those jurisdictions where voting was required, employees usually tended to give their leaders majority approval to take strike action.

The view is held by some proponents of strike voting that in the absence of some kind of control, strikes may be, and frequently are, called by trade union leaders without majority approval. Moreover, they say that even if approval is forthcoming, it may be so obtained that the workers involved are not in fact expressing their genuine wish to strike.[20] This can happen when union leaders follow undemocratic procedures. For example, strikes may be called without any vote being taken among the rank and file; others may be called on the basis of a swift show of hands or a voice vote. Even where secret ballot votes are conducted by the union, the ballot boxes may be "rigged", or officials may misrepresent the count to produce a decision favouring their own position. It is alleged that irrespective of the methods used by union leaders at branch meetings to obtain strike authorization, certain other practices may be adopted that make the majority authorization obtained an inaccurate reflection of members' attitudes. For example, a union-held strike vote may be taken early in the negotiations; the issues at stake may be misconstrued, glossed over, or omitted, so that workers do not fully understand what is involved in the dispute and the possible consequences of a strike vote. Workers may be advised by their leaders that majority approval to strike is not in fact a directive to do so, but nothing more than an expression of confidence in their negotiators, which will enable them to obtain a better settlement management.[21]

Even where union leaders do follow democratic procedure, proponents of strike vote legislation declare that strikes may still take place without true majority consent. This can happen, they assert, because of poor attendances at union meetings and because nonunion workers in the bargaining unit are prohibited from attending such meetings and voting on matters that concern them. For the above reasons, therefore, advocates of strike voting assert that appropriate legislation should be enacted to safeguard the rights of all workers involved and minimize industrial unrest.

Counterarguments

Those who oppose a strike vote requirement do not deny that majority authorization to strike is necessary, or that union leaders may sometimes bring about work stoppages that have not been approved by the majority involved. They question, however, whether costly and time-consuming government sponsored votes are needed to ascertain if a majority of the employees in the unit involved favour strike action. Most union leaders, it is argued, act responsibly where a strike issue is involved and adhere to the normal democratic trade union government [22] procedures laid down for them by their constitutions. Should union leaders consistently fail to abide by these procedures, it would ultimately mean their dismissal from office--a result few officials would risk.[23] Trade unionists assert that the union represents the best judgement and will of the workers, and like any competent organization is perfectly capable of managing its own internal affairs. Contrary to opinion, it is declared, union leaders do not authorize strikes except as a last resort, when all peaceful means of reaching a fair settlement have failed, and only after obtaining prior approval from the membership. Most constitutions specify the penalty involved for failure to observe provisions whose aim is to make it difficult rather than easy for locals to call a strike. Strike-prone leaders would soon exhaust the union's strike fund. Spokesmen for organized labour also maintain that a strike vote requirement is proposed in the name of democracy on the assumption that most unions follow unethical practices and that harassing tactics need to be contrived to break down the security of the union. Supporters of such legislation seem to assume that if workers are given the chance to vote in a government-sponsored secret ballot, they will vote to repudiate their leaders. But opponents argue that there is little evidence to support these views.

   The opinion that strike voting tends to reduce industrial unrest is not shared by critics of such legislation. Union leaders state, and many impartial observers agree, that such a provision tends to impede the process of negotiations and make labour-management relations worse rather than better.[24] Authorities assert that the strike vote elections in the U.S. during World War II and under the "last offer" ballots of the Taft-Hartley Act caused more strikes than would have occurred in their absence. In the course of a strike vote, it is said, workers usually see the issue as a loyalty contest and the survival of their union in the face of an external attack from management, abetted by the government; they tend to resist this invasion of their domestic affairs by voting affirmatively. To maintain, as some do, that most strikes result largely because of the machination of union leaders is absurd; some strikes, union leaders declare, are initiated by the employees themselves - often despite the strenuous opposition of their leaders. To suggest, therefore, that the threat of strikes would dissolve and industrial unrest be reduced if only employees, untrammeled by their leaders, could express their real wishes by secret ballot in a strike vote is unsupported by the facts. Strike voting does not eliminate or reduce strikes, as the wartime experience of both the U.S. and Canadian governments bears out and as postwar results in two Canadian provinces substantiate. Thus, it is argued, for a government to espouse strike vote legislation would put the weight of government against the union and strike at the heart of collective bargaining; such action would effectively deny the union the right to make decisions on the most critical issue. To put the issue in the form of a vote to all employees in the unit, as distinguished from union members, is to deprive labour unions of their power to bargain on behalf of the unit.[25] Finally, union officials argue that a supervised strike vote militates against sound labour-management relations by seeking to abridge the right to strike, and thus impairs a fundamental freedom.

Conclusions

The aim here has been to provide a background against which arguments and counterarguments involved in the proposed extension of government-sponsored strike voting could be evaluated, but readers should note that the above analysis has been predicated on the assumption that unions and their members follow the procedures laid down by their constitutions and the law. Where these are ignored (as commonly happens in Britain) and wildcat strikes are frequent occurrences, then requiring a strike ballot authorization is unlikely to make much difference. The authorities must first diagnose the causes of widespread unofficial strikes before appropriate solutions can be introduced. Under relatively normal conditions, however, where both labour and management abide by the rules of the game, the following conclusions appear valid.

The data on strike authorization gathered from Canadian and U.S. sources during both World War II and the postwar period reveal broadly similar results. The findings support the conventional view that, in the majority of cases, when employees are called upon to support their union officers in negotiations they will generally do so, even to the point of authorizing strike action. This was so in all of the jurisdictions examined, although the proportion of affirmative votes varied. To deny strike authority might be construed as a vote of nonconfidence and might weaken the bargaining power of a union's negotiation committee in collective bargaining.

The evidence does not, however, permit any firm conclusion to be drawn regarding the efficacy or advantage of mandatory votes in preventing strikes. That strike authorization was withheld in a number of cases need not imply that strikes were avoided solely because of the strike vote requirement. It is possible that had there been no supervised vote, strikes would not have occurred in any case, whether or not union leaders obtained affirmation when sounding out members' opinions.

The evidence derived from the data can in no way support or deny the contention that strikes should not be permitted to occur unless a majority of the workers involved in a dispute signify their approval by secret ballot. It therefore remains a matter of opinion where honest differences may exist. But it is clear that the controversy over strike authorization arises, to a large extent, over differences of opinion on the procedures some think trade unions now follow and procedures they believe unions ought to follow before calling a strike. To maintain, as many do, that strike balloting will quench this controversy by fulfilling the dual objectives of reducing the number of work stoppages and making sure that strikes are authorized by a majority of the rank and file, does not appear convincing in the light of this investigation. There is no evidence to support either claim. Indeed, union officials in North America argue, with justice, that the weight of evidence leans to their side, in that the strike control provisions imposed by their constitutions are there specifically to keep strikes to a minimum and to ensure that such strikes as are called have first been approved by the membership.

Perhaps the lesson for Britain and other countries plagued by a relatively high incidence of wildcat strikes is for the state to require unions to be responsible for their own internal affairs but accountable to an enforcement agency. *Direct* government intervention in what is essentially a domestic matter should be a last resort.

Notes

1. See "Select Committee in Improper Activities in the Labor or Management Field", U.S. Senate, 85th Cong., 1st Sess., 1957. See also John Hutchinson, "Corruption in American Trade Unions", *Political Quarterly*, vol. 28, no. 3 (July-September 1957).

2. See White Paper on proposals for action following the *Report of Royal Commission on Trade Unions and Employers Associations, 1965-1968* The Donovan Report, Cmnd. 3623 (HMSO, 1968) ; and the *Report of Royal Commission Enquiry into Labour Disputes* (The Rand Report) (Toronto: Queen's Printer, 1968). See also *Proposals to Deal with National Emergency Strikes* (Washington, D.C.: American Enterprise Institute, 1969). Also, for less recent views, see *Proceedings and Reports of Public Enquiry in Labour Relations and Wage Conditions* (Ottawa, 1943-44); Report of Committee on Industrial Relations to House of Commons, 17 August 1946, and Hearings before House Standing Committee on Industrial Relations, June and July 1947; Minutes of *Proceedings and Evidence* on Bill no. 195 (The Industrial Relations and Disputes Investigation Act), April 1948; and *Hearings on Proposed Revisions of the Labor-Management Relations Act, 1947,* Committee on Labor and Public Welfare, U.S. Senate, 83rd Cong., 2d Sess., part 6, 1954.

3. House Document 291, 83rd U.S. Cong., 2d Sess.

4. *Report of Royal Commission*, p. 114.

5. *Industrial Disputes Investigation Act*, 1907, Statutes of Canada, ch. 20 as amended by ch. 14, 1925.

6. Data furnished by the Department of Labour, Ottawa.

7. *War Labor Disputes Act*, 1943, U.S. Stat. 163, ch. 144. For an authoritative work on U.S. experience with strike voting see H.S. Parnes, *Union Strike Votes: Current Practice and Proposed Controls*, Res. report, ser. no. 92 (Princeton, N.J.: Princeton University, Dept. of Economics and Sociology, 1956). I have drawn liberally on the methodology and research of Parnes's publication.

8. National Labor Relations Board, *Eleventh Annual Report* (1946), appendix B, p. 91.

9. *The Alberta Labour Act*, 1973, ch. 33, sec. 123. For a detailed analysis of strike voting in Alberta and British Columbia, see F. R. Anton, *Government Supervised Strike Voting* (Toronto: C.C.H. Canadian Ltd., 1961).

10. Information supplied by members of the Board of Industrial Relations.

11. Compiled from annual bulletins and records of the Alberta Board of Industrial Relations.

12. *Industrial Conciliation and Arbitration Act*, 1937, Statutes of B.C., ch. 31, sec. 44.

13. Statutes of B.C., 1947, ch. 44.

14. *The Labour Gazette XLVIII* (May 1948), p. 453; and *The Labour Gazette* (August 1948), p. 880; also the *Vancouver Daily Province* (28 February, 4, 12, 17 March, and 2 April 1947).

15. *Labor Mediation Act*, Stats. of Michigan, 1939, Act no. 176 as amended by Act no. 230 (1949) and Act no. 86 (1954).

16. F. Whitney, *Government and Collective Bargaining* (Philadelphia: Lippincott, 1951), p. 529. Also Federal Mediation and Conciliation Service, *First Annual Report* (1948), p. 57.

17. See testimony of M. M. Maclean, Assistant Deputy Minister of Labour, Ottawa, at the Public Enquiry into Labour Relations and Wage Conditions in Canada, in *Proceedings and Reports* (Ottawa, 1943-1944), p. 85.

18. Department of Labour, *Strikes and Lockouts in Canada* (Ottawa, 1952-1968).

19. "Strike Control Provisions in Union Constitutions", *Monthly Labor Review* 77 (May 1954), pp. 497–500. Also, "Unions' Strike Vote Provisions", and "Strike Authorization Procedures", *Management Record,* May 1954, p. 186, and November 1954, p. 429, respectively.

20. See K.G.J.C. Knowles, *Strikes: A Study in Industrial Conflict* (Oxford: Blackwell, 1954), p. 121.

21. It is not unusual for unions to urge their members to vote for a strike. In a recent ballot among Yorkshire miners the posters read:
The issue before the members is clear. You either support your union in its fight to obtain higher wages and better conditions or you support Government policy and as a consequence weaken the union now and in the future. VOTE YES.
Over 90 per cent of the miners in that country did so.

22. See *Monthly Labor Review*, p. 498; and *Management Record*, p. 431.

23. V.L. Allen, *Power in Trade Unions* (London: Longmans Green, 1954), pp. 158–164.

24. See F. Whitney, *Government and Collective Bargaining*, p. 529; also H. S. Parnes, *Union Strike Votes*, pp. 140–141.

25. See testimony of Archibald Cox, Walter Reuther, and George Meany at *Hearings on Proposed Revisions of the Labor-Management Relations Act*, pp. 3394, 3051, and 3590, respectively. For an important analogue to this issue of eligibility to vote see also Otto Kahn-Freund, "Industrial Disputes and Compulsory Arbitration", *The Listener* (27 December 1956), pp. 1058–59.

31. Administration of the Agreement

by J. Douglas Muir

The collective bargaining process, with its ever-present threat of
a work stoppage, is the glamorous part of labour-management relations that receives front-page newspaper coverage and the bulk of
the public's attention. However, the actual bargaining activity
may last for only a couple of months a year or even every other
year. Another process that is equally important and lasts
throughout the year is the collective agreement administration
process.

The result of collective bargaining is the labour-management
agreement. This agreement sets out the basic rules and rights
governing management and the union in their dealings with each
other. It contains clauses dealing with wages and fringe benefits,
hours and overtime, promotions and transfers, layoffs and discharge, work assignments and incentives, union security and management rights and numerous other matters. Each clause, therefore,
establishes either a "right" or an "obligation" on the part of
either management, the union, or the employee. These rights or
obligations, as established through the negotiation procedure, are
the result of compromises made during the final stages of the bargaining process. These compromises may have been made under considerable pressure and the actual wording of the clauses may have
been developed during the small hours of the morning. In many
cases the wording of the clauses may not have been fully thought
out and the understanding of the parties at the time may have been
slightly different. Even in those cases where pressure and mis-
understanding are not present it is seldom possible for the parties to develop a clause that will be applicable to all situations
at any period of time. Owing to the conditions under which bargaining takes place, many contractual clauses are themselves written in rather broad terms. The day-to-day job of the personnel
manager, the foreman, and the shop stewards in labour relations is
to apply the principles of the labour agreement. To effectively
apply these broad principles to specific problems it is imperative
that both parties really want the agreement to work and are willing to display a degree of flexibility in making it work. This
flexibility and a degree of trust are the elements necessary for
successful labour-management relations and must be present for the
effective administration of the collective agreement.

Supervisory management and the personnel office must daily initiate actions in the general areas covered by the collective
agreement. Whenever such action is initiated there is always the
possibility of management's decision running counter to the provisions of the agreement. For example, even with the best of
faith, a supervisor may transfer one employee when the union believes the agreement would provide for the movement of another;
he may assign work to an employee which the employee believes
calls for a higher rate of pay than he is given; he may deny an

employee a paid holiday to which the employee believes he is entitled; he may suspend an employee for an infraction of shop rules and the employee may claim such action to be unfair. The list of examples could be extended but the important point to note is that such conflict may arise out of honest differences in interpreting the agreement. To handle such matters a procedure has been developed through which such controversies can be resolved--the grievance procedure.

All of the labour statutes in Canada require that every collective agreement contain a provision for the final settlement by arbitration of all differences between the parties concerning the interpretation, application or operation, or any alleged violation of the collective agreement. Thus, by law, all disputes in Canada arising out of the collective agreement (these are known as "rights disputes") must be referred to a grievance procedure, and the final stage of all grievance procedures must refer the dispute to an arbitrator for a final and binding decision which thereby resolves the dispute. There can be no strikes or lockouts during the term of the agreement, which gives rise to the need for binding arbitration to resolve conflicts over rights disputes.

Grievances should be distinguished from complaints. Any action of the employer that an employee or the union does not like may be the basis for a complaint. Some complaints are also grievances. The essence of a grievance is a charge that the labour-management contract has been violated. Grievances may be divided into six main groups.

(1)   Grievances arising out of *violations* of the agreement by the employer. No dispute over the meaning of the agreement or over facts is involved - the employer, for some reason (ignorance, carelessness, or some other), has simply violated the agreement.

(2)   Grievances arising out of *disagreements over facts,* such as when a worker is disciplined for an offence that he denies having committed.

(3)   Grievances arising out of a disagreement over the *meaning of* the agreement between the union and the employer. These include cases where the scope of the agreement is in dispute. Even carefully written agreements may give rise to disputes over what the agreement means in specific situations. Included in this group are grievances that arise from omissions in the agreement. For example, an agreement may contain no provision against the employer's contracting out work, but include a wage scale for various occupations. Does inclusion of the wage scale mean that the employer is prohibited from contracting out work done by the employees for which the agreement includes a wage scale?

(4)   Grievances involving the *method of applying the agreement.* For example, an agreement provides that overtime shall be divided equally among the employees who do a given kind of work. But the agreement does not say during how long a period management must make an equal division of overtime.

(5)   Grievances involving differences of opinion as to the reasonableness or *fairness of various actions* by management. The union, while admitting that a worker was at fault, may contend that the discipline imposed is too severe. Or workers may complain

that a standard is too high or a piece rate too low.

(6)   Grievances arising from *application of seniority rules*. The rule may indicate that seniority will prevail provided the senior employee has "sufficient ability" to do the job. What is meant by "sufficient" ability? Is it ability to do the job at once, ability to attain a satisfactory level of output within a week, a month, or some other period, or ability to learn the job?

The grievance procedure is really a conference technique by which the two parties decide how a rule (which both accept) should be applied in a particular situation. The process is an appeals procedure, by which any individual who believes that he has been wronged can enter a claim and have it heard. If it is denied at one level, he can appeal it to a higher authority through a series of stages. In the first instance, if the foreman turns the employee down, the employee may go to his union shop steward. The steward is a worker's representative at the shop level; his jurisdiction corresponds roughly to that of the foreman. The shop steward's primary job is to keep the men in his department active in the union and to represent them whenever they have a grievance.

The shop steward will listen to the employee, get all the facts, and then talk to the foreman. If he thinks the employee's action. If the foreman persists in his judgement, however, the steward will help the employee put his grievance in writing. The foreman too will summarize his position in writing, and by doing so the grievance becomes formal and is processed to the second step of the procedure.

The particular union and company officials who are designated to handle the appeals stages of the grievance procedure vary from situation to situation. In a typical case, however, in the second stage of the procedure the employee's grievance is presented by a chief shop steward (or by the chairman of the local union's grievance committee) to the company's departmental supervisor. If the grievance is still not resolved to the union's satisfaction, the union can then take the grievance to a third step, in which the union grievance committee or the local union president argues the case with the plant personnel manager or the general plant manager. If settlement is still not reached, a national or international representative of the union can take the employee's case to the company's top management at head office.

If the company's reply still denies the employee his claim and if the union is still convinced that the employee is right, and with all the bilateral appeals stages now exhausted, the union can take the case to arbitration.

Grievances should be settled as near the point of origin as possible, that is, by the worker's immediate supervisor. However, most grievances require at least one appeal before being settled. Usually complaints that can be settled by the immediate supervisor never become formal grievances anyway. In addition, many employees consider that shop stewards are not fulfilling their jobs if they don't process grievances at least one step above the immediate supervisor. Technical grievances often require at least one appeal before there is adequate discussion and explanation. A grievance procedure that settles a large proportion of routine grievances within the first two steps is considered to be functioning very well, provided management is not giving away its rights in doing so. The level of the grievance procedure at which the grievance is resolved depends to a large extent upon the type of grievance, the nature of the issue, and the personalities involved. For example, grievances involving interpretation or application of the contract to several departments or perhaps the entire plant obviously cannot be settled at the lower steps. The higher steps are required because settlement involves major policy issues.

The number of steps in the grievance procedure and the personnel participating at each step will vary from company to company. The purpose of a multistep grievance procedure is to permit different personnel of the company and the union to take a fresh look at the problems of each of the preceding stages. Equally important, it provides the parties every opportunity to gather all the relevant facts and to review past practices that may bear upon the grievance. In this manner, there is an excellent chance for the grievance to be settled without resorting to arbitration, and in a manner consistent with the terms of the collective agreement.

The grievance procedure provides the parties with an excellent opportunity to discuss employee complaints and, in so doing, to promote a better understanding of management, employee, and union problems. In this manner, the grievance procedure may be regarded as the "psychotherapy" of industrial relations. Small problems can be discussed and settled promptly before they become major and troublesome issues in the plant. Serious problems can be analyzed in a rational manner and resolved speedily, peacefully, and in keeping with the terms of the collective bargaining contract. The rights of employees, employers, and unions contained in the collective agreement can be protected in an orderly fashion. Thus the grievance procedure not only serves as a means of enforcing the collective agreement, but it also provides the parties with the opportunity to discuss various problems. This may lead to the adoption of policies that will reduce the number of grievances in the future.

The grievance procedure should not be regarded as a device whereby companies or unions can "win" a grievance. It should be viewed as a means for developing a better climate of labour relations in the company. It is the basis of the "working relationship" between the company and the union. This does not mean that rights guaranteed in the collective agreement should be waived or compromised, but that in discharging obligations under the grievance procedure the parties should understand the broader implications involved in the processing of complaints. Company and union representatives who regard the grievance procedure in this light gear their behaviour, arguments, and general approach toward the improvement of labour relations. In short, the grievance procedure should not be regarded as an end in itself. It should be viewed as a channel of communication between the company, the union, and the employees for the promotion of mutual understanding and for the improvement of the labour relations environment.

The binding arbitration feature of the grievance procedure as the final stage is beneficial to both management and labour. It assures the employee that his complaint of unjust treatment will be given a fair hearing, right on up to the judgement of an impartial outside judge (a lawyer, a professor, a minister, or a professional arbitrator), and that he will be "made whole" for any loss that he has suffered. He is guaranteed his "day in court". At the same time, management is assured that there will be no walkout in protest over its actions. Thus management has gained the advantage of uninterrupted production, while the employees and the union have gained the assurance that justice will be accorded them.

The significance of this grievance procedure can hardly be overstressed. It is one of the truly great accomplishments of Canadian industrial relations. For all its defects - the bypassing of some of the appeals stages, its use by the union as a political device to convince the employees that it is looking out for their interests, the slowness with which it sometimes operates - it constitutes a social invention of great importance.

The grievance process is considered by many to be the "heart" of collective bargaining. The negotiation of the agreement occurs perhaps every two years, but the grievance procedure takes care of the gripes and individual problems that are bound to arise in any plant or shop every day.

Bibliography

Books

Alford, R. *Party and Society*. Chicago: Rand McNally, 1963.

Allen, V.L. *Power in Trade Unions*. London: Longmans Green, 1954.

Anton, F.R. *Government Supervised Strike Voting*. Toronto: C.C.H. Canadian Ltd., 1961.

Ashenfelter, O., and Rees, A., eds. *Discrimination in Labor Markets*. Princeton: Princeton University Press, 1973.

Barnett, George E. *Chapters on Machinery and Labor*. Cambridge: Harvard University Press, 1926.

Center for Labor and Management. *Collective Bargaining Simulation*. Iowa: University of Iowa Press, n.d.

Chamberlain, Neil W. *Collective Bargaining*. New York: McGraw-Hill, 1951.

Commons, John R. *A Documentary History of American Industrial Society*. 11 vols. Glendale, Calif.: Arthur H. Clark Co., 1910-1911.

-------. *Legal Foundations of Capitalism*. Madison: University of Wisconsin Press, 1959.

Crispo, John. *International Unionism: A Study in Canadian-American Relations*. Toronto: McGraw-Hill, 1967.

-------. *The Role of International Unionism*. Washington: Canadian-American Committee, 1967.

Cunningham, W.B. *Compulsory Conciliation and Collective Bargaining: The New Brunswick Experience*. Montreal: McGill University Industrial Relations Centre, 1958.

Dankert, Clyde E., et al., eds. *Hours of Work*. New York: Harper and Row, 1965.

Doeringer, Peter, and Piore, Michael. *Internal Labour Markets and Manpower Analysis*. Lexington, Mass.: D.C. Heath, 1971.

Downie, Bryan M. *Relationships Between Canadian-American Wage Settlements: An Empirical Study of Five Industries*. Kingston, Ont.: Industrial Relations Centre, Queen's University, 1970.

Dunlop, John T. *Industrial Relations Systems*. New York: Holt, Rinehart and Winston, 1958.

Etzioni, Amitai. *Complex Organizations*. New York: Holt, Rinehart and Winston, 1961.

Fidell, Linda, and Dehamater, John, eds. *Women in the Professions*. Beverly Hills: Sage Publications, 1971.

Galenson, Marjorie. *Women and Work: An International Comparison*. Ithaca, N.Y.: New York School of Industrial and Labor Relations, Cornell University, 1973.

Gunderson, Morley. *Factors Influencing Male-Female Wage Differentials in Ontario*. Toronto: Ontario Ministry of Labour Research Branch, 1974.

Hameed, S.M.A., and Cullen, D., eds. *Work and Leisure in Canada*. Edmonton: University of Alberta, 1971.

Hameed, S.M.A., and Paul, G.S., eds. *3 or 4 Day Work Week*. Edmonton: University of Alberta, 1974.

Herman, Edward E. *Determination of the Appropriate Bargaining by Labour Relations Boards in Canada*. Ottawa: Department of Labour, 1966.

Horowitz, Gad. *Canadian Labour in Politics*. Toronto: University of Toronto Press, 1968.

Jamieson, Stuart M. *Industrial Relations in Canada*. Ithaca, N.Y.: Cornell University Press, 1957.

--------. *Industrial Relations in Canada*. Toronto: Macmillan, 1973.

Judek, S. *Women in the Public Service*. Ottawa: Economics and Research Branch, Canada Department of Labour, 1968.

Kerr, et al. *Industrialism and Industrial Man*. Cambridge: Harvard University Press, 1960.

Keynes, J.M. *The General Theory of Employment, Interest and Money*. New York: Harcourt Brace and Co., 1951.

Knowles, K.G.J.C. *Strikes: A Study in Industrial Conflict*. Oxford: Blackwell, 1954.

Knowles, Stanley. *The New Party*. Toronto: McClelland and Stewart, 1961.

Korman, A.R. *Industrial and Organizational Psychology*. Englewood Cliffs, N.J.: Prentice-Hall, 1971.

Kornhauser, A. *The Industrial Conflict*. New York: McGraw-Hill, 1956.

Kruger, Arthur, and Meltz, N.M., eds. *The Canadian Labour Market: Readings in Manpower Economics*. Toronto: University of Toronto, Centre for Industrial Relations, 1968.

Kujawa, Duane. *International Relations Management in the Automobile Industry: A Comparative Study of Chrysler, Ford and General Motors*. New York: Praeger, 1971.

Lawler, E.E. *Pay and Organizational Effectiveness*. New York: McGraw-Hill, 1971.

Lipset, S.M. *Agrarian Socialism*. Berkeley, Calif.: University of California Press, 1950.

Litvak, I., and Mallen, B., eds. *Marketing: Canada*. Toronto: McGraw-Hill, 1964.

Logan, H.P. *Trade Unions in Canada*. Toronto: Macmillan, 1948.

Maslow, A.H. *Motivation and Personality*. New York: Harper, 1954.

McClelland, D.C. *The Achieving Society*. New York: Irvington Books, 1961.

McHenry, Dean. *The Third Force in Canada*. Berkeley, Calif.: University of California Press, 1950.

Miller, R.U., and Isbester, A.F., eds. *Canadian Labour in Transition*. Toronto: Prentice-Hall, 1971.

Morse, N.C. *Satisfaction in the White-Collar Job*. Ann Arbor: University of Michigan, Institute for Social Research, Survey Research Center, 1953.

Morton, Desmond. *NDP: The Dream of Power*. Toronto: Hakkert, 1974.

Ostry, Sylvia. *The Female Worker in Canada*. Ottawa: Information Canada, 1968.

Parnes, H.S. *Union Strike Votes: Current Practice and Proposed Controls*. Princeton, N.J.: Princeton University, Department of Economics and Sociology, 1956.

Perlman, Selig. *The Theory of the Labour Movement*. New York: Macmillan, 1928.

Perman, Mark. *Labour Union Theories in America*. Illinois: Row, Peterson and Co., 1958.

Piel, G. *Consumers of Abundance*. Centre for the Study of Democratic Institutions, 1961.

Reynolds, L.G. *The Structure of Labor Markets: Wages and Labor Mobility in Theory and Practice*. New York: Harper, 1951.

Roethlisberger and Dickson. *Management and the Worker*. Cambridge: Harvard University Press, 1943.

Ross, A.M., and Hartman, P. *Changing Patterns of Industrial Conflict*. New York: Wiley, 1960.

Scotton, Clifford A. *Canadian Labour and Politics*. Ottawa: Canadian Labour Congress, n.d.

Seidman, Joel, ed. *Trade Union, Government and Collective Bargaining: Some Critical Issues*. New York: Praeger, 1970.

Smith, Adam. *An Enquiry Into the Nature and Causes of Wealth of Nations*. Edinburgh: A. and C. Black, 1850.

Smith, K.U. *Behaviour, Organization and Work: A New Approach to Industrial Behavioural Science*. Madison: College Printing and Typing, 1962.

Somers, G.G. *Labor, Management and Social Policy*. Madison: University of Wisconsin Press, 1963.

Somers, G.G., ed. *Essays in Industrial Relations Theory*. Ames, Iowa: Iowa State University Press, 1969.

Tannenbaum, Frank. *A Philosophy of Labour*. New York: Alfred A. Knopf, 1951.

Thurow, Lester. *Poverty and Discrimination*. Washington: Brookings Institute, 1969.

Tremblay, M.A., and Fortin, G. *Les comportements économiques de la famille salariee du Quebec*. Quebec: Laval University Press, 1964.

Ulman, Lloyd. *Challenges to Collective Bargaining*. Englewood Cliffs, N.J.: Prentice-Hall, 1967.

Van Horne, James. *Financial Management and Policy*. 2d ed. Englewood Cliffs, N.J.: Prentice-Hall, 1971.

Weber, Arnold, ed. *The Structure of Collective Bargaining*. New York: Free Press, 1961.

Whitney, F. *Government and Collective Bargaining*. Philadelphia: Lippincott, 1951.

Woods, A.D., and Ostry, S. *Labour Policy and Labour Economics in Canada*. Toronto: Macmillan, 1962.

Zif, Jay, and Otlewski, Robert. *Contract Negotiations*. New York: Macmillan, 1971.

Articles and Periodicals

Arrow, Kenneth.   "The Theory of Discrimination."   In *Discrimination in Labor Markets,* edited by O. Ashenfelter and A. Rees. Princeton: Princeton University Press, 1973.

Ball, R.J., and St. Cyr, E.B.A.   "Short-term Employment Functions in British Manufacturing Industry."   *Review of Economic Studies* 33 (1966).

Barbash, Jack.   "The Elements of Industrial Relations."   *British Journal of Industrial Relations* 4 (October 1964).

Bergmann, Barbara.   "The Effect on White Incomes of Discrimination in Employment."   *Journal of Political Economy* 79 (March-April 1971).

Blake, David H.   "Multi-National Corporation, International Union and International Collective Bargaining."   In *Transnational Industrial Relations,* edited by Hans Gunter.   International Institute for Labour Studies, 1972.

Blakely, Arthur.   "Four-Day Work Week Liked."   *Edmonton Journal,* Friday, 4 May 1973.

Blandy, Richard.   "Equal Pay in Australia."   *Journal of Industrial Relations,* April 1963.

Brechling, F., and O'Brien, P.   "Short-run Employment Functions in Manufacturing Industries: An International Comparison."   *Review of Economics and Statistics* 49 (1967).

Brown, J. Douglas.   "University Research in IR."   *IRRA Annual Proceedings,* 28-29 December 1952.

Canada Department of Labour.   *Labour Gazette XLVIII* (May 1948).

———.   *Labour Gazette* XLVIII (August 1948).

———.   *Labour Gazette,* April 1972.

———.   "Labour Facing Greatest Challenge."   *Labour Gazette,* August 1972.

———.   "The Canada Labour Code and the Shorter Week."   *Labour Gazette,* April 1973.

———.   *Labour Gazette,* October 1974.

———.   *News,* 7 August 1974.

Canadian Hospital, January 1972.

Canadian Labour Congress. *Canadian Labour Movement,* 1 November 1974.

Caplan, Gerald L. "Insight: Perspectives on Party Conflict." *New Democrat,* May-June 1973.

Cardin, Jean-Réal. "Collective Bargaining and the Professional Employee in Quebec." In *Collective Bargaining and the Professional Employer*. Toronto: Industrial Relations Centre, University of Toronto, 1966.

Chamberlain, Neil. "Determinants of Collective Bargaining Structure." In *Challenges to Collective Bargaining,* edited by Lloyd Ulman. Englewood Cliffs, N.J.: Prentice-Hall, 1967.

———————. "The Structure of Bargaining Units in the United States." *Industrial and Labour Relations Review,* vol. 10, no. 1 (October 1956).

Craig, Alton, and Waisglass, Harry. "Collective Bargaining Perspectives." *Relations Industrielles,* vol. 23, no. 4 (October 1968).

Downie, Bryan M. "Centralized Collective Bargaining: U.S.-Canadian Experience." *Industrial Relations Quarterly Review,* vol. 26, no. 1. Quebec: Laval University Press, 1971.

Dunlop, John T. "Research in IR: Past and Present." *IRRA Proceedings,* 1954.

Dymond, W.R., and Saunders, George. "Hours of Work in Canada." In *Hours of Work,* edited by Clyde E. Dankert, et al. New York: Harper and Row, 1965.

Eckstein, O., and Wilson, T.A. "The Determination of Money Wages in American Industry." *Quarterly Journal of Economics* 74 (1962).

Edgeworth, P. "Equal Pay to Men and Women for Equal Work." *Economic Journal* 32 (December 1922).

Fawcett, M. "Equal Pay for Equal Work." *Economic Journal* 28 (March 1918).

Feinsinger, N. "Law and the Public Interest in Labor-Management Relations." In *Labor, Management and Social Policy,* edited by G.G. Somers. Madison: University of Wisconsin Press, 1963.

Festinger, L. "A Theory of Social Comparison Processes." *Human Relations* 7 (1954).

Freeman, Richard. "Decline of Labor Market Discrimination and Economic Analysis." *American Economic Review Papers and Proceedings* 63 (May 1973).

Gunderson, Morley. "Determinants of Individual Success in On-the-Job Training." *Journal of Human Resources,* vol. 8, no. 4 (Fall 1973).

Hameed, S.M.A. "A Theory of Collective Bargaining." *Industrial Relations,* vol. 25, no. 3 (August 1970).

-------. "Canadian Election Bargaining: Analysis and Prospect." In *Canadian Labour in Transition,* edited by R.U. Miller and A.F. Isbester. Toronto: Prentice-Hall, 1971.

-------. "Economic and Institutional Determinants of the Average Work Week in Canada." In *Work and Leisure in Canada,* edited by S.M.A. Hameed and D. Cullen. Edmonton: University of Alberta, 1971.

-------. "Theory and Research in the Field of Industrial Relations." *British Journal of Industrial Relations,* vol. V, no. 2 (July 1967).

Henerman, Herbert G. "Toward a General Conceptual System of Industrial Relations: How Do We Get There?" In *Essays in Industrial Relations Theory,* edited by G.G. Somers. Ames, Iowa: Iowa State University Press, 1969.

Henle, Peter. "Recent Growth of Paid Leisure for U.S. Workers." *Monthly Labor Review,* 1962.

Hulin, C.L., and Smith, P.C. "Sex Differences in Job Satisfaction." *Journal of Applied Psychology* 48 (1964).

Hutchinson, John. "Corruption in American Trade Unions." *Political Quarterly,* vol. 28, no. 3 (July-September 1957).

Isaac, J.E. "Compulsory Arbitration and Collective Bargaining Reconsidered." *Journal of Industrial Relations,* vol. 16, no. 1 (March 1974).

Kahn-Freund, Otto. "Industrial Disputes and Compulsory Arbitration." *The Listener,* 27 December 1956.

Kanungo, R.N., Misra, S., and Dayal, I. "Relationship of Job Involvement to Perceived Importance and Satisfaction of Employee Needs." *International Review of Applied Psychology,* 1975, in press.

Kerr and Seigal. "The Inter Industry Property to Strike - An International Comparison." In A. Kornhauser, *The Industrial Conflict.* New York: McGraw-Hill, 1956.

Kruger, A.M. "The Direction of Unionism in Canada." In *Canadian Labour in Transition,* edited by R.U. Miller and A.F. Isbester. Toronto: Prentice-Hall, 1971.

Kuh, E. "A Productivity Theory of Wage Levels - An Alternative to the Phillips Curve." *Review of Economic Studies* 34 (1967).

Kumar, Pradeep. "Differentials in Wage Rates of Unskilled Labour in Manufacturing Industries." *Industrial and Labour Relations Review,* vol. 26, no. 1 (October 1972).

Larson, C. "Equal Pay for Women in the United Kingdom." *International Labour Review* 103 (January 1971).

Levitan, Sar A. "Can We Afford Not to Reduce Hours of Work?" *Challenge,* June 1965.

Livernash, E. Robert. "New Developments in Bargaining Structure." In *Trade Union, Government and Collective Bargaining: Some Critical Issues,* edited by Joel Seidman. New York: Praeger, 1970.

——————. "The Relation of Power to the Structure and Process of Collective Bargaining." *The Journal of Law and Economics* VI (October 1963).

Lortie, Guy. "Evolution de l'action politique de la CSN." *Relations Industrielles,* vol. 22, no. 4 (n.d.).

Madison, B. "Women's Liberation and Social Welfare in the Soviet Union." *Social Service Review,* 1971.

Management Record 431, n.d.

Mandel, William. "Soviet Women in the Work Force and Professions." In *Women in the Professions,* edited by Linda Fidell and John Dehamater. Beverly Hills: Sage Publications, 1971.

Miller, Richard U. "Organized Labour and Politics in Canada." In *Canadian Labour in Transition,* edited by R.U. Miller and A.F. Isbester. Toronto: Prentice-Hall, 1971.

Monthly Labor Review, December 1926.

Monthly Labor Review 498, n.d.

New Democrat, July-August 1968.

Ottawa Citizen, 13 May 1967.

Paltiel, Khayyam Z. "Party and Candidate Expenditures in the Canadian General Election of 1972." *Canadian Journal of Political Science,* June 1974.

Parenteau, K. "The Impact of Industrialization in Quebec." In *Marketing: Canada,* edited by I. Litvak and B. Mallen. Toronto: McGraw-Hill, 1964.

Parsons, K.   "The Basis of Commons' Progressive Approach to Public Policy." In *Labor, Management and Social Policy,* edited by G.G. Somers. Madison: University of Wisconsin Press, 1963.

Porter, I.W.   "A Study of Perceived Need Satisfactions in Bottom and Middle Management Jobs." *Journal of Applied Psychology* 45 (1961).

Rees, A.   "Industrial Conflict and Business Fluctuations." *Journal of Political Economy* 60 (October 1952).

Reuber, G.L.   "Wage Adjustments in Canadian Industry, 1953-66." *Review of Economic Studies* 37 (1970).

Ripley, F.C.   "An Analysis of the Eckstein-Wilson Wage Determination Model." *Quarterly Journal of Economics* 80 (1966).

Robinson, K.R.   "PSAC Priority - A Shorter Week." *Canadian Labour,* November 1971.

Rosen, Sherwin.   "Unionism and the Occupational Wage Structure in the United States." *International Economic Review,* vol. III, no. 2 (June 1970).

Ross, David P.   "Leisure as a Response to Technological Change in the Economic System." In *Work and Leisure in Canada,* edited by S.M.A. Hameed and D. Cullen. Edmonton: University of Alberta, 1971.

Sawhill, E.   "The Economics of Discrimination Against Women: Some New Findings." *Journal of Human Resources* 8 (Summer 1973).

Shister, Joseph.   "Collective Bargaining." In *A Decade of Industrial Relations Research, 1946-1956.* New York: Harper and Bros., 1958.

Smigel, Erwin O.   "The Problem of Leisure Time in an Industrial Society." In *Computer Technology - Concepts for Management.* Industrial Relations Counselors, May 1964.

Somers, G.G.   "Bargaining Power and Industrial Relations Theory." In *Essays in Industrial Relations Theory,* edited by G.G. Somers. Ames, Iowa: Iowa State University Press, 1969.

Sparks, G.R., and Wilton, D.A.   "Determinants of Negotiated Wage Increases: An Empirical Analysis." *Econometrica* 39 (1971).

Spector, A.J.   "Expectations, Fulfillment, and Morale." *Journal of Abnormal and Social Psychology* 52 (1956).

Steinberg, Rafael.   "Professionals in Unions Cite Old Reasons: Pay, Security." *New York Times,* 28 July 1974.

Stiglitz, Joseph. "Approaches to the Economics of Discrimination." *American Economic Review Papers and Proceedings* 63 (May 1973).

Streeten, P. "Economics and Value Judgement." *Quarterly Journal of Economics,* November 1950.

"Strike Authorization Procedures." *Management Record,* November 1954.

"Strike Control Provisions in Union Constitutions." *Monthly Labor Review* 77 (May 1954).

Toronto Star, 22 July 1972.

Ibid., 20 January 1973.

Ibid., 24 January 1973.

Ibid., 26 February 1973.

Ibid., 5 May 1973.

Tripp, L. Reed. "Collective Bargaining Theory." In *Labor, Management and Social Policy,* edited by G.G. Somers. Madison: University of Wisconsin Press, 1963.

––––––––. "The Industrial Relations Discipline in American Universities." *ILRR,* July 1964.

"Unions' Strike Vote Provisions." *Management Record,* May 1954.

Vancouver Daily Province, 28 February 1947.

Ibid., 4 March 1947.

Ibid., 12 March 1947.

Ibid., 17 March 1947.

Ibid., 2 April 1947.

Vancouver Sun, 10 July 1974.

Vangsness, Kari. "Equal Pay in Norway." *International Labour Review* 103 (April 1971).

Whyte, W.F. "Human Relations – A Progress Report." In *Complex Organizations,* edited by Amitai Etzioni. New York: Holt, Rinehart and Winston, 1961.

Winder, J.W.L. "Structural Unemployment." In *The Canadian Labour Market: Readings in Manpower Economics,* edited by A. Kruger and N.M. Meltz. Toronto: Centre for Industrial Relations, University of Toronto, 1968.

Woytinsky, Wladimir. "Hours of Labour." In *Encyclopedia of Social Sciences,* vol. 7 (1937).

Yerbury, D., and Isaac, J.E. "Recent Trends in Collective Bargaining in Australia." *International Labour Review,* vol. 103, no. 5 (May 1971).

Zakuta, Leo. "Membership in a Becalmed Protest Movement." *Canadian Political Science* 24 (May 1958).

Government Reports and Documents, and Special Studies

Bodkin, R.G., Bond, E.P., Reuber, G.L., and Robinson, T.R. *Price Stability and High Employment: The Options for Canadian Economic Policy.* Special Study no. 5, for the Economic Council of Canada. Ottawa: Queen's Printer, 1967.

Canadian Labour Congress. *Report of Proceedings.* First Convention, 23-27 April 1956.

Compressed Work Week in Ontario, The. Research Branch, Ontario Ministry of Labour, September 1972.

Cox, Archibald. Address given at the 7th Annual Meeting of the National Academy of Arbitration, 22 January 1954.

Craig, Alton W.J. "A Model for the Analysis of Industrial Relations Systems." Mimeographed. 1967.

Crispo, John. "Multi-National Corporations and International Unions: Their Impact on Canadian Industrial Relations." Study prepared for a conference on Industrial Relations and the Multinational Corporation, sponsored by the University of Chicago Graduate School of Business, May 1973. To be published by the University of Chicago Press.

Economic Council of Canada. *Third Annual Review: Prices, Productivity and Employment.*

-------. *Fourth Annual Review.* Ottawa: Queen's Printer, 1967.

-------. *Fifth Annual Review: The Challenge and Growth of Change.* Ottawa: Queen's Printer, September 1968.

Federal Mediation and Conciliation Service. *First Annual Report,* 1948.

Government of Canada. *Strikes and Lockouts in Canada.* Ottawa: Department of Labour, 1952-1968.

Gray, Hon. Herb, P.C. *Special Report on Foreign Direct Investment in Canada*. Ottawa, 1972.

"Hearings before House Standing Committee on Industrial Relations", June and July 1947.

Herman, E.E., Skinner, G.S., and Leftwich, H.M. "The Bargaining Unit." Study for the Task Force on Labour Relations. Ottawa, 1968.

Holmes, R. "Male-Female Earnings Differentials in Canada." Discussion Paper 74-5-2, Simon Fraser University, Department of Economics and Commerce, 1974.

Jamieson, S.M. "French and English in the Institutional Structure of Montreal: A Study of the Social and Economic Division of Labor." M.A. thesis, McGill University, 1938.

-------. *Times of Trouble - Labour Unrest and Industrial Conflict in Canada, 1900-66*. Task Force on Labour Relations, Study no. 22. Ottawa: Privy Council, 1968.

Kaun, David E. "Economics of the Minimum Wage: The Effects of the Fair Labor Standards Acts, 1945-1960." Ph.D. thesis, Stanford University, 1964.

Kovacs, A.E. "A Study of Joint Labour-Management Committees at the Provincial Level in the Provinces of Canada." Task Force on Labour Relations, Project no. 56. Ottawa, April 1968.

Kruger, Arthur. *Human Adjustment to Industrial Conversion*. Task Force on Labour Relations, Project no. 45. Ottawa: Privy Council, 1968.

March, R.R. *Public Opinion and Industrial Relations*. Study for the Task Force on Labour Relations. Ottawa: Privy Council, 1968.

Minutes of *Proceedings and Evidence* on Bill no. 195, April 1948.

National Labour Relations Board. *Eleventh Annual Report*. Appendix B. Ottawa, 1946.

Proceedings and Reports of Public Inquiry into Labour Relations and Wage Conditions. Ottawa, 1943-44.

Proposals to Deal with National Emergency Strikes. Washington, D.C.: American Enterprise Institute, 1969.

"Report of Committee on Industrial Relations to House of Commons", 17 August 1946.

Report of the Royal Commission on the Relations of Labour and Capital in Canada. Appendix F. Ottawa, 1889.

Report of Royal Commission Inquiry into Labour Disputes.   Toronto: Queen's Printer, 1968.

Report of Royal Commission on Trade Unions and Employers Associations, 1965-1968.   Toronto: Queen's Printer, 1968.

Report of the Royal Commission on Bilingualism and Biculturalism. *III The Work World.*   Ottawa: Queen's Printer, 1969.

Report of the Task Force on Labour Relations. *Canadian Industrial Relations.*   Ottawa: Privy Council, December 1968.

Reuber, G.L.   *Wage Determination in Canadian Manufacturing Industries.*   Task Force on Labour Relations, Study no. 19.   Ottawa: Privy Council, 1970.

Robson, R., and Lapointe, M.   *A Comparison of Men's and Women's Salaries and Employment Fringe Benefits in the Academic Professions.*   Study no. 2, for the Royal Commission on the Status of Women in Canada.   Ottawa: Information Canada, 1971.

Samson Belair Riddell Stead Inc.   *Report on the Compressed Work Week,* September 1972.

Schaffer, H.B.   *Shorter Work Week.*   Editorial Research Report, vol. 2, no. 22, 1954.

Scott, F.   "Federal Jurisdiction over Labour Relations."   Paper delivered to the 11th Annual Conference of the McGill University Industrial Relations Centre, September 1959.

(U.S.) Senate, Committee on Labor and Public Welfare, *Hearings on Proposed Revisions of the Labor-Management Relations Act,* 83rd Cong., 2d sess. part 6, 1954.

-------, House Document 291, 83rd Cong., 2d sess.

-------, Select Committee in Improper Activities in the Labor or Management Field, 85th Cong., 1st sess., 1957.

Shorter Work Week, A: Some Costs and Consequences for British Columbia.   Vancouver: Commercial and Industrial Research Foundation, 1967.

Simmons, C. Gordon.   "Co-ordinated Bargaining by Unions and Employers."   Study for the Task Force on Labour Relations.   Ottawa, 1968.

Siok, R.B.   "Job Motivation: An Eclectic Approach."   M.B.A. thesis, Faculty of Management, McGill University, 1971.

Solasse, Bernard.   *Syndicalisme, consommation et société de consommation.*   Task Force on Labour Relations, Study no. 3. Ottawa: Privy Council, 1968.

Statistics Canada. *Annual Report of the Minister of Industry, Trade and Commerce Under the Corporations and Labour Unions Return Act, 1969*. Part II. Ottawa: Queen's Printer, 1971.

Statutes of British Columbia, *Industrial Conciliation and Arbitration Act, 1937*.

Statutes of Canada, *Industrial Disputes Investigation Act, 1907*.

———, *Newfoundland Trade Union Act, 1968*.

———, *Quebec Labour Code, 1969*.

———, *Ontario Labour Relations Act, 1970*.

———, *Canada Labour Code, 1971*.

———, *Prince Edward Island Labour Act, 1971*.

———, *Industrial Relations Act of New Brunswick, 1972*.

———, *Nova Scotia Trade Unions Act, 1972*.

———, *Alberta Labour Act, 1973*.

———, *Labour Code of British Columbia, 1973*.

———, *Labour Relations Act of Manitoba, 1973*.

———, *Saskatchewan Trade Union Act, 1973*.

Statutes of Michigan, *Labor Mediation Act*, Stat. 939, Act. no. 176.

U.S., *War Labor Disputes Act*, Stat. 163, 1943.

Vanderkamp, John. "The Time Pattern of Industrial Conflict in Canada, 1901-1966." Study for the Task Force on Labour Relations. Ottawa, 1968.

Whittingham, Frank. *Minimum Wages in Ontario: Analysis and Measurement Problems*. Research Series, no. 11, Industrial Research Centre, Queen's University, 1970.

Women in the Labour Force: Facts and Figures. Ottawa: Information Canada, 1973.

Zaida, M.A. *A Study of the Effects of the $1.25 Minimum Wage under the Canada Labour (Standards) Code*. Task Force on Labour Relations, Study no. 16. Ottawa: Privy Council, March 1970.